VOL. 1

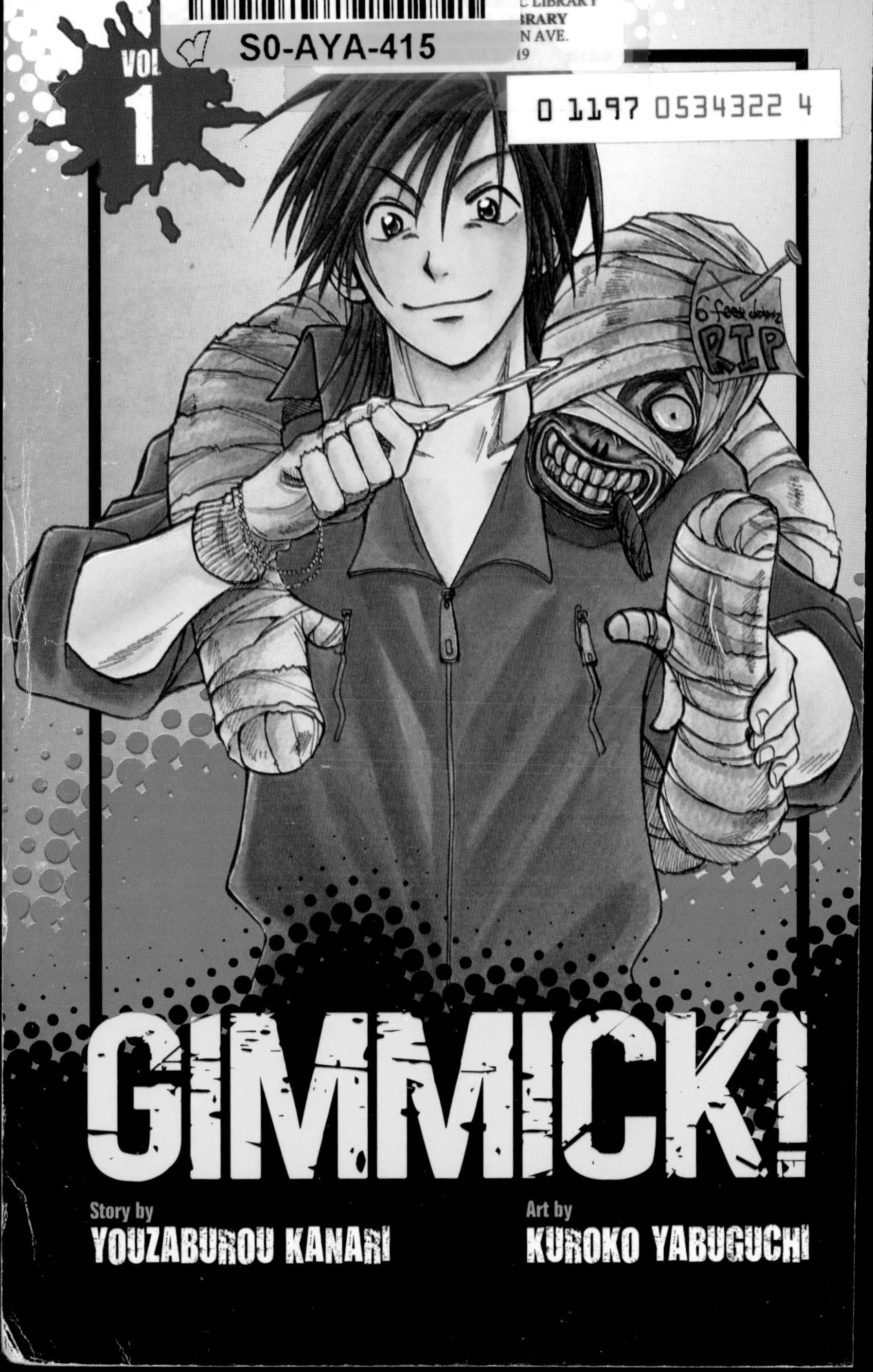
6 feet down
RIP

GIMMICK!

Story by
YOUZABUROU KANARI

Art by
KUROKO YABUGUCHI

GIMMICK!

CONTENTS

VOL 1

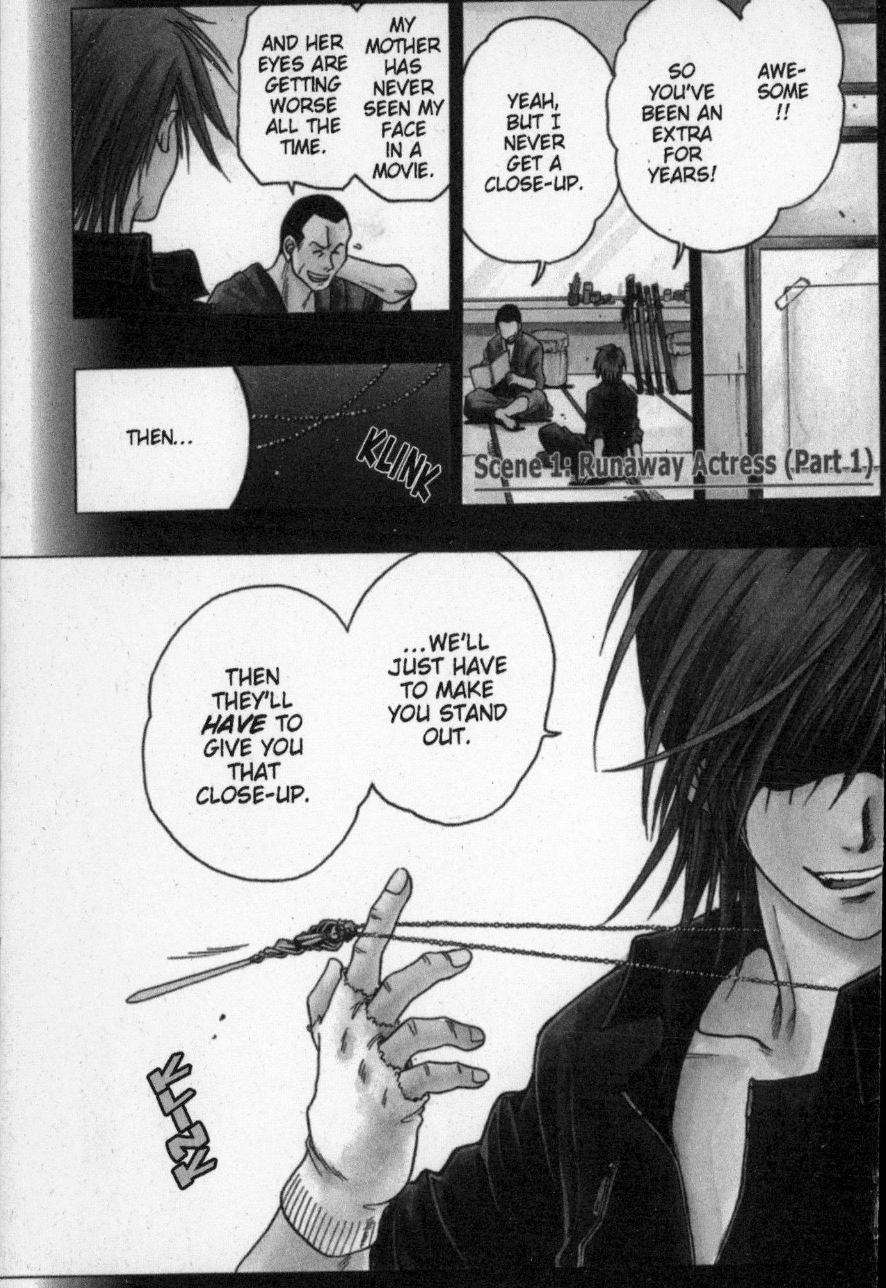
AWESOME!!
SO YOU'VE BEEN AN EXTRA FOR YEARS!
YEAH, BUT I NEVER GET A CLOSE-UP.
Scene 1: Runaway Actress (Part 1)
MY MOTHER HAS NEVER SEEN MY FACE IN A MOVIE.
AND HER EYES ARE GETTING WORSE ALL THE TIME.
KLINK
THEN...
...WE'LL JUST HAVE TO MAKE YOU STAND OUT.
THEN THEY'LL *HAVE* TO GIVE YOU THAT CLOSE-UP.
KLIZZ

Scene 1:
Runaway Actress (Part 1)

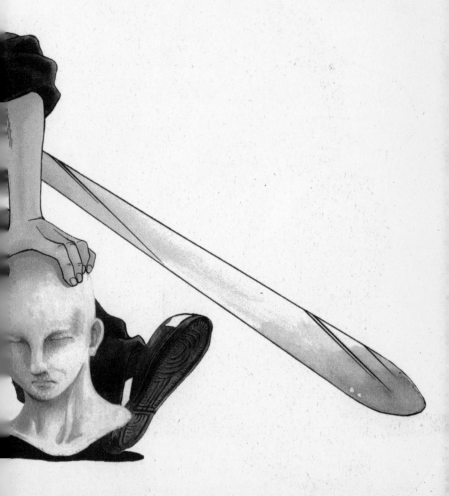

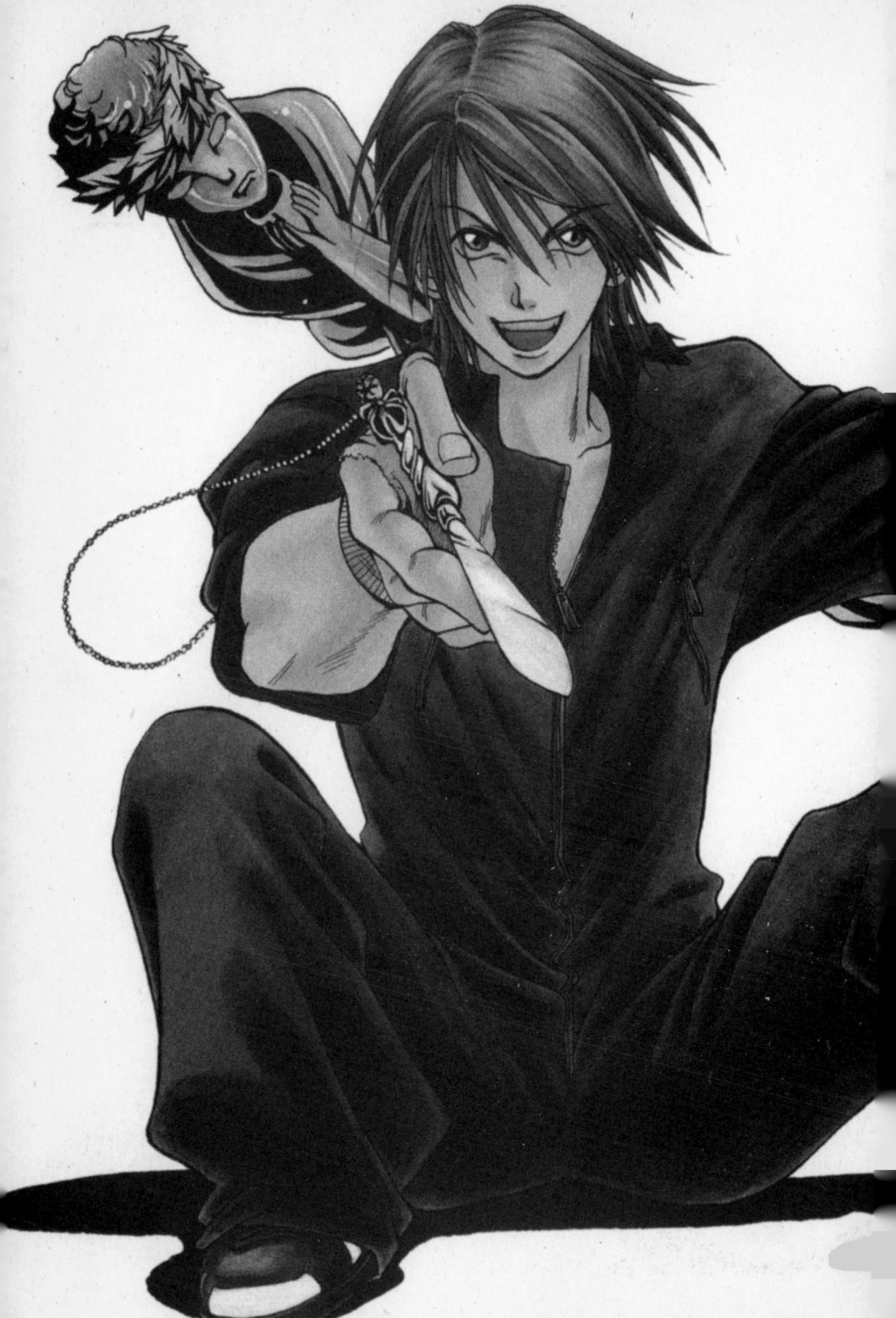

GIMMICK!

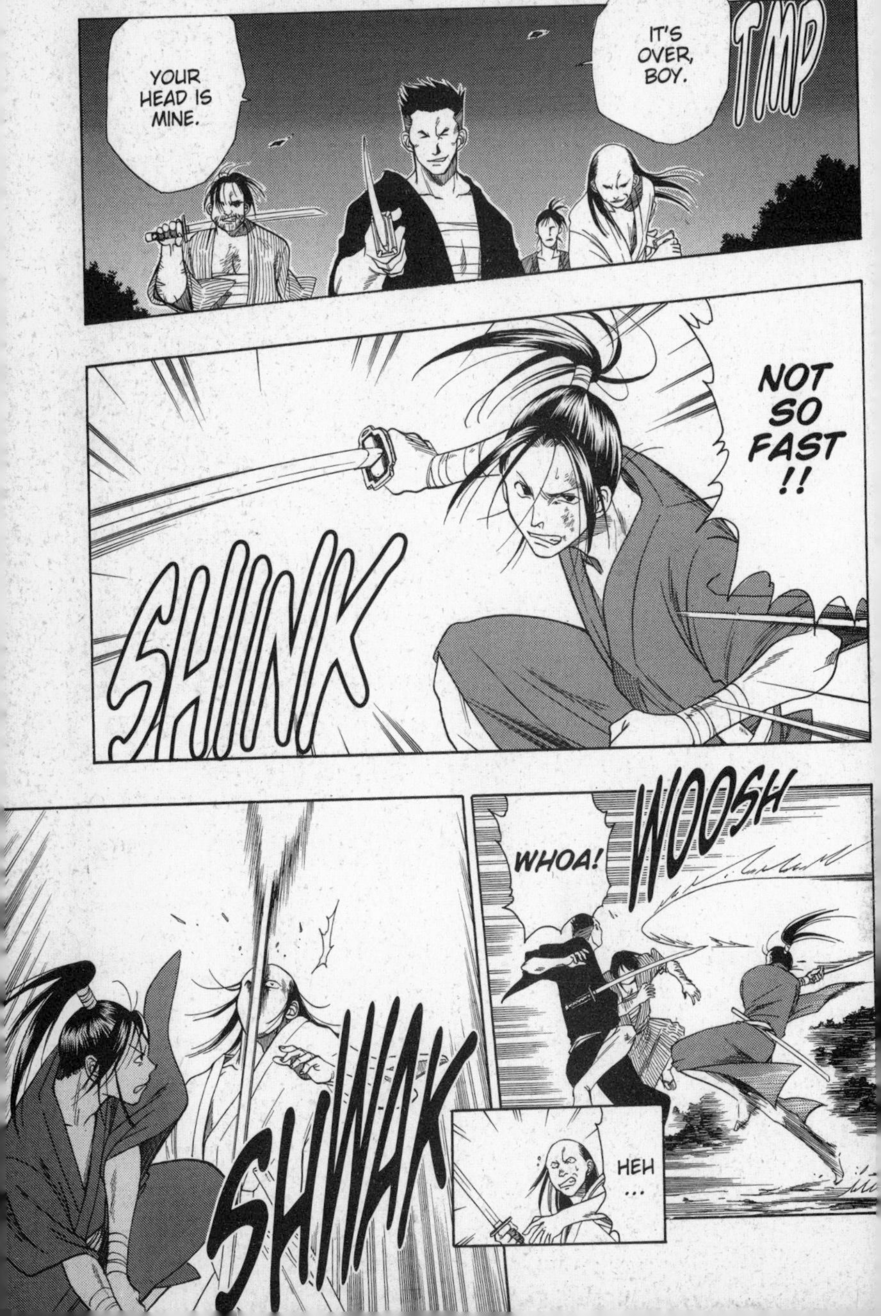
TMP
IT'S OVER, BOY.
YOUR HEAD IS MINE.
NOT SO FAST!!
SHINK
WOOSH
WHOA!
HEH ...
SHWAK

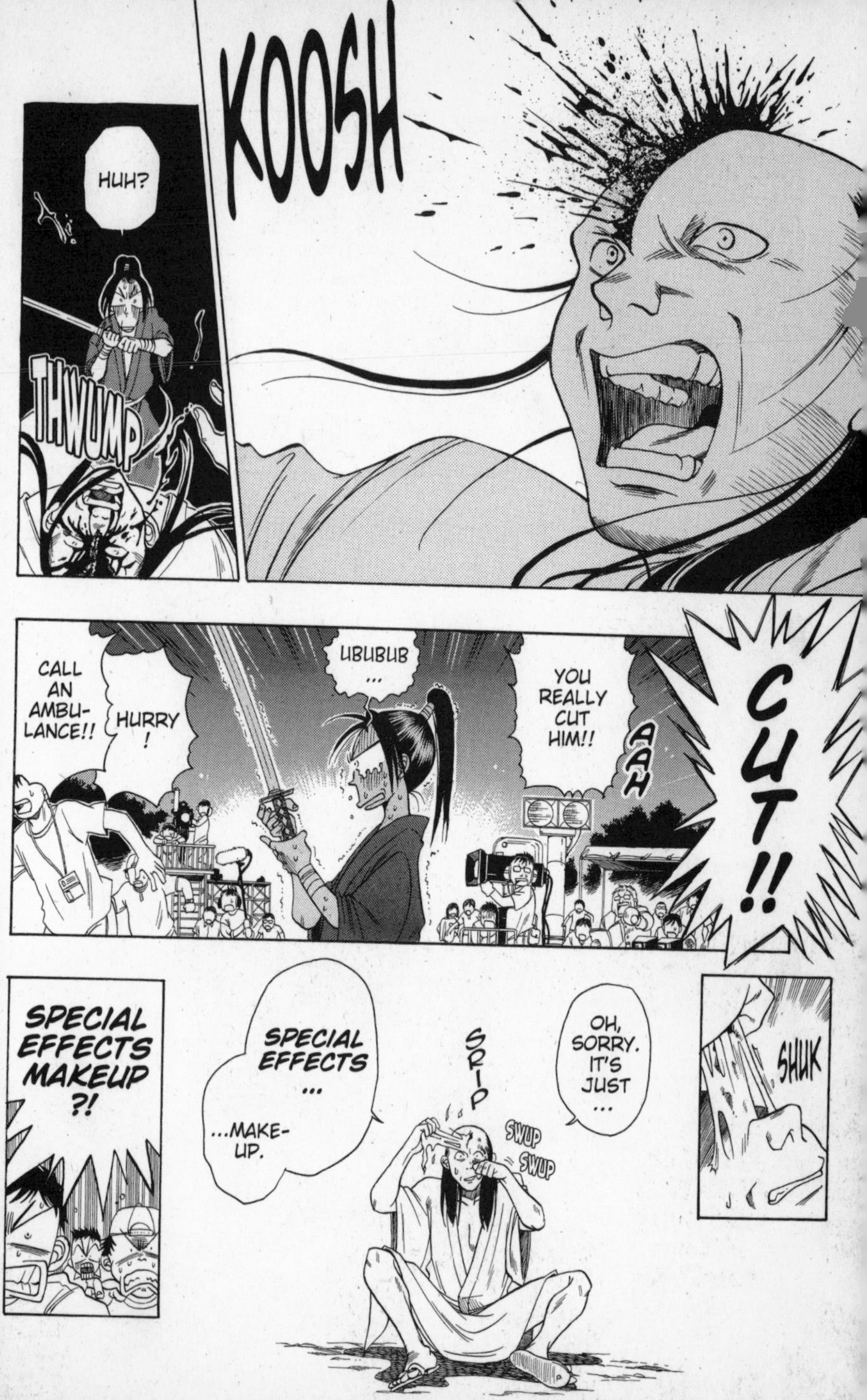
KOOSH
HUH?
THWUMP
CUT!!
AAH
YOU REALLY CUT HIM!!
UBUBUB...
HURRY!
CALL AN AMBULANCE!!
SHUK
OH, SORRY. IT'S JUST...
SRIP
SWUP SWUP
SPECIAL EFFECTS...
...MAKE-UP.
SPECIAL EFFECTS MAKEUP?!

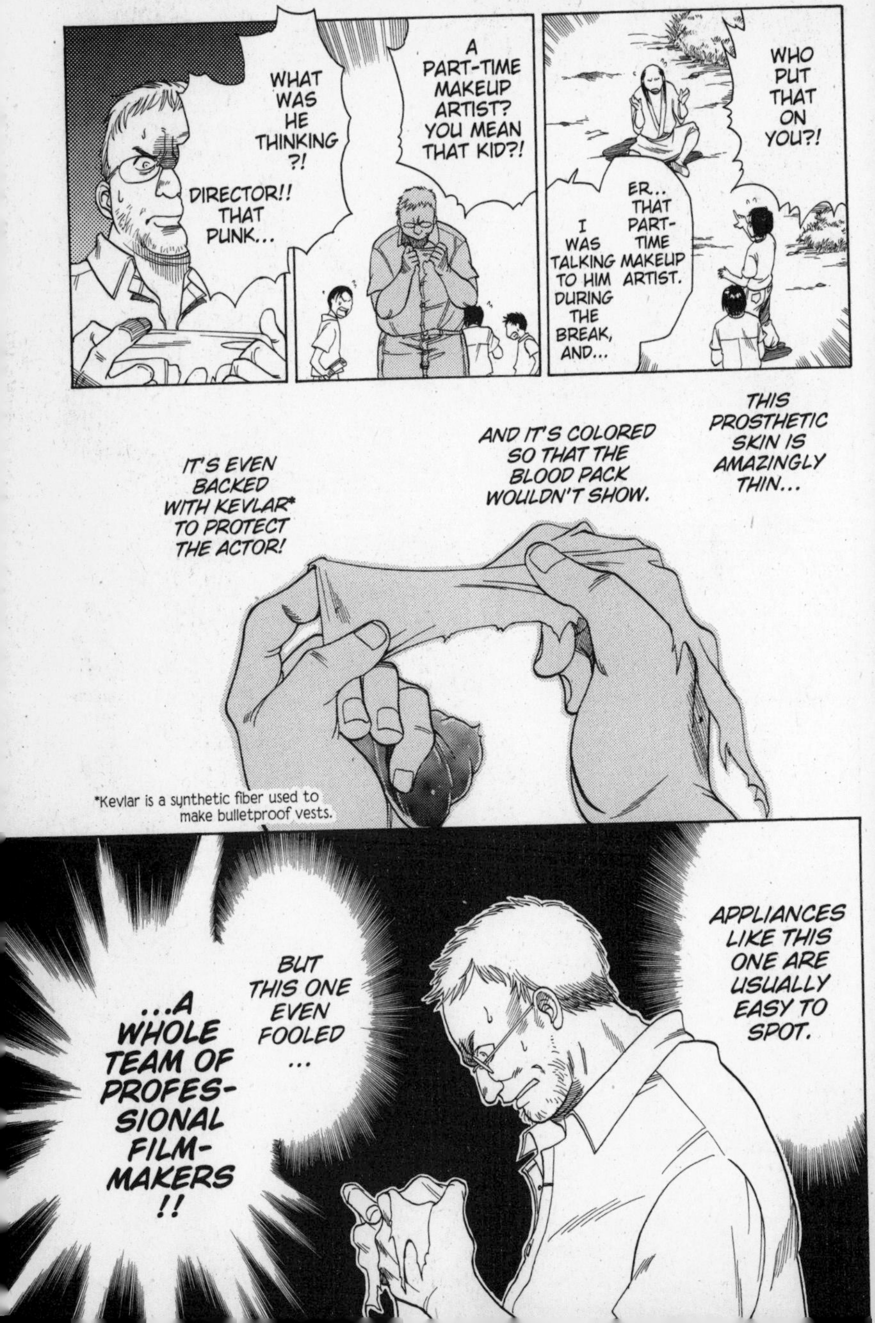
WHO PUT THAT ON YOU?!
ER... THAT PART-TIME MAKEUP ARTIST.
I WAS TALKING TO HIM DURING THE BREAK, AND...
A PART-TIME MAKEUP ARTIST? YOU MEAN THAT KID?!
WHAT WAS HE THINKING ?!
DIRECTOR!! THAT PUNK...
THIS PROSTHETIC SKIN IS AMAZINGLY THIN...
AND IT'S COLORED SO THAT THE BLOOD PACK WOULDN'T SHOW.
IT'S EVEN BACKED WITH KEVLAR* TO PROTECT THE ACTOR!
APPLIANCES LIKE THIS ONE ARE USUALLY EASY TO SPOT.
BUT THIS ONE EVEN FOOLED ...
...A WHOLE TEAM OF PROFES-SIONAL FILM-MAKERS !!

*Kevlar is a synthetic fiber used to make bulletproof vests.

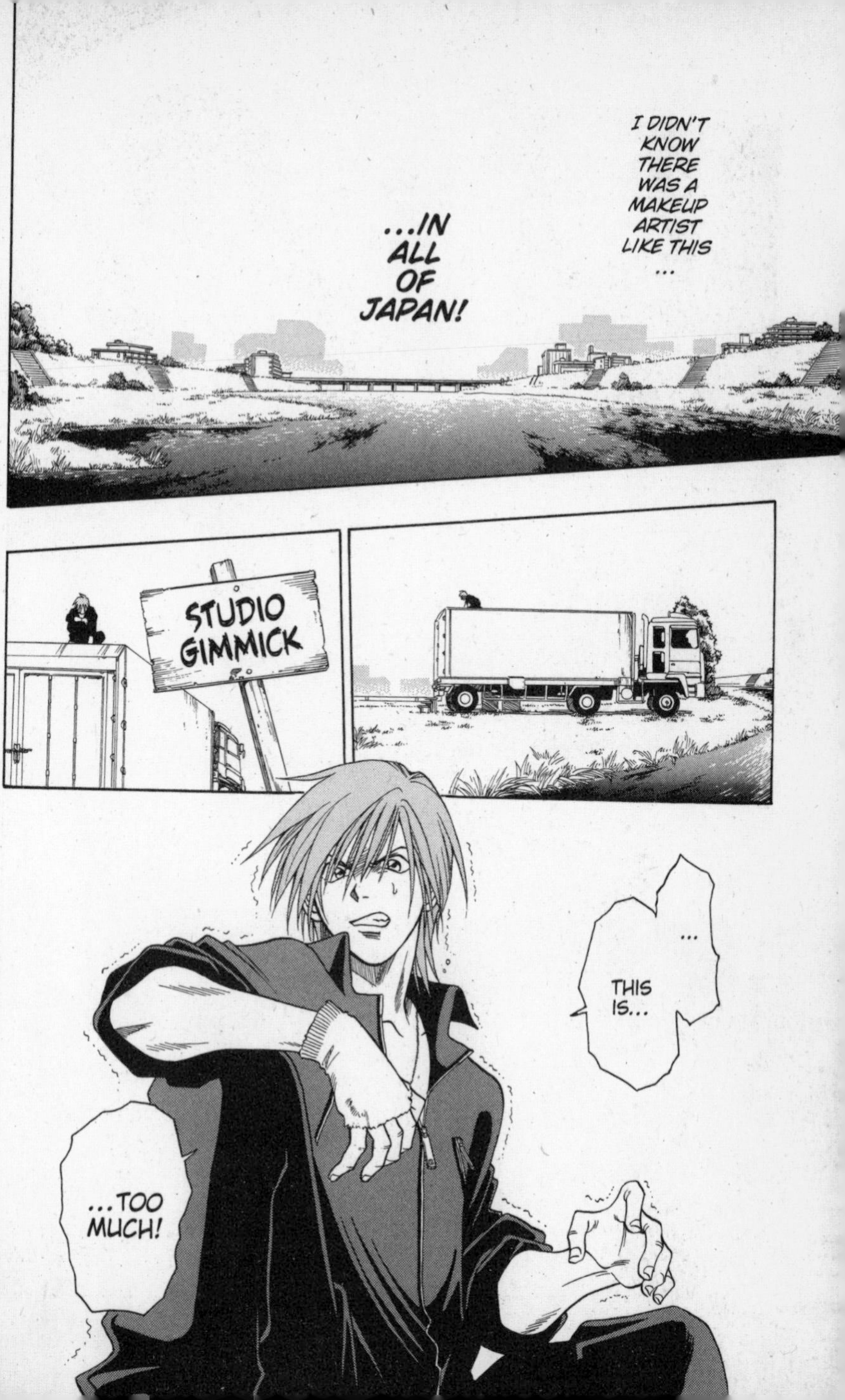
I DIDN'T KNOW THERE WAS A MAKEUP ARTIST LIKE THIS ...
...IN ALL OF JAPAN!
STUDIO GIMMICK
... THIS IS...
...TOO MUCH!

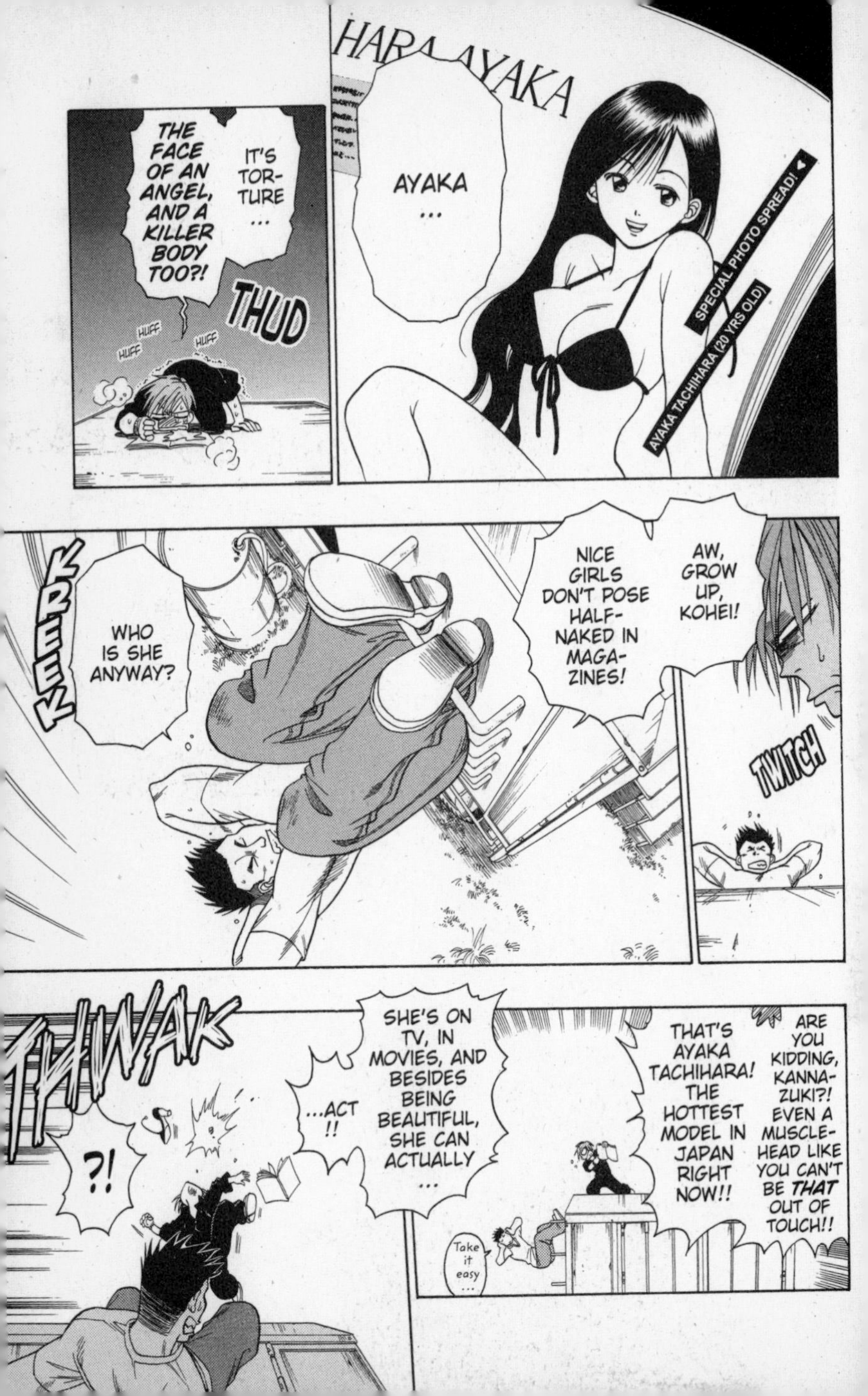
HARA AYAKA
AYAKA ...
SPECIAL PHOTO SPREAD! ♥
AYAKA TACHIHARA (20 YRS OLD)
IT'S TORTURE ...
THE FACE OF AN ANGEL, AND A KILLER BODY TOO?!
THUD
HUFF
HUFF
HUFF
TWITCH
AW, GROW UP, KOHEI!
NICE GIRLS DON'T POSE HALF-NAKED IN MAGAZINES!
WHO IS SHE ANYWAY?
KREEK
ARE YOU KIDDING, KANNAZUKI?! EVEN A MUSCLEHEAD LIKE YOU CAN'T BE *THAT* OUT OF TOUCH!!
THAT'S AYAKA TACHIHARA! THE HOTTEST MODEL IN JAPAN RIGHT NOW!!
Take it easy ...
SHE'S ON TV, IN MOVIES, AND BESIDES BEING BEAUTIFUL, SHE CAN ACTUALLY ...
...ACT !!
?!
THWAK

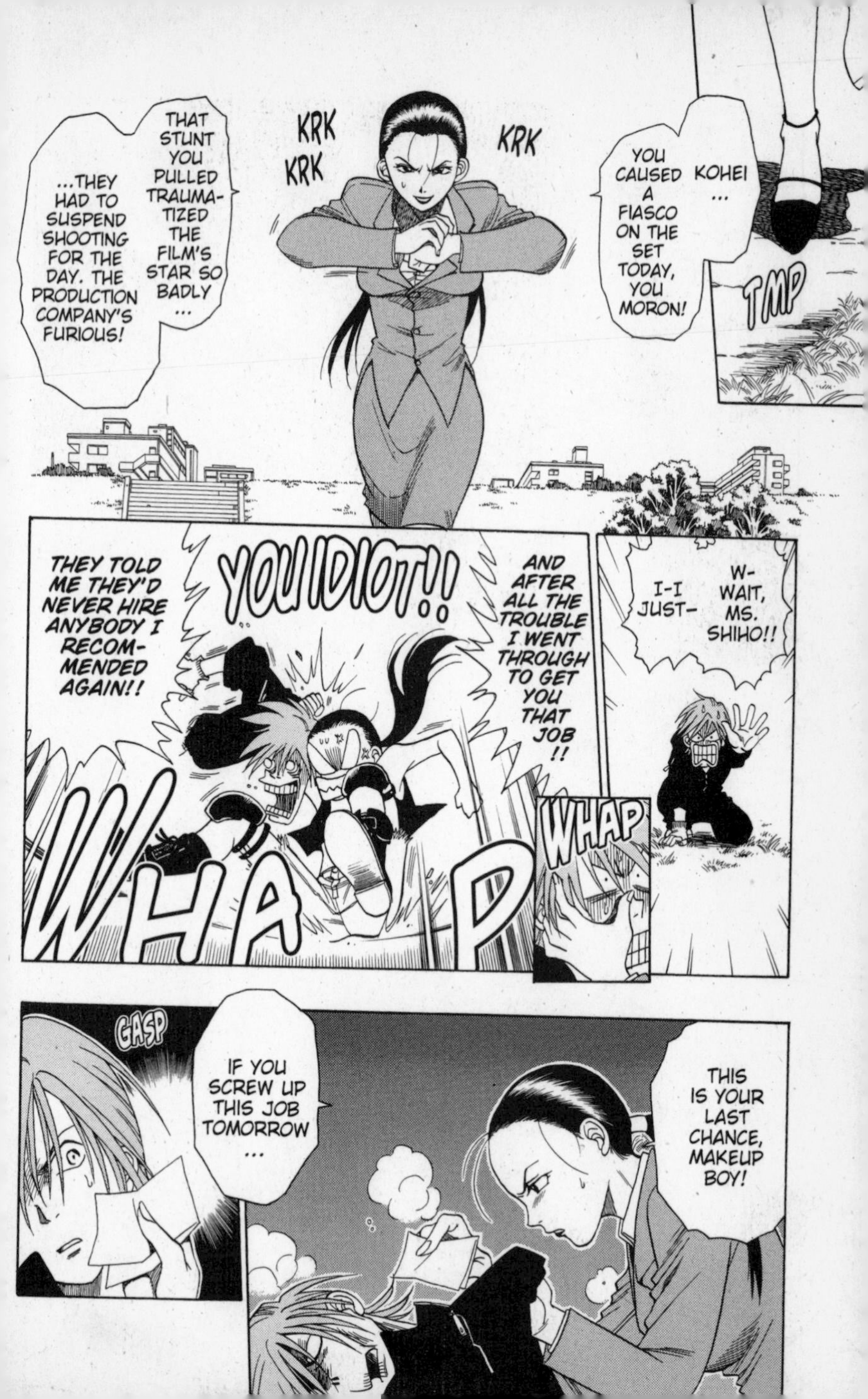
KOHEI ...
YOU CAUSED A FIASCO ON THE SET TODAY, YOU MORON!
TMP
KRK
KRK
KRK
THAT STUNT YOU PULLED TRAUMATIZED THE FILM'S STAR SO BADLY ...
...THEY HAD TO SUSPEND SHOOTING FOR THE DAY. THE PRODUCTION COMPANY'S FURIOUS!
W-WAIT, MS. SHIHO!!
I-I JUST-
WHAP
AND AFTER ALL THE TROUBLE I WENT THROUGH TO GET YOU THAT JOB!!
YOU IDIOT!!
THEY TOLD ME THEY'D NEVER HIRE ANYBODY I RECOMMENDED AGAIN!!
WHAP
THIS IS YOUR LAST CHANCE, MAKEUP BOY!
IF YOU SCREW UP THIS JOB TOMORROW ...
GASP

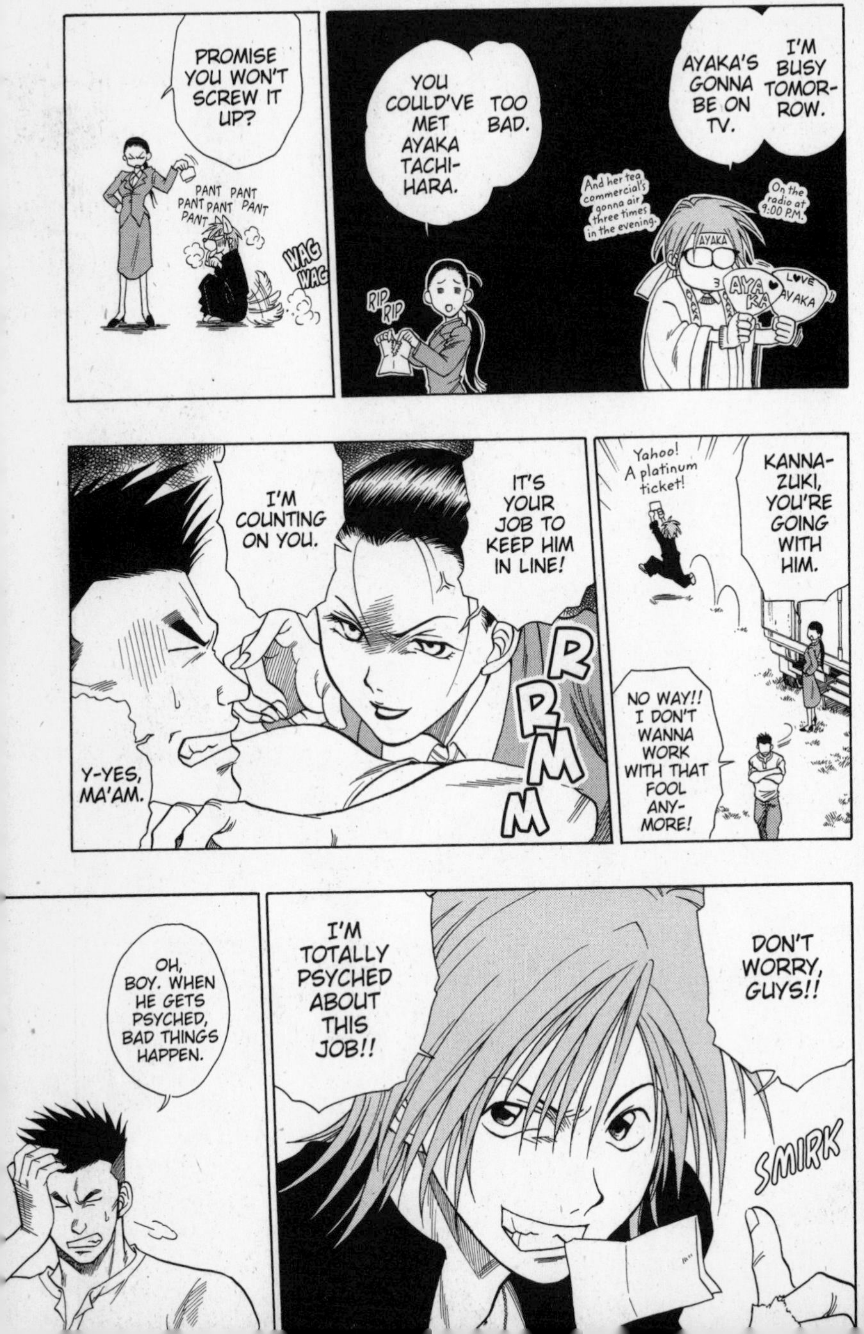

I'M BUSY TOMORROW.
AYAKA'S GONNA BE ON TV.
On the radio at 9:00 P.M.
And her tea commercial's gonna air three times in the evening.
AYAKA
AYAKA
LOVE AYAKA
TOO BAD.
YOU COULD'VE MET AYAKA TACHIHARA.
RIP RIP
PROMISE YOU WON'T SCREW IT UP?
PANT PANT PANT PANT PANT
WAG WAG
KANNAZUKI, YOU'RE GOING WITH HIM.
Yahoo! A platinum ticket!
NO WAY!! I DON'T WANNA WORK WITH THAT FOOL ANYMORE!
IT'S YOUR JOB TO KEEP HIM IN LINE!
I'M COUNTING ON YOU.
RRMM
Y-YES, MA'AM.
DON'T WORRY, GUYS!!
I'M TOTALLY PSYCHED ABOUT THIS JOB!!
SMIRK
OH, BOY. WHEN HE GETS PSYCHED, BAD THINGS HAPPEN.

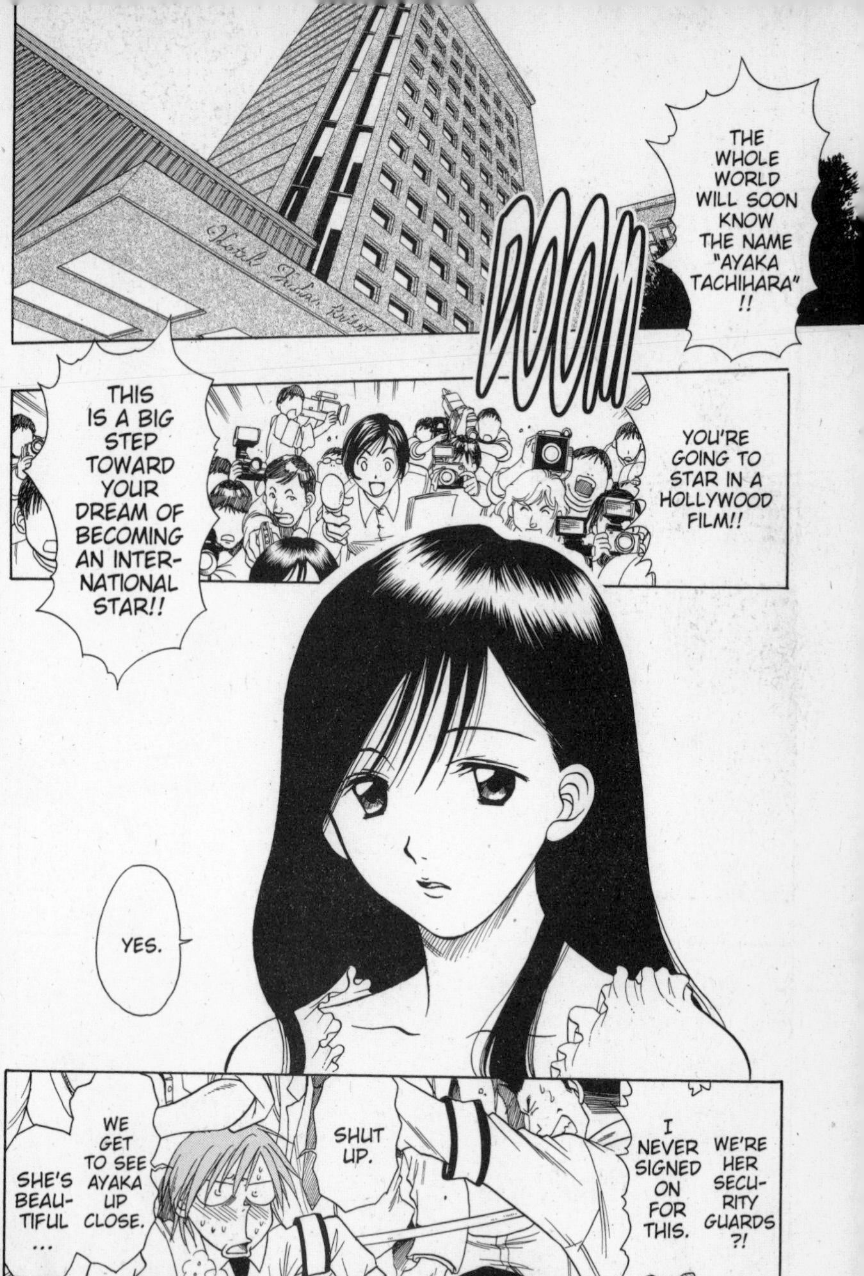
THE WHOLE WORLD WILL SOON KNOW THE NAME "AYAKA TACHIHARA"!!
DOOM
YOU'RE GOING TO STAR IN A HOLLYWOOD FILM!!
THIS IS A BIG STEP TOWARD YOUR DREAM OF BECOMING AN INTER-NATIONAL STAR!!
YES.
WE'RE HER SECU-RITY GUARDS?!
I NEVER SIGNED ON FOR THIS.
SHUT UP.
WE GET TO SEE AYAKA UP CLOSE.
SHE'S BEAU-TIFUL...

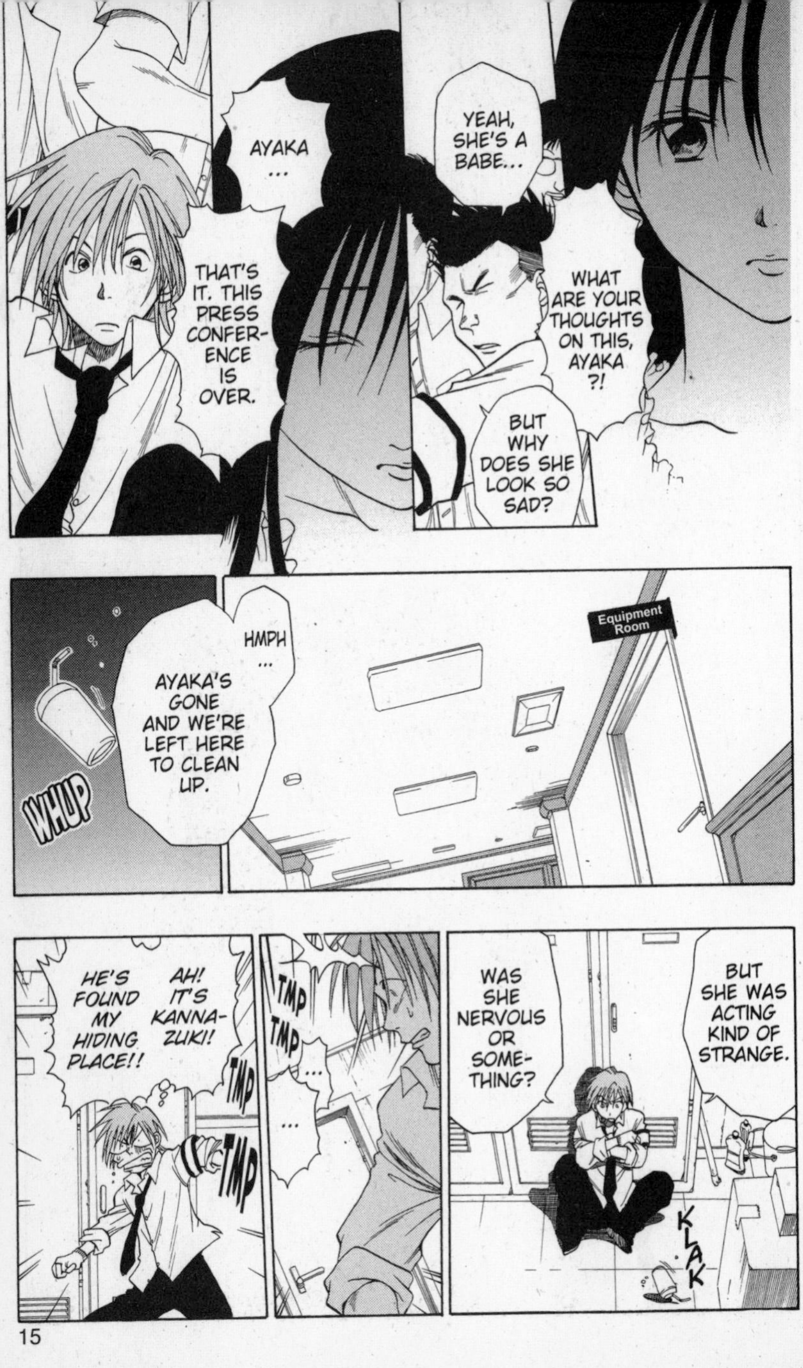
YEAH, SHE'S A BABE...
WHAT ARE YOUR THOUGHTS ON THIS, AYAKA?!
BUT WHY DOES SHE LOOK SO SAD?
AYAKA ...
THAT'S IT. THIS PRESS CONFERENCE IS OVER.
Equipment Room
HMPH ...
AYAKA'S GONE AND WE'RE LEFT HERE TO CLEAN UP.
WHUP
BUT SHE WAS ACTING KIND OF STRANGE.
WAS SHE NERVOUS OR SOMETHING?
KLAK
TMP
TMP
...
...
TMP
TMP
AH! IT'S KANNA-ZUKI!
HE'S FOUND MY HIDING PLACE!!

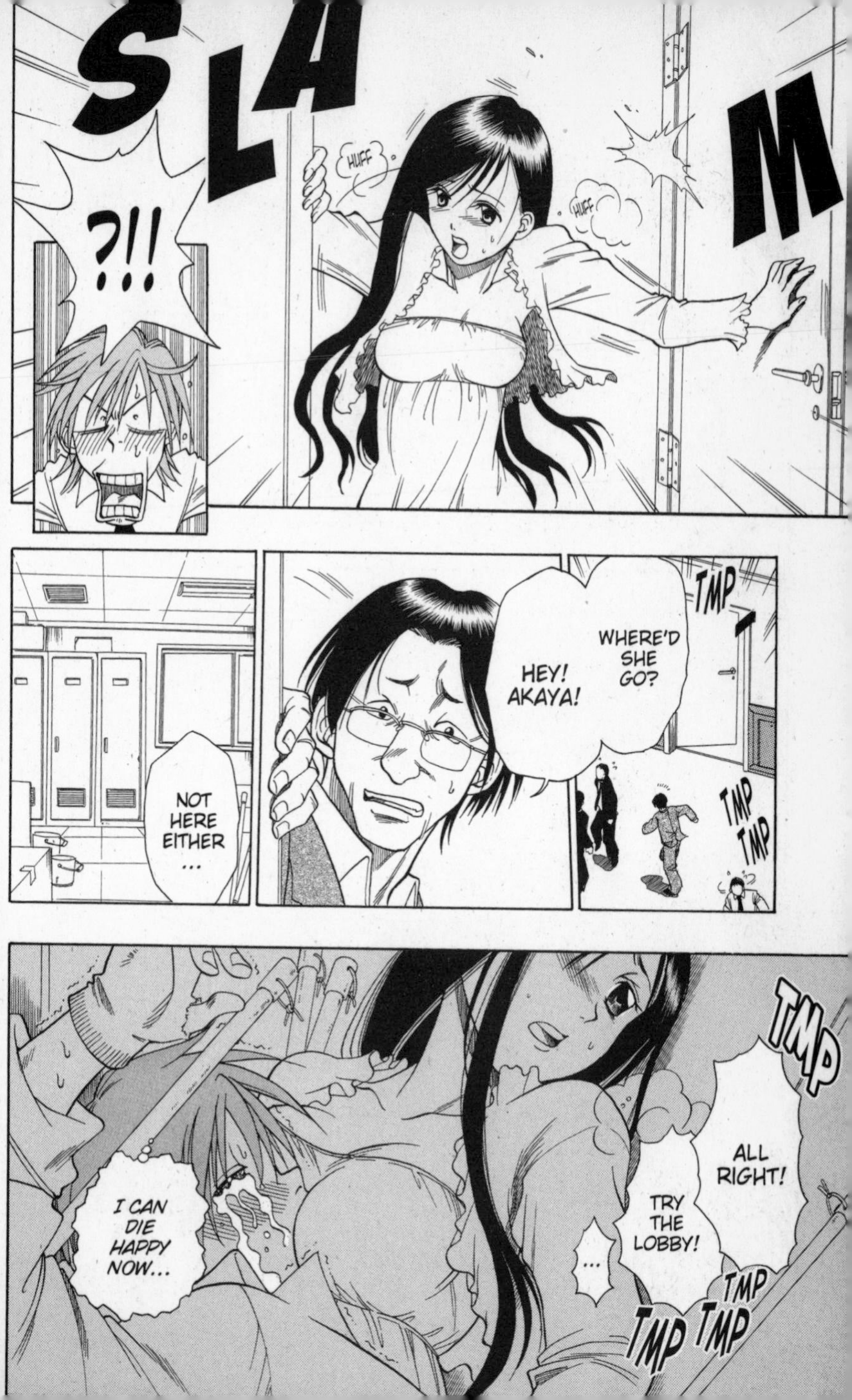
SLAM
HUFF
HUFF
?!!
TMP
WHERE'D SHE GO?
HEY! AKAYA!
TMP TMP
NOT HERE EITHER ...
TMP
ALL RIGHT!
TRY THE LOBBY!
TMP TMP
TMP
...
I CAN DIE HAPPY NOW...

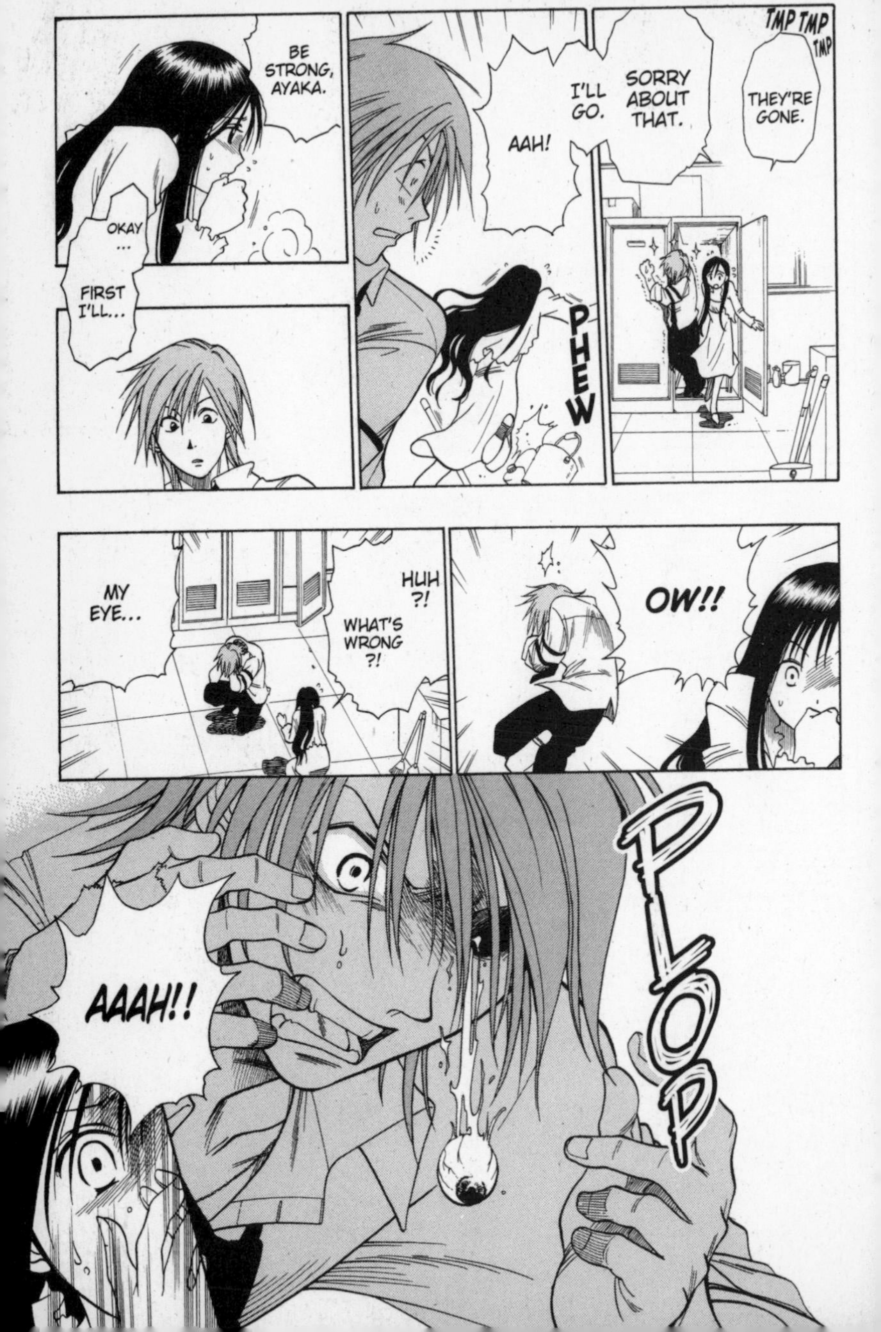
TMP TMP TMP
THEY'RE GONE.
SORRY ABOUT THAT. I'LL GO.
AAH!
PHEW
BE STRONG, AYAKA.
OKAY...
FIRST I'LL...
OW!!
HUH?!
WHAT'S WRONG?!
MY EYE...
PLOP
AAAH!!

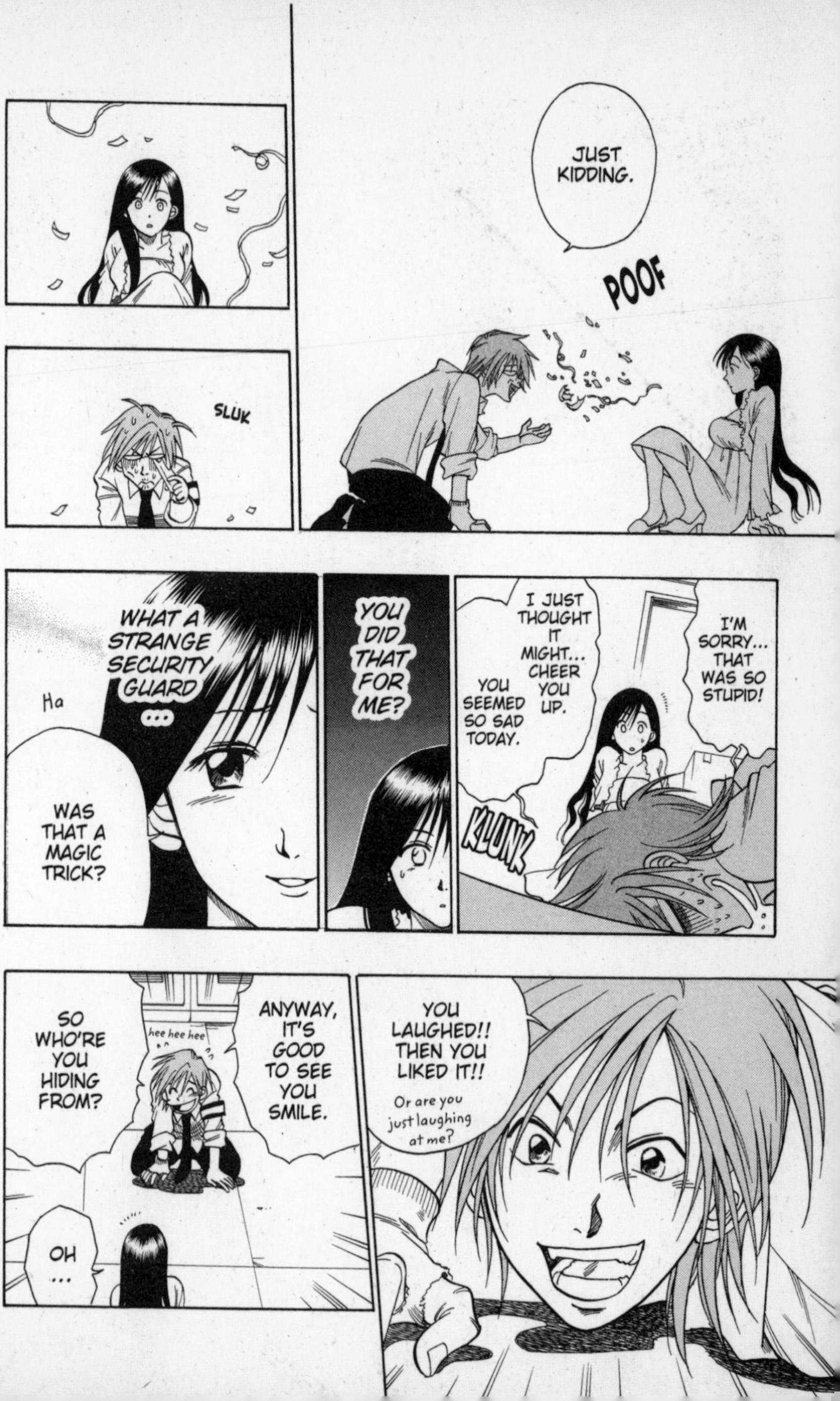
JUST KIDDING.
POOF
SLUK
I'M SORRY... THAT WAS SO STUPID!
I JUST THOUGHT IT MIGHT... CHEER YOU UP.
YOU SEEMED SO SAD TODAY.
KLUNK
YOU DID THAT FOR ME?
WHAT A STRANGE SECURITY GUARD...
Ha
WAS THAT A MAGIC TRICK?
YOU LAUGHED!! THEN YOU LIKED IT!!
Or are you just laughing at me?
ANYWAY, IT'S GOOD TO SEE YOU SMILE.
hee hee hee
SO WHO'RE YOU HIDING FROM?
OH...

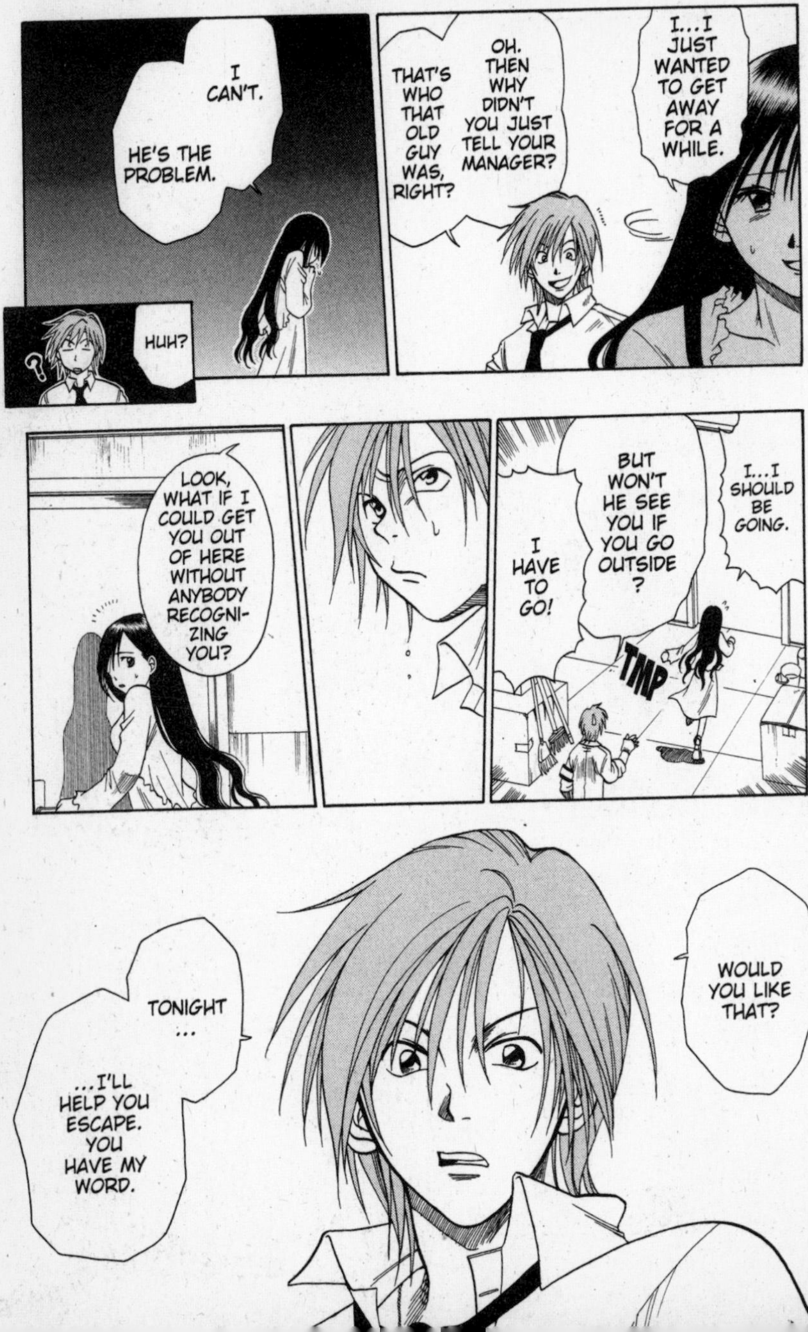
I...I JUST WANTED TO GET AWAY FOR A WHILE.
OH. THEN WHY DIDN'T YOU JUST TELL YOUR MANAGER?
THAT'S WHO THAT OLD GUY WAS, RIGHT?
I CAN'T.
HE'S THE PROBLEM.
HUH?
I...I SHOULD BE GOING.
BUT WON'T HE SEE YOU IF YOU GO OUTSIDE?
I HAVE TO GO!
TMP
LOOK, WHAT IF I COULD GET YOU OUT OF HERE WITHOUT ANYBODY RECOGNI-ZING YOU?
WOULD YOU LIKE THAT?
TONIGHT...
...I'LL HELP YOU ESCAPE. YOU HAVE MY WORD.

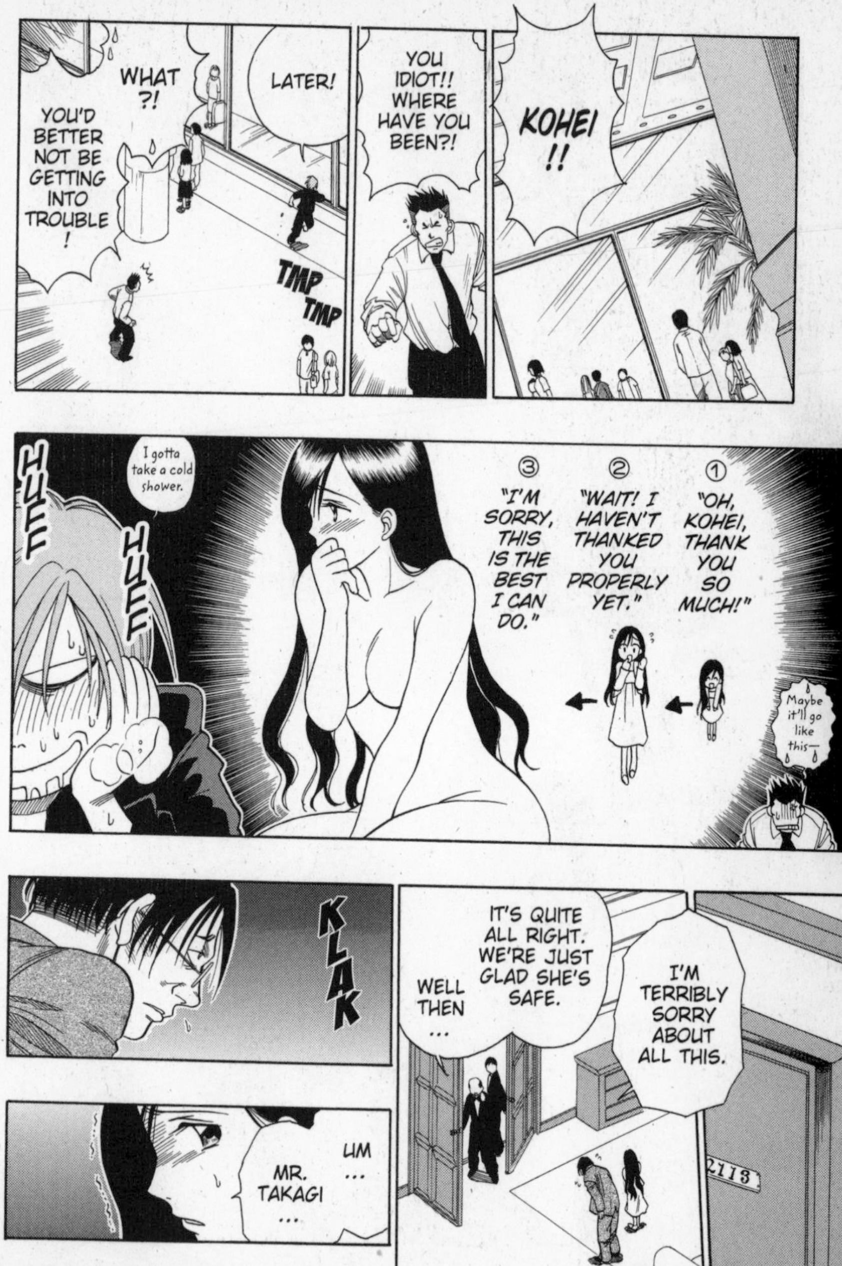
KOHEI !!
YOU IDIOT!! WHERE HAVE YOU BEEN?!
LATER!
WHAT ?!
YOU'D BETTER NOT BE GETTING INTO TROUBLE !
TMP TMP
Maybe it'll go like this—
① "OH, KOHEI, THANK YOU SO MUCH!"
② "WAIT! I HAVEN'T THANKED YOU PROPERLY YET."
③ "I'M SORRY, THIS IS THE BEST I CAN DO."
I gotta take a cold shower.
HUFF HUFF
I'M TERRIBLY SORRY ABOUT ALL THIS.
IT'S QUITE ALL RIGHT. WE'RE JUST GLAD SHE'S SAFE.
WELL THEN ...
2113
KLAK
UM ...
MR. TAKAGI ...

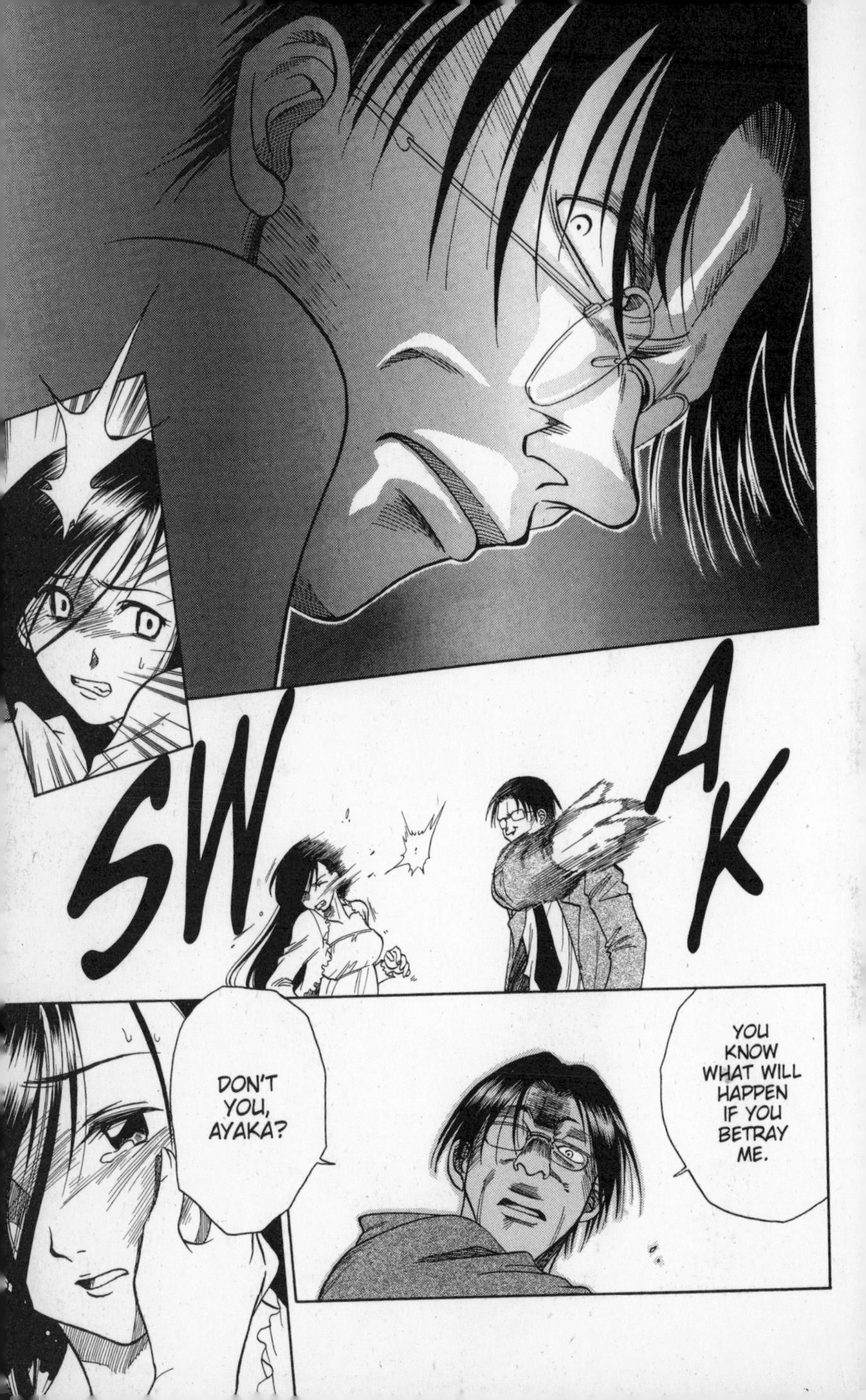
SWAK
YOU KNOW WHAT WILL HAPPEN IF YOU BETRAY ME.
DON'T YOU, AYAKA?

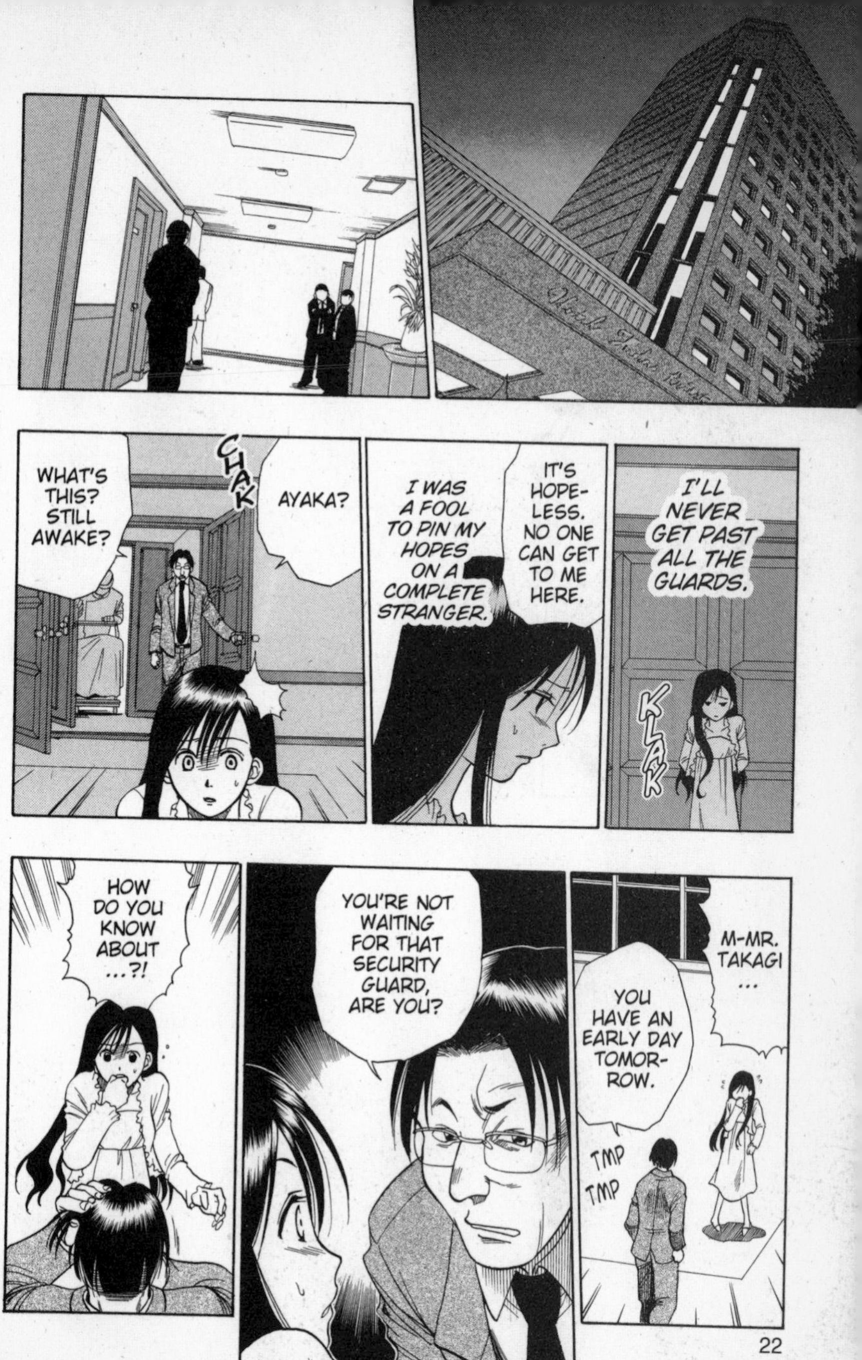
I'LL NEVER GET PAST ALL THE GUARDS.
KLAK
IT'S HOPELESS. NO ONE CAN GET TO ME HERE.
I WAS A FOOL TO PIN MY HOPES ON A COMPLETE STRANGER.
CHAK
AYAKA?
WHAT'S THIS? STILL AWAKE?
M-MR. TAKAGI ...
YOU HAVE AN EARLY DAY TOMORROW.
TMP
TMP
YOU'RE NOT WAITING FOR THAT SECURITY GUARD, ARE YOU?
HOW DO YOU KNOW ABOUT ...?!

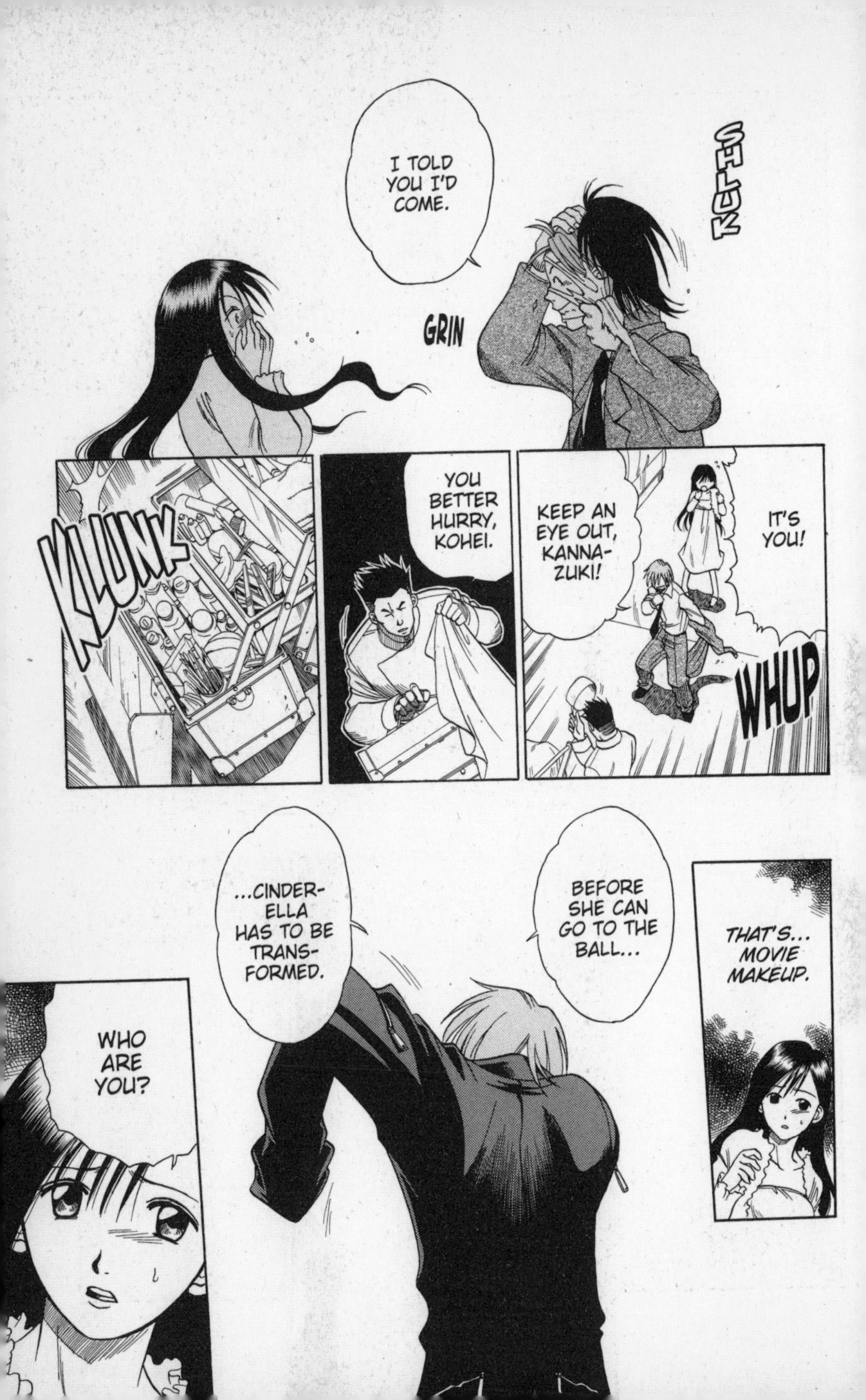
SHLUK
I TOLD YOU I'D COME.
GRIN
IT'S YOU!
KEEP AN EYE OUT, KANNA-ZUKI!
WHUP
YOU BETTER HURRY, KOHEI.
KLUNK
THAT'S... MOVIE MAKEUP.
BEFORE SHE CAN GO TO THE BALL...
...CINDER-ELLA HAS TO BE TRANS-FORMED.
WHO ARE YOU?

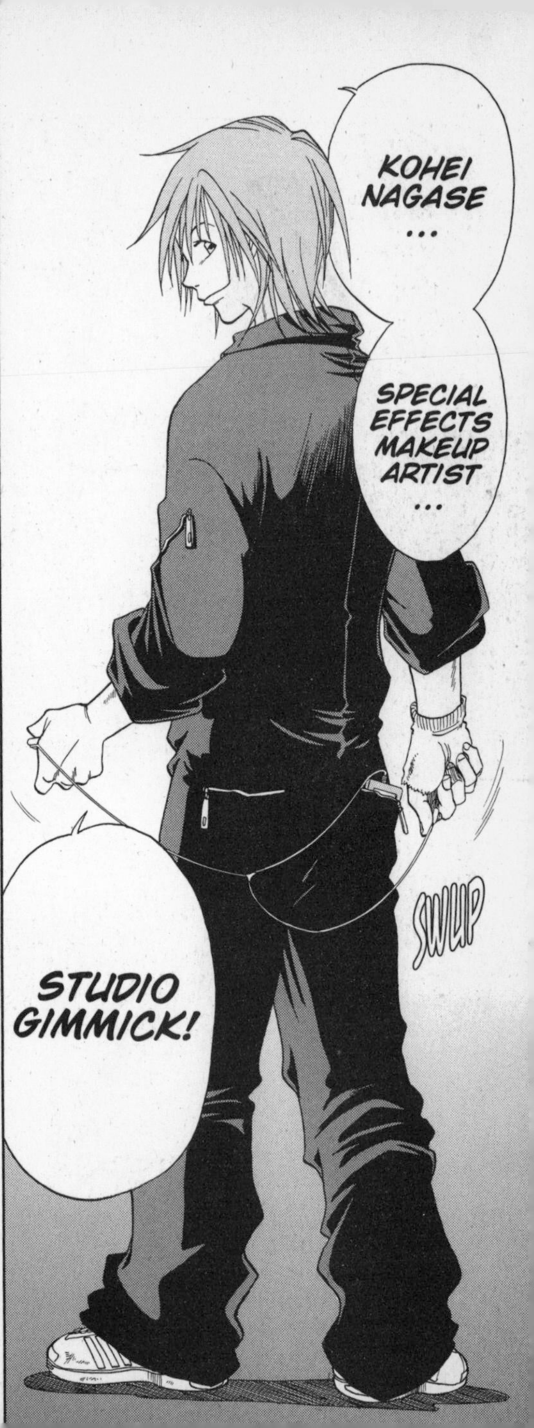
KOHEI NAGASE ...
SPECIAL EFFECTS MAKEUP ARTIST ...
SWUP
STUDIO GIMMICK!

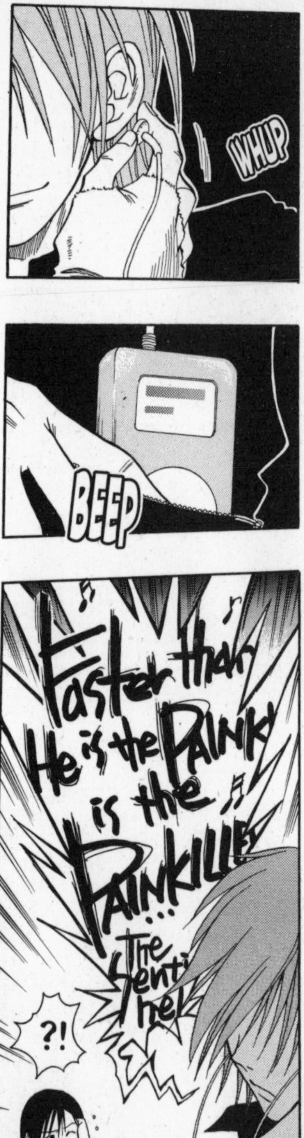
WHUP
BEEP
Faster than
He is the PAINK
is the
PAINKILLE
...
?!

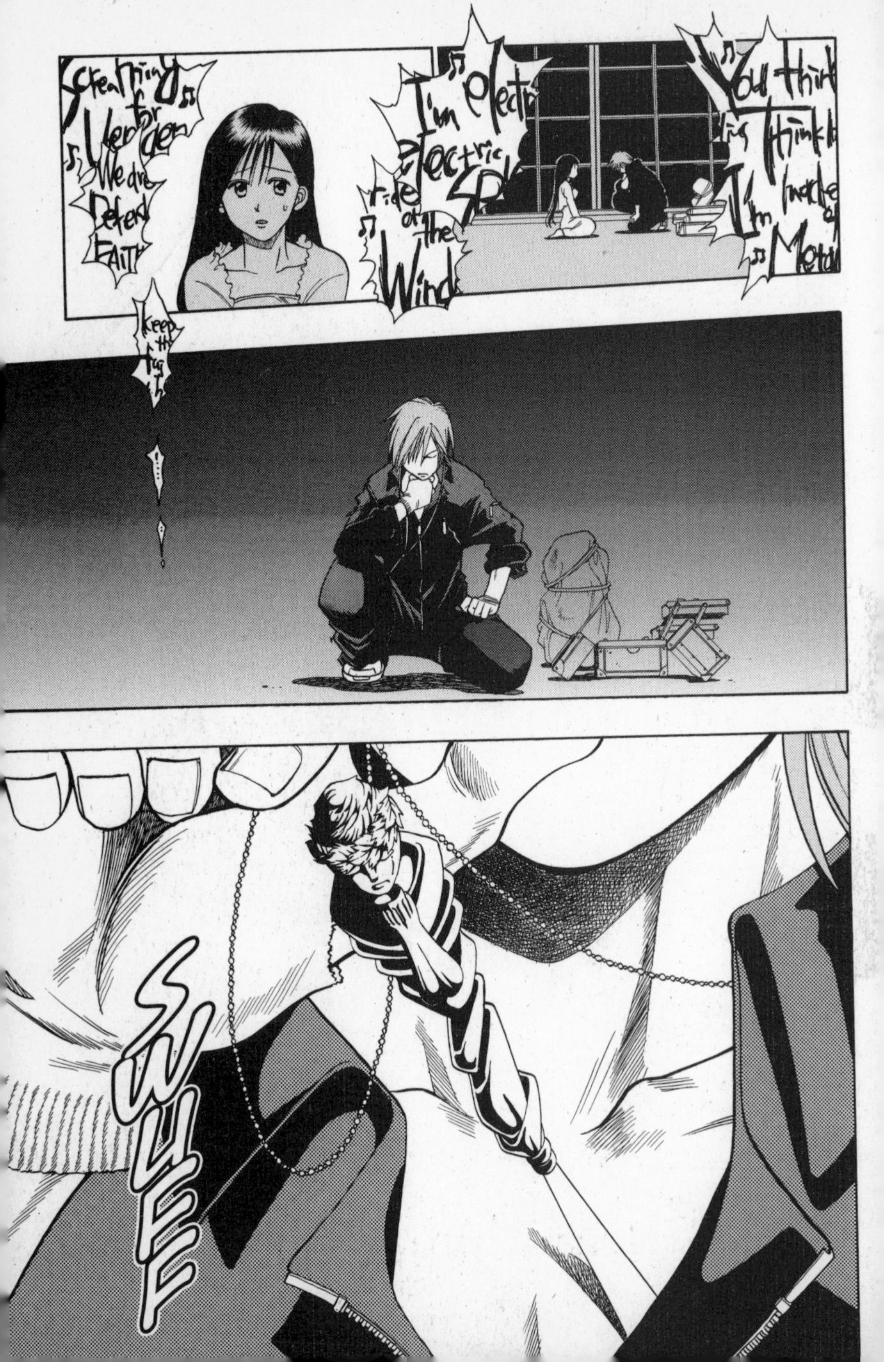

♫ You think
Think
I'm
♫ Metal
♫ I'm electric
electric
♫ ride on the Wind
Screaming for ♫
♫ We are Defenders Faith
Keep the faith
...!
SWEEE

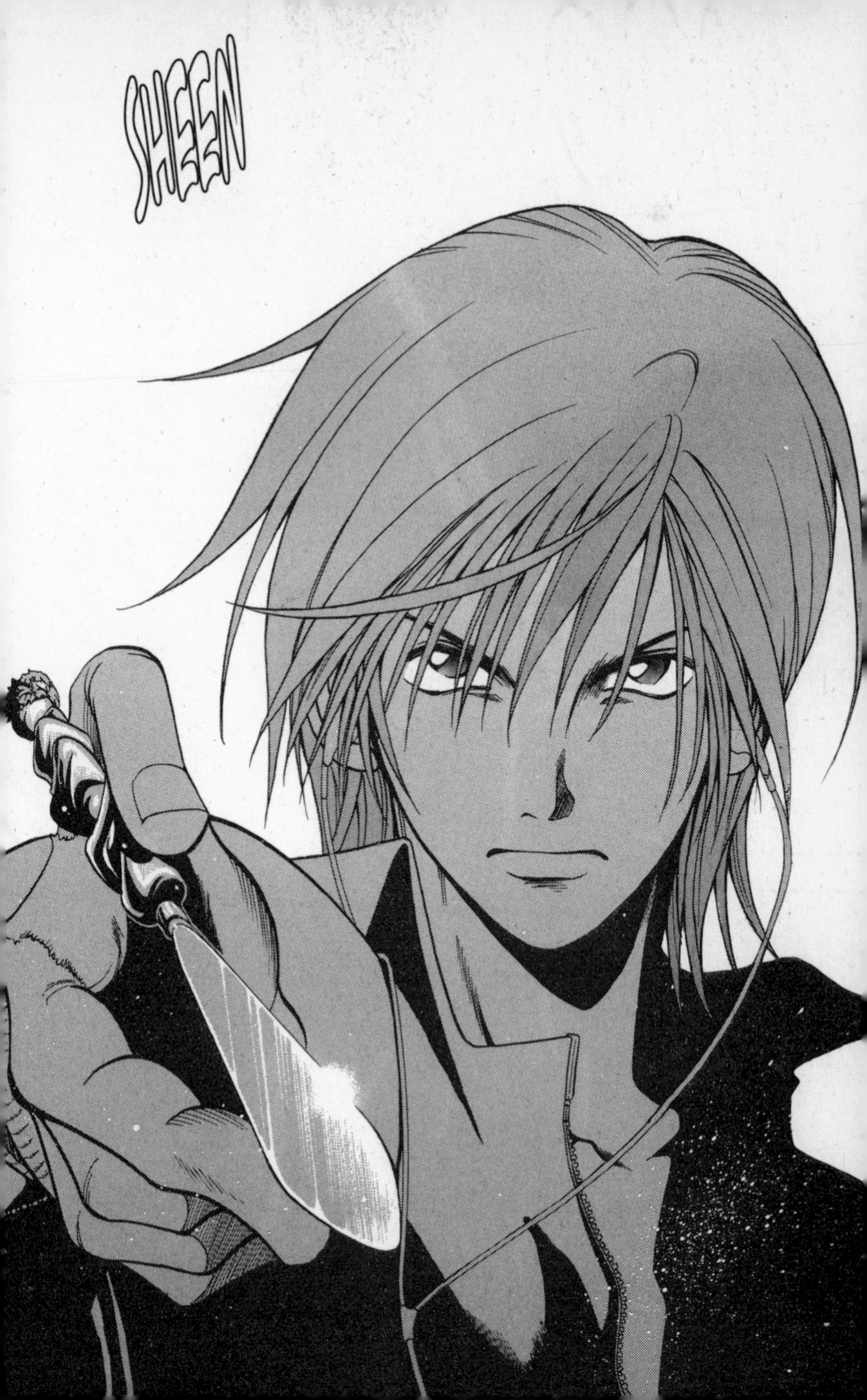
SHEEN

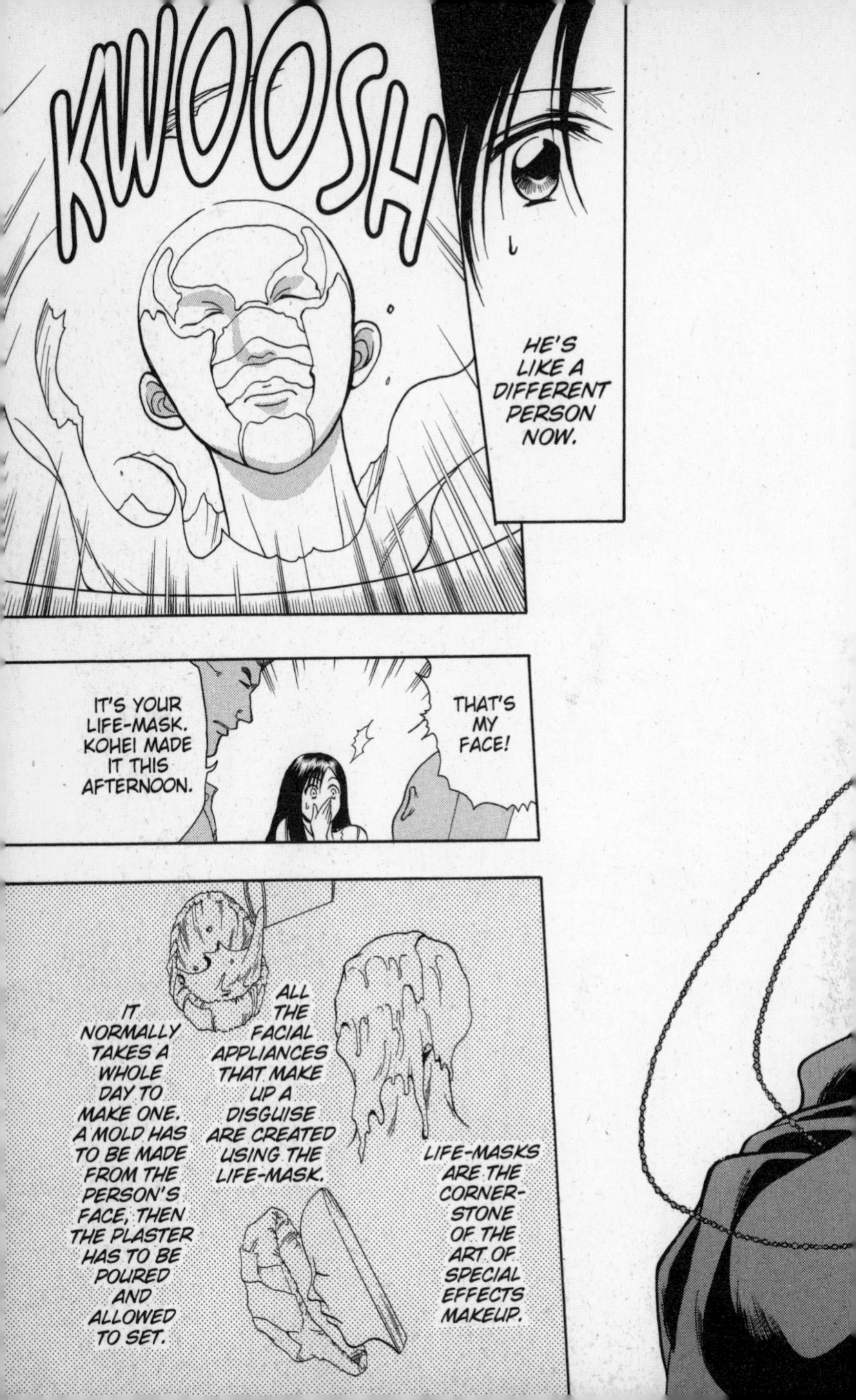
KWOOSH
HE'S LIKE A DIFFERENT PERSON NOW.
THAT'S MY FACE!
IT'S YOUR LIFE-MASK. KOHEI MADE IT THIS AFTERNOON.
LIFE-MASKS ARE THE CORNER-STONE OF THE ART OF SPECIAL EFFECTS MAKEUP.
ALL THE FACIAL APPLIANCES THAT MAKE UP A DISGUISE ARE CREATED USING THE LIFE-MASK.
IT NORMALLY TAKES A WHOLE DAY TO MAKE ONE. A MOLD HAS TO BE MADE FROM THE PERSON'S FACE, THEN THE PLASTER HAS TO BE POURED AND ALLOWED TO SET.

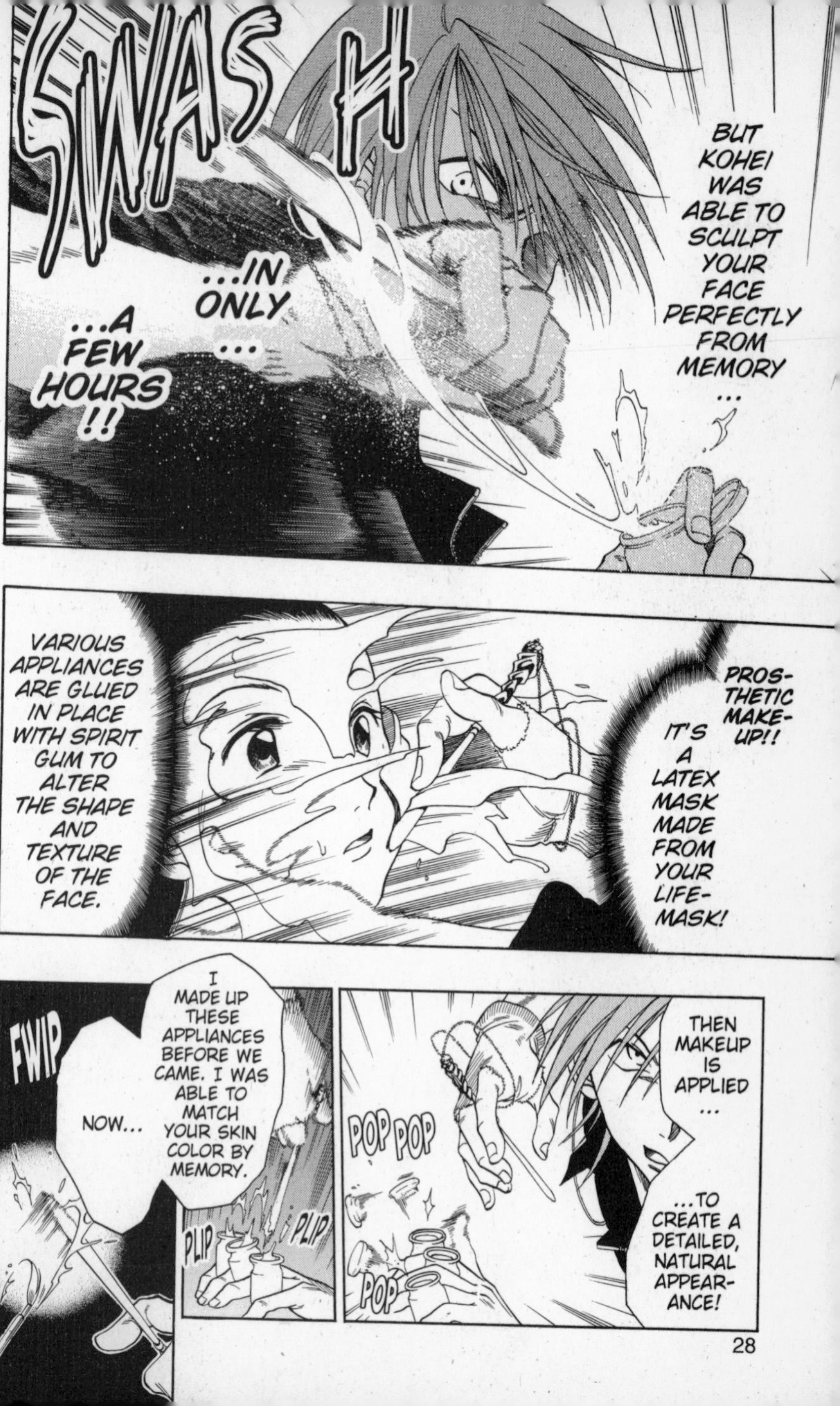
SWASH
BUT KOHEI WAS ABLE TO SCULPT YOUR FACE PERFECTLY FROM MEMORY ...
...IN ONLY ...
...A FEW HOURS !!
PROSTHETIC MAKE-UP!!
IT'S A LATEX MASK MADE FROM YOUR LIFE-MASK!
VARIOUS APPLIANCES ARE GLUED IN PLACE WITH SPIRIT GUM TO ALTER THE SHAPE AND TEXTURE OF THE FACE.
THEN MAKEUP IS APPLIED ...
POP POP
POP
...TO CREATE A DETAILED, NATURAL APPEARANCE!
I MADE UP THESE APPLIANCES BEFORE WE CAME. I WAS ABLE TO MATCH YOUR SKIN COLOR BY MEMORY.
PLIP
PLIP
FWIP
NOW...

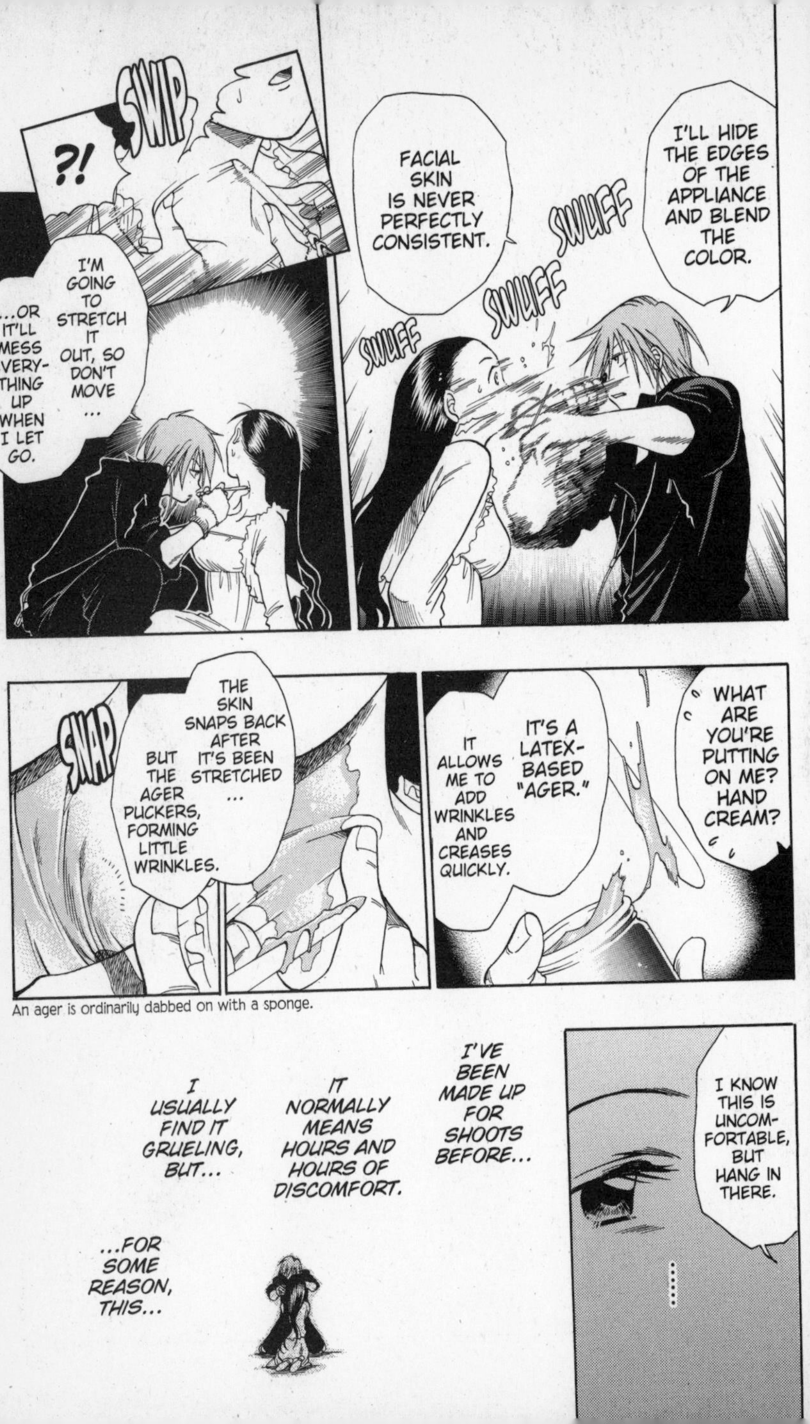
I'LL HIDE THE EDGES OF THE APPLIANCE AND BLEND THE COLOR.
FACIAL SKIN IS NEVER PERFECTLY CONSISTENT.
SWUFF
SWUFF
SWUFF
SWIP
?!
I'M GOING TO STRETCH IT OUT, SO DON'T MOVE...
...OR IT'LL MESS EVERYTHING UP WHEN I LET GO.
WHAT ARE YOU'RE PUTTING ON ME? HAND CREAM?
IT'S A LATEX-BASED "AGER."
IT ALLOWS ME TO ADD WRINKLES AND CREASES QUICKLY.
THE SKIN SNAPS BACK AFTER IT'S BEEN STRETCHED...
BUT THE AGER PUCKERS, FORMING LITTLE WRINKLES.
SNAP
I KNOW THIS IS UNCOMFORTABLE, BUT HANG IN THERE.
......
I'VE BEEN MADE UP FOR SHOOTS BEFORE...
IT NORMALLY MEANS HOURS AND HOURS OF DISCOMFORT.
I USUALLY FIND IT GRUELING, BUT...
...FOR SOME REASON, THIS...
An ager is ordinarily dabbed on with a sponge.

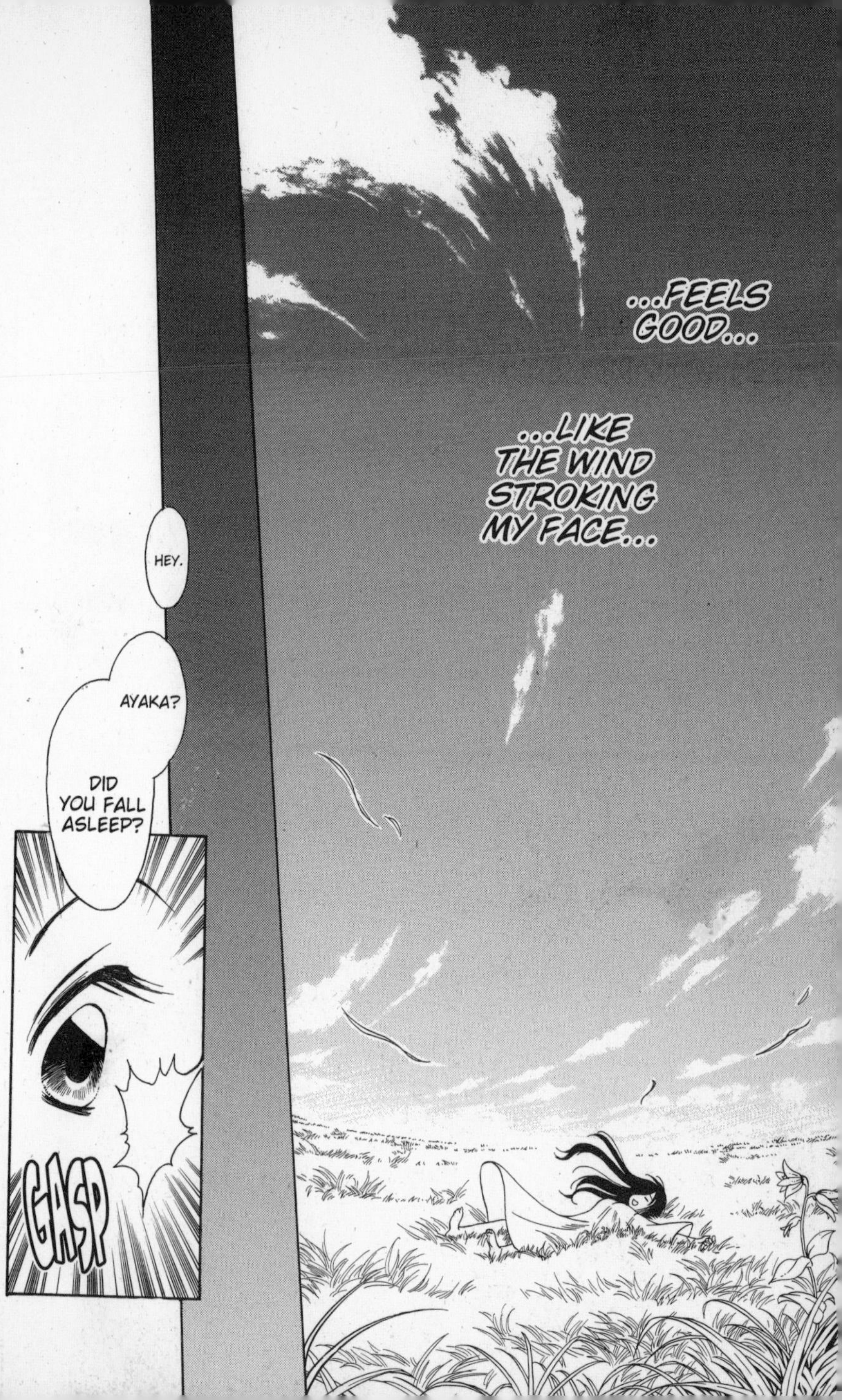
...FEELS GOOD...
...LIKE THE WIND STROKING MY FACE...
HEY.
AYAKA?
DID YOU FALL ASLEEP?
GASP

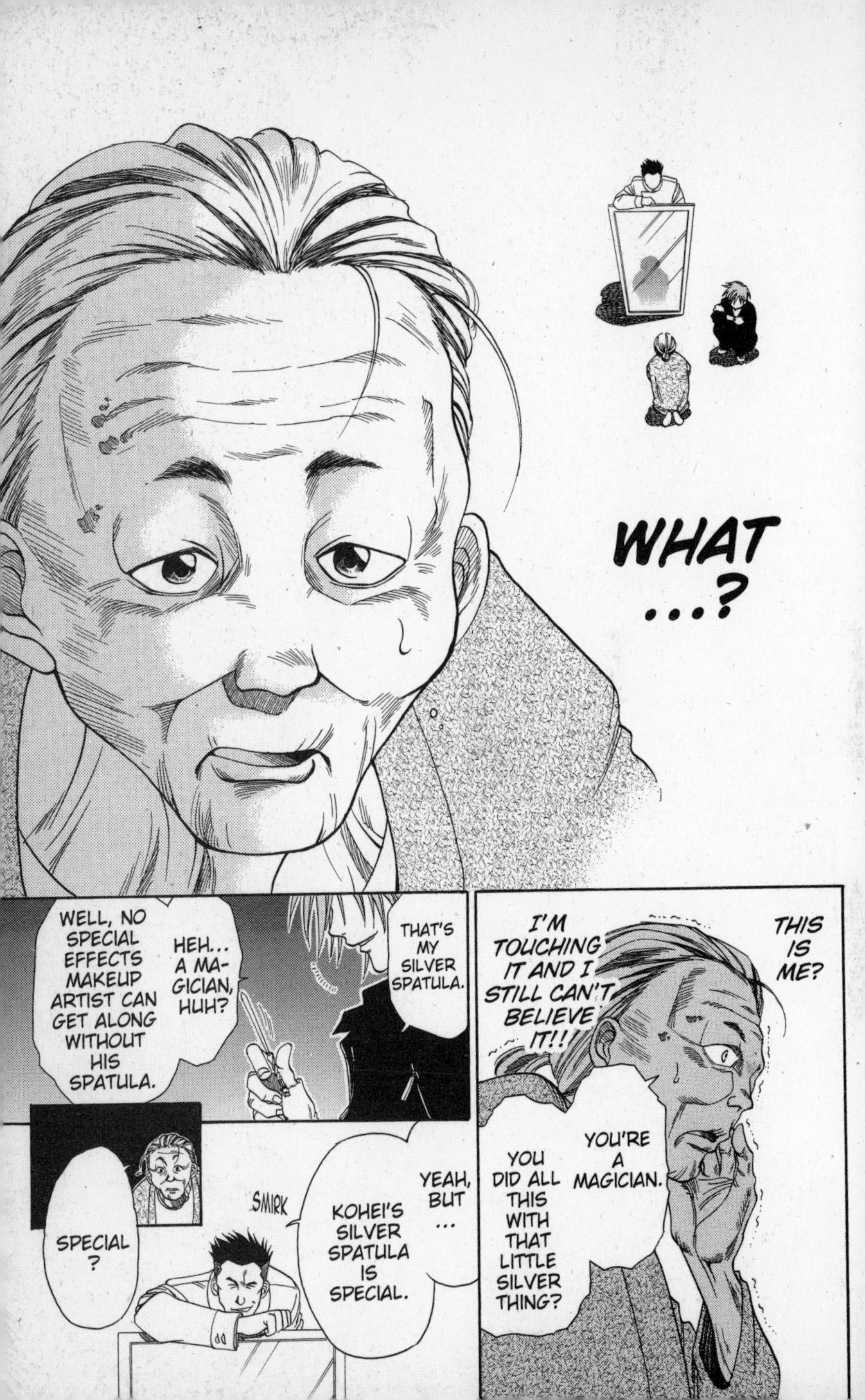
WHAT ...?
THIS IS ME?
I'M TOUCHING IT AND I STILL CAN'T BELIEVE IT!!
YOU'RE A MAGICIAN.
YOU DID ALL THIS WITH THAT LITTLE SILVER THING?
THAT'S MY SILVER SPATULA.
HEH... A MAGICIAN, HUH?
WELL, NO SPECIAL EFFECTS MAKEUP ARTIST CAN GET ALONG WITHOUT HIS SPATULA.
YEAH, BUT ...
KOHEI'S SILVER SPATULA IS SPECIAL.
SMIRK
SPECIAL?

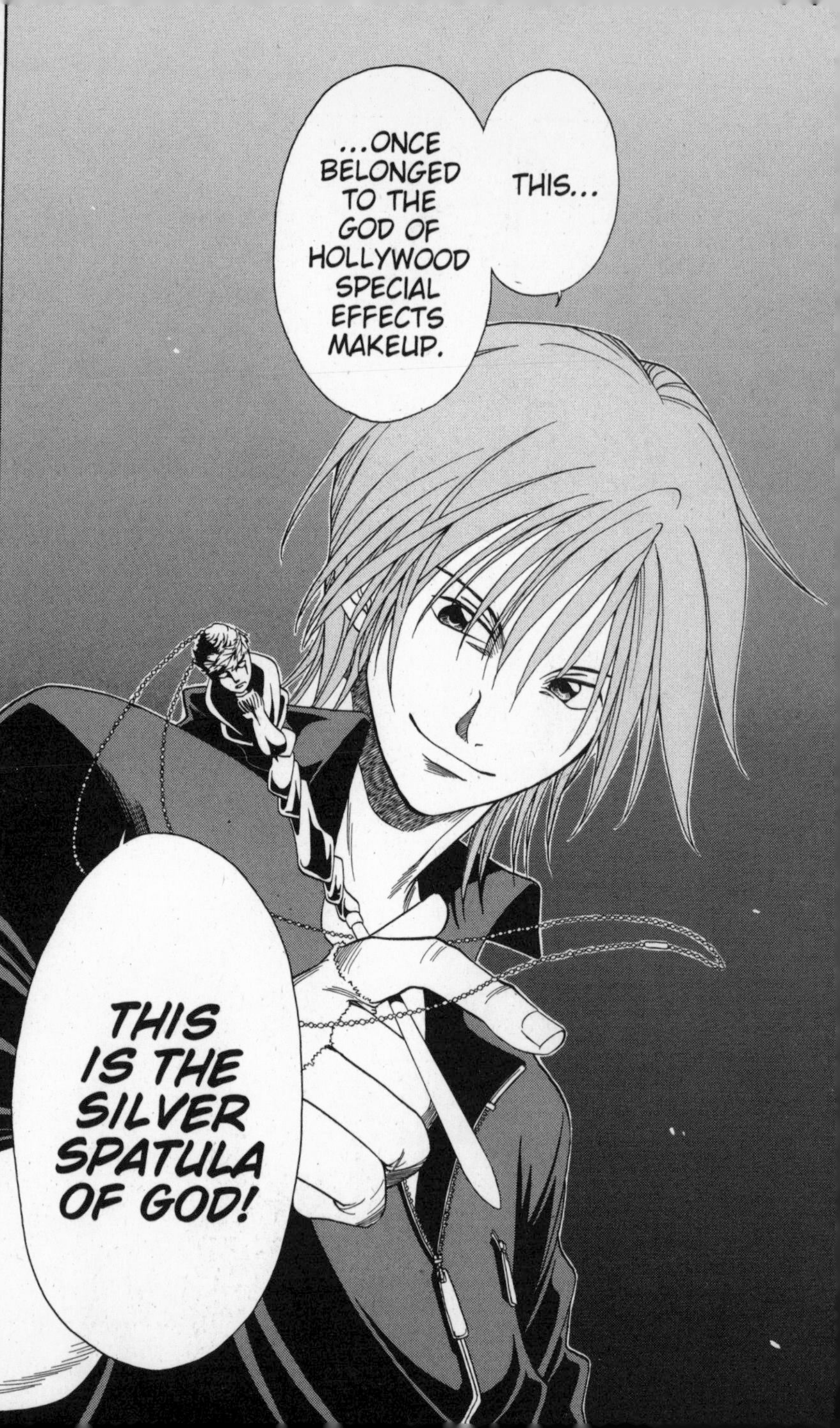
THIS...
...ONCE BELONGED TO THE GOD OF HOLLYWOOD SPECIAL EFFECTS MAKEUP.
THIS IS THE SILVER SPATULA OF GOD!

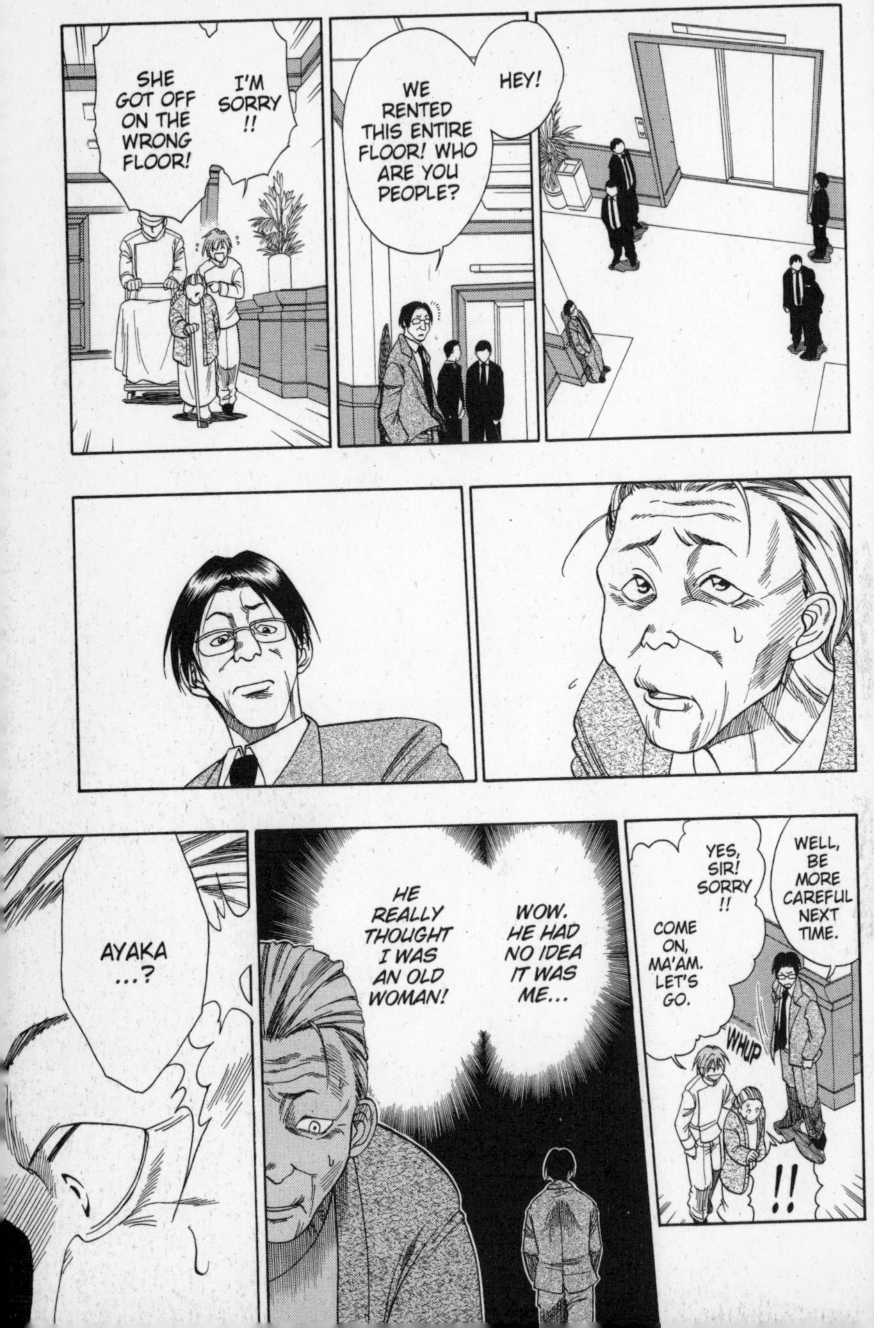
HEY!
WE RENTED THIS ENTIRE FLOOR! WHO ARE YOU PEOPLE?
I'M SORRY !!
SHE GOT OFF ON THE WRONG FLOOR!
WELL, BE MORE CAREFUL NEXT TIME.
YES, SIR! SORRY !!
COME ON, MA'AM. LET'S GO.
WHUP
!!
WOW. HE HAD NO IDEA IT WAS ME...
HE REALLY THOUGHT I WAS AN OLD WOMAN!
AYAKA ...?

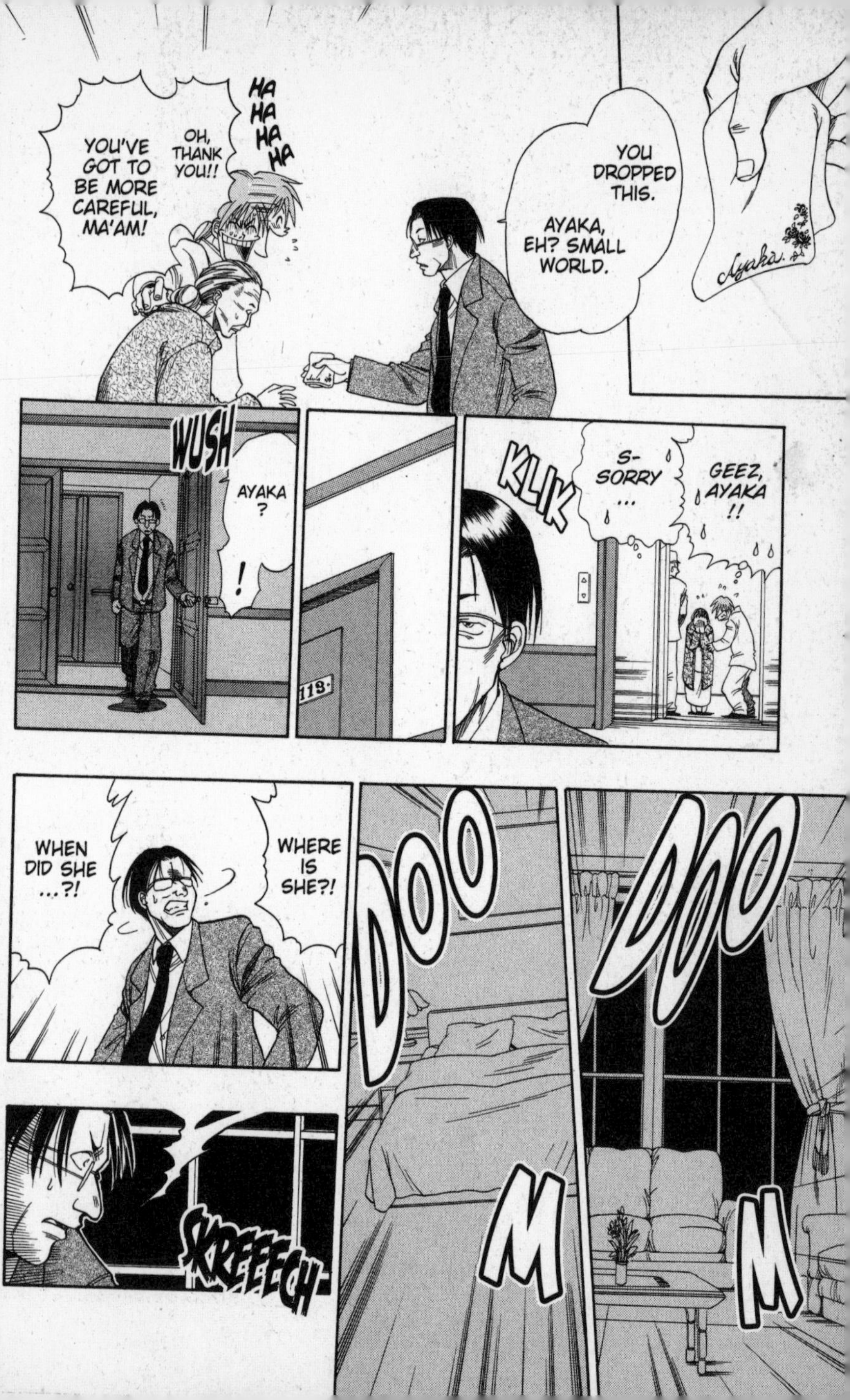

Ayaka.
YOU DROPPED THIS.
AYAKA, EH? SMALL WORLD.
HA HA HA HA
OH, THANK YOU!!
YOU'VE GOT TO BE MORE CAREFUL, MA'AM!
KLIK
GEEZ, AYAKA!!
S-SORRY...
113
WUSH
AYAKA?
!
DOOM
DOOM
WHERE IS SHE?!
WHEN DID SHE ...?!
SKREEEECH

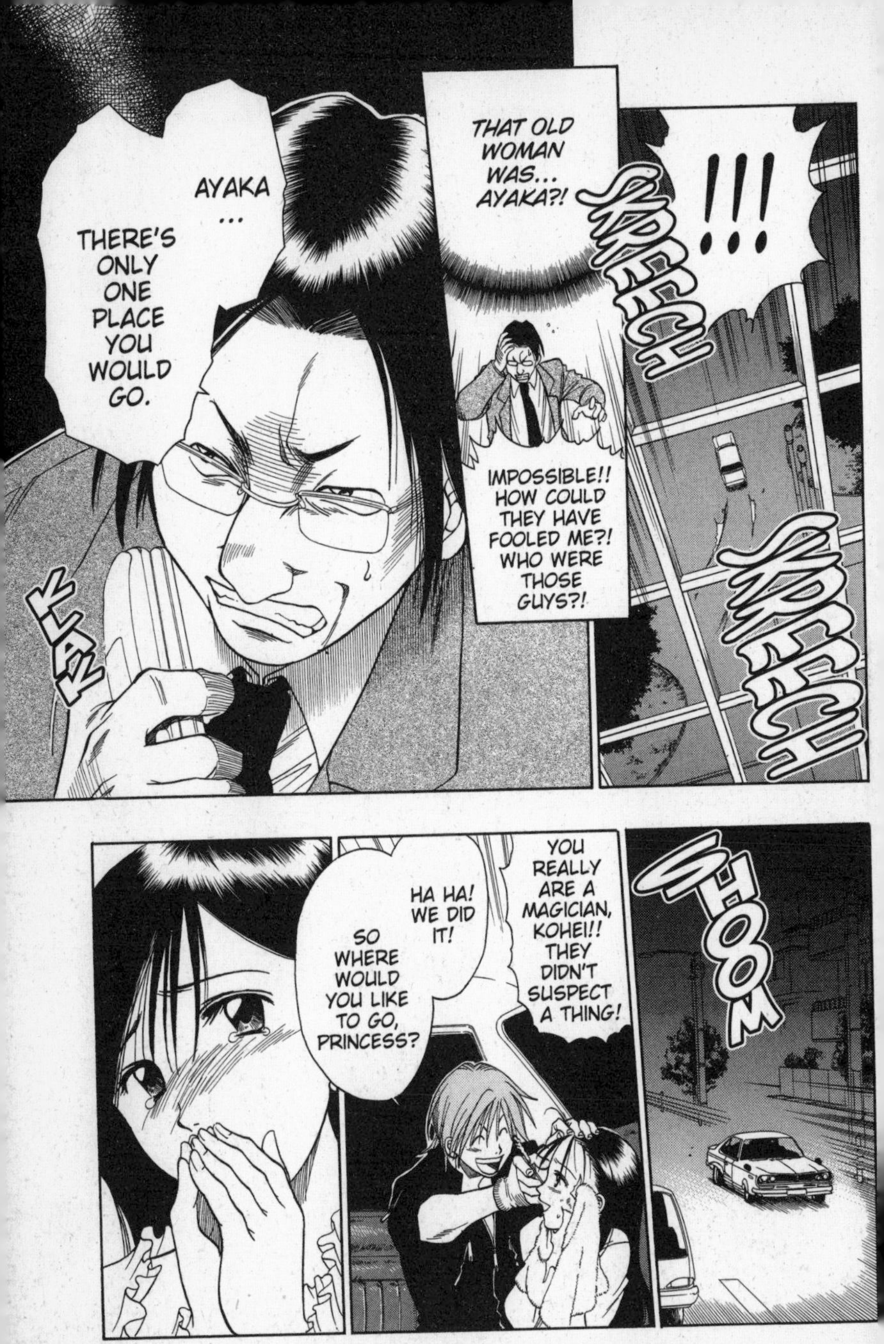
!!!
SKREECH
SKREECH
THAT OLD WOMAN WAS... AYAKA?!
IMPOSSIBLE!! HOW COULD THEY HAVE FOOLED ME?! WHO WERE THOSE GUYS?!
AYAKA...
THERE'S ONLY ONE PLACE YOU WOULD GO.
VROOM
YOU REALLY ARE A MAGICIAN, KOHEI!! THEY DIDN'T SUSPECT A THING!
HA HA! WE DID IT!
SO WHERE WOULD YOU LIKE TO GO, PRINCESS?

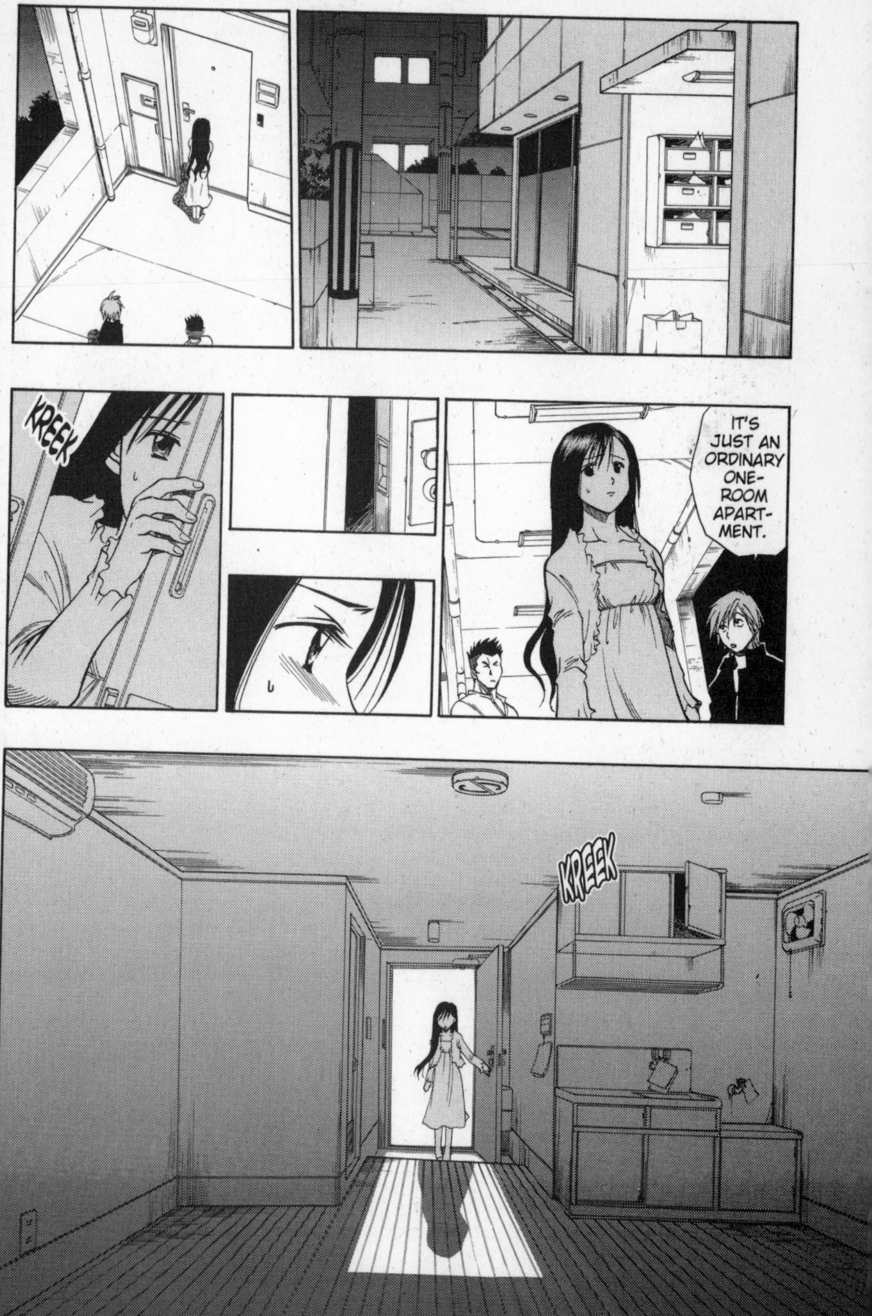
IT'S JUST AN ORDINARY ONE-ROOM APART-MENT.
KREEK
KREEK

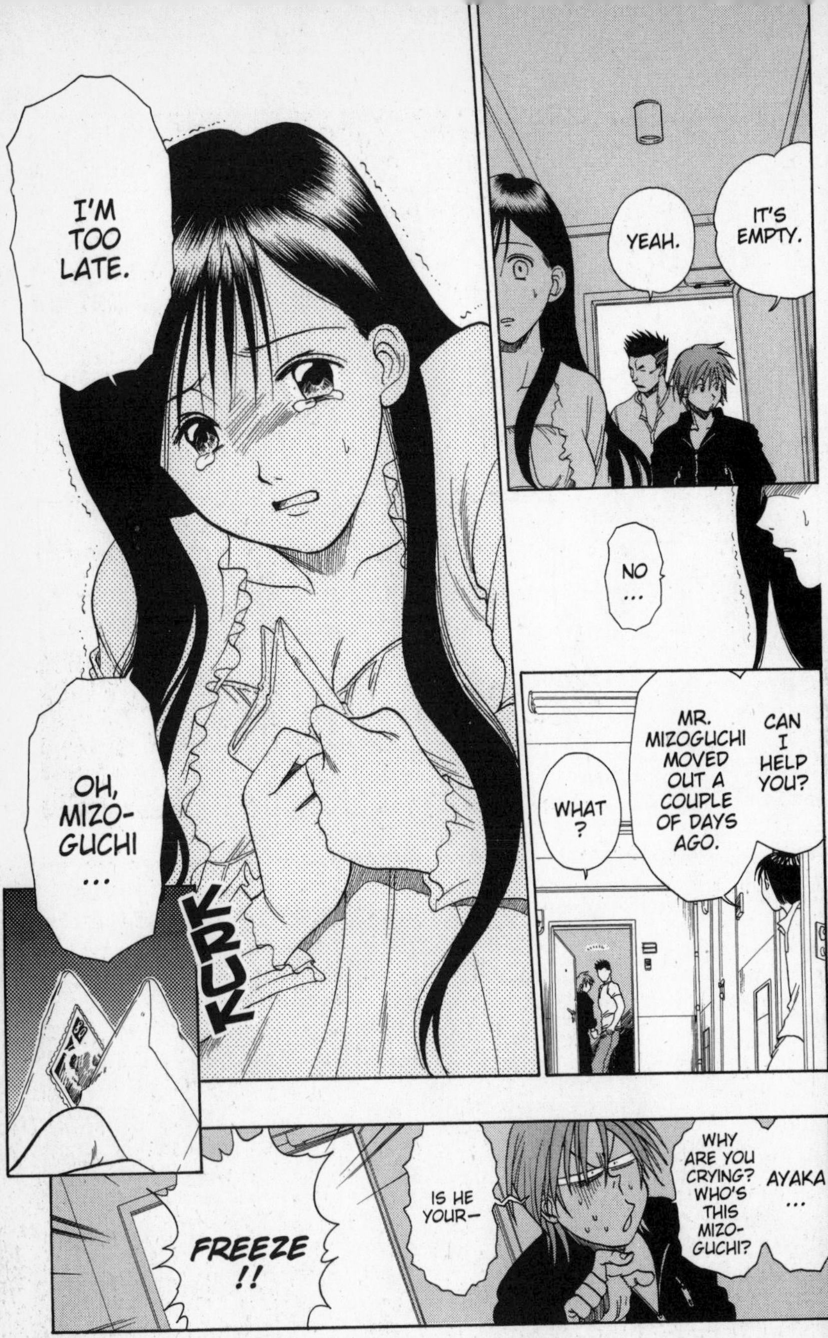
IT'S EMPTY.
YEAH.
NO ...
CAN I HELP YOU?
MR. MIZOGUCHI MOVED OUT A COUPLE OF DAYS AGO.
WHAT?
I'M TOO LATE.
OH, MIZO-GUCHI ...
KRUK
AYAKA ...
WHY ARE YOU CRYING? WHO'S THIS MIZO-GUCHI?
IS HE YOUR—
FREEZE !!

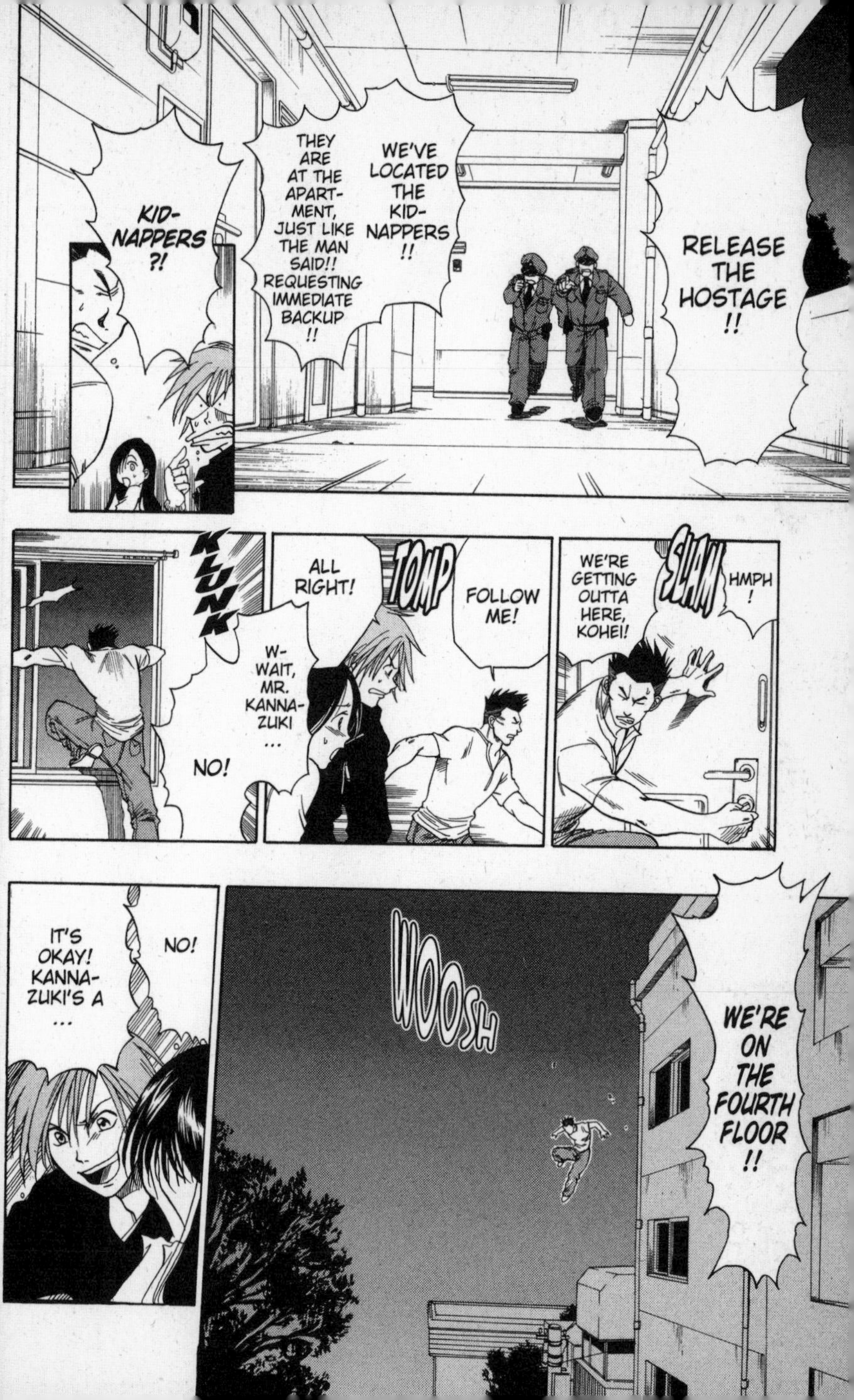
RELEASE THE HOSTAGE !!
WE'VE LOCATED THE KID-NAPPERS !!
THEY ARE AT THE APART-MENT, JUST LIKE THE MAN SAID!! REQUESTING IMMEDIATE BACKUP !!
KID-NAPPERS ?!
HMPH !
SLAM
WE'RE GETTING OUTTA HERE, KOHEI!
FOLLOW ME!
TOMP
ALL RIGHT!
W-WAIT, MR. KANNA-ZUKI ...
KLUNK
NO!
WE'RE ON THE FOURTH FLOOR !!
WOOSH
NO!
IT'S OKAY! KANNA-ZUKI'S A ...

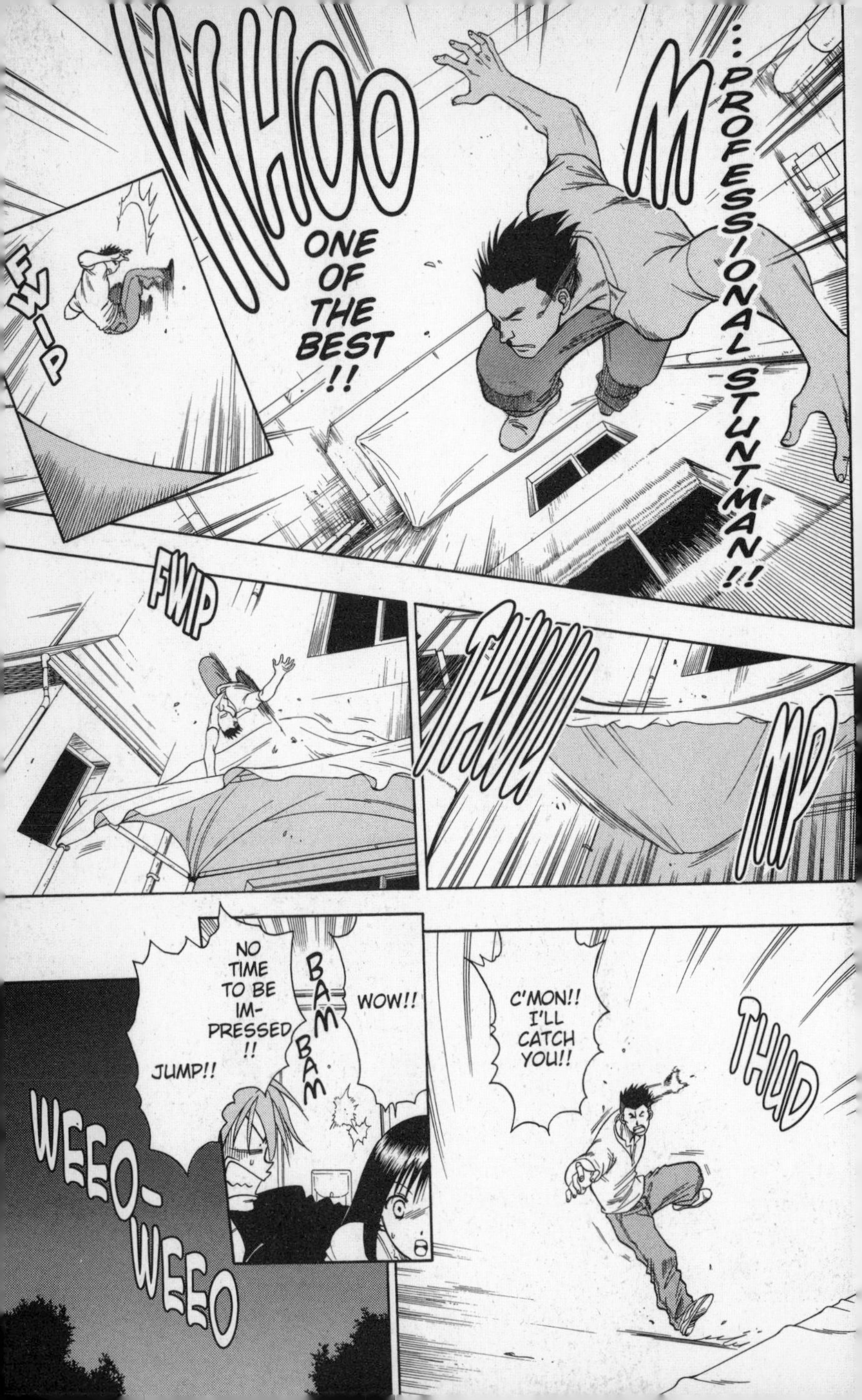

...PROFESSIONAL STUNTMAN!!
WHOOM
ONE OF THE BEST!!
FWIP
THUMP
FWIP
THUD
C'MON!! I'LL CATCH YOU!!
WOW!!
BAM BAM
NO TIME TO BE IM-PRESSED!!
JUMP!!
WEEO-WEEO

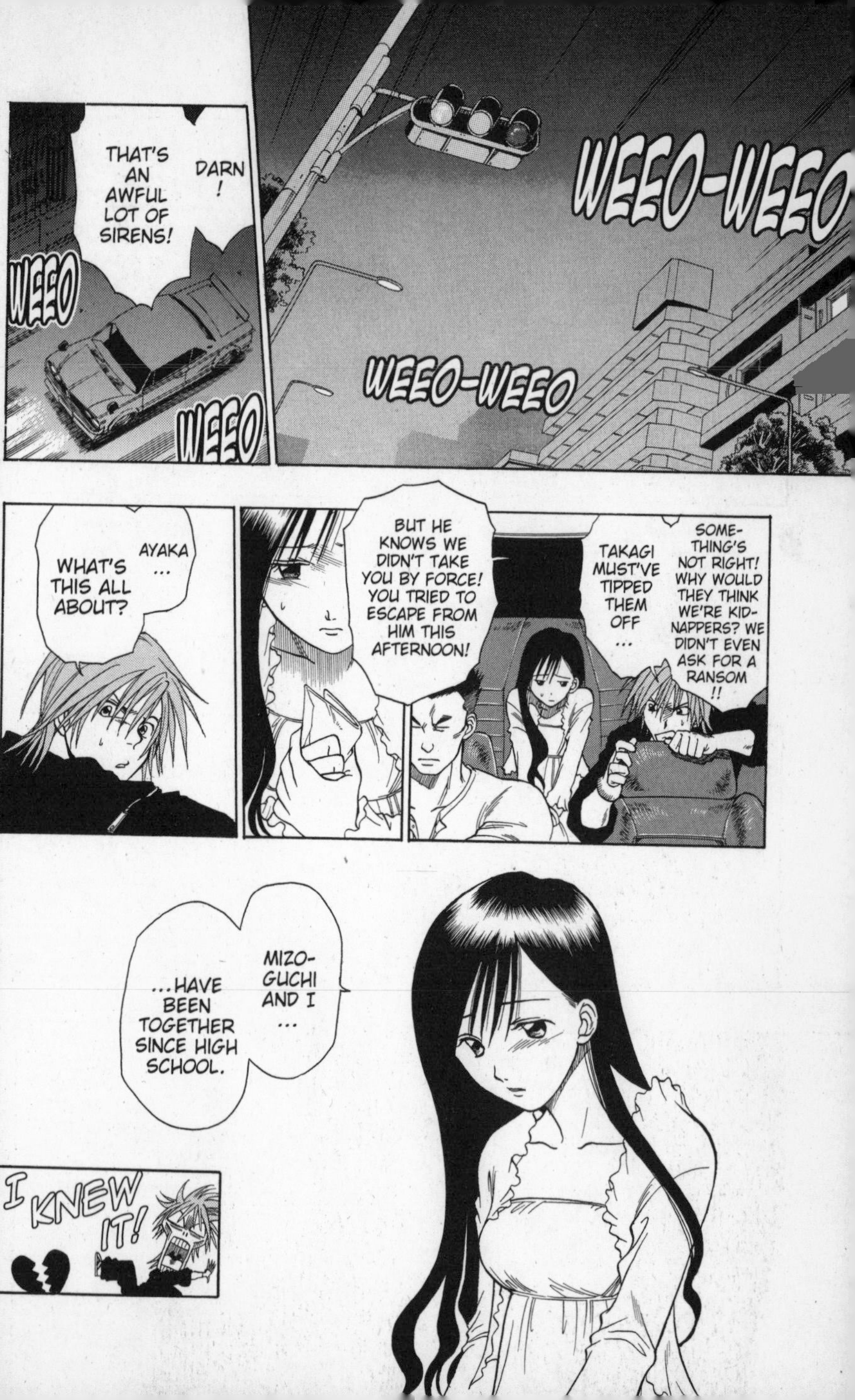
WEEO-WEEO
WEEO-WEEO
DARN!
THAT'S AN AWFUL LOT OF SIRENS!
WEEO
WEEO
SOME-THING'S NOT RIGHT! WHY WOULD THEY THINK WE'RE KID-NAPPERS? WE DIDN'T EVEN ASK FOR A RANSOM!!
TAKAGI MUST'VE TIPPED THEM OFF...
BUT HE KNOWS WE DIDN'T TAKE YOU BY FORCE! YOU TRIED TO ESCAPE FROM HIM THIS AFTERNOON!
AYAKA...
WHAT'S THIS ALL ABOUT?
MIZO-GUCHI AND I...
...HAVE BEEN TOGETHER SINCE HIGH SCHOOL.
I KNEW IT!

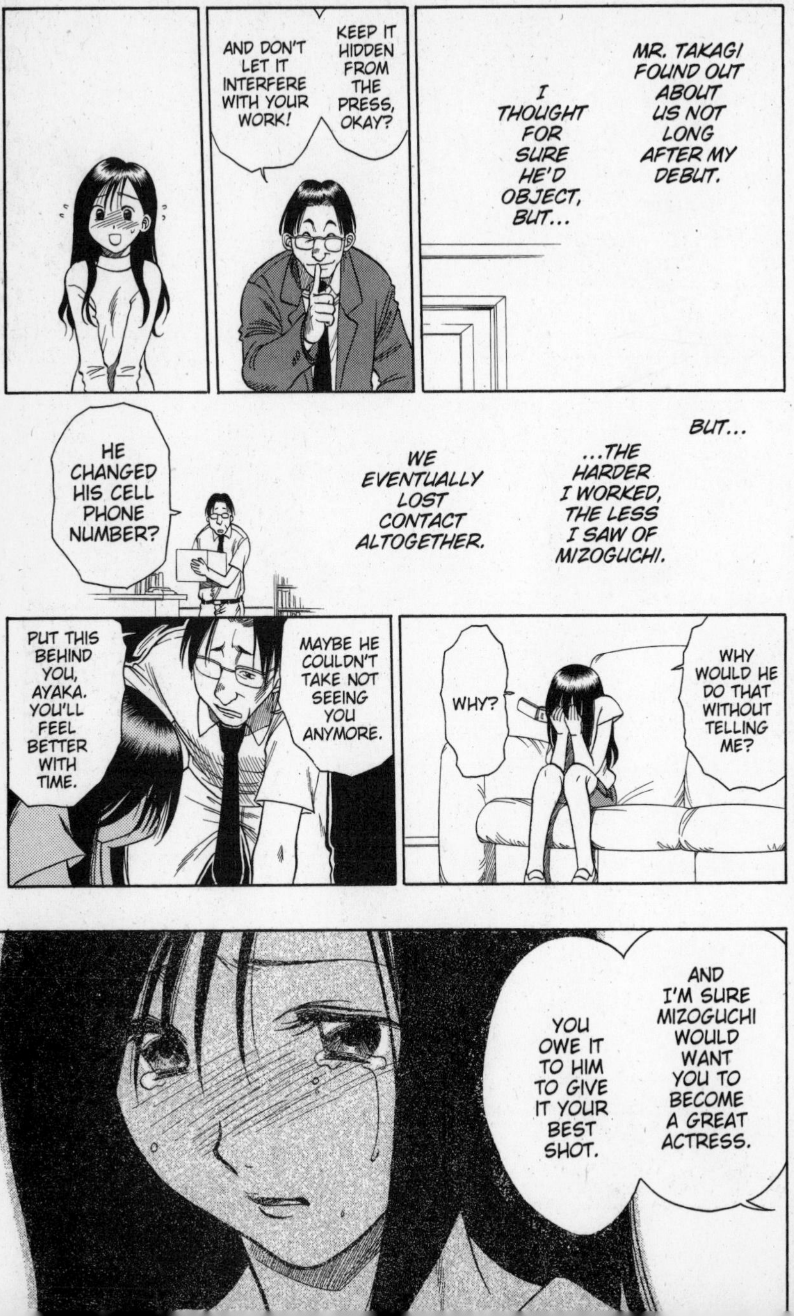
MR. TAKAGI FOUND OUT ABOUT US NOT LONG AFTER MY DEBUT.
I THOUGHT FOR SURE HE'D OBJECT, BUT...
KEEP IT HIDDEN FROM THE PRESS, OKAY?
AND DON'T LET IT INTERFERE WITH YOUR WORK!
BUT...
...THE HARDER I WORKED, THE LESS I SAW OF MIZOGUCHI.
WE EVENTUALLY LOST CONTACT ALTOGETHER.
HE CHANGED HIS CELL PHONE NUMBER?
WHY WOULD HE DO THAT WITHOUT TELLING ME?
WHY?
MAYBE HE COULDN'T TAKE NOT SEEING YOU ANYMORE.
PUT THIS BEHIND YOU, AYAKA. YOU'LL FEEL BETTER WITH TIME.
AND I'M SURE MIZOGUCHI WOULD WANT YOU TO BECOME A GREAT ACTRESS.
YOU OWE IT TO HIM TO GIVE IT YOUR BEST SHOT.

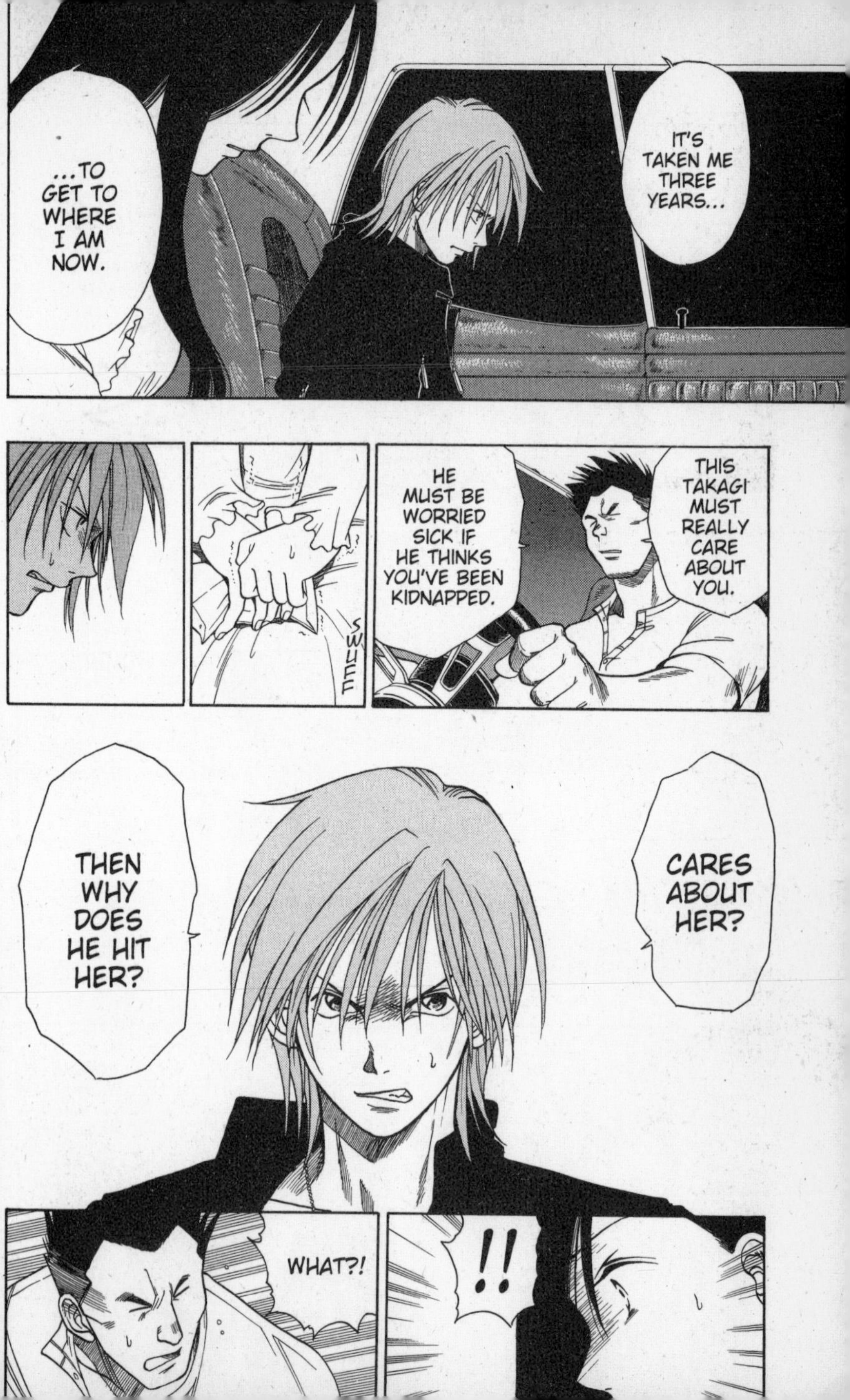
IT'S TAKEN ME THREE YEARS...
...TO GET TO WHERE I AM NOW.
THIS TAKAGI MUST REALLY CARE ABOUT YOU.
HE MUST BE WORRIED SICK IF HE THINKS YOU'VE BEEN KIDNAPPED.
SWUFF
CARES ABOUT HER?
THEN WHY DOES HE HIT HER?
!!
WHAT?!

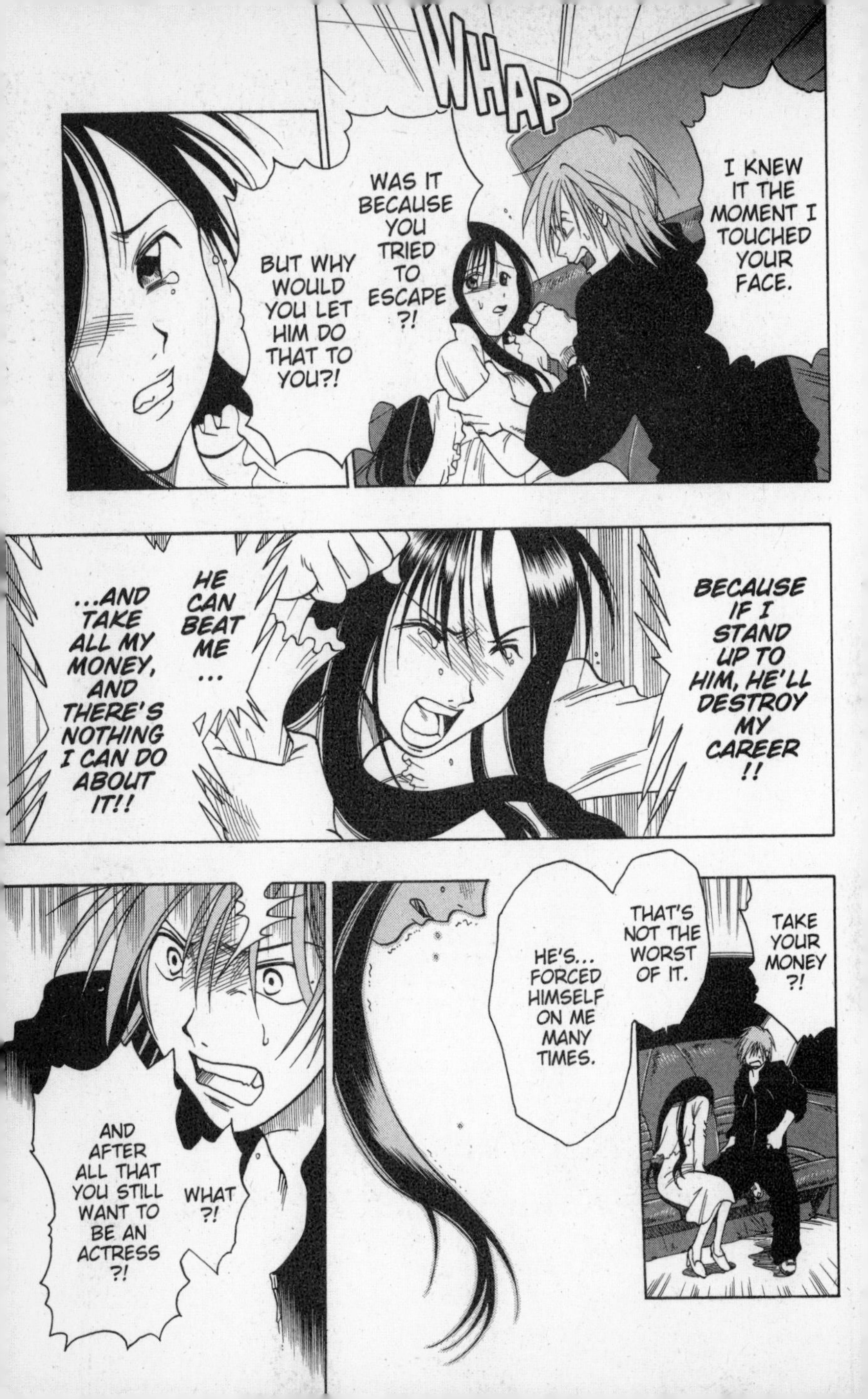
WHAP
I KNEW IT THE MOMENT I TOUCHED YOUR FACE.
WAS IT BECAUSE YOU TRIED TO ESCAPE?!
BUT WHY WOULD YOU LET HIM DO THAT TO YOU?!
BECAUSE IF I STAND UP TO HIM, HE'LL DESTROY MY CAREER!!
HE CAN BEAT ME...
...AND TAKE ALL MY MONEY, AND THERE'S NOTHING I CAN DO ABOUT IT!!
TAKE YOUR MONEY?!
THAT'S NOT THE WORST OF IT.
HE'S... FORCED HIMSELF ON ME MANY TIMES.
WHAT?!
AND AFTER ALL THAT YOU STILL WANT TO BE AN ACTRESS?!

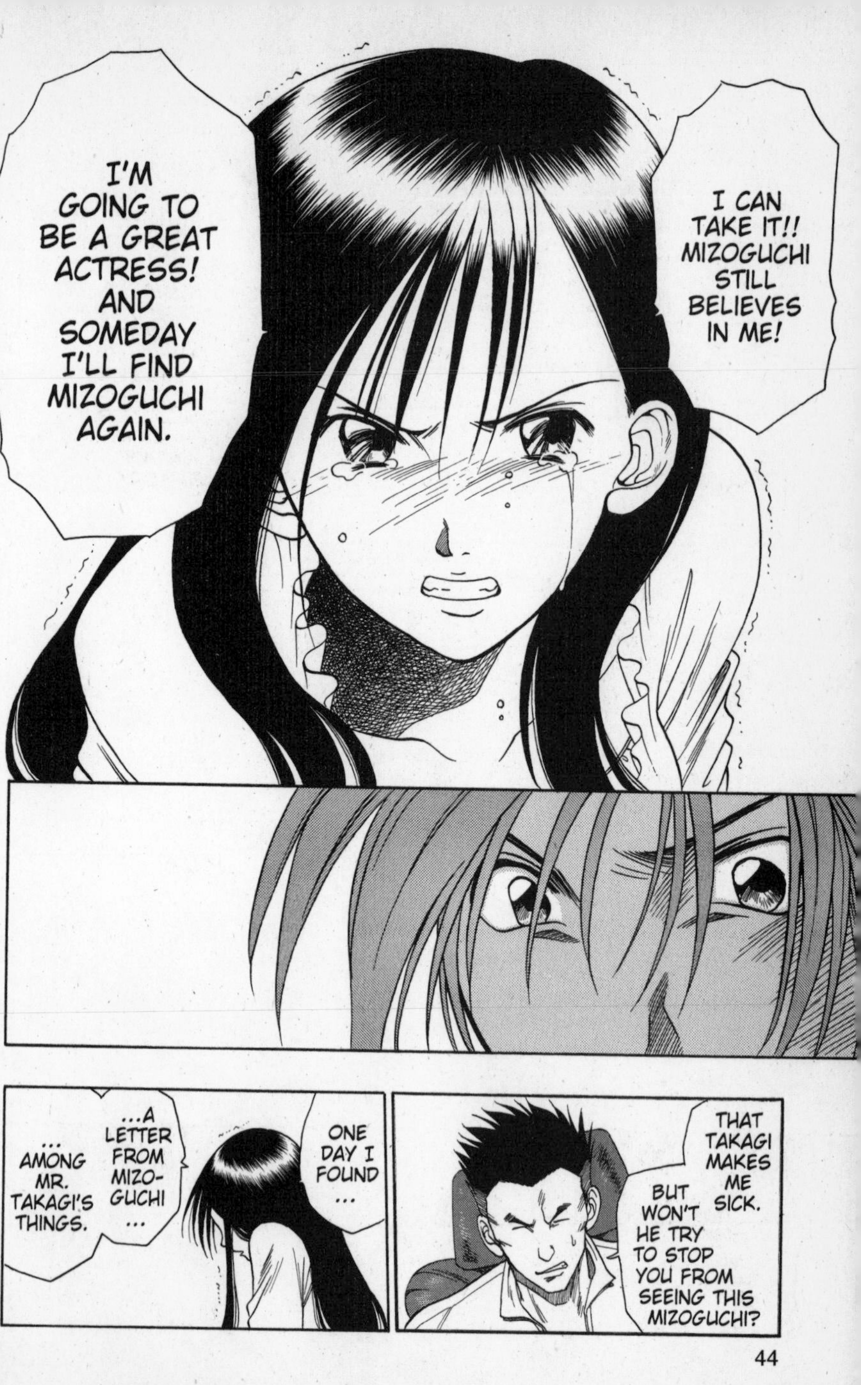
I CAN TAKE IT!! MIZOGUCHI STILL BELIEVES IN ME!
I'M GOING TO BE A GREAT ACTRESS! AND SOMEDAY I'LL FIND MIZOGUCHI AGAIN.
THAT TAKAGI MAKES ME SICK.
BUT WON'T HE TRY TO STOP YOU FROM SEEING THIS MIZOGUCHI?
ONE DAY I FOUND...
...A LETTER FROM MIZO-GUCHI...
...AMONG MR. TAKAGI'S THINGS.

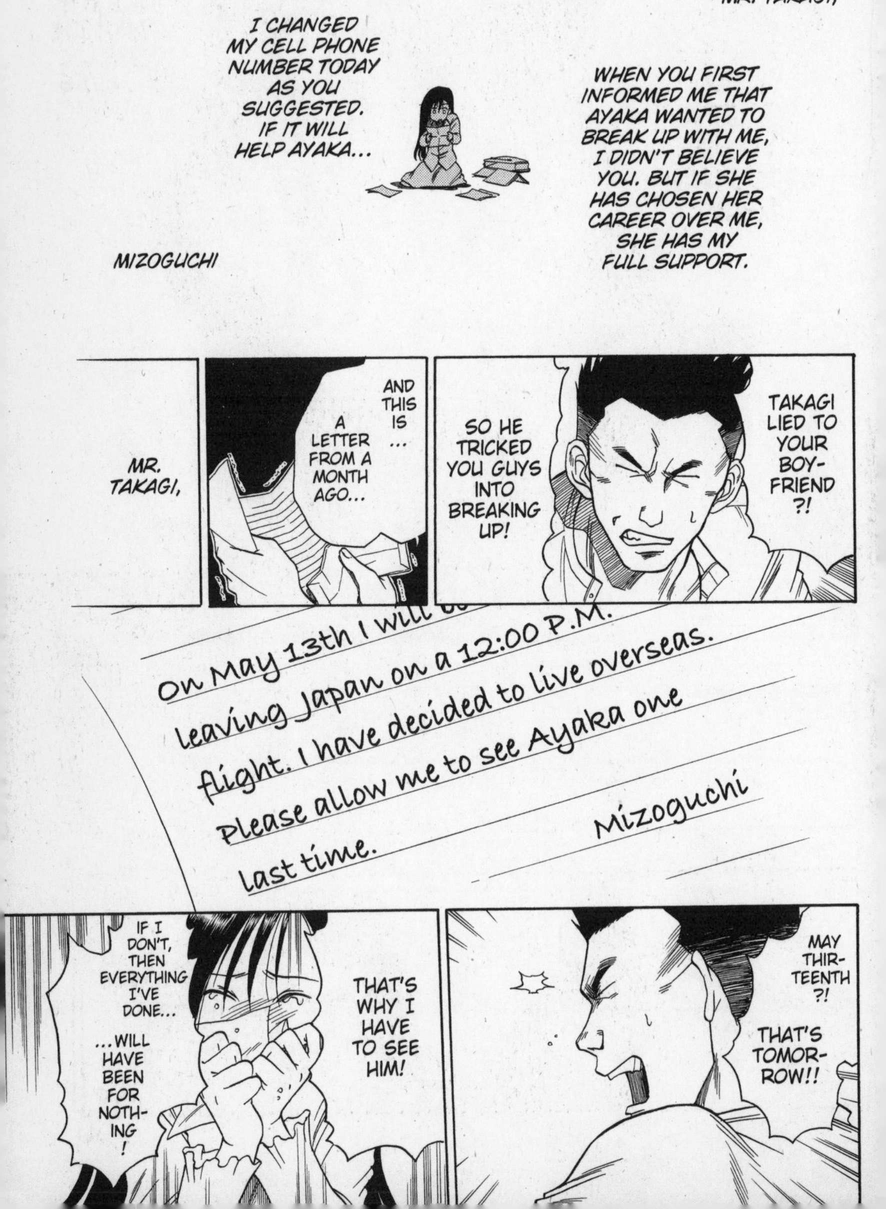

MR. TAKAGI,
WHEN YOU FIRST INFORMED ME THAT AYAKA WANTED TO BREAK UP WITH ME, I DIDN'T BELIEVE YOU. BUT IF SHE HAS CHOSEN HER CAREER OVER ME, SHE HAS MY FULL SUPPORT.
I CHANGED MY CELL PHONE NUMBER TODAY AS YOU SUGGESTED. IF IT WILL HELP AYAKA...
MIZOGUCHI
TAKAGI LIED TO YOUR BOY-FRIEND?!
SO HE TRICKED YOU GUYS INTO BREAKING UP!
AND THIS IS...
A LETTER FROM A MONTH AGO...
MR. TAKAGI,
On May 13th I will
leaving Japan on a 12:00 P.M.
flight. I have decided to live overseas.
Please allow me to see Ayaka one
last time.
Mizoguchi
MAY THIRTEENTH?!
THAT'S TOMORROW!!
THAT'S WHY I HAVE TO SEE HIM!
IF I DON'T, THEN EVERYTHING I'VE DONE...
...WILL HAVE BEEN FOR NOTHING!

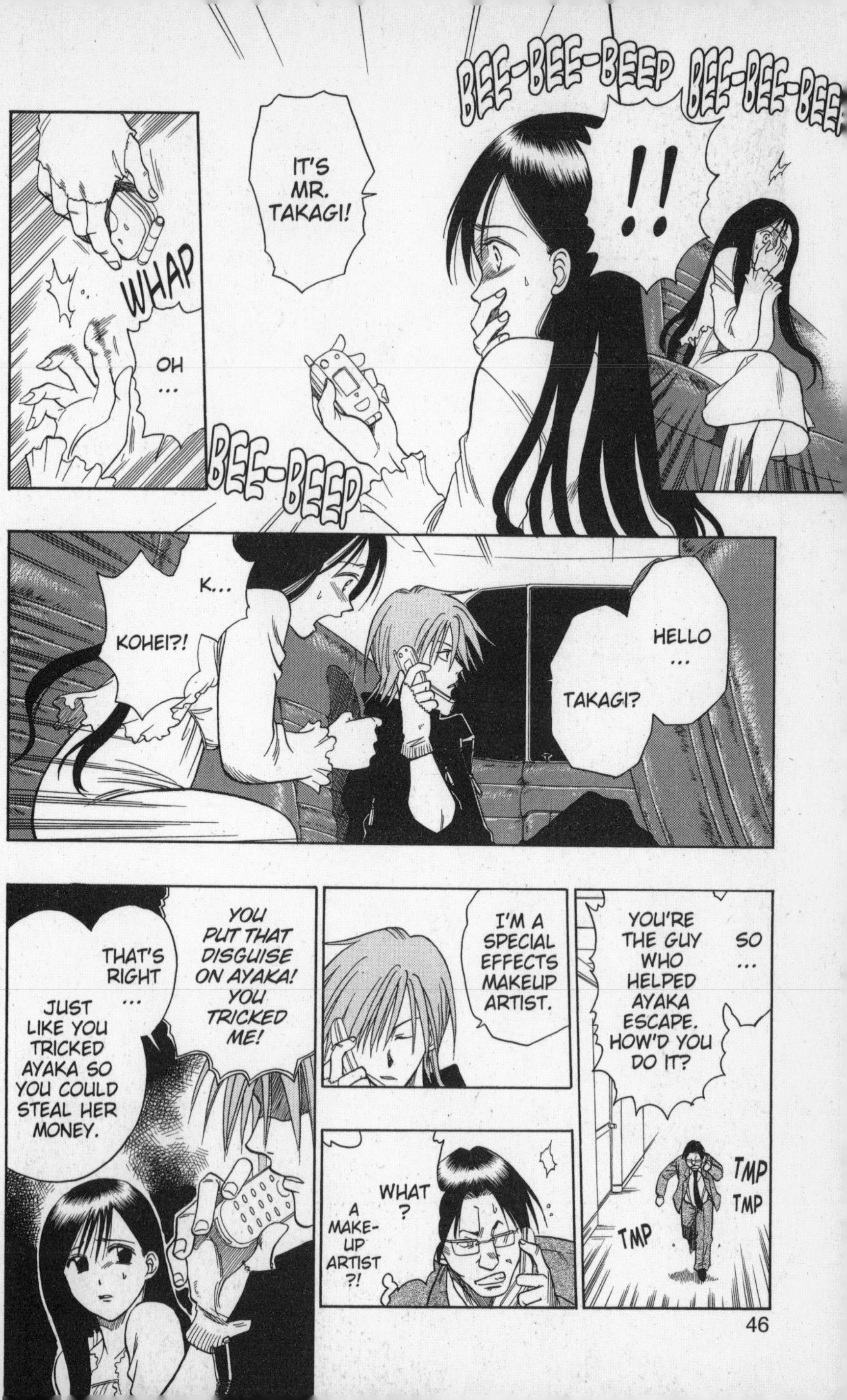
BEE-BEE-BEEP BEE-BEE-BEE
!!
IT'S MR. TAKAGI!
BEE-BEEP
WHAP
OH ...
HELLO ... TAKAGI?
K...
KOHEI?!
SO ...
YOU'RE THE GUY WHO HELPED AYAKA ESCAPE. HOW'D YOU DO IT?
TMP
TMP
TMP
I'M A SPECIAL EFFECTS MAKEUP ARTIST.
WHAT ?
A MAKE-UP ARTIST ?!
YOU PUT THAT DISGUISE ON AYAKA! YOU TRICKED ME!
THAT'S RIGHT ...
JUST LIKE YOU TRICKED AYAKA SO YOU COULD STEAL HER MONEY.

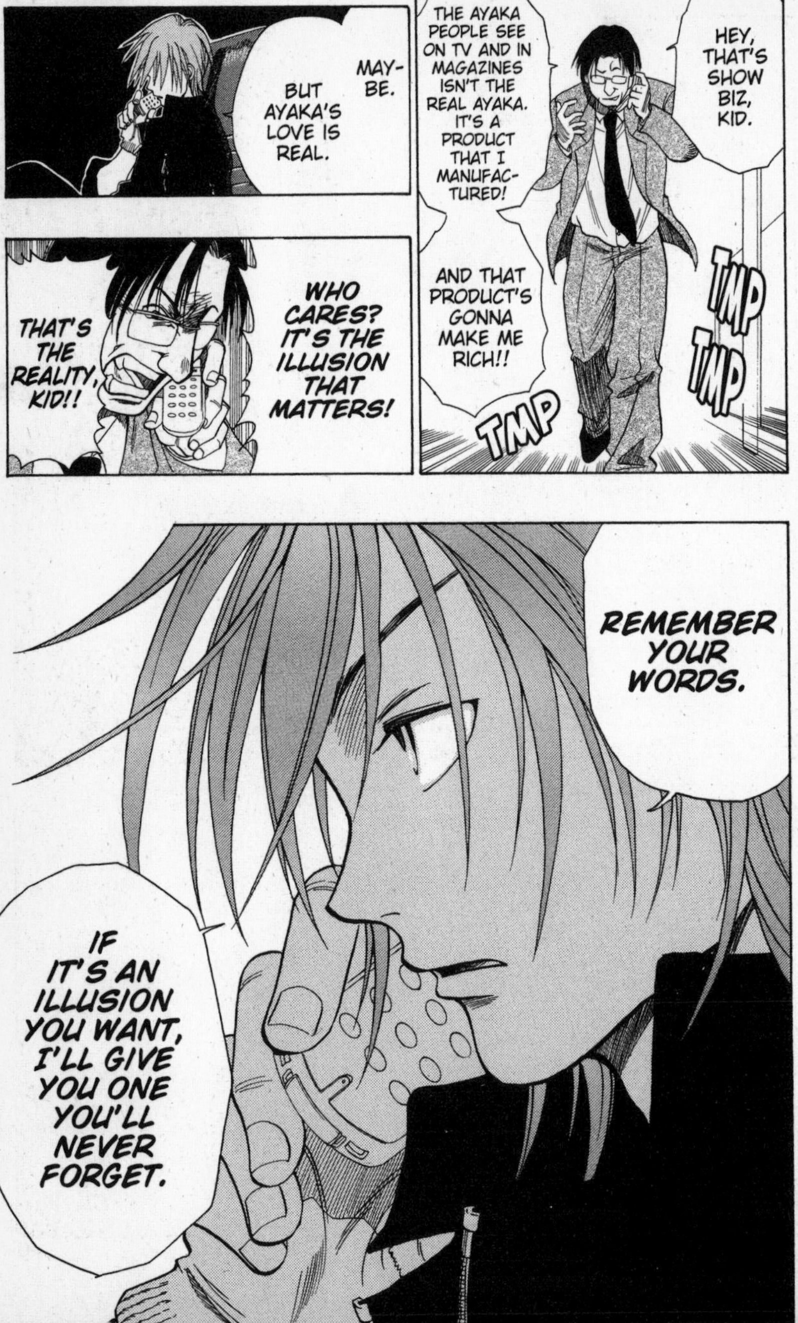
HEY, THAT'S SHOW BIZ, KID.
THE AYAKA PEOPLE SEE ON TV AND IN MAGAZINES ISN'T THE REAL AYAKA. IT'S A PRODUCT THAT I MANUFACTURED!
AND THAT PRODUCT'S GONNA MAKE ME RICH!!
TMP
TMP
TMP
MAY-BE.
BUT AYAKA'S LOVE IS REAL.
WHO CARES? IT'S THE ILLUSION THAT MATTERS!
THAT'S THE REALITY, KID!!
REMEMBER YOUR WORDS.
IF IT'S AN ILLUSION YOU WANT, I'LL GIVE YOU ONE YOU'LL NEVER FORGET.

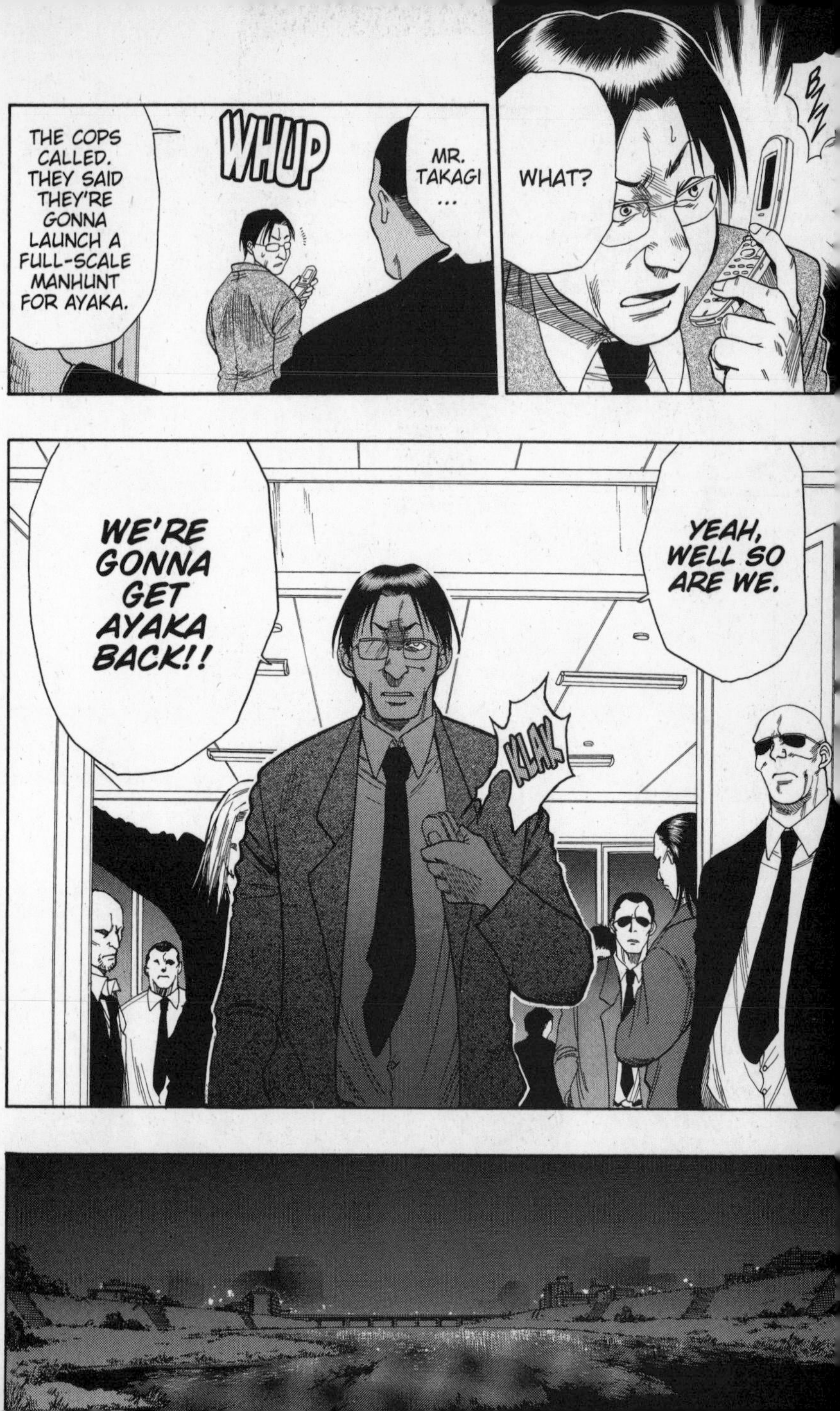
BZZ
WHAT?
MR. TAKAGI ...
WHUP
THE COPS CALLED. THEY SAID THEY'RE GONNA LAUNCH A FULL-SCALE MANHUNT FOR AYAKA.
WE'RE GONNA GET AYAKA BACK!!
KLAK
YEAH, WELL SO ARE WE.

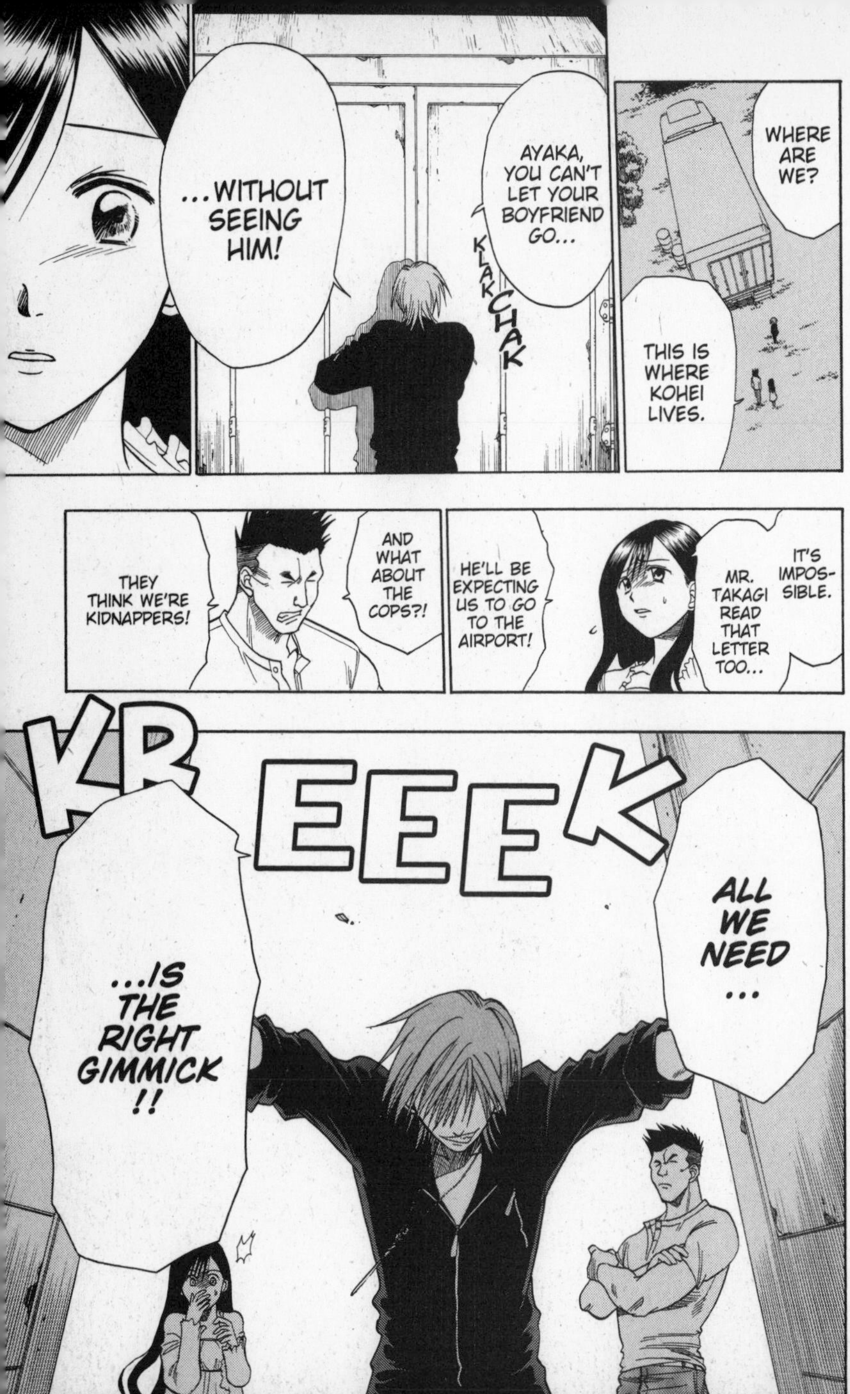
WHERE ARE WE?
THIS IS WHERE KOHEI LIVES.
AYAKA, YOU CAN'T LET YOUR BOYFRIEND GO...
KLAK CHAK
...WITHOUT SEEING HIM!
IT'S IMPOSSIBLE.
MR. TAKAGI READ THAT LETTER TOO...
HE'LL BE EXPECTING US TO GO TO THE AIRPORT!
AND WHAT ABOUT THE COPS?!
THEY THINK WE'RE KIDNAPPERS!
KREEEK
ALL WE NEED...
...IS THE RIGHT GIMMICK!!

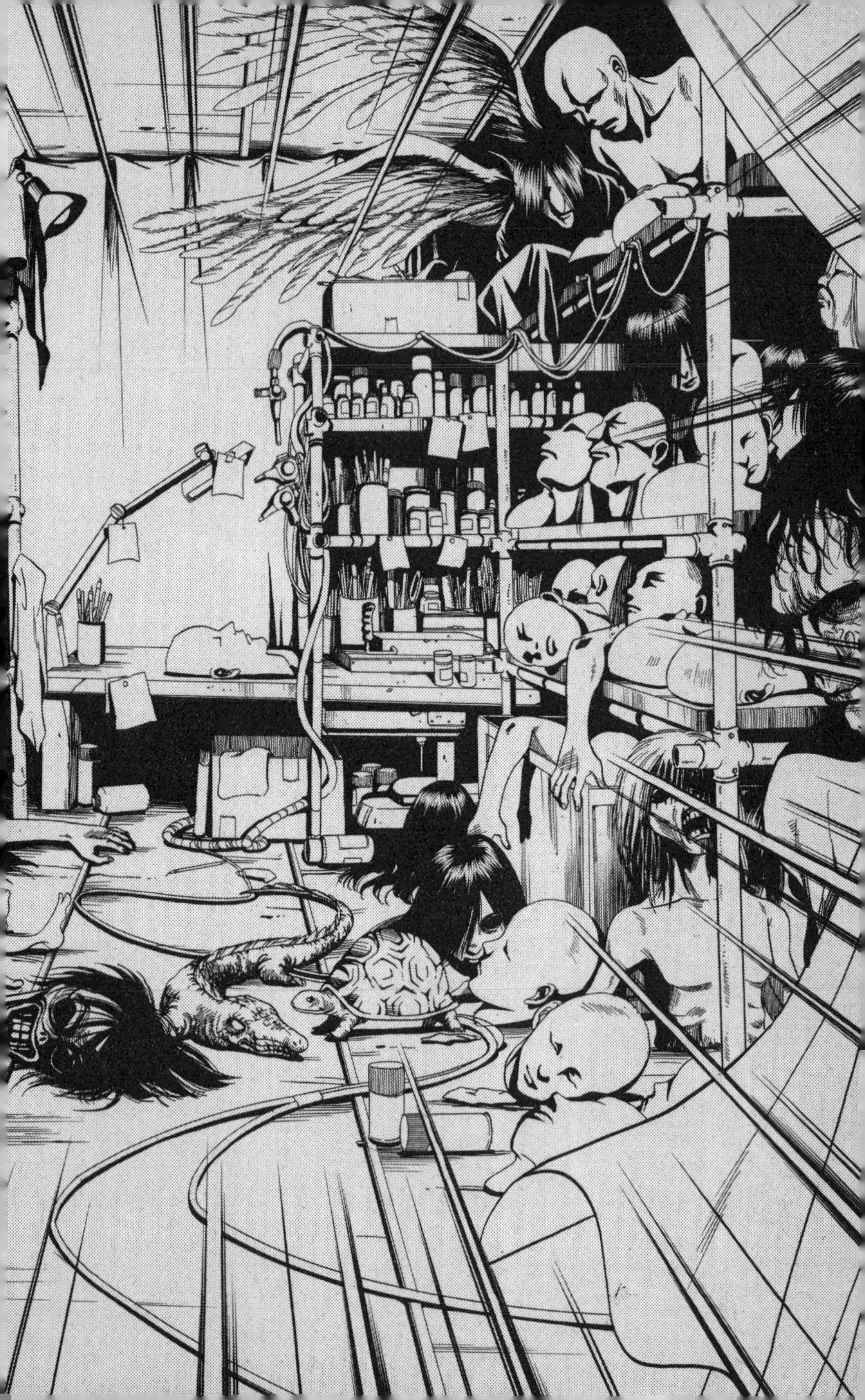

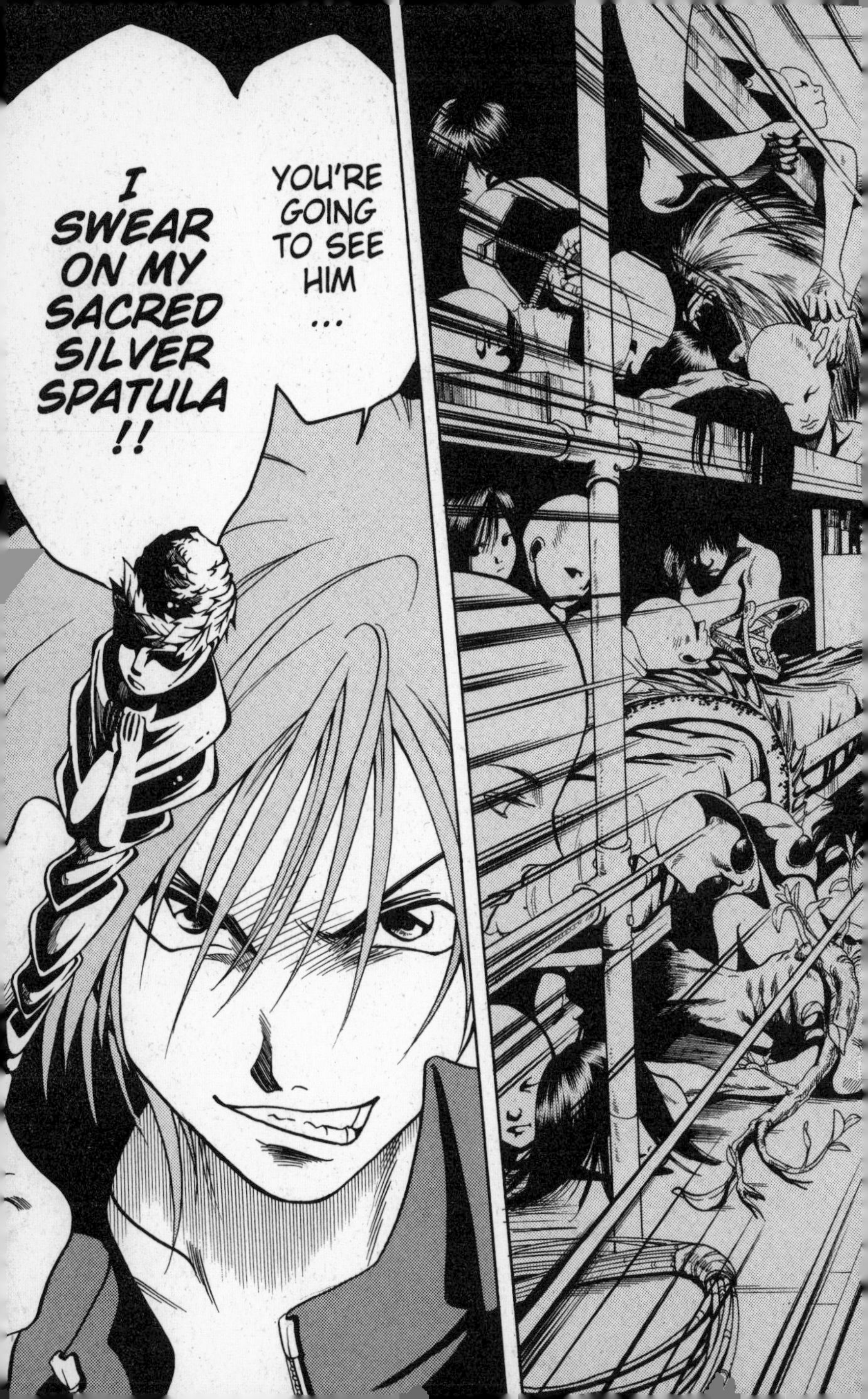
YOU'RE GOING TO SEE HIM ...
I SWEAR ON MY SACRED SILVER SPATULA !!

GIMMICK!

Scene 2: Runaway Actress (Part 2)

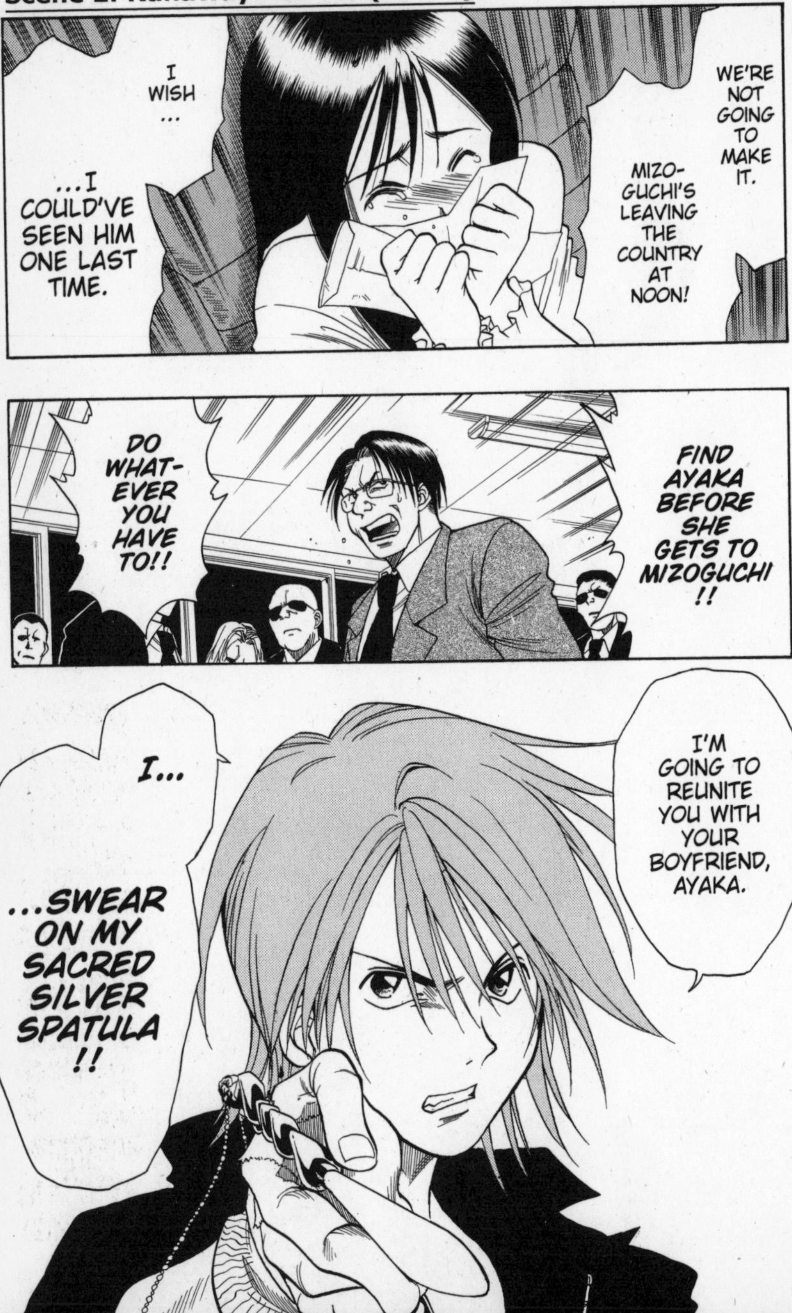

WE'RE NOT GOING TO MAKE IT.
MIZOGUCHI'S LEAVING THE COUNTRY AT NOON!
I WISH...
...I COULD'VE SEEN HIM ONE LAST TIME.
FIND AYAKA BEFORE SHE GETS TO MIZOGUCHI!!
DO WHATEVER YOU HAVE TO!!
I'M GOING TO REUNITE YOU WITH YOUR BOYFRIEND, AYAKA.
I...
...SWEAR ON MY SACRED SILVER SPATULA!!

Scene 2: Runaway Actress (Part 2)

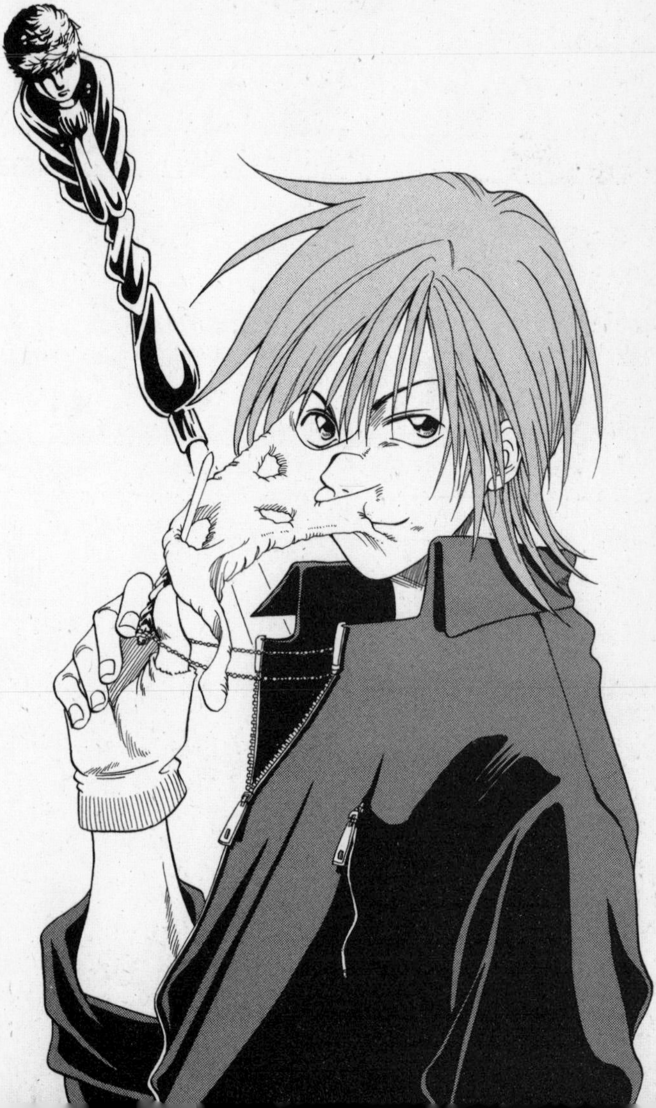

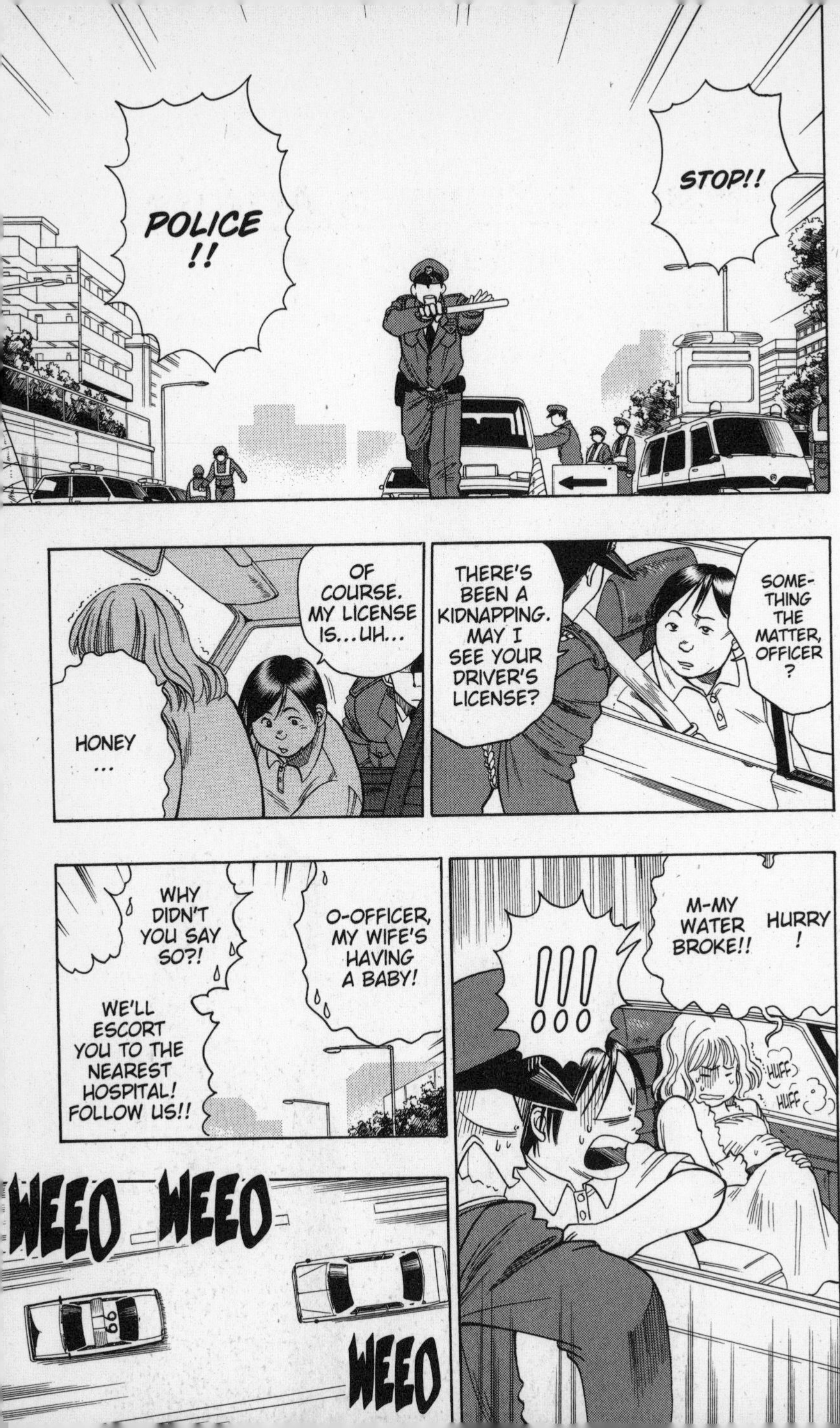
STOP!!
POLICE!!
SOMETHING THE MATTER, OFFICER?
THERE'S BEEN A KIDNAPPING. MAY I SEE YOUR DRIVER'S LICENSE?
OF COURSE. MY LICENSE IS...UH...
HONEY...
HURRY!
M-MY WATER BROKE!!
HUFF
HUFF
!!!
O-OFFICER, MY WIFE'S HAVING A BABY!
WHY DIDN'T YOU SAY SO?!
WE'LL ESCORT YOU TO THE NEAREST HOSPITAL! FOLLOW US!!
WEEO WEEO
WEEO

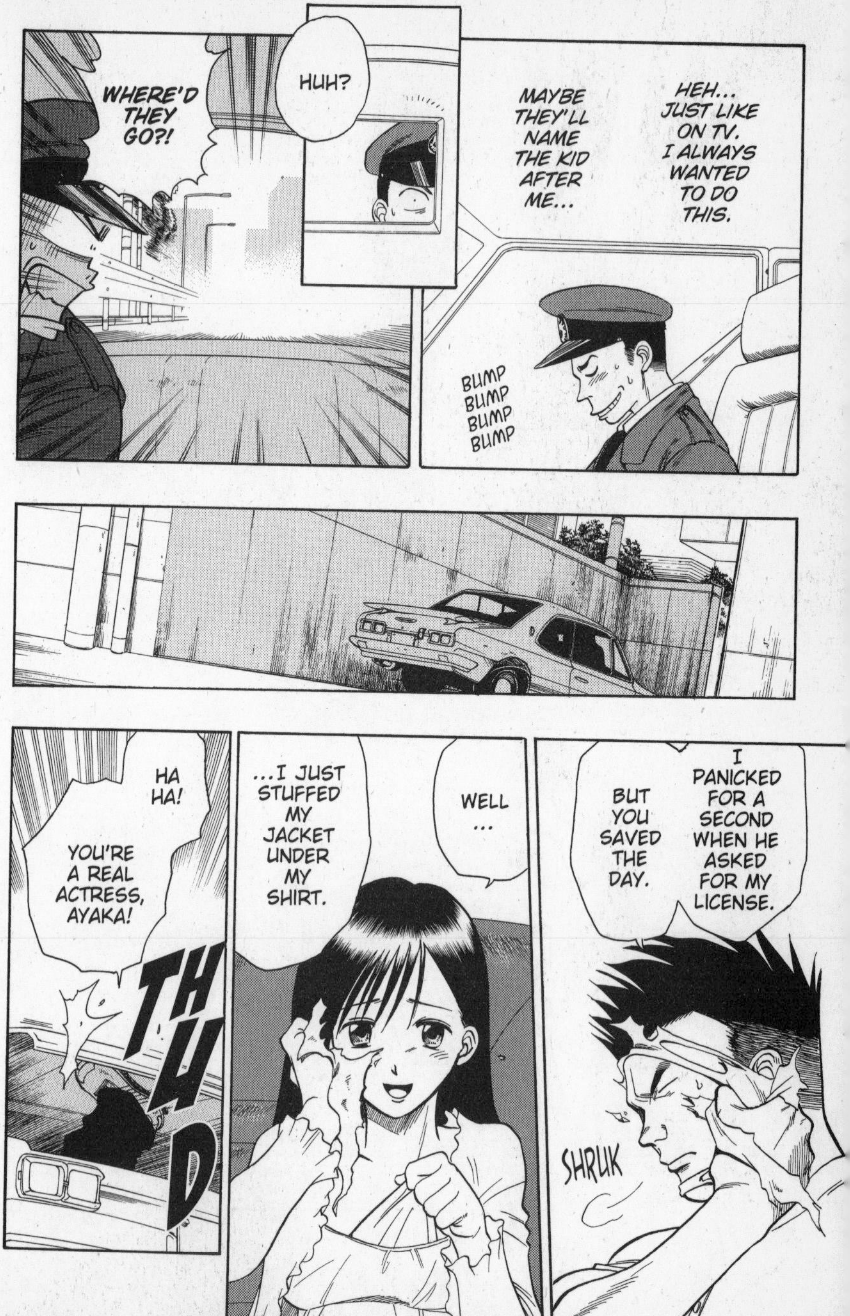
HEH... JUST LIKE ON TV. I ALWAYS WANTED TO DO THIS.
MAYBE THEY'LL NAME THE KID AFTER ME...
BUMP BUMP BUMP BUMP
HUH?
WHERE'D THEY GO?!
I PANICKED FOR A SECOND WHEN HE ASKED FOR MY LICENSE.
BUT YOU SAVED THE DAY.
SHRUK
WELL ...
...I JUST STUFFED MY JACKET UNDER MY SHIRT.
HA HA!
YOU'RE A REAL ACTRESS, AYAKA!
THUD

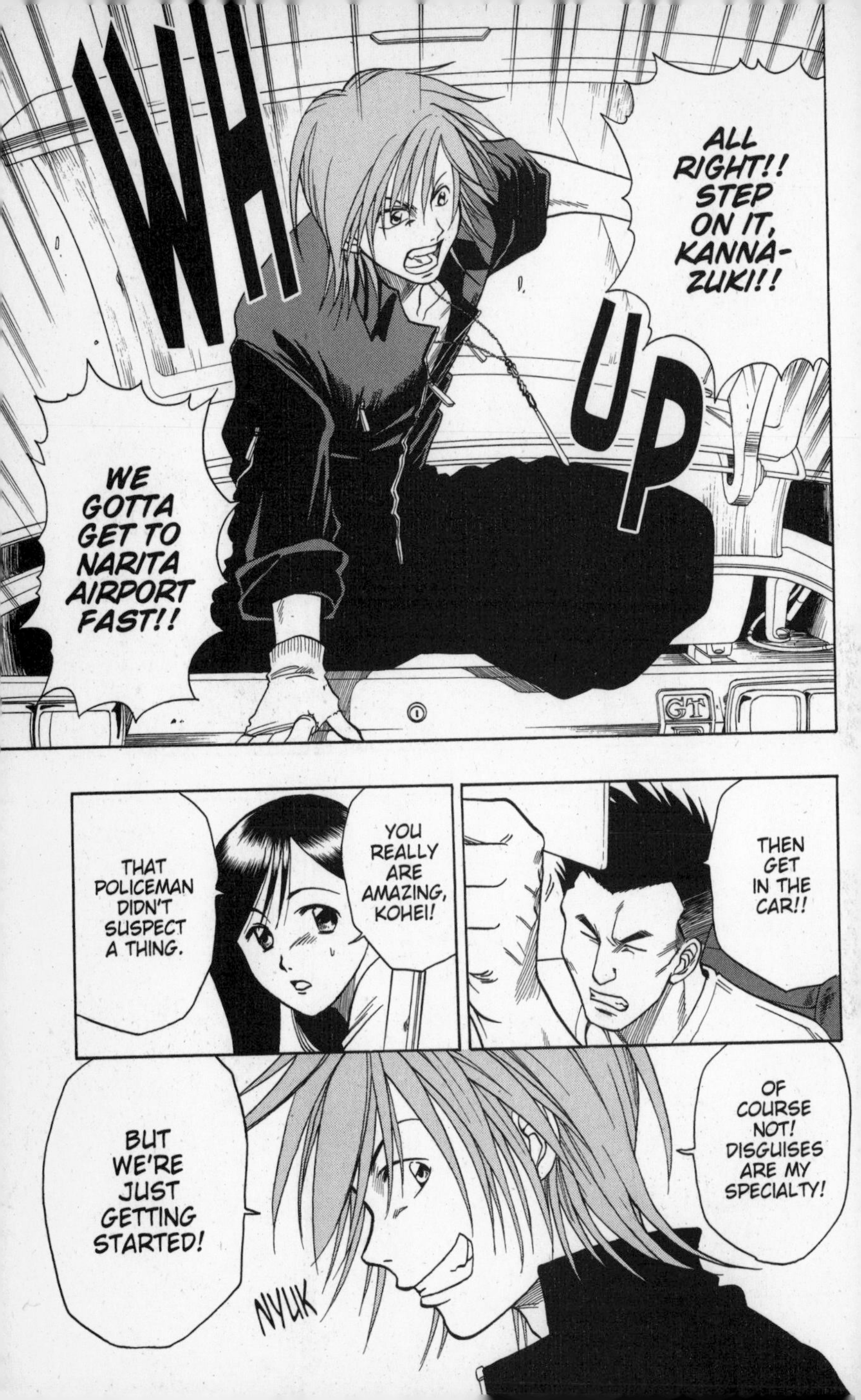
ALL RIGHT!! STEP ON IT, KANNA-ZUKI!!
WH UP
WE GOTTA GET TO NARITA AIRPORT FAST!!
THEN GET IN THE CAR!!
YOU REALLY ARE AMAZING, KOHEI!
THAT POLICEMAN DIDN'T SUSPECT A THING.
OF COURSE NOT! DISGUISES ARE MY SPECIALTY!
BUT WE'RE JUST GETTING STARTED!
NYUK

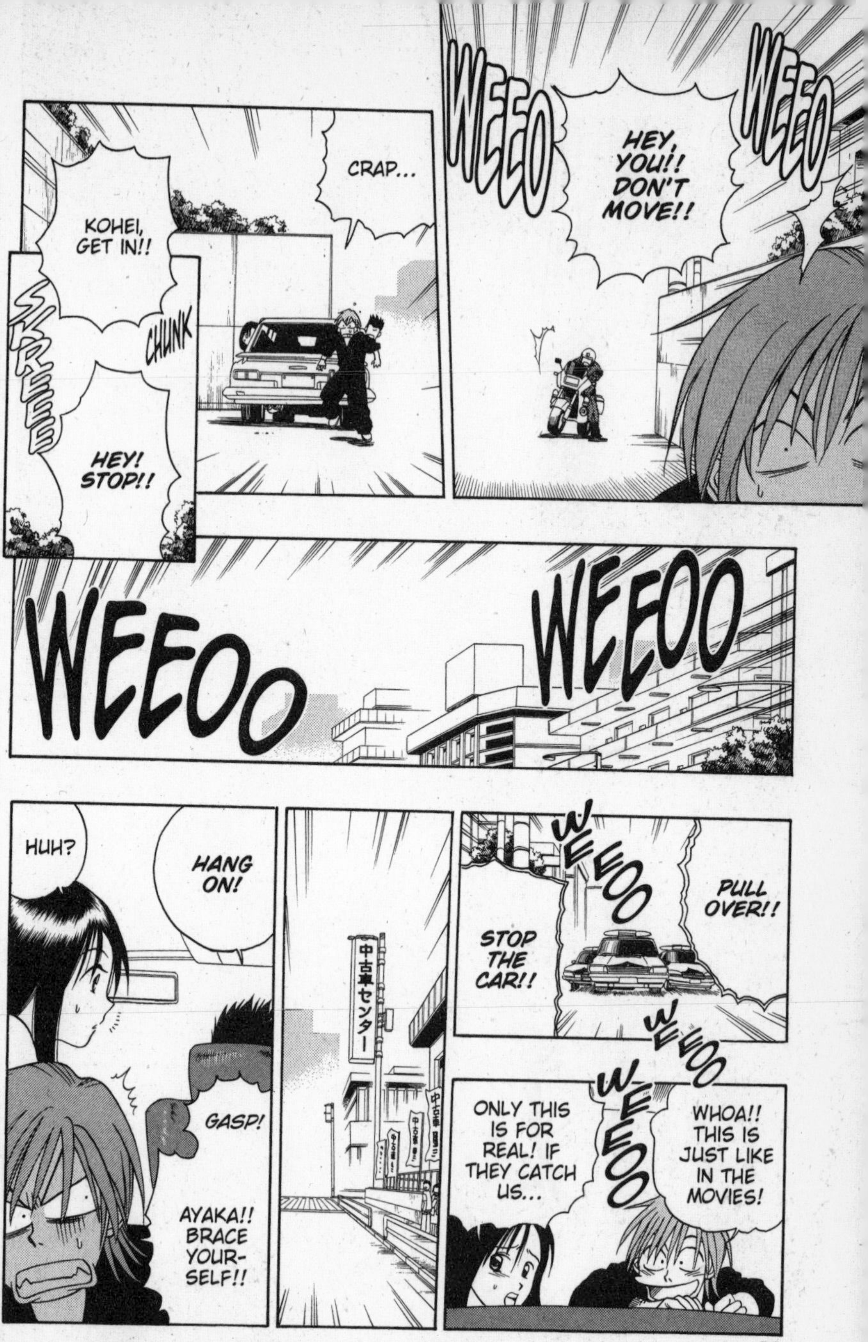
WEEO
HEY, YOU!! DON'T MOVE!!
WEEO
CRAP...
KOHEI, GET IN!!
CHUNK
HEY! STOP!!
SKREEE
WEEOO
WEEOO
PULL OVER!!
WEEOO
STOP THE CAR!!
WEEOO
WHOA!! THIS IS JUST LIKE IN THE MOVIES!
WEEOO
ONLY THIS IS FOR REAL! IF THEY CATCH US...
中古車センター
HANG ON!
HUH?
GASP!
AYAKA!! BRACE YOURSELF!!

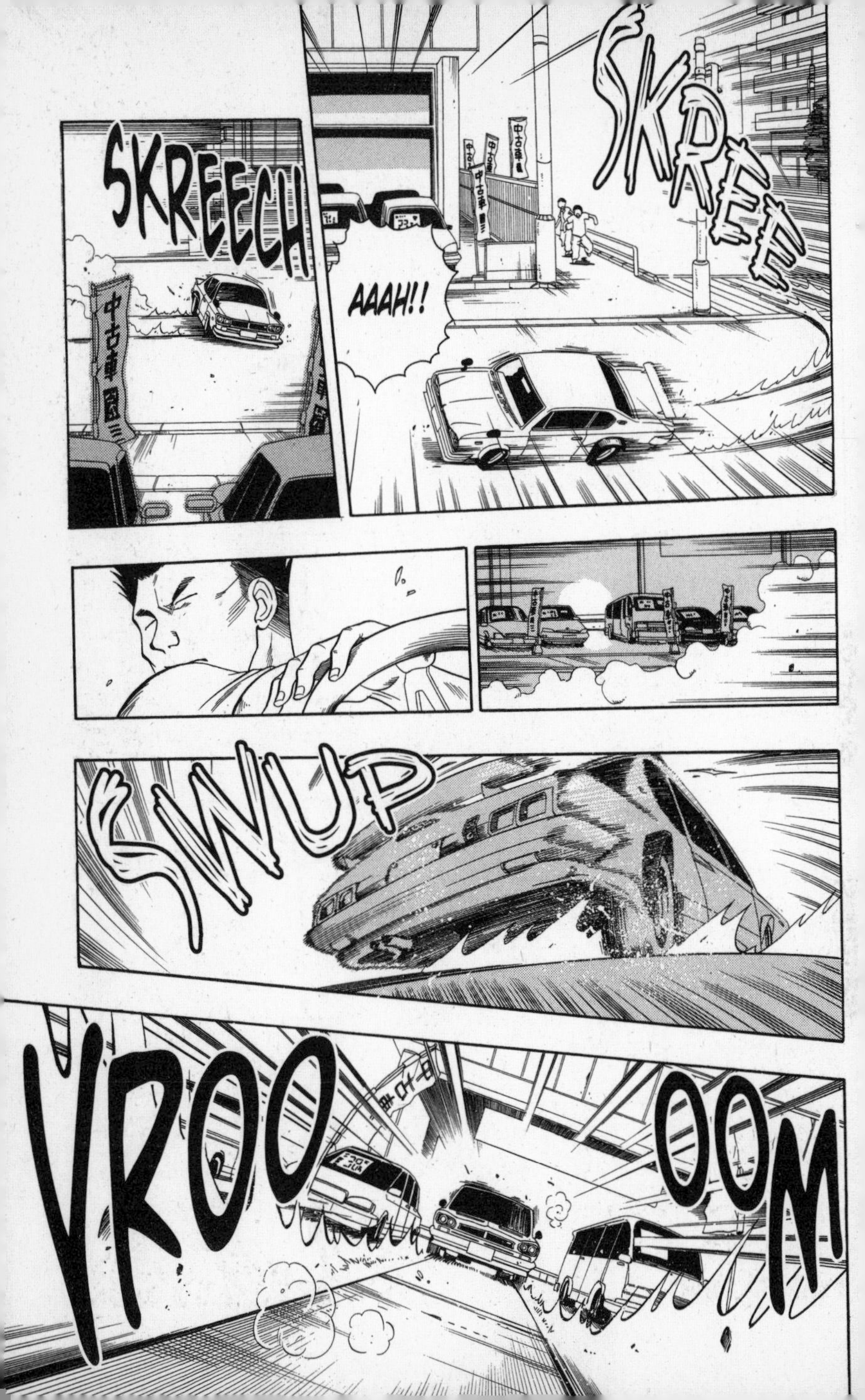
SKREE
AAAH!!
SKREECH
SWUP
VROOOOM

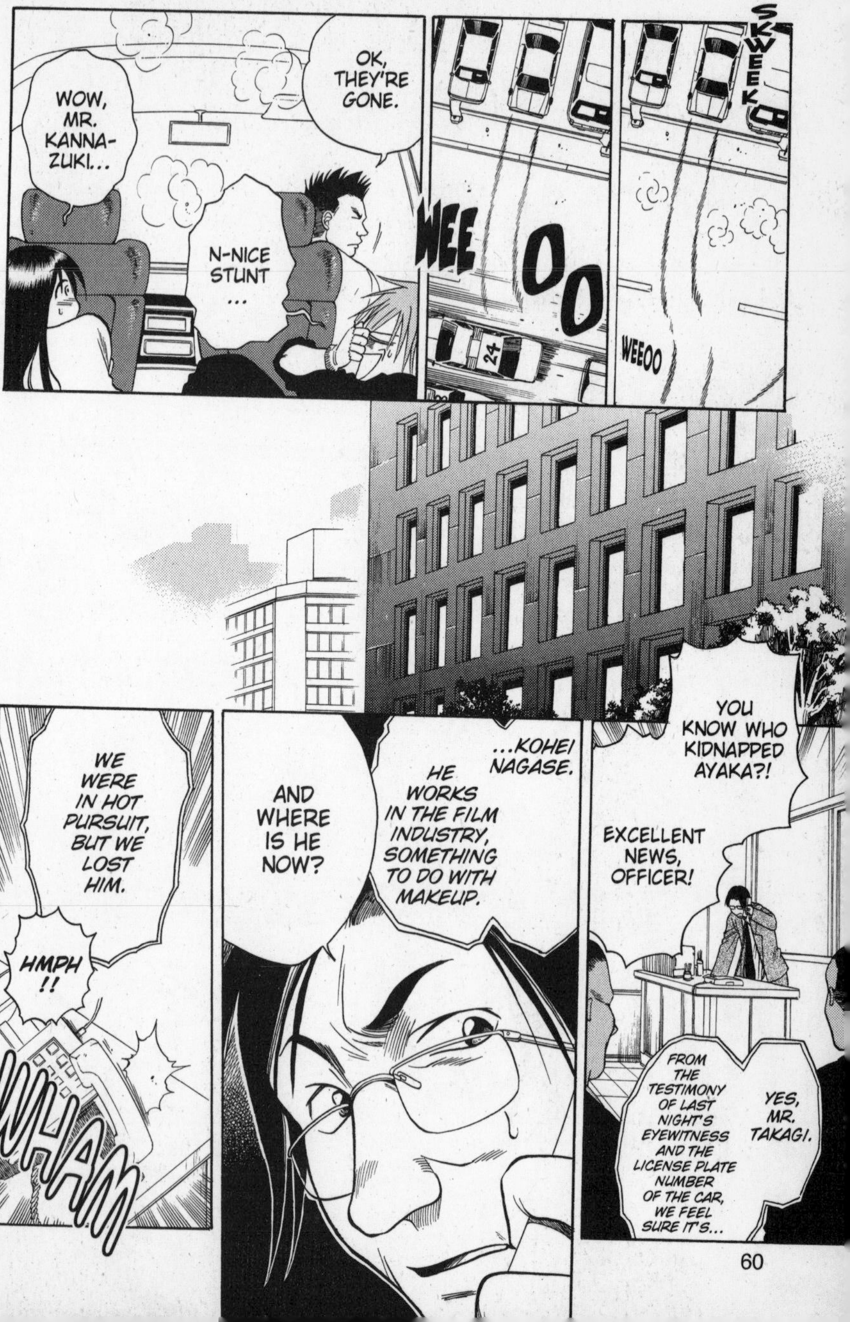
SKWEEK
WEEOO
WEE OO
OK, THEY'RE GONE.
WOW, MR. KANNA-ZUKI...
N-NICE STUNT ...
YOU KNOW WHO KIDNAPPED AYAKA?!
EXCELLENT NEWS, OFFICER!
YES, MR. TAKAGI.
FROM THE TESTIMONY OF LAST NIGHT'S EYEWITNESS AND THE LICENSE PLATE NUMBER OF THE CAR, WE FEEL SURE IT'S...
...KOHEI NAGASE.
HE WORKS IN THE FILM INDUSTRY, SOMETHING TO DO WITH MAKEUP.
AND WHERE IS HE NOW?
WE WERE IN HOT PURSUIT, BUT WE LOST HIM.
HMPH !!
WHAM

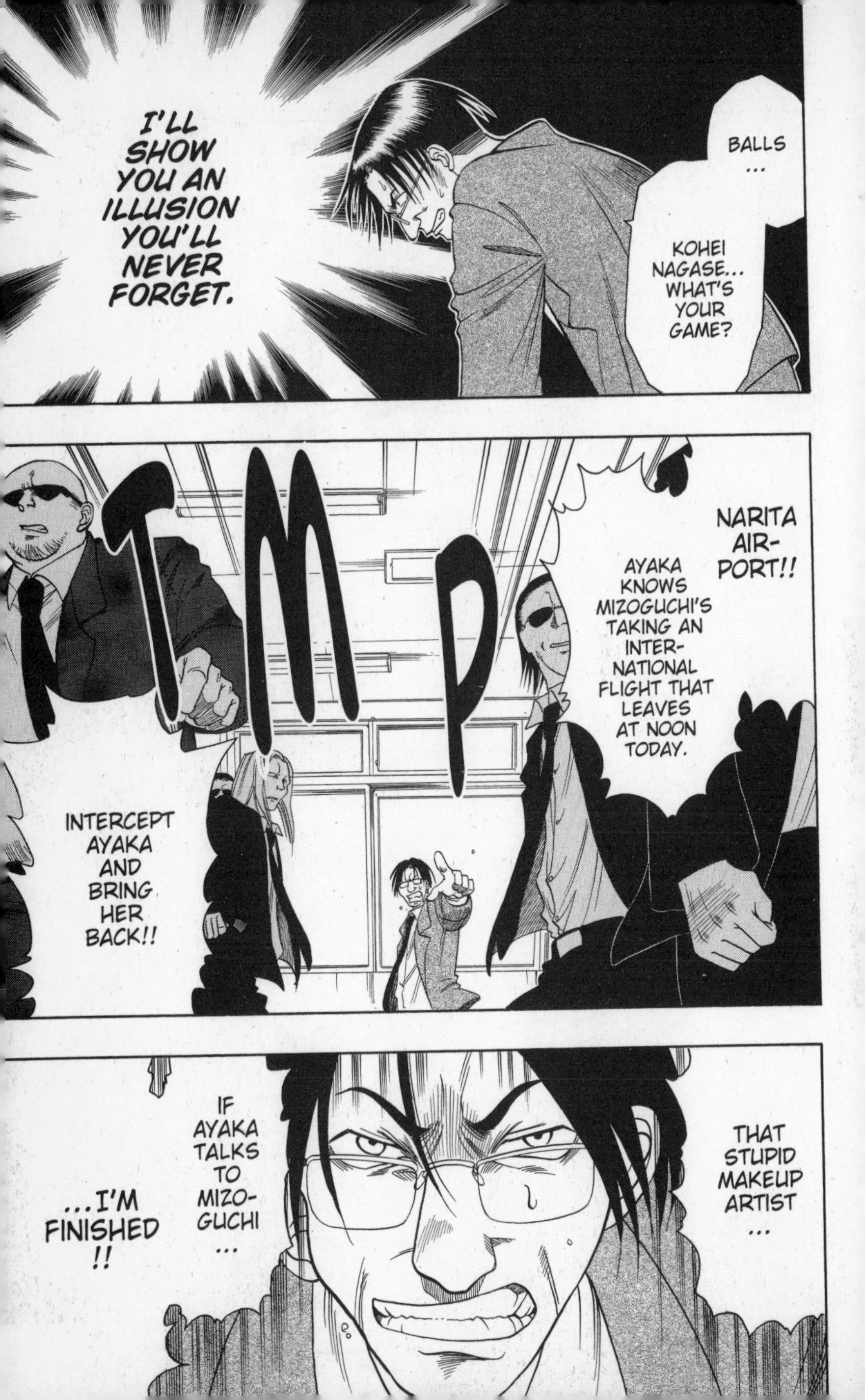
BALLS...
KOHEI NAGASE... WHAT'S YOUR GAME?
I'LL SHOW YOU AN ILLUSION YOU'LL NEVER FORGET.
NARITA AIRPORT!!
AYAKA KNOWS MIZOGUCHI'S TAKING AN INTERNATIONAL FLIGHT THAT LEAVES AT NOON TODAY.
TMP
INTERCEPT AYAKA AND BRING HER BACK!!
THAT STUPID MAKEUP ARTIST...
IF AYAKA TALKS TO MIZOGUCHI...
...I'M FINISHED!!

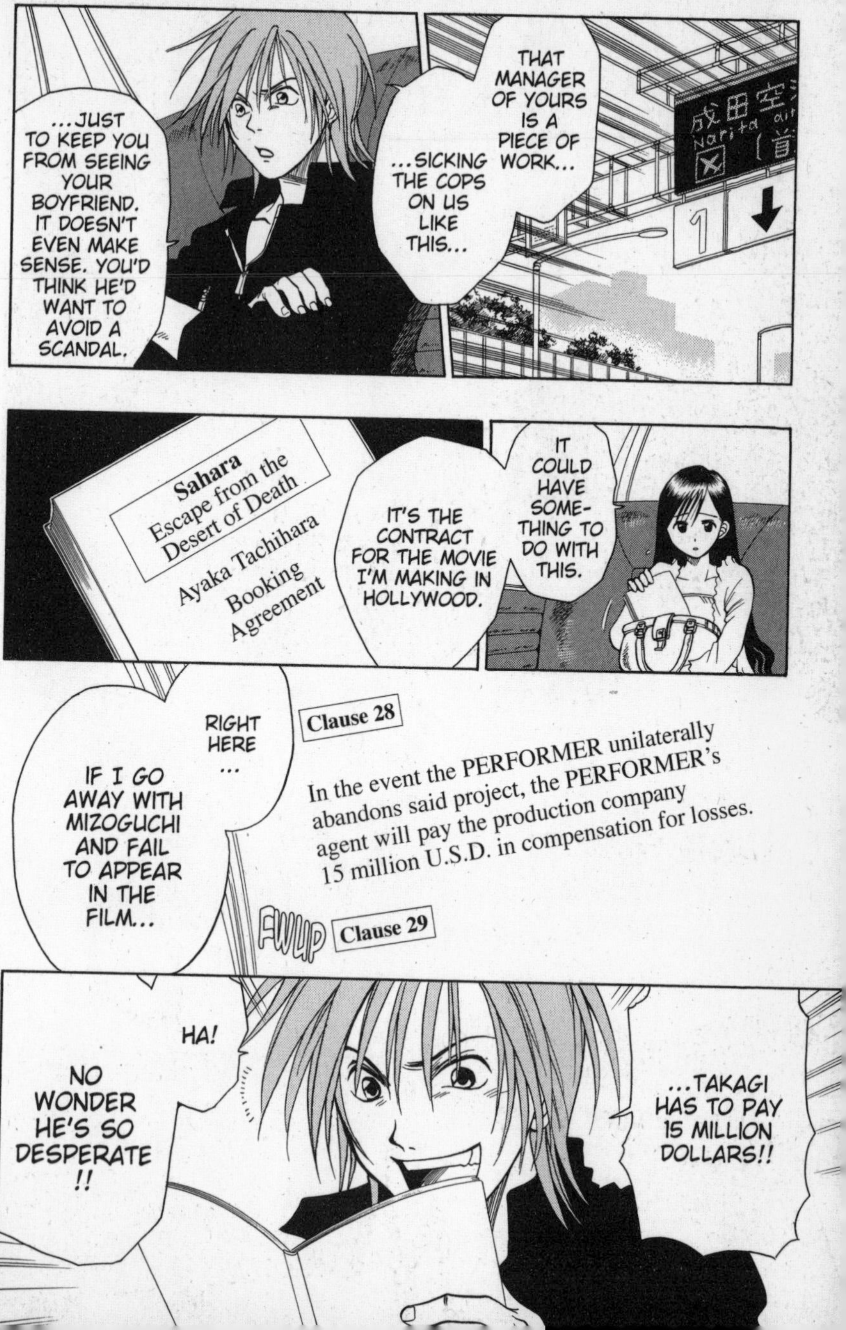
THAT MANAGER OF YOURS IS A PIECE OF WORK...
...SICKING THE COPS ON US LIKE THIS...
...JUST TO KEEP YOU FROM SEEING YOUR BOYFRIEND. IT DOESN'T EVEN MAKE SENSE. YOU'D THINK HE'D WANT TO AVOID A SCANDAL.
IT COULD HAVE SOME-THING TO DO WITH THIS.
IT'S THE CONTRACT FOR THE MOVIE I'M MAKING IN HOLLYWOOD.
Sahara
Escape from the Desert of Death
Ayaka Tachihara
Booking Agreement
RIGHT HERE ...
Clause 28
In the event the PERFORMER unilaterally abandons said project, the PERFORMER's agent will pay the production company 15 million U.S.D. in compensation for losses.
IF I GO AWAY WITH MIZOGUCHI AND FAIL TO APPEAR IN THE FILM...
FWUP
Clause 29
...TAKAGI HAS TO PAY 15 MILLION DOLLARS!!
HA!
NO WONDER HE'S SO DESPERATE !!

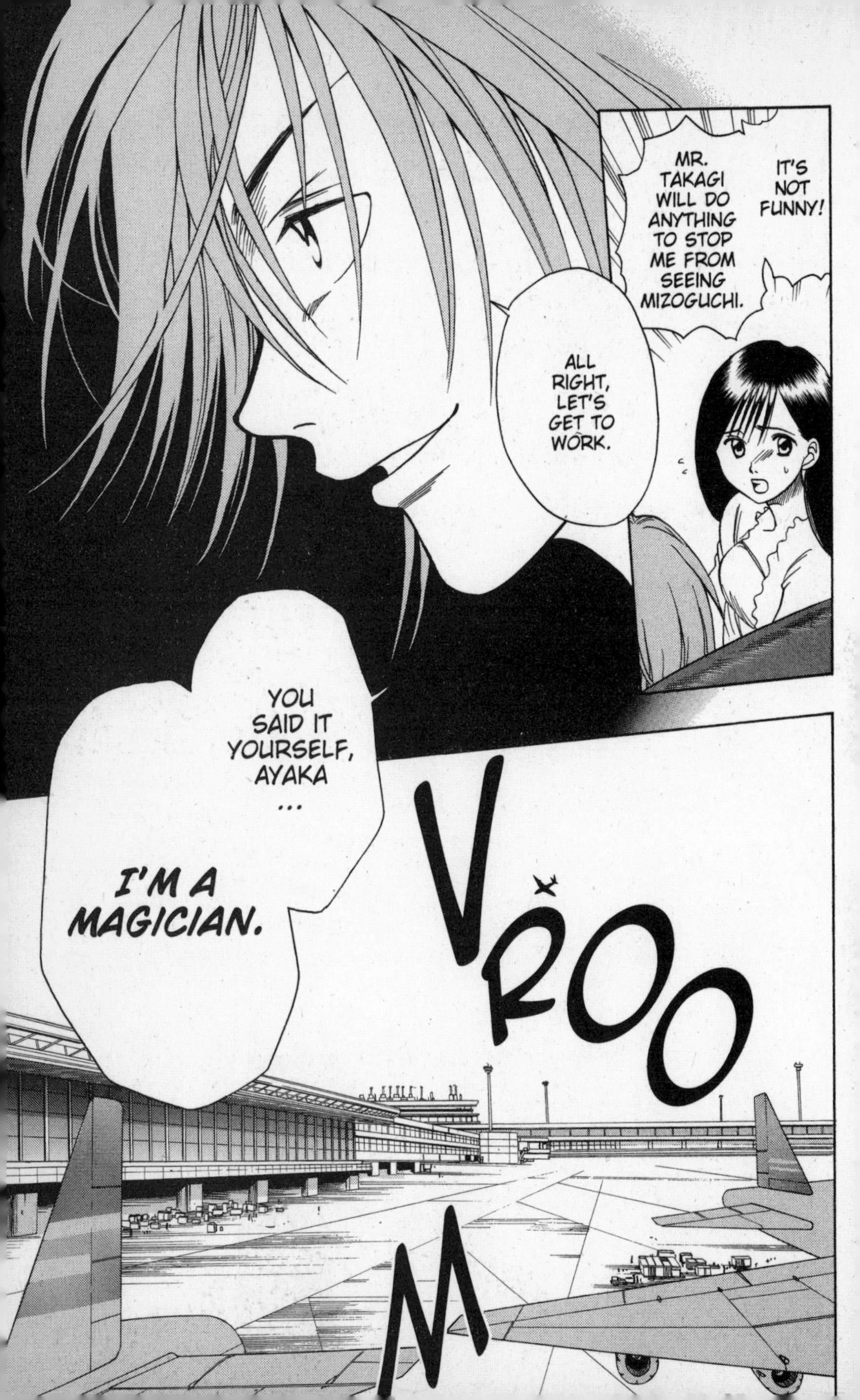
IT'S NOT FUNNY!
MR. TAKAGI WILL DO ANYTHING TO STOP ME FROM SEEING MIZOGUCHI.
ALL RIGHT, LET'S GET TO WORK.
YOU SAID IT YOURSELF, AYAKA ...
I'M A MAGICIAN.
VROOOM

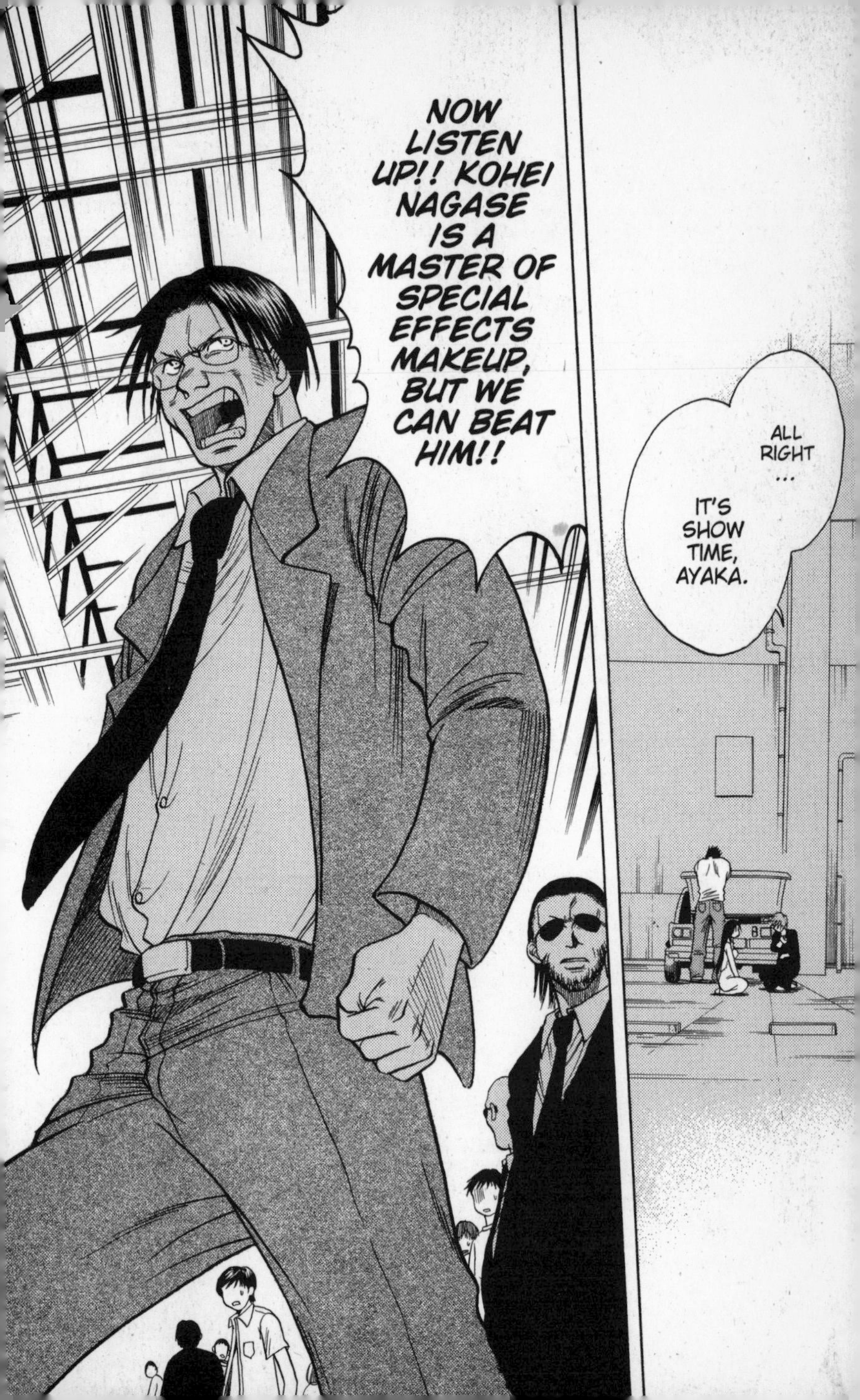
ALL RIGHT ...
IT'S SHOW TIME, AYAKA.
NOW LISTEN UP!! KOHEI NAGASE IS A MASTER OF SPECIAL EFFECTS MAKEUP, BUT WE CAN BEAT HIM!!

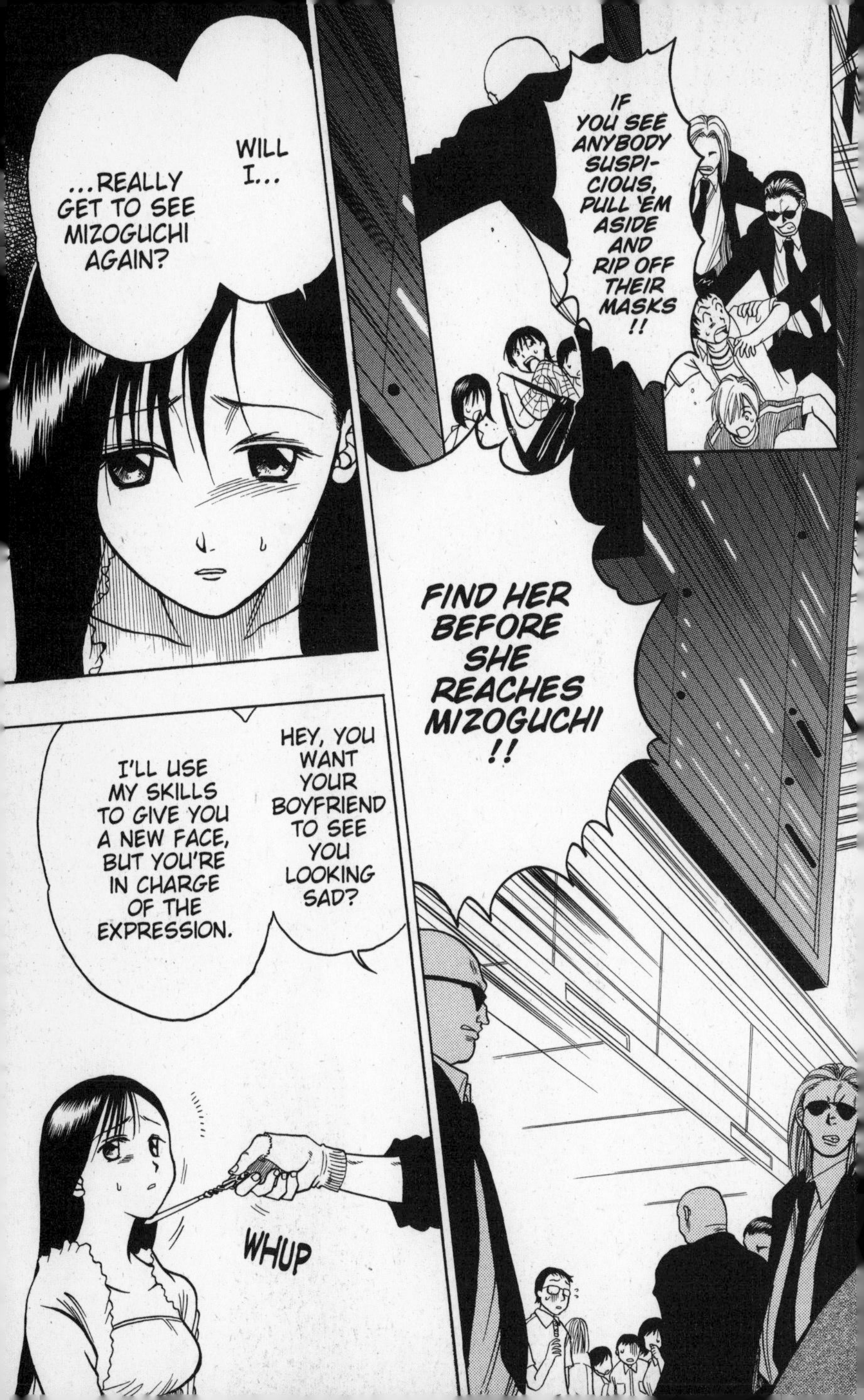
IF YOU SEE ANYBODY SUSPICIOUS, PULL 'EM ASIDE AND RIP OFF THEIR MASKS!!
FIND HER BEFORE SHE REACHES MIZOGUCHI!!
WILL I...
...REALLY GET TO SEE MIZOGUCHI AGAIN?
HEY, YOU WANT YOUR BOYFRIEND TO SEE YOU LOOKING SAD?
I'LL USE MY SKILLS TO GIVE YOU A NEW FACE, BUT YOU'RE IN CHARGE OF THE EXPRESSION.
WHUP

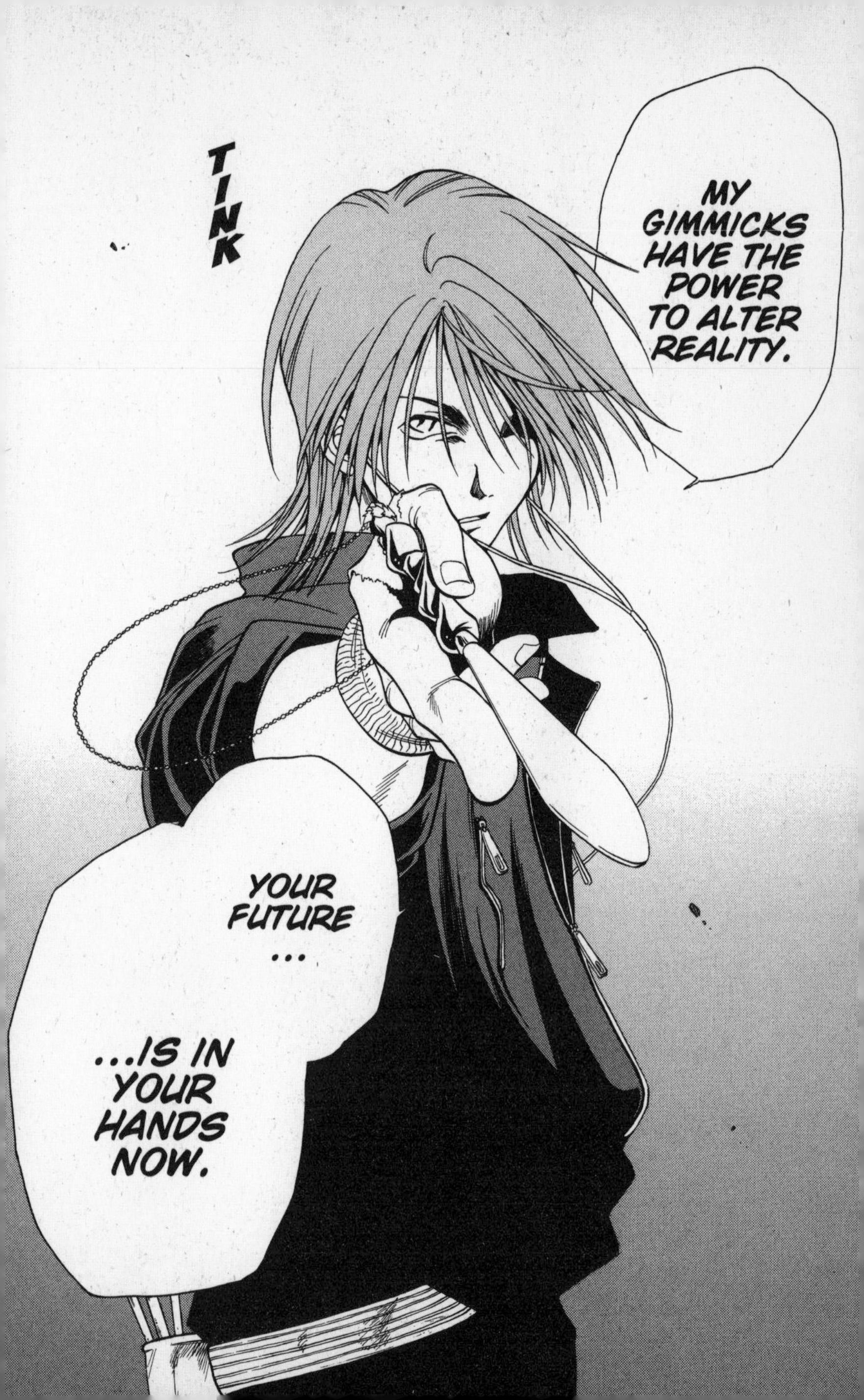
MY GIMMICKS HAVE THE POWER TO ALTER REALITY.
TINK
YOUR FUTURE ...
...IS IN YOUR HANDS NOW.

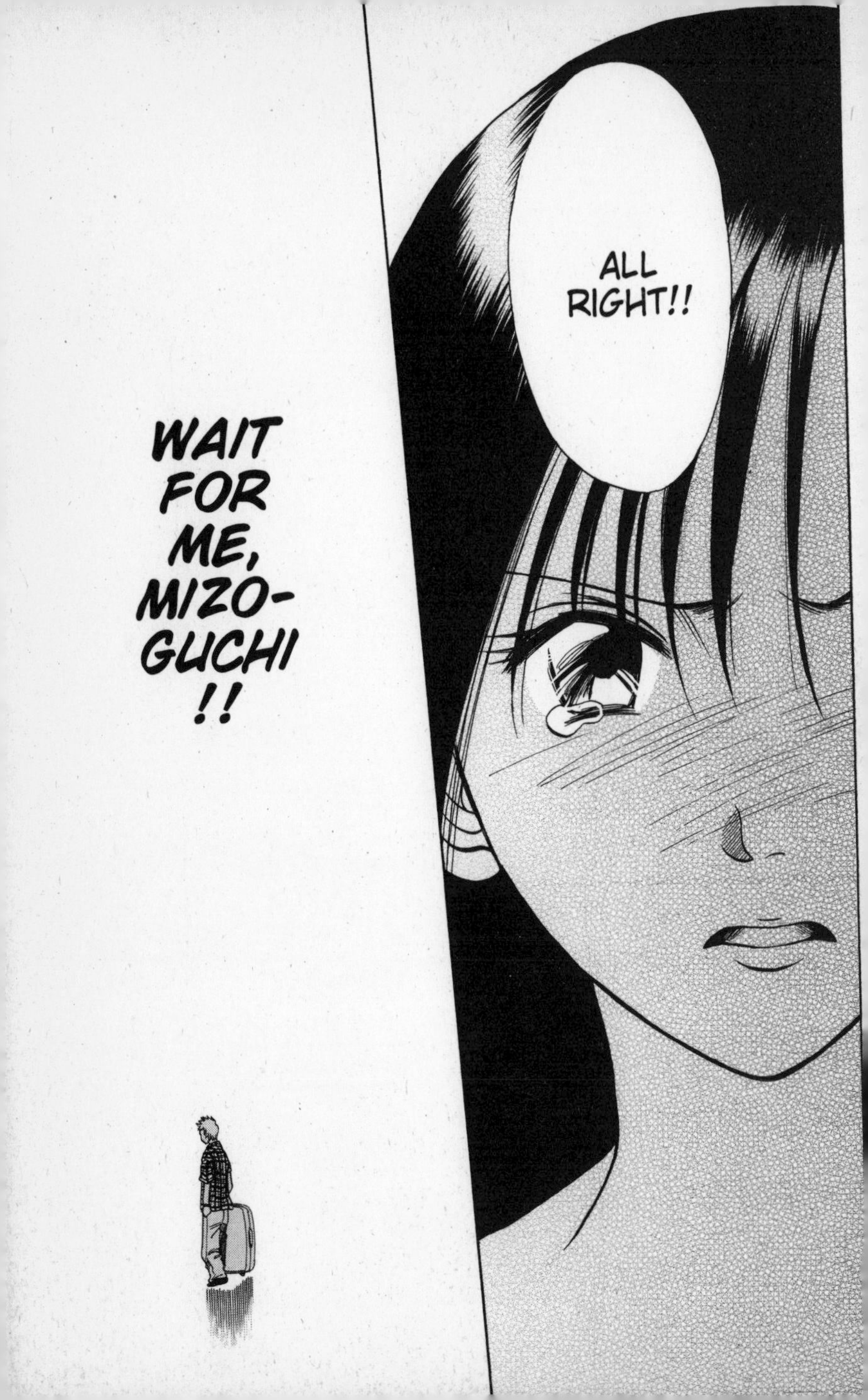
ALL RIGHT!!
WAIT FOR ME, MIZOGUCHI!!

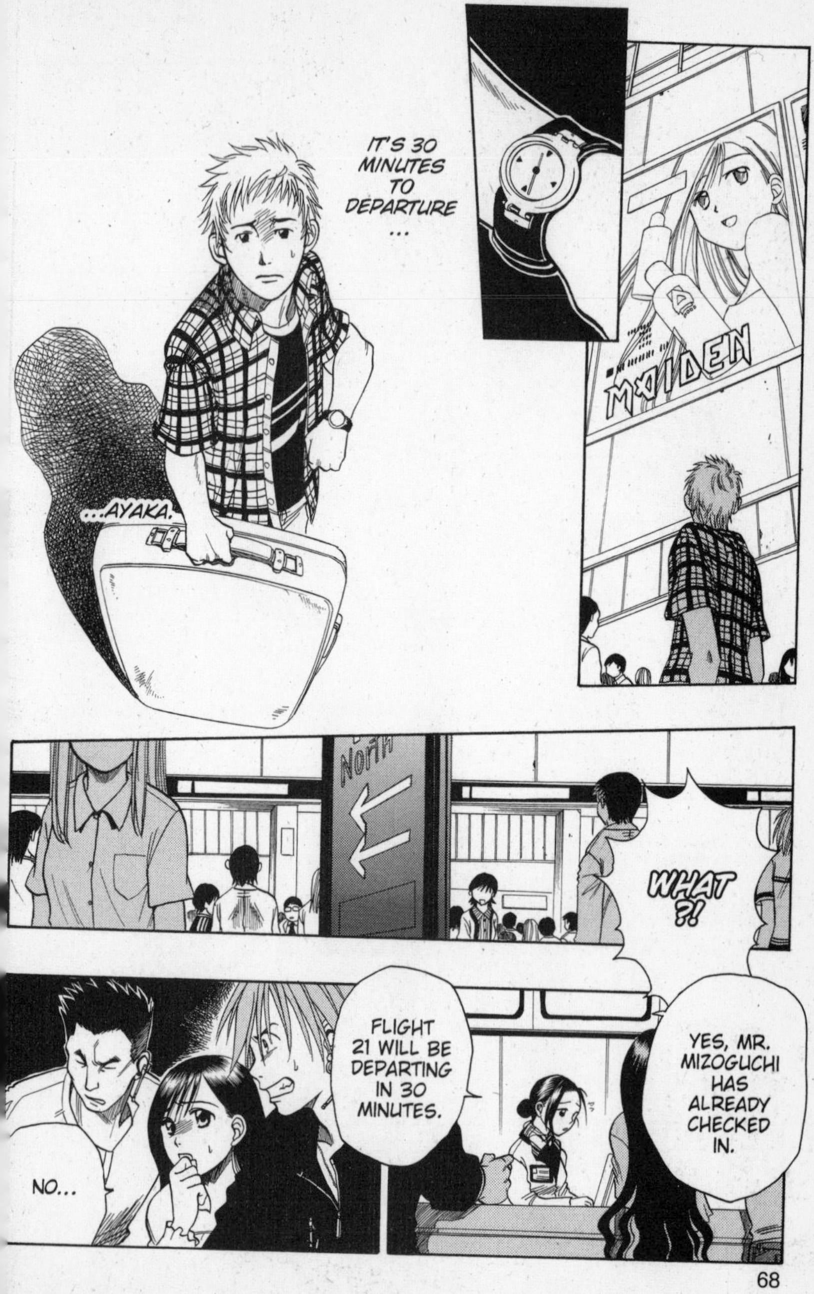
MAIDEN
IT'S 30 MINUTES TO DEPARTURE ...
...AYAKA.
WHAT ?!
North
YES, MR. MIZOGUCHI HAS ALREADY CHECKED IN.
FLIGHT 21 WILL BE DEPARTING IN 30 MINUTES.
NO...

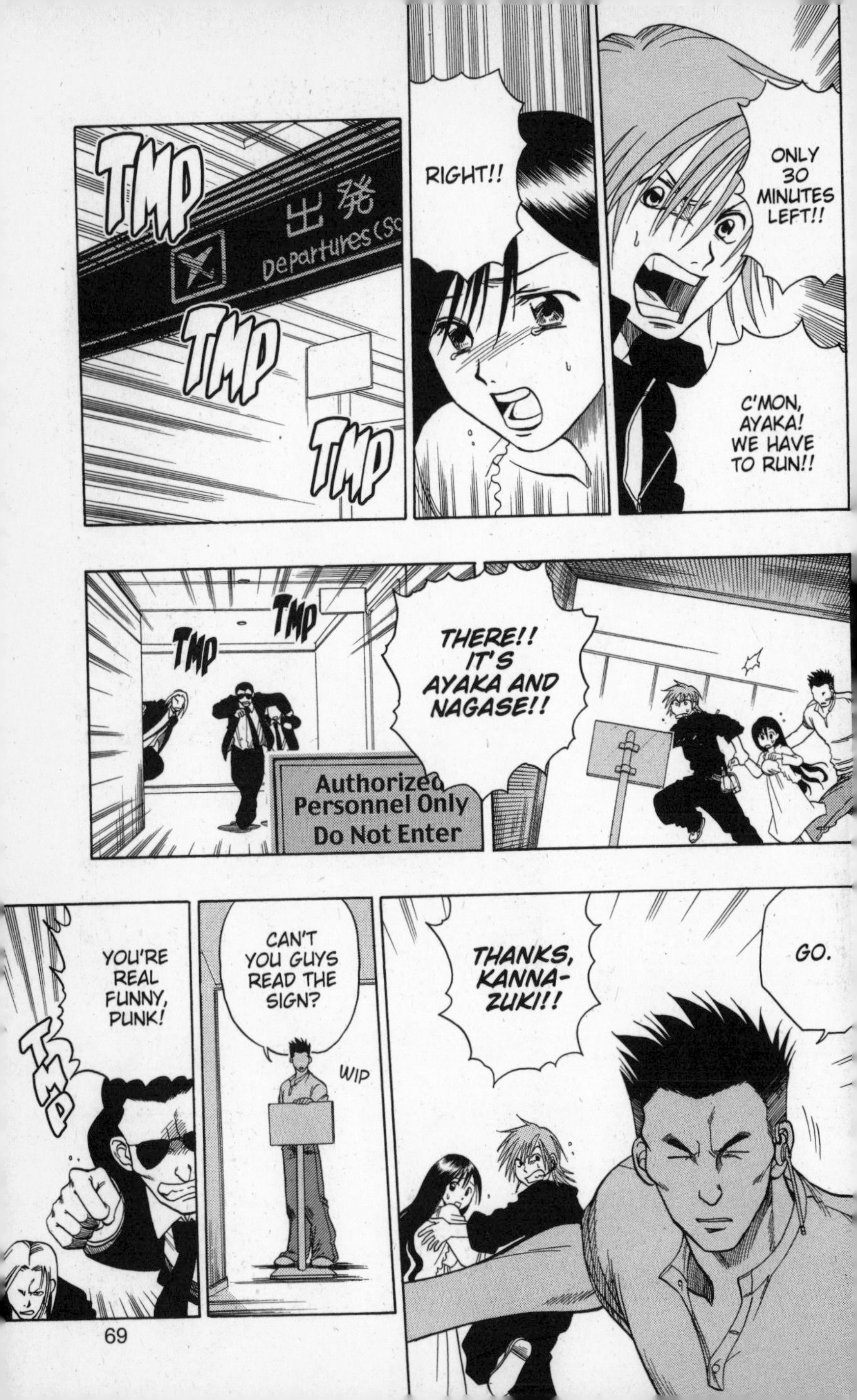
ONLY 30 MINUTES LEFT!!
C'MON, AYAKA! WE HAVE TO RUN!!
RIGHT!!
TMP
出発
Departures (Sc
TMP
TMP
THERE!! IT'S AYAKA AND NAGASE!!
TMP
TMP
Authorized Personnel Only
Do Not Enter
GO.
THANKS, KANNA-ZUKI!!
CAN'T YOU GUYS READ THE SIGN?
WIP
YOU'RE REAL FUNNY, PUNK!
TMP

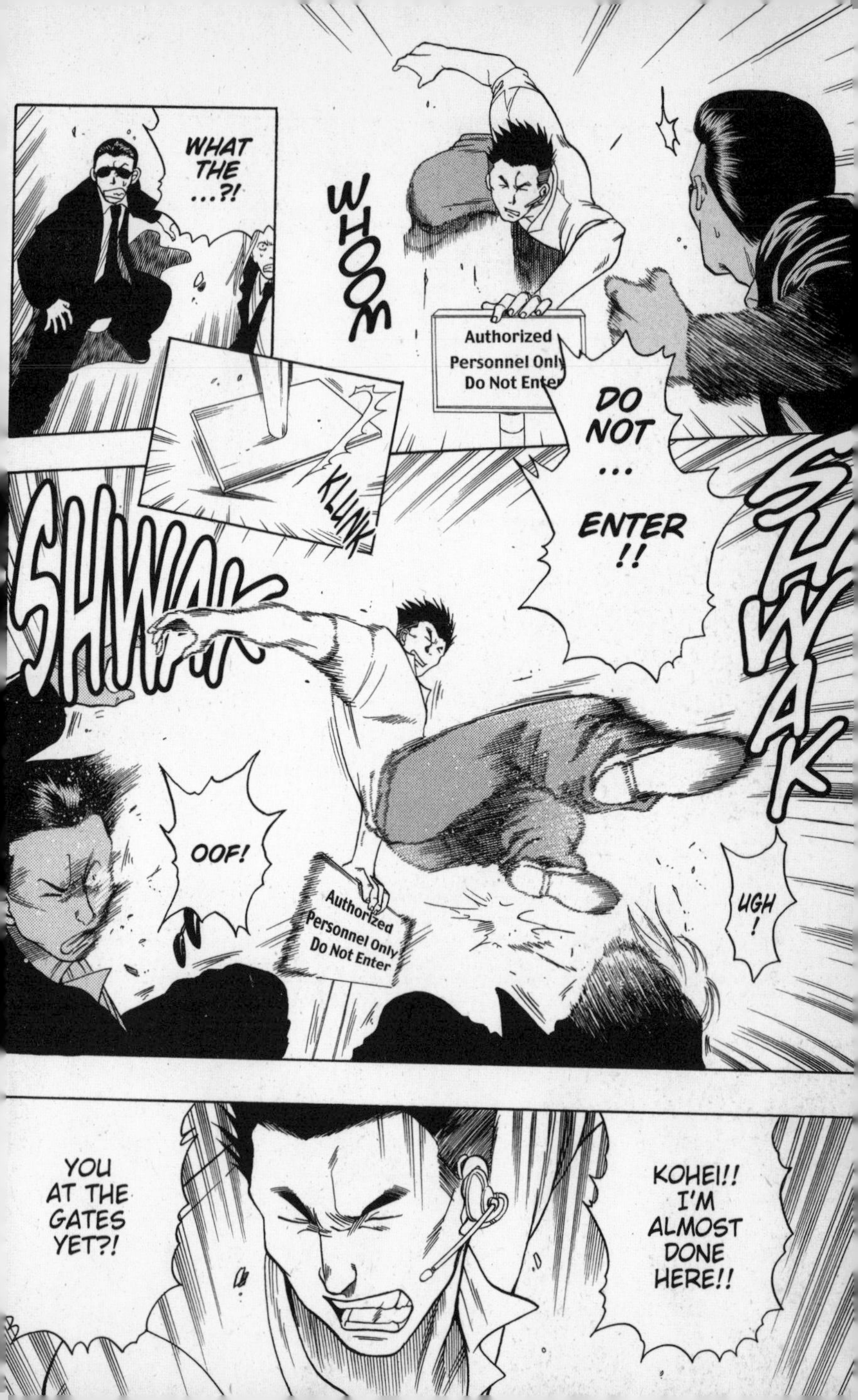

WHOOM
Authorized Personnel Only Do Not Enter
DO NOT ... ENTER!!
WHAT THE ...?!
KLUNK
SHWAK
UGH!
SHWAK
OOF!
Authorized Personnel Only Do Not Enter
KOHEI!! I'M ALMOST DONE HERE!!
YOU AT THE GATES YET?!

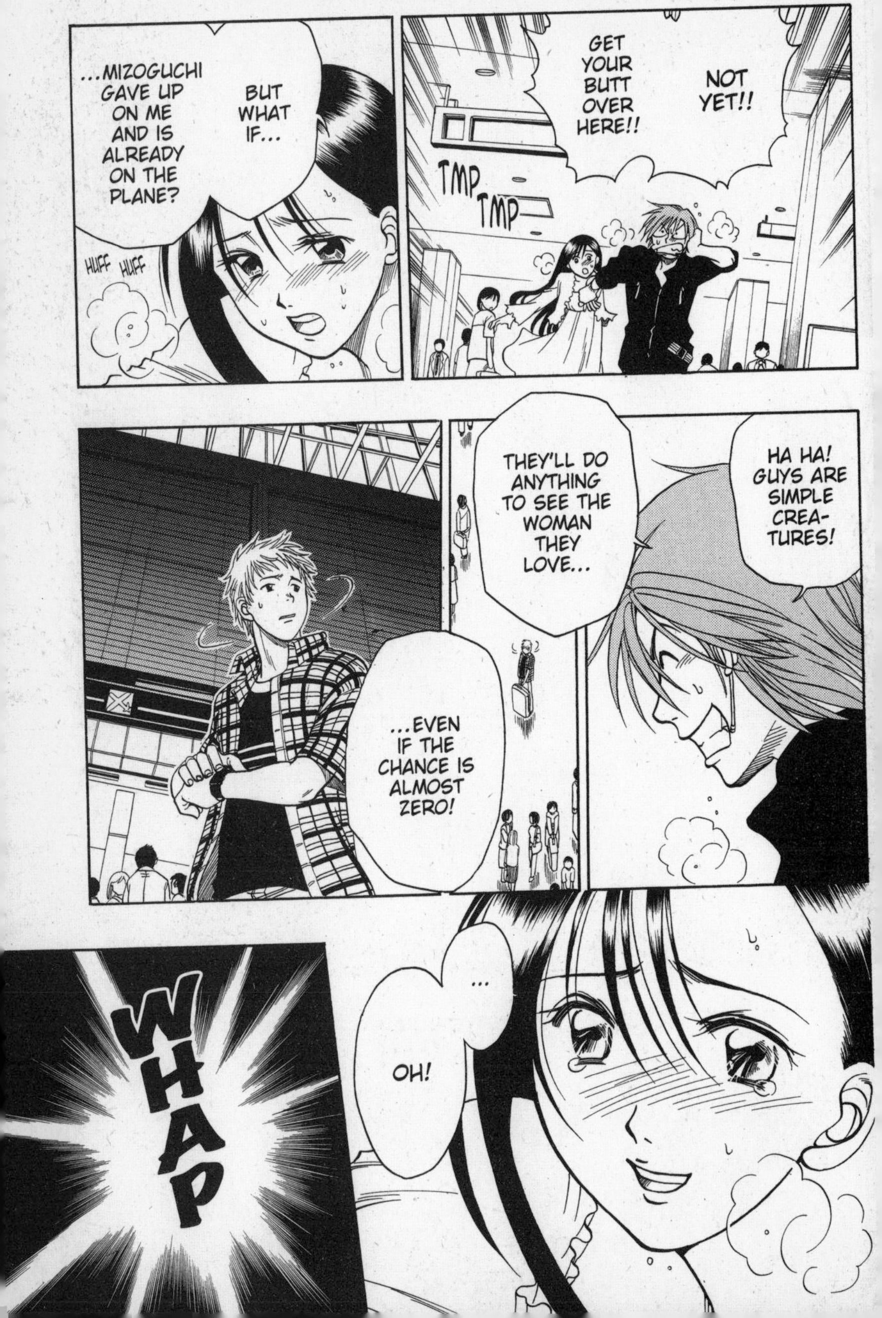
NOT YET!!
GET YOUR BUTT OVER HERE!!
TMP TMP
BUT WHAT IF...
...MIZOGUCHI GAVE UP ON ME AND IS ALREADY ON THE PLANE?
HUFF HUFF
HA HA! GUYS ARE SIMPLE CREA-TURES!
THEY'LL DO ANYTHING TO SEE THE WOMAN THEY LOVE...
...EVEN IF THE CHANCE IS ALMOST ZERO!
...
OH!
WHAP

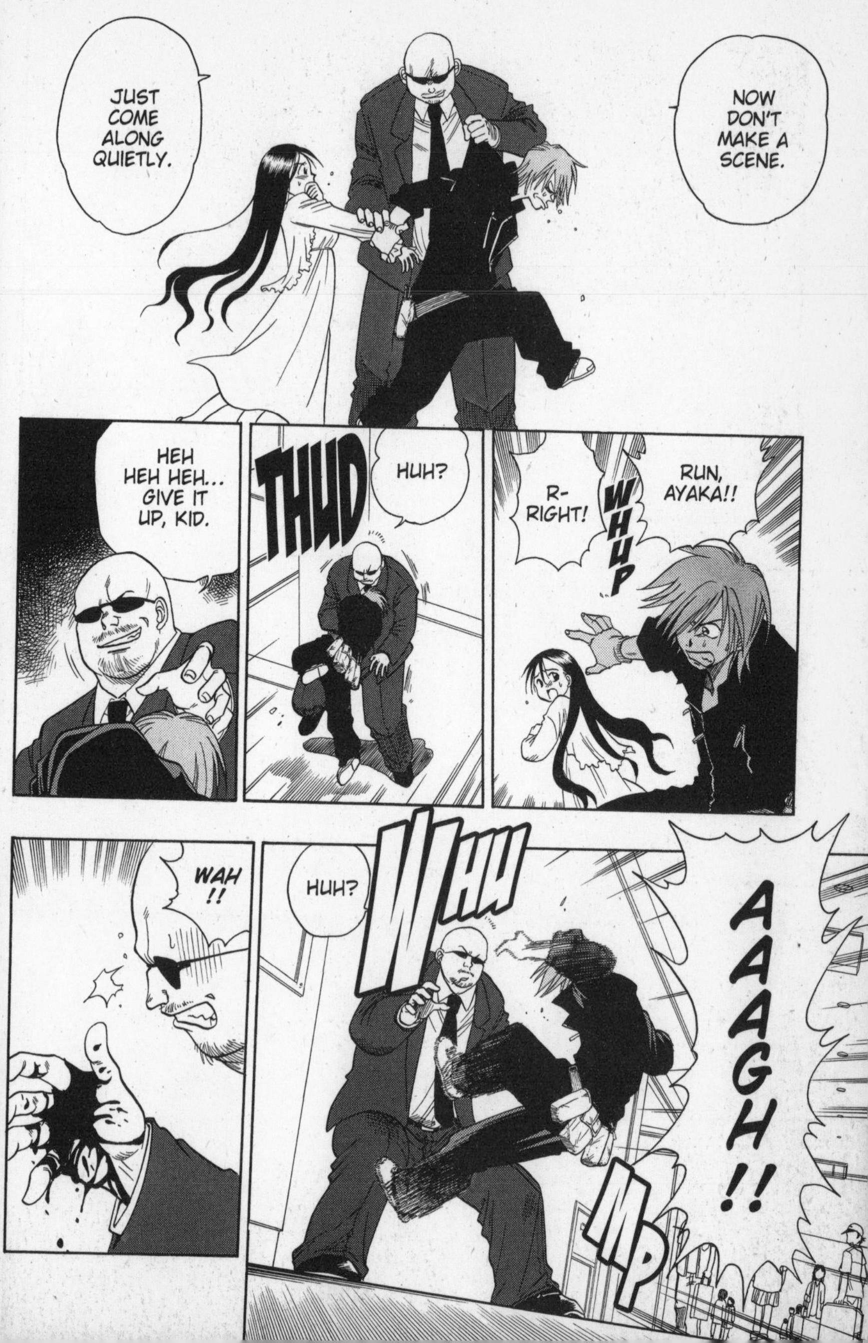
NOW DON'T MAKE A SCENE.
JUST COME ALONG QUIETLY.
RUN, AYAKA!!
WHUP
R-RIGHT!
THUD
HUH?
HEH HEH HEH... GIVE IT UP, KID.
AAAAGH!!
WHU
MP
HUH?
WAH!!

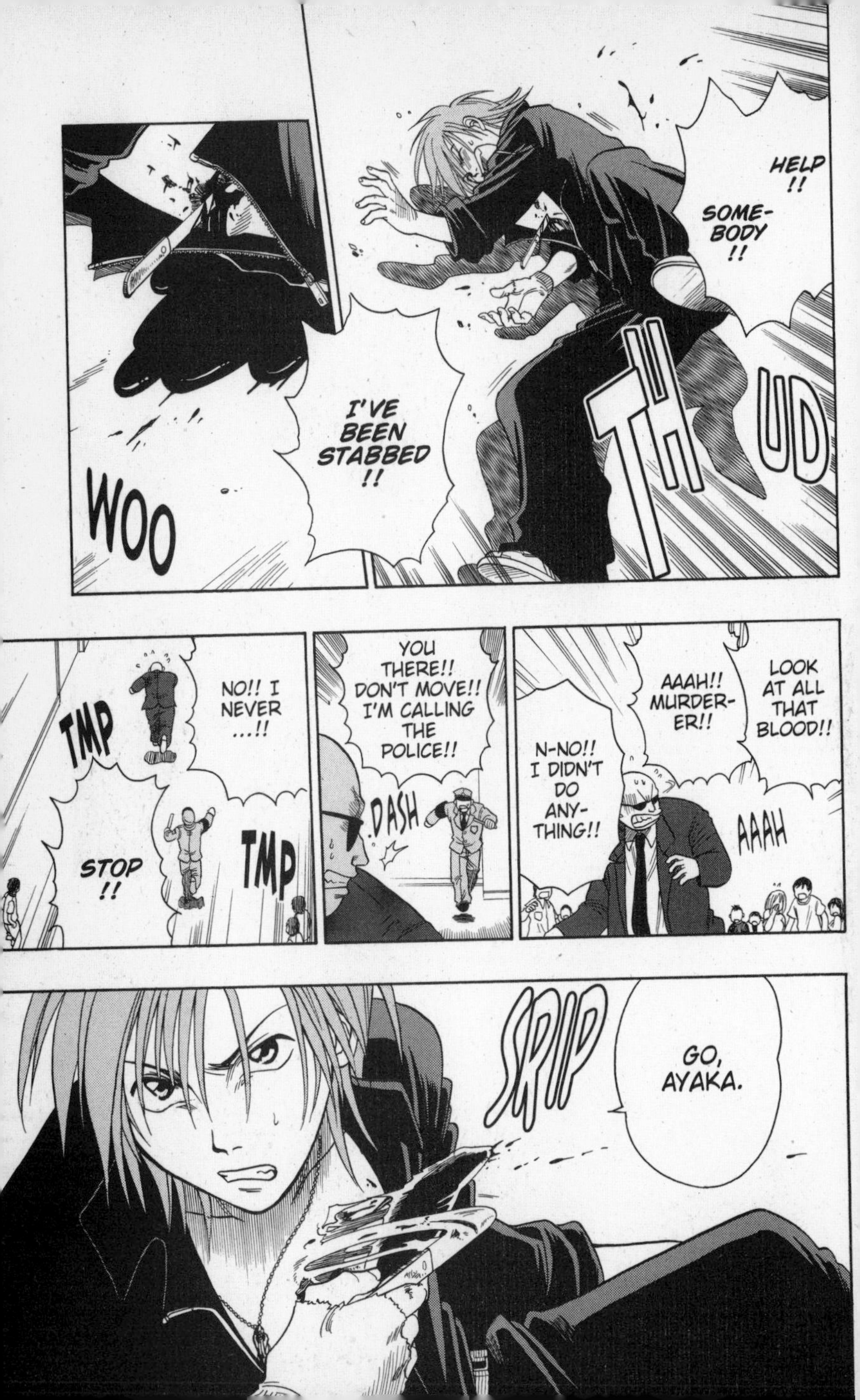
HELP!!
SOMEBODY!!
THUD
I'VE BEEN STABBED!!
WOO
LOOK AT ALL THAT BLOOD!!
AAAH!! MURDERER!!
N-NO!! I DIDN'T DO ANYTHING!!
AAAH
YOU THERE!! DON'T MOVE!! I'M CALLING THE POLICE!!
DASH
NO!! I NEVER ...!!
TMP
TMP
STOP!!
SRIP
GO, AYAKA.

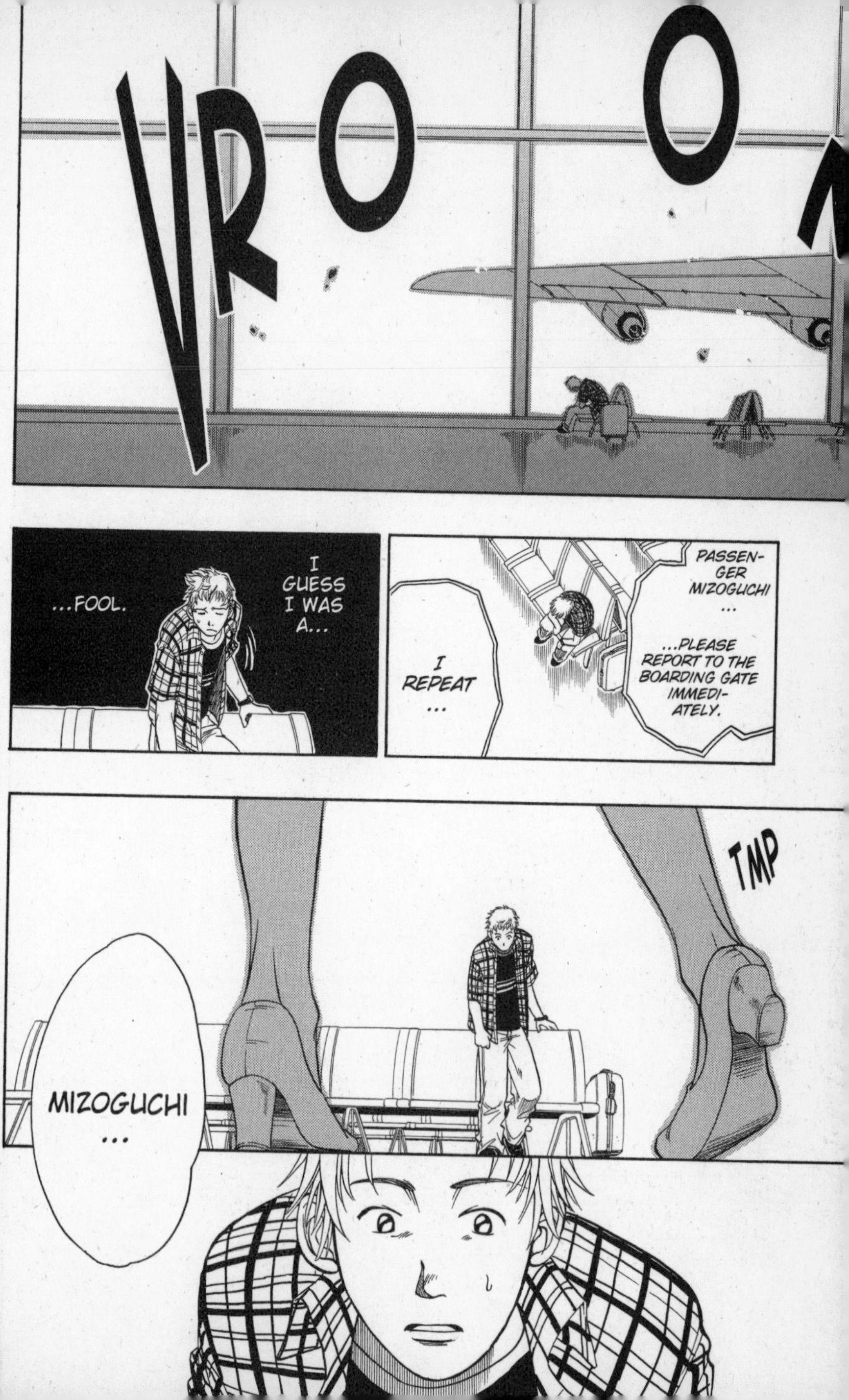
VROOOM
PASSEN-GER MIZOGUCHI...
...PLEASE REPORT TO THE BOARDING GATE IMMEDI-ATELY.
I REPEAT...
I GUESS I WAS A...
...FOOL.
TMP
MIZOGUCHI...

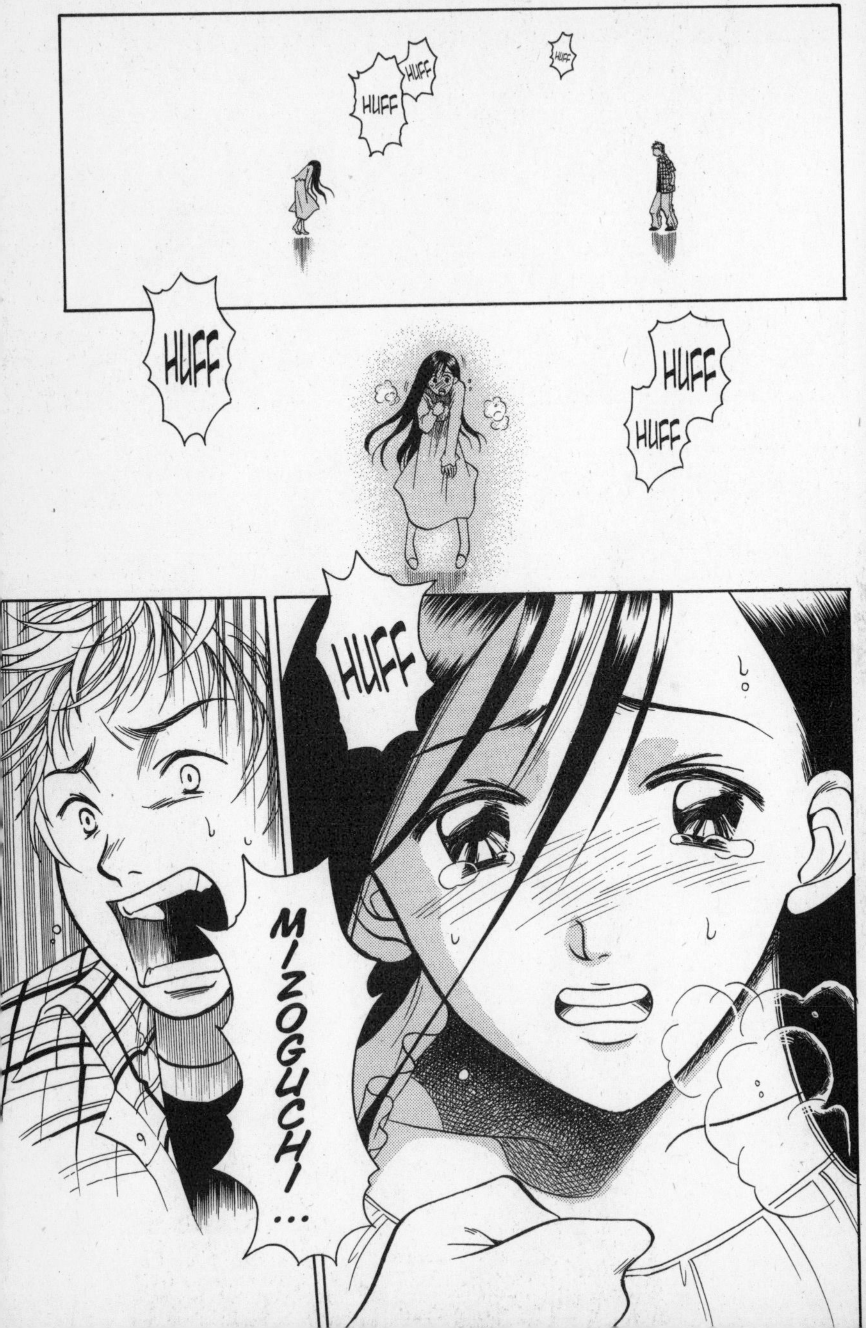

HUFF
HUFF
HUFF
HUFF
HUFF
HUFF
HUFF
MIZOGUCHI...

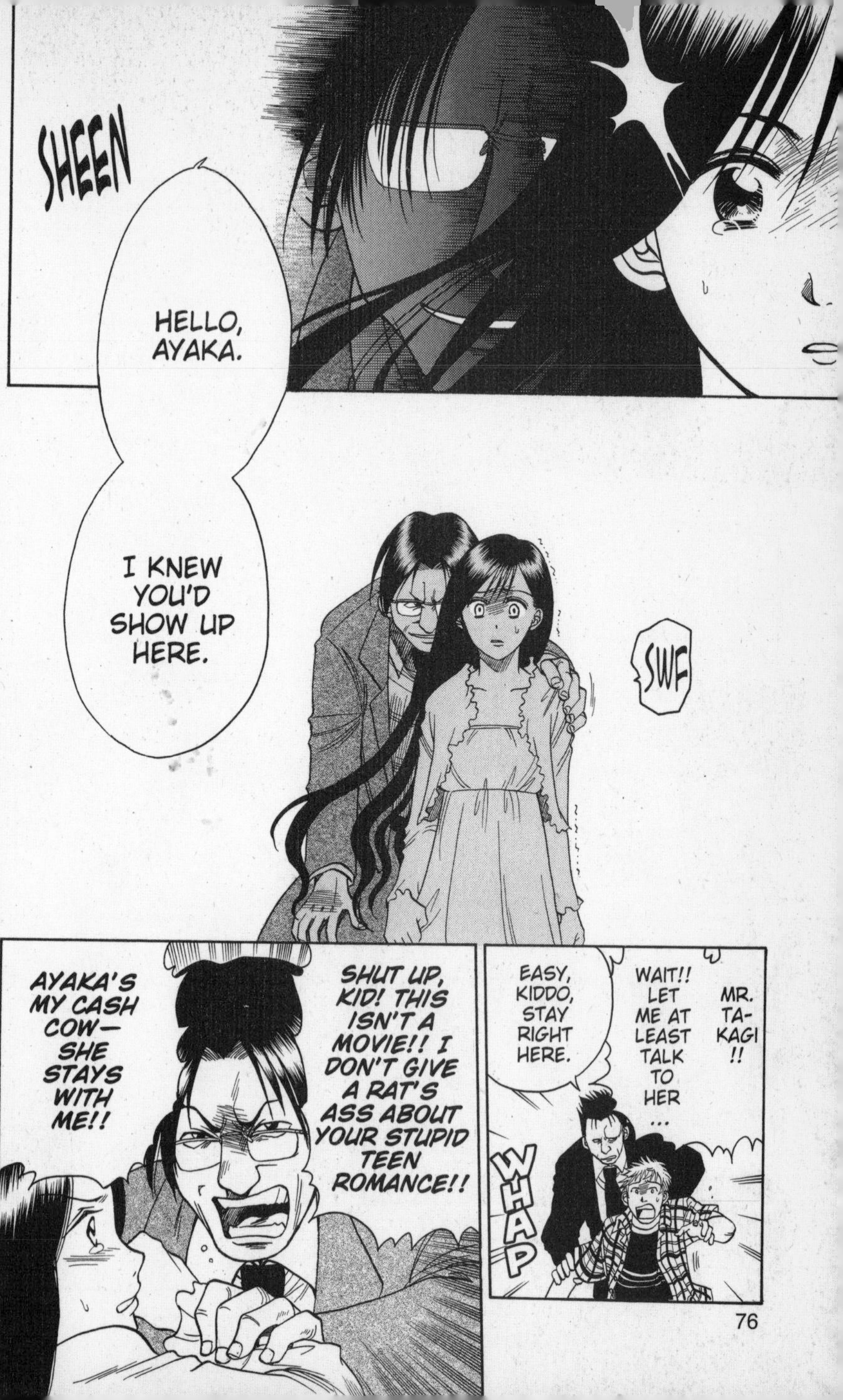
SHEEN
HELLO, AYAKA.
I KNEW YOU'D SHOW UP HERE.
SWF
MR. TA-KAGI!!
WAIT!! LET ME AT LEAST TALK TO HER...
EASY, KIDDO, STAY RIGHT HERE.
WHAP
SHUT UP, KID! THIS ISN'T A MOVIE!! I DON'T GIVE A RAT'S ASS ABOUT YOUR STUPID TEEN ROMANCE!!
AYAKA'S MY CASH COW— SHE STAYS WITH ME!!

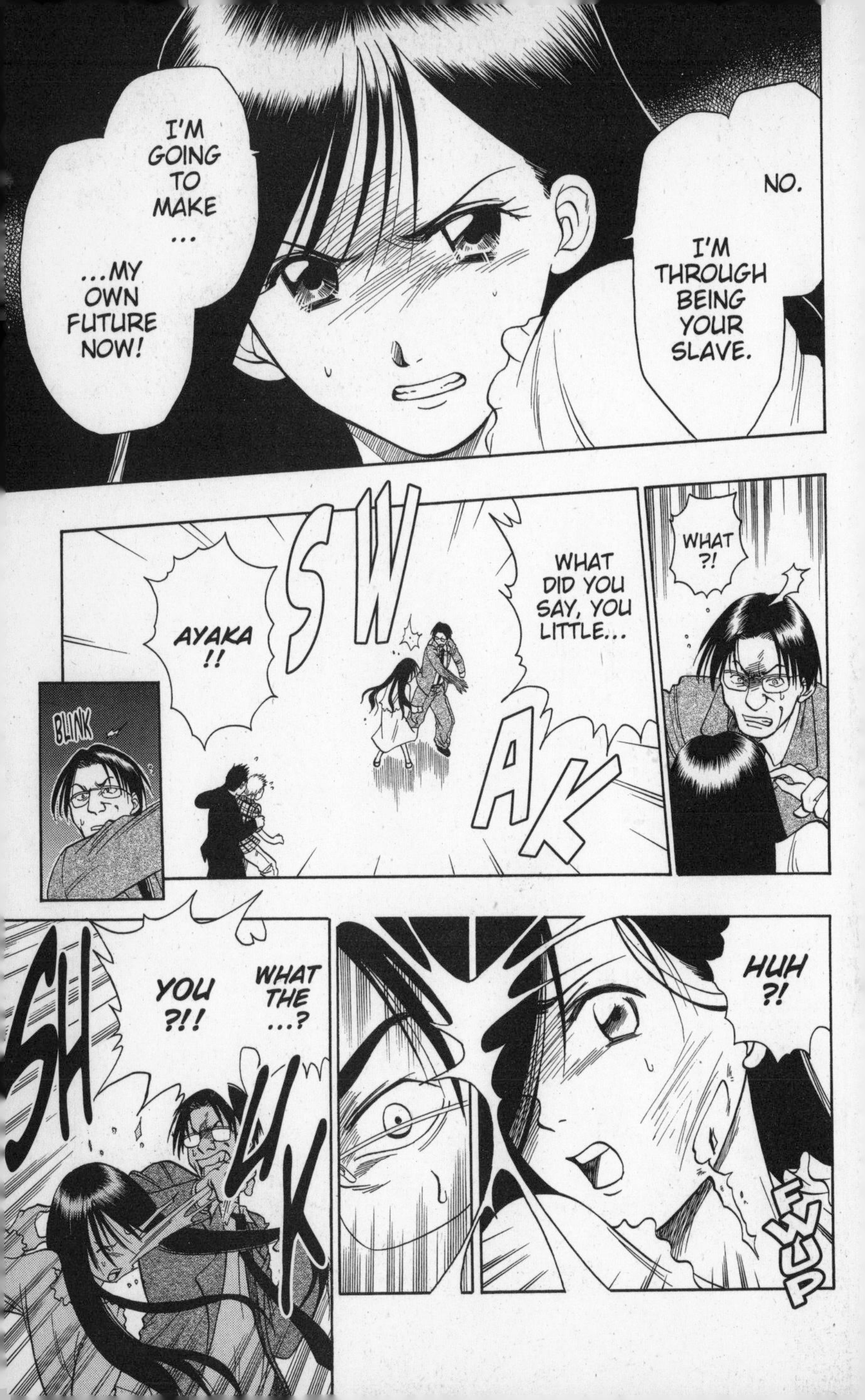
NO.
I'M THROUGH BEING YOUR SLAVE.
I'M GOING TO MAKE ...
...MY OWN FUTURE NOW!
WHAT ?!
WHAT DID YOU SAY, YOU LITTLE...
SW AK
AYAKA !!
BLINK
HUH ?!
FWUP
WHAT THE ...?
YOU ?!!
SH UK

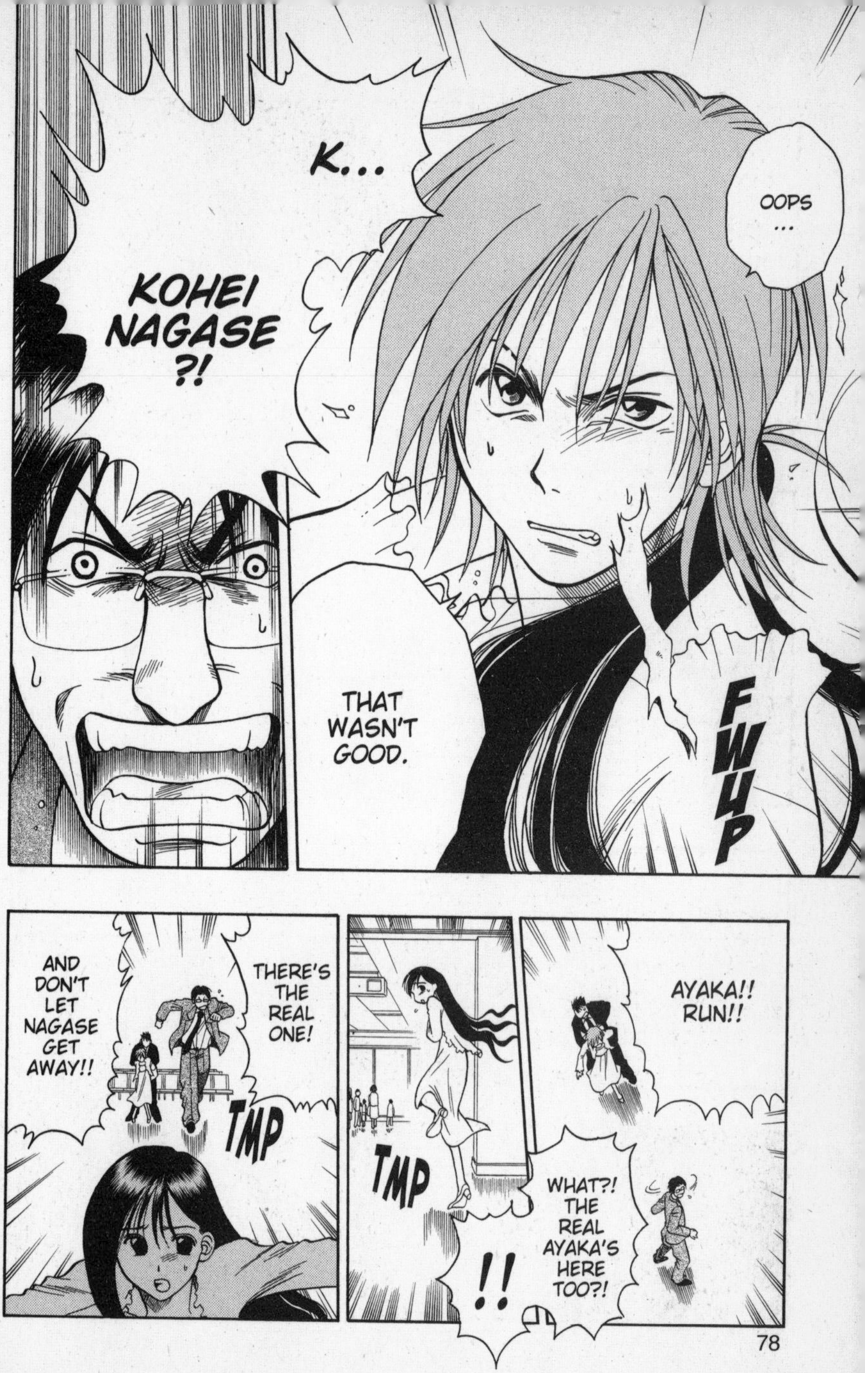
OOPS ...
THAT WASN'T GOOD.
FWUP
K...
KOHEI NAGASE ?!
AYAKA!! RUN!!
WHAT?! THE REAL AYAKA'S HERE TOO?!
TMP
!!
THERE'S THE REAL ONE!
AND DON'T LET NAGASE GET AWAY!!
TMP

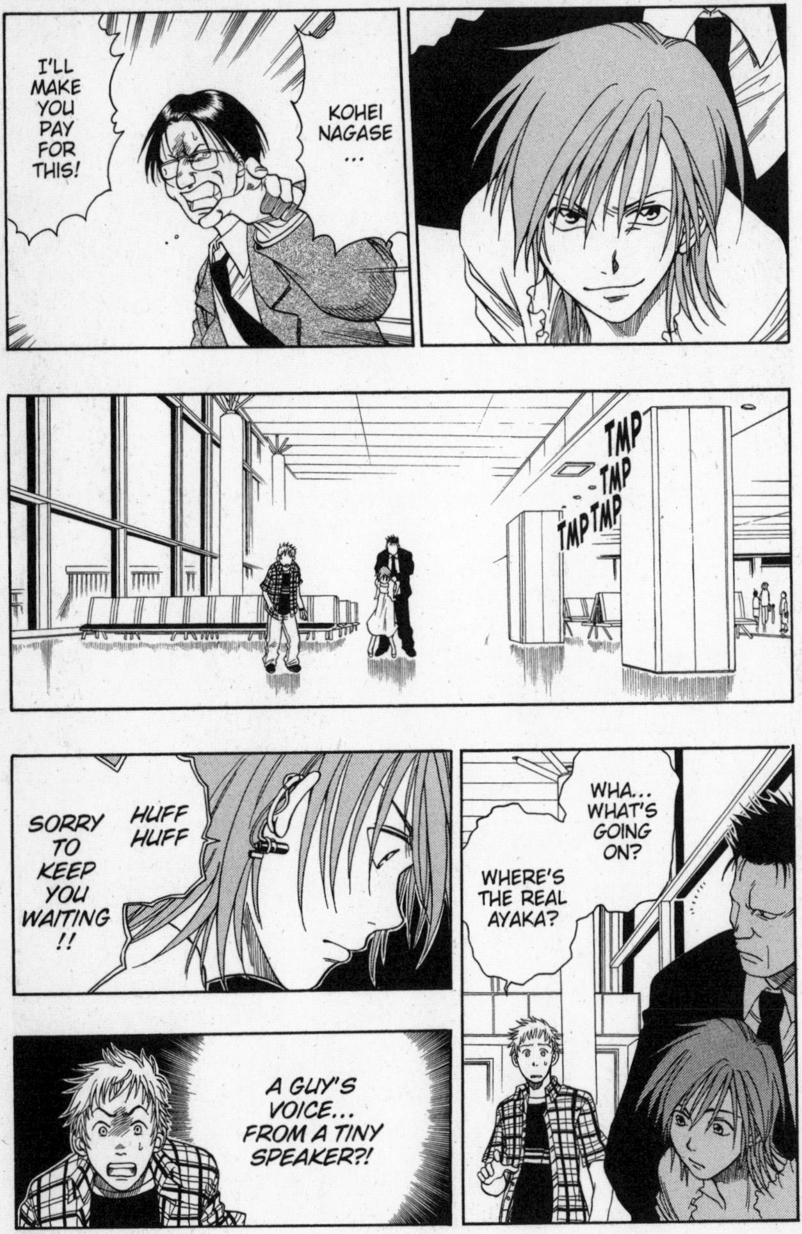
KOHEI NAGASE...
I'LL MAKE YOU PAY FOR THIS!
TMP TMP TMPTMP
WHA... WHAT'S GOING ON?
WHERE'S THE REAL AYAKA?
HUFF HUFF
SORRY TO KEEP YOU WAITING!!
A GUY'S VOICE... FROM A TINY SPEAKER?!

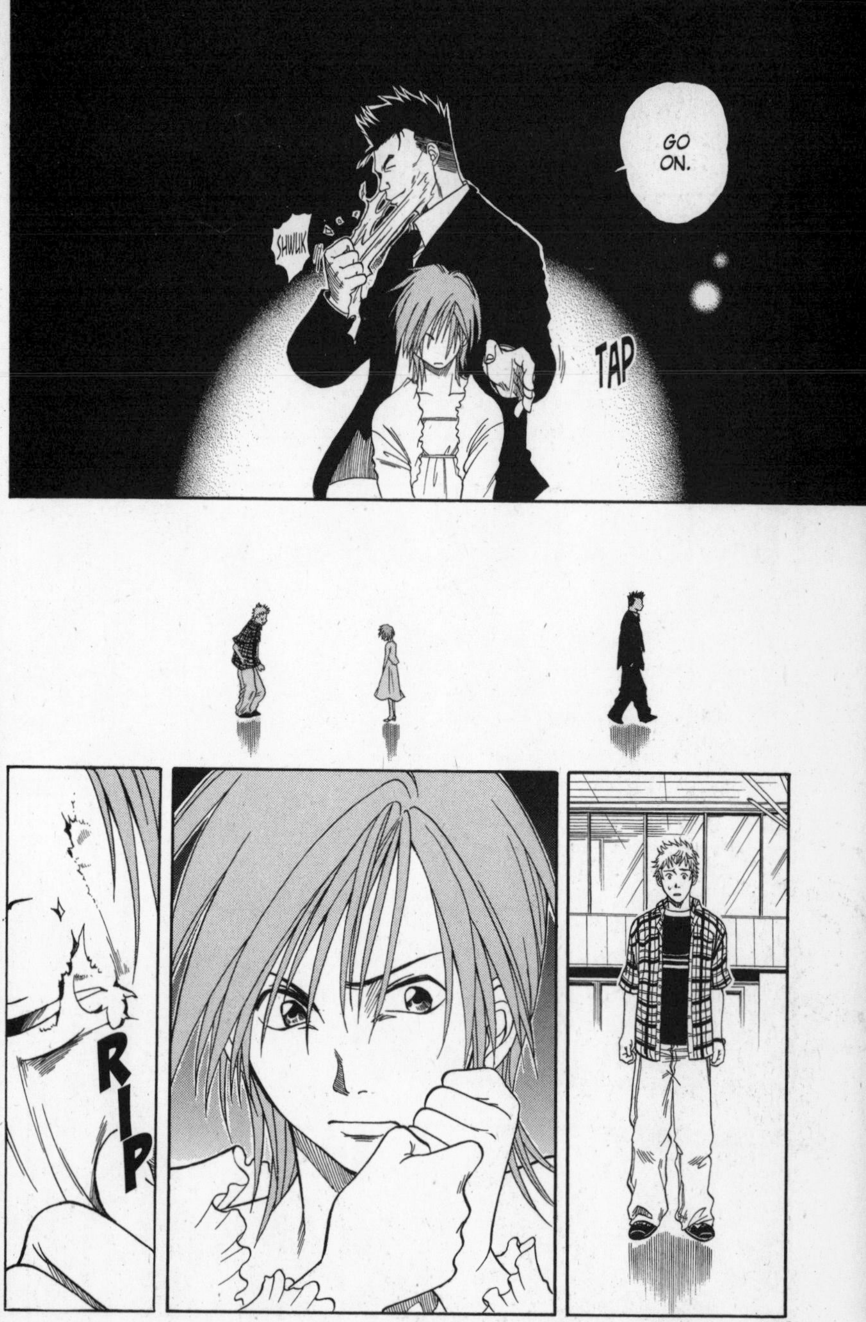
GO ON.
TAP
SHWUK
RIP

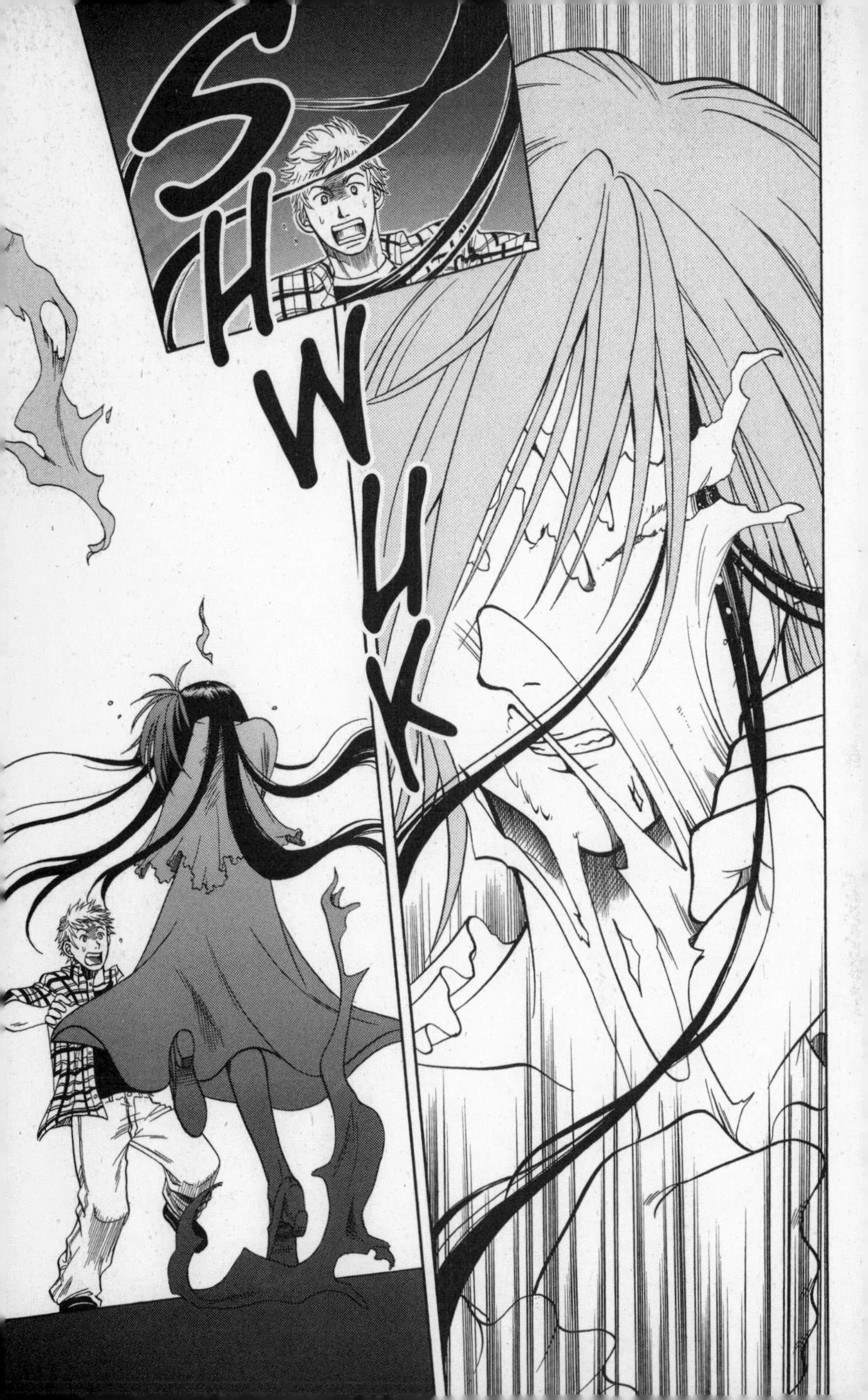
SHWUK

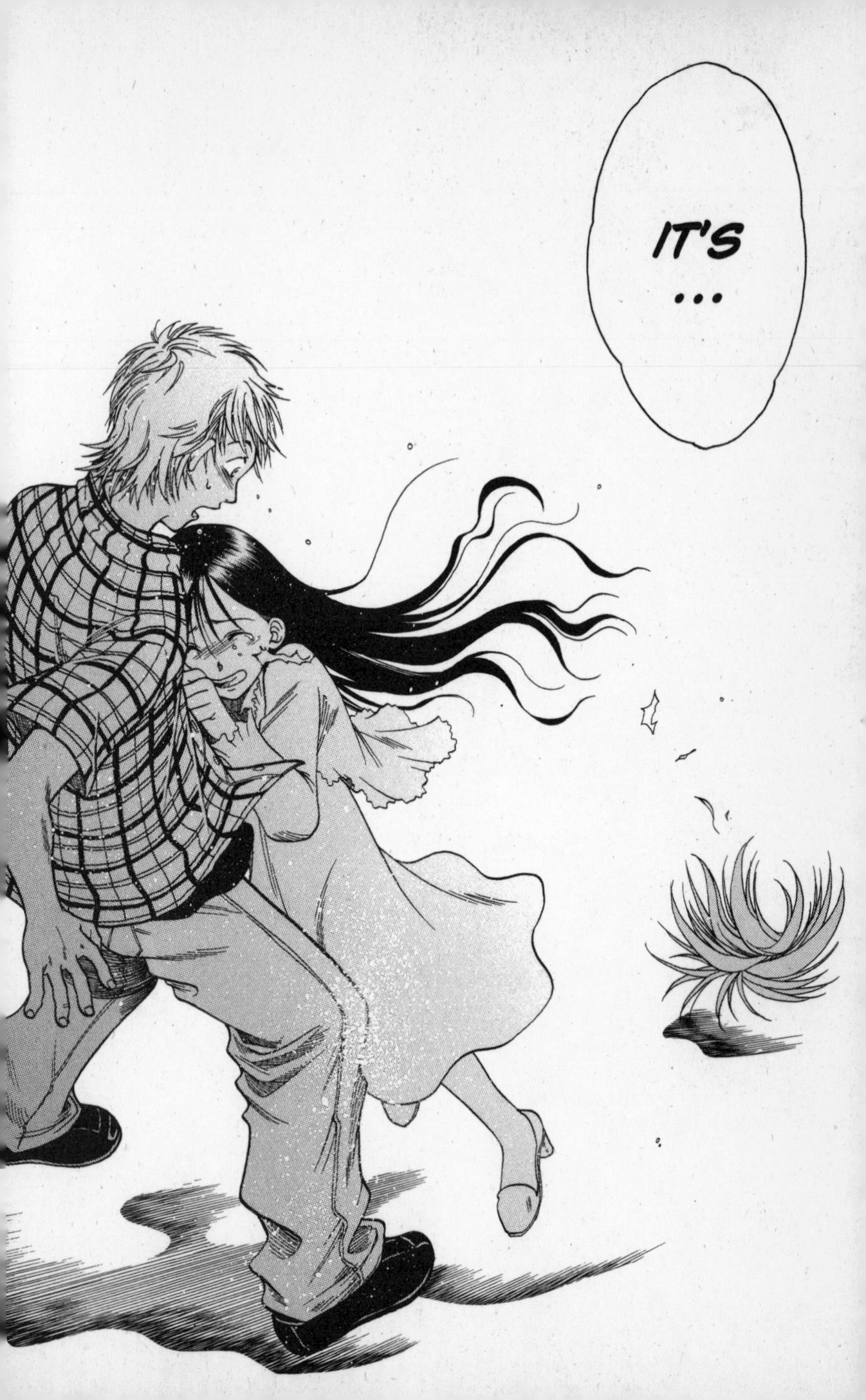
IT'S ...

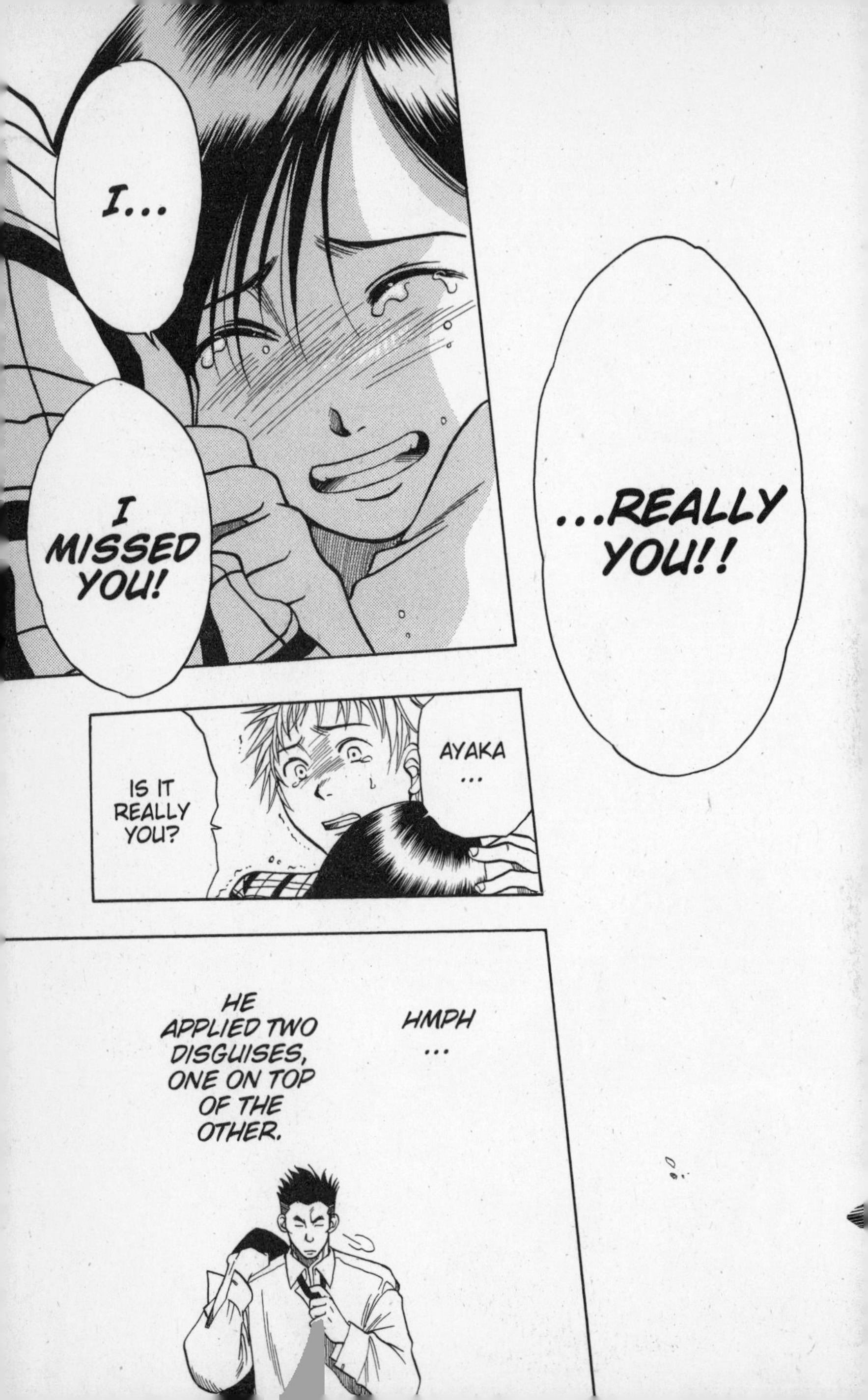
...REALLY YOU!!
I...
I MISSED YOU!
AYAKA ...
IS IT REALLY YOU?
HMPH ...
HE APPLIED TWO DISGUISES, ONE ON TOP OF THE OTHER.

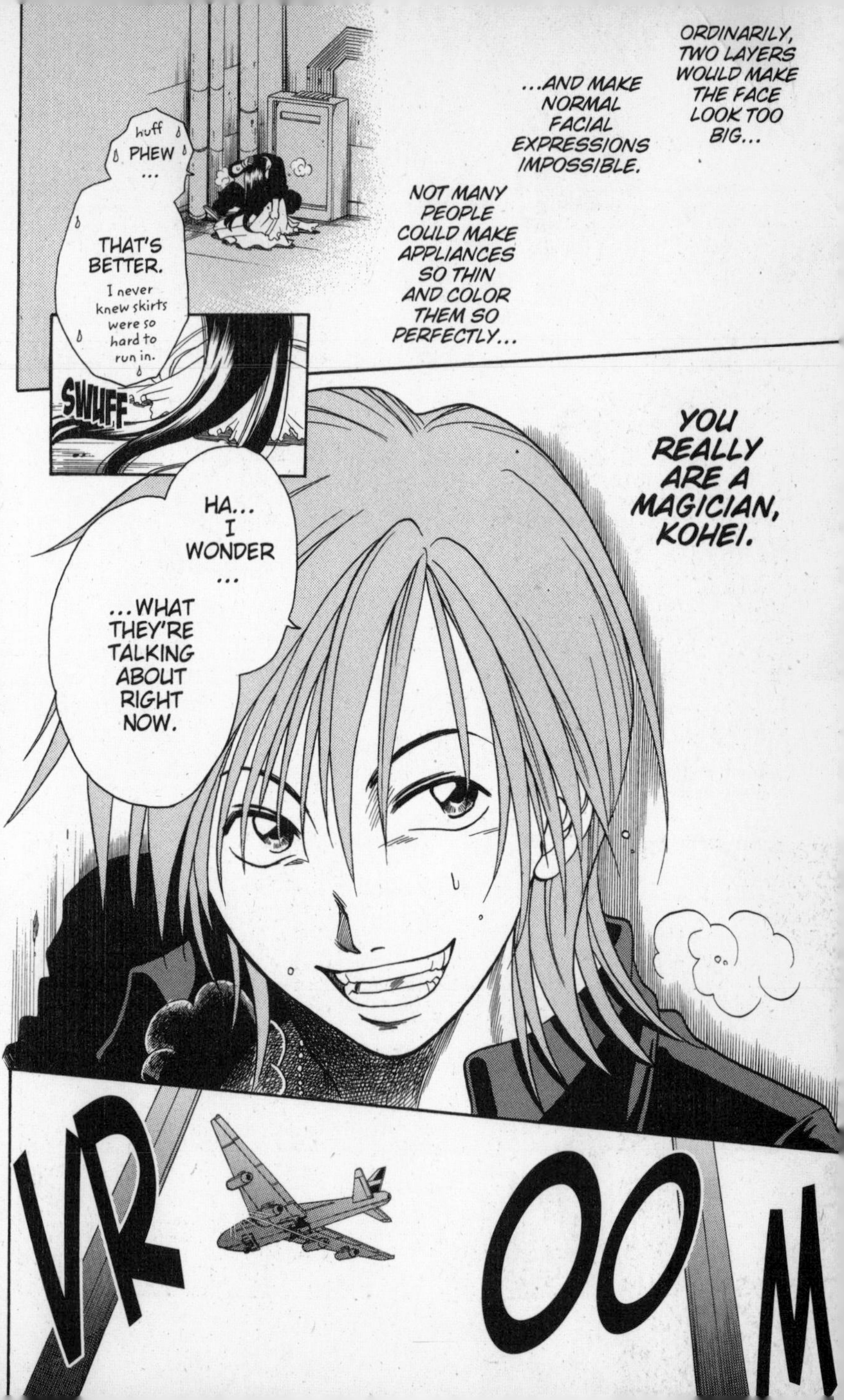

ORDINARILY, TWO LAYERS WOULD MAKE THE FACE LOOK TOO BIG...
...AND MAKE NORMAL FACIAL EXPRESSIONS IMPOSSIBLE.
NOT MANY PEOPLE COULD MAKE APPLIANCES SO THIN AND COLOR THEM SO PERFECTLY...
huff PHEW ...
THAT'S BETTER.
I never knew skirts were so hard to run in.
SWUFF
YOU REALLY ARE A MAGICIAN, KOHEI.
HA... I WONDER ...
...WHAT THEY'RE TALKING ABOUT RIGHT NOW.
VROOM

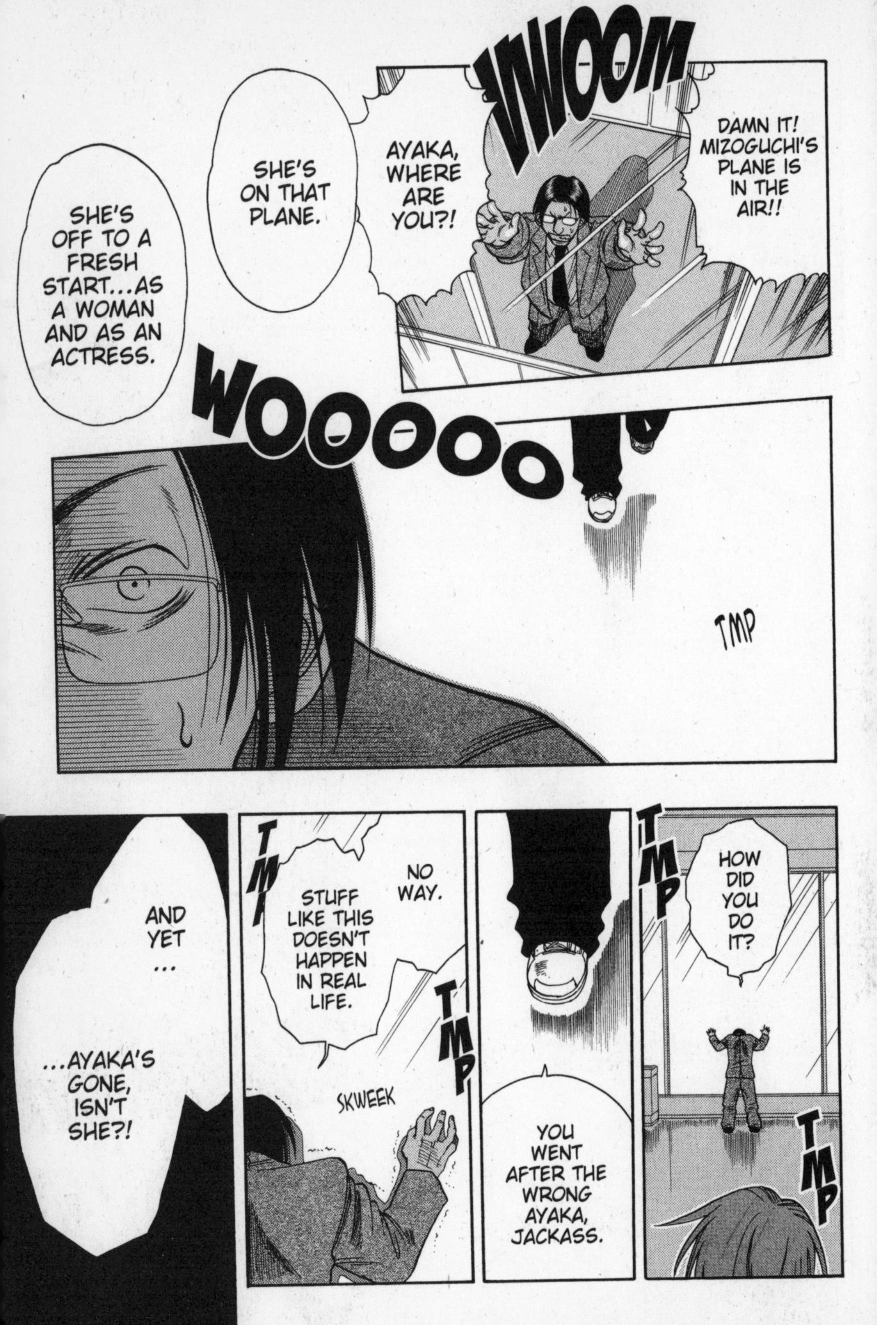
VWOOM
DAMN IT! MIZOGUCHI'S PLANE IS IN THE AIR!!
AYAKA, WHERE ARE YOU?!
SHE'S ON THAT PLANE.
SHE'S OFF TO A FRESH START...AS A WOMAN AND AS AN ACTRESS.
WOOOOO
TMP
TMP
HOW DID YOU DO IT?
TMP
YOU WENT AFTER THE WRONG AYAKA, JACKASS.
TM
NO WAY.
STUFF LIKE THIS DOESN'T HAPPEN IN REAL LIFE.
TMP
SKWEEK
AND YET ...
...AYAKA'S GONE, ISN'T SHE?!

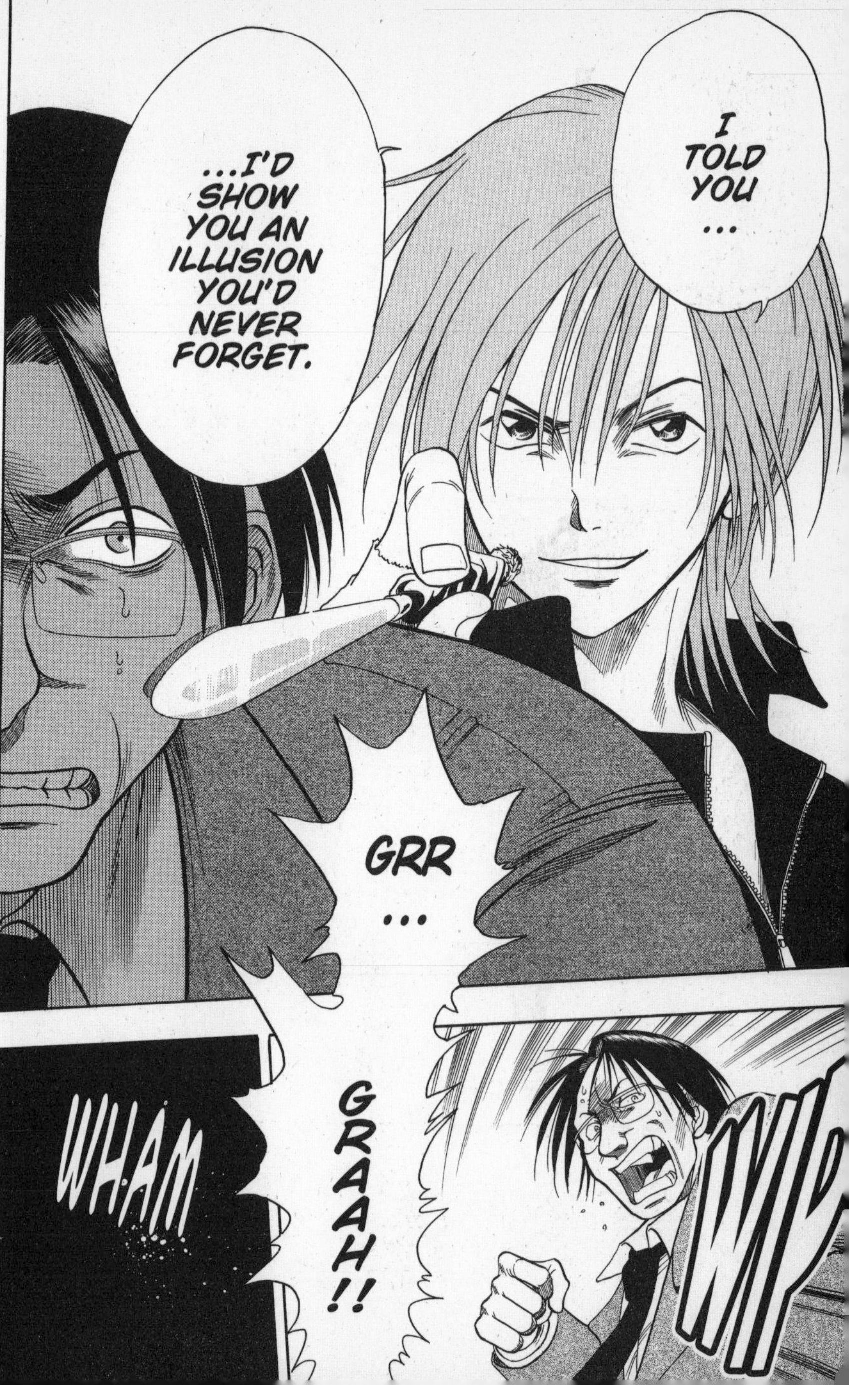
I TOLD YOU ...
...I'D SHOW YOU AN ILLUSION YOU'D NEVER FORGET.
GRR ...
GRAAH!!
WHAM

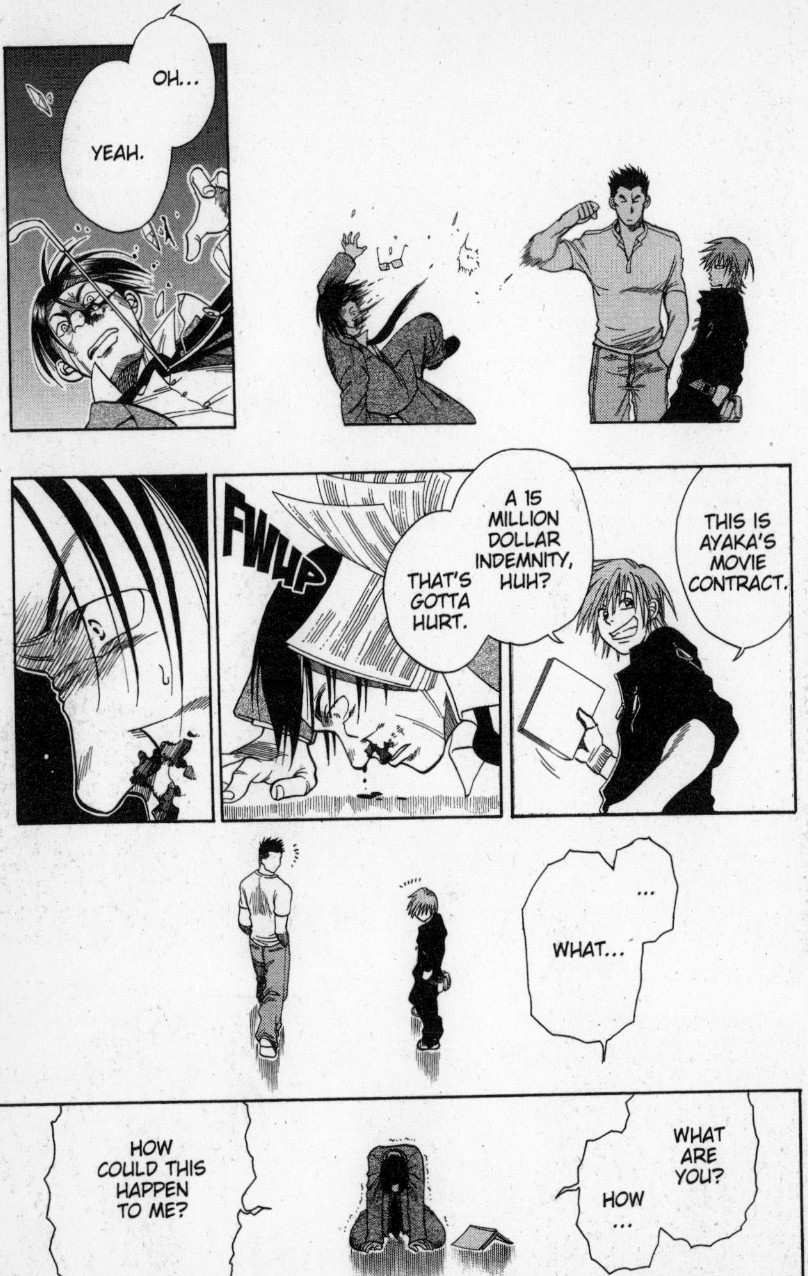
OH...
YEAH.
THIS IS AYAKA'S MOVIE CONTRACT.
A 15 MILLION DOLLAR INDEMNITY, HUH?
THAT'S GOTTA HURT.
FWUP
...
WHAT...
WHAT ARE YOU?
HOW ...
HOW COULD THIS HAPPEN TO ME?

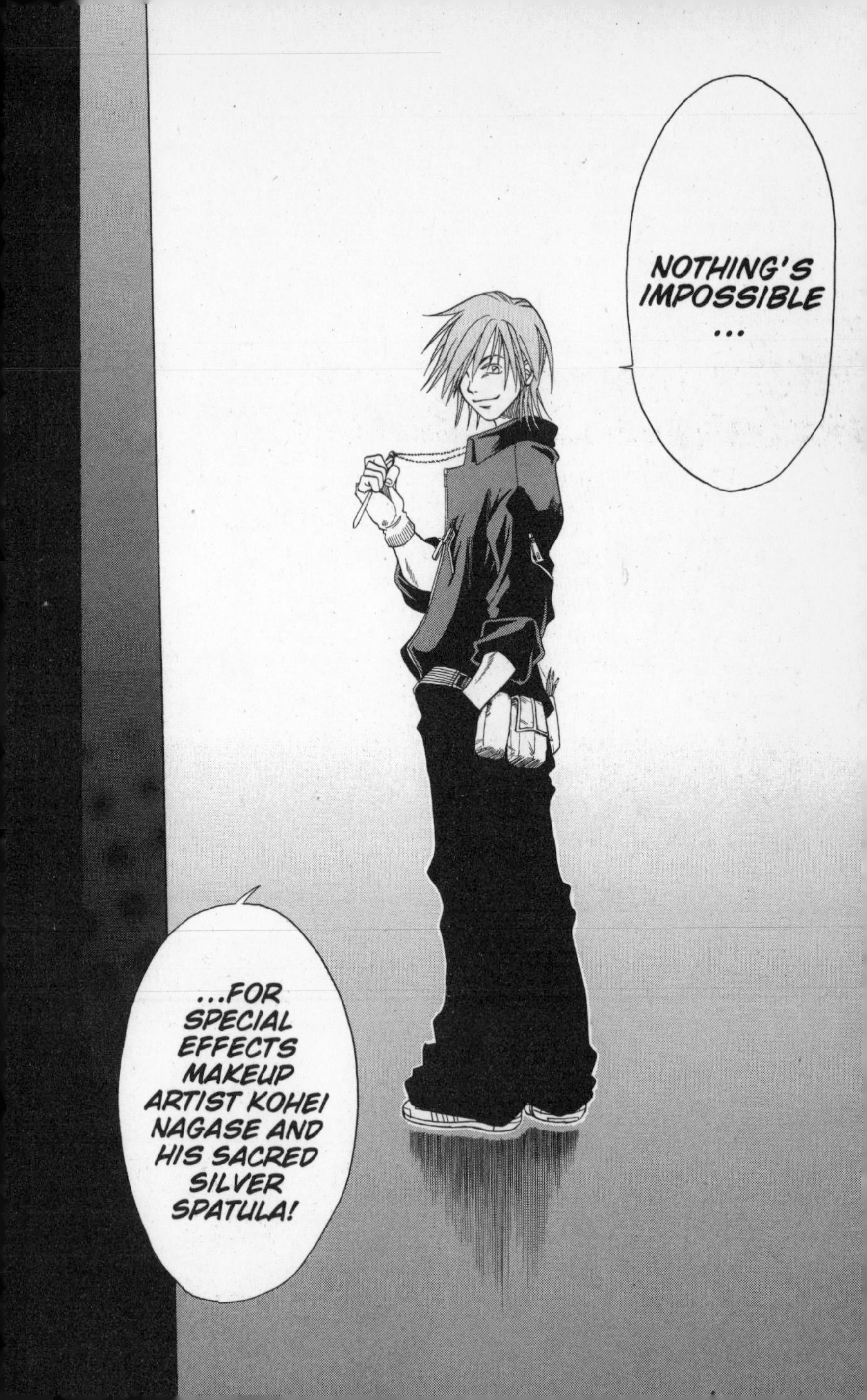
NOTHING'S IMPOSSIBLE ...
...FOR SPECIAL EFFECTS MAKEUP ARTIST KOHEI NAGASE AND HIS SACRED SILVER SPATULA!

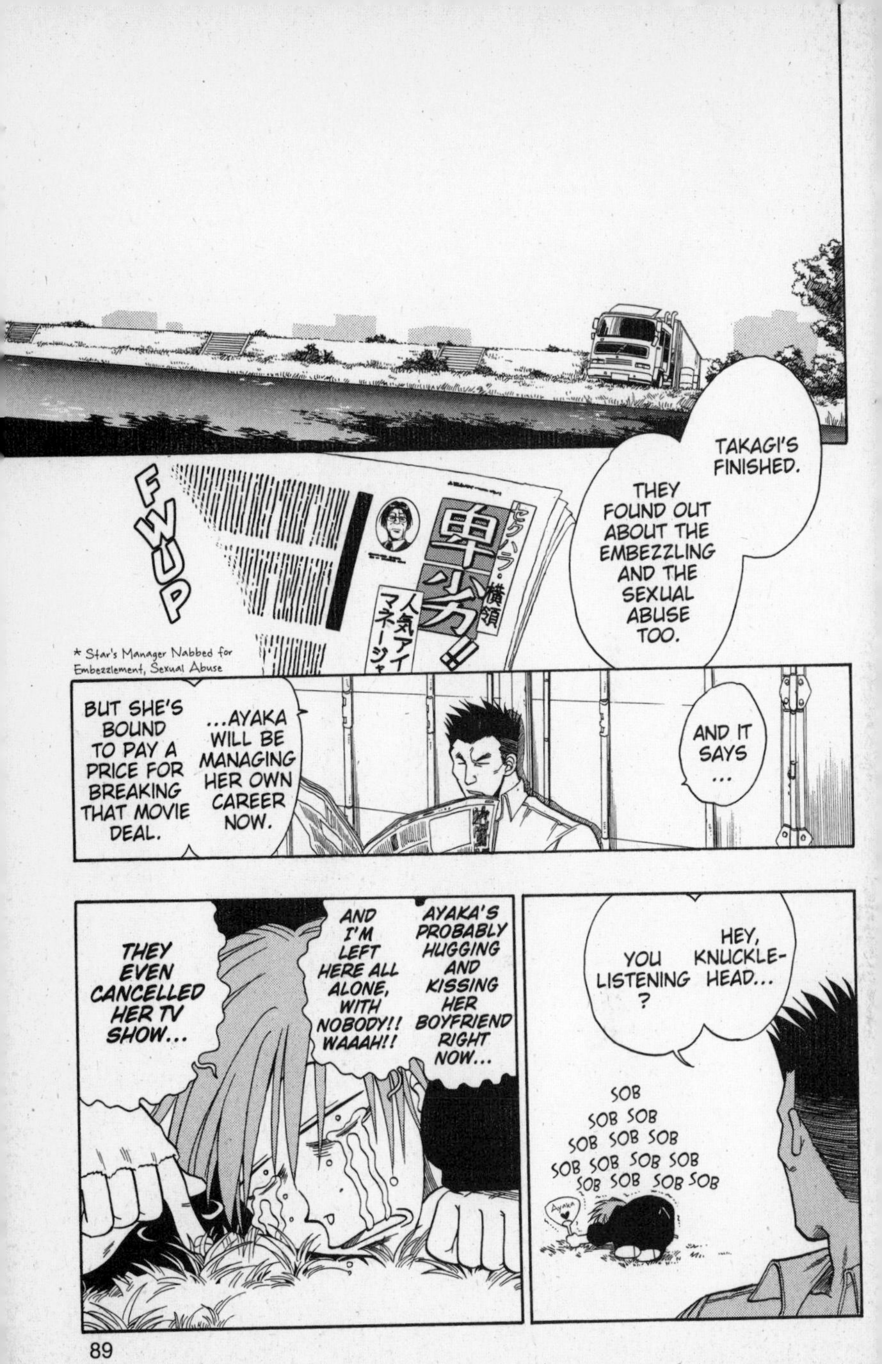
TAKAGI'S FINISHED.
THEY FOUND OUT ABOUT THE EMBEZZLING AND THE SEXUAL ABUSE TOO.
FWUP
セクハラ・横領
* Star's Manager Nabbed for Embezzlement, Sexual Abuse
AND IT SAYS ...
...AYAKA WILL BE MANAGING HER OWN CAREER NOW.
BUT SHE'S BOUND TO PAY A PRICE FOR BREAKING THAT MOVIE DEAL.
HEY, KNUCKLE-HEAD...
YOU LISTENING?
SOB SOB SOB SOB SOB SOB SOB SOB SOB SOB SOB SOB SOB SOB
Ayaka
AYAKA'S PROBABLY HUGGING AND KISSING HER BOYFRIEND RIGHT NOW...
AND I'M LEFT HERE ALL ALONE, WITH NOBODY!! WAAAH!!
THEY EVEN CANCELLED HER TV SHOW...

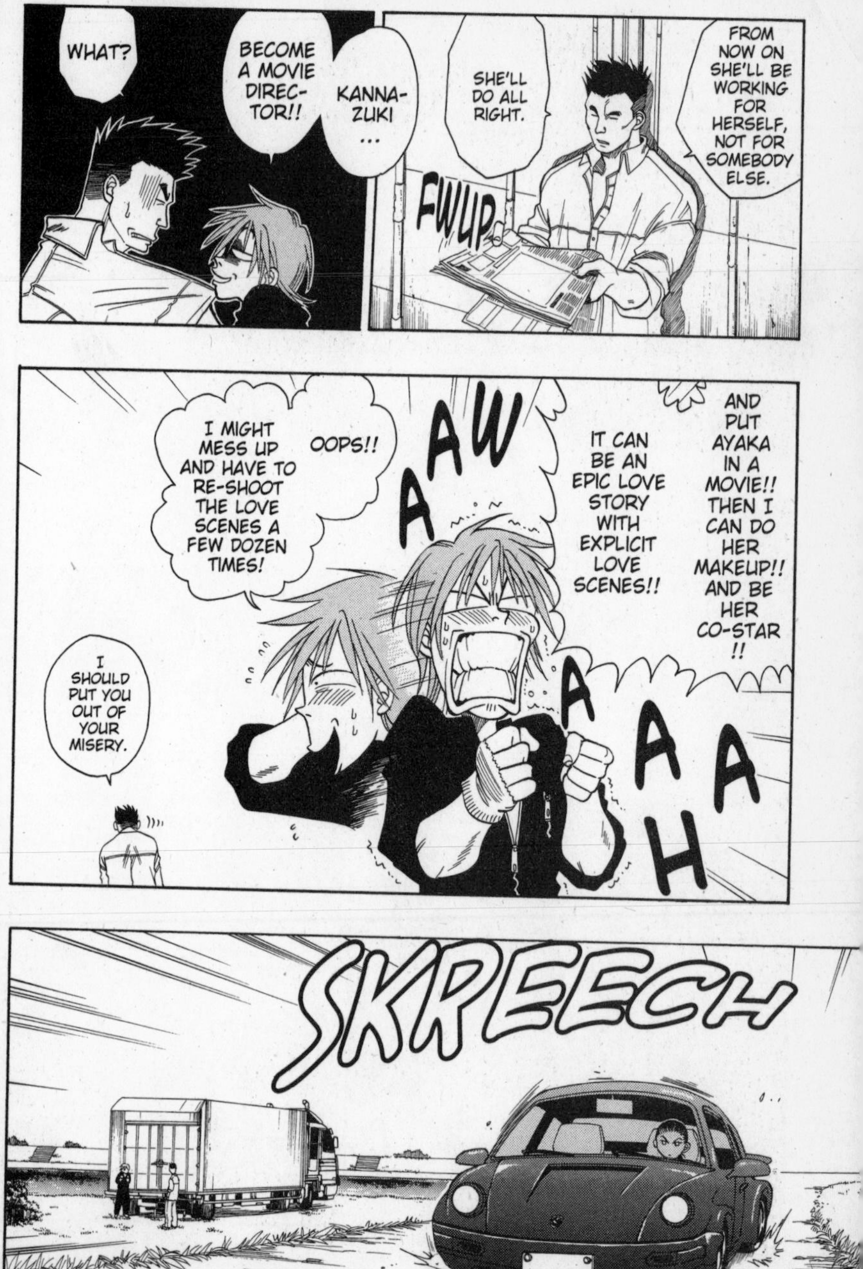
FROM NOW ON SHE'LL BE WORKING FOR HERSELF, NOT FOR SOMEBODY ELSE.
SHE'LL DO ALL RIGHT.
FWUP
KANNA-ZUKI ...
BECOME A MOVIE DIREC-TOR!!
WHAT?
AND PUT AYAKA IN A MOVIE!! THEN I CAN DO HER MAKEUP!! AND BE HER CO-STAR!!
IT CAN BE AN EPIC LOVE STORY WITH EXPLICIT LOVE SCENES!!
AAW
AAAAH
OOPS!!
I MIGHT MESS UP AND HAVE TO RE-SHOOT THE LOVE SCENES A FEW DOZEN TIMES!
I SHOULD PUT YOU OUT OF YOUR MISERY.
SKREECH

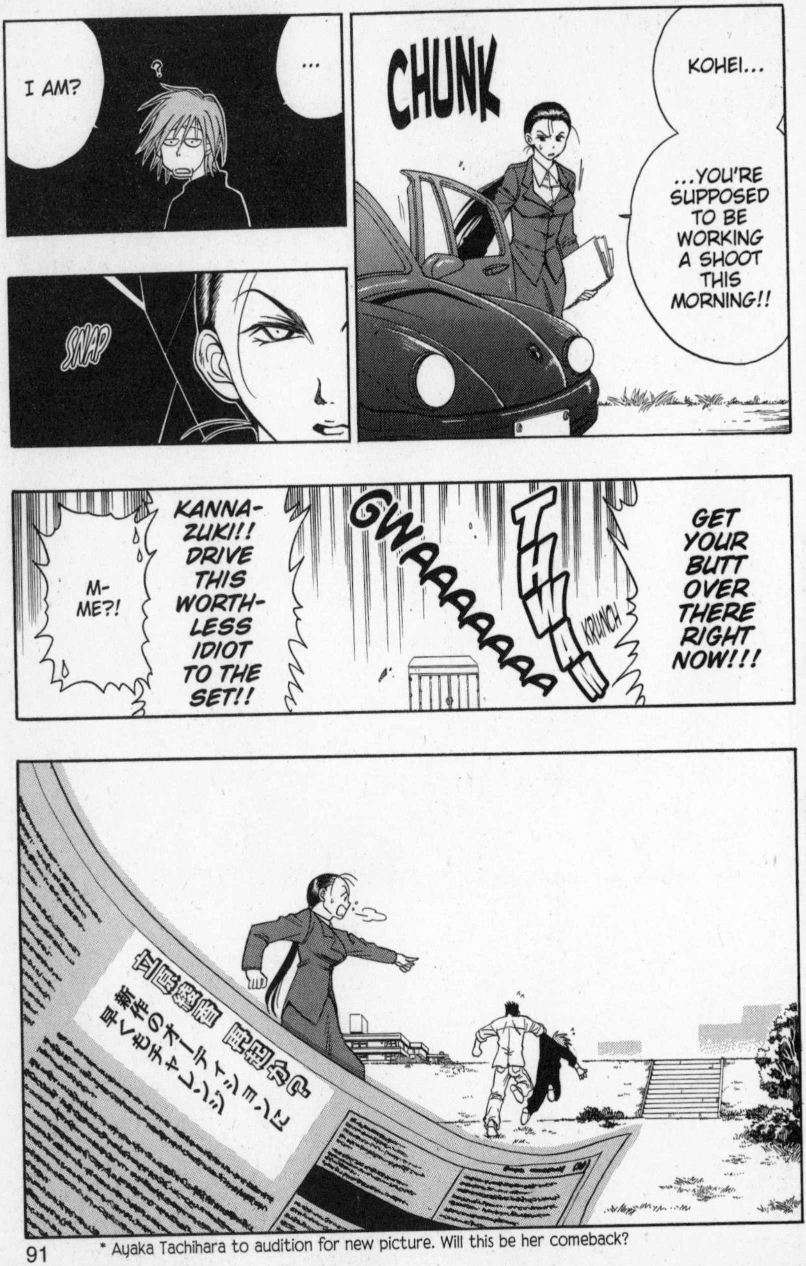
CHUNK
KOHEI...
...YOU'RE SUPPOSED TO BE WORKING A SHOOT THIS MORNING!!
...
I AM?
SNAP
GET YOUR BUTT OVER THERE RIGHT NOW!!!
THWAM
KRUNCH
GWAAAAAAA
KANNAZUKI!! DRIVE THIS WORTHLESS IDIOT TO THE SET!!
M-ME?!
立原綾香 再起か?!
新作のオーディションに
早くもチャレンジ

* Ayaka Tachihara to audition for new picture. Will this be her comeback?

Scene 3: Monster House of Terror (Part 1)

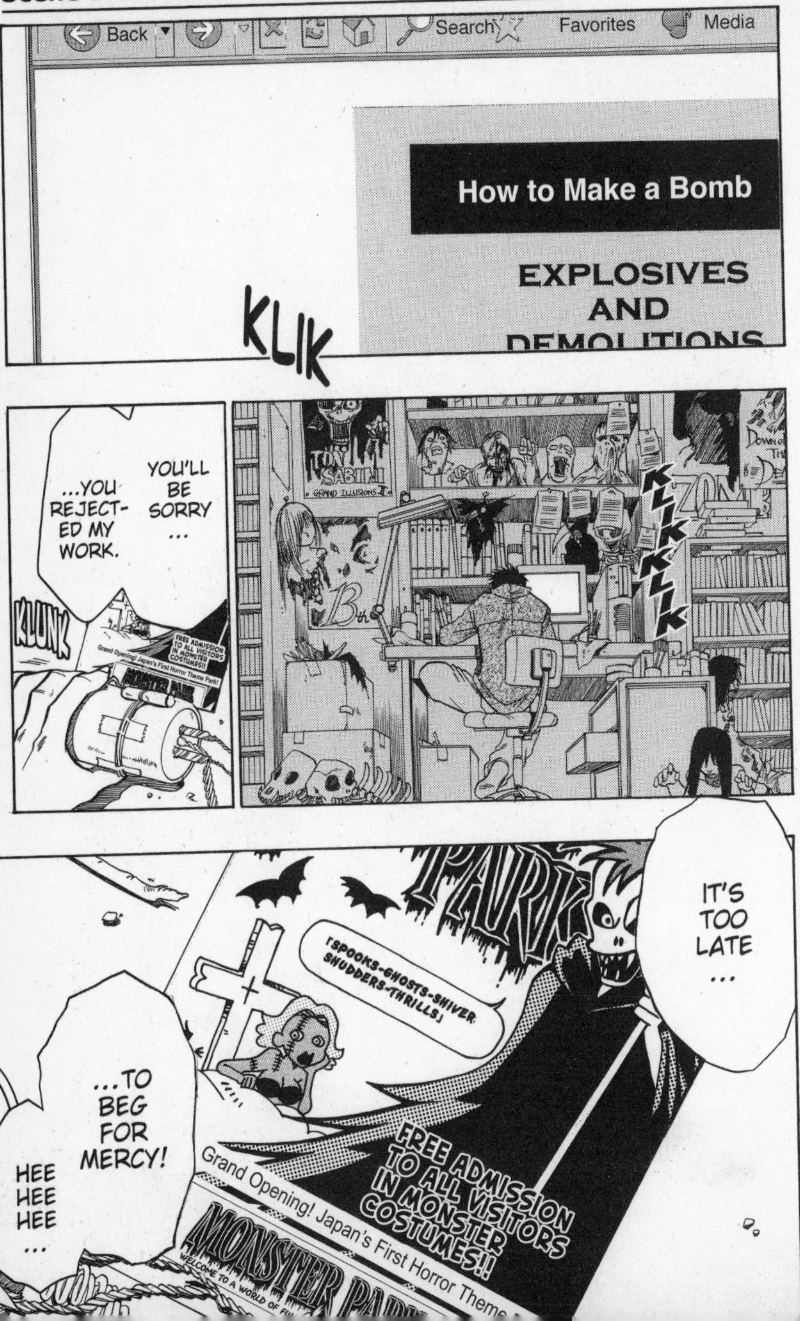
Back
Search
Favorites
Media
How to Make a Bomb
EXPLOSIVES
AND
KLIK
KLIK KLIK KLIK
YOU'LL BE SORRY...
...YOU REJECTED MY WORK.
KLUNK
FREE ADMISSION TO ALL VISITORS IN MONSTER COSTUMES!!
Grand Opening! Japan's First Horror Theme Park!
MONSTER PARK
IT'S TOO LATE...
「SPOOKS-GHOSTS-SHIVER SHUDDERS-THRILLS」
FREE ADMISSION TO ALL VISITORS IN MONSTER COSTUMES!!
Grand Opening! Japan's First Horror Theme
...TO BEG FOR MERCY!
HEE HEE HEE...

Scene 3:

Monster House of Terror (Part 1)

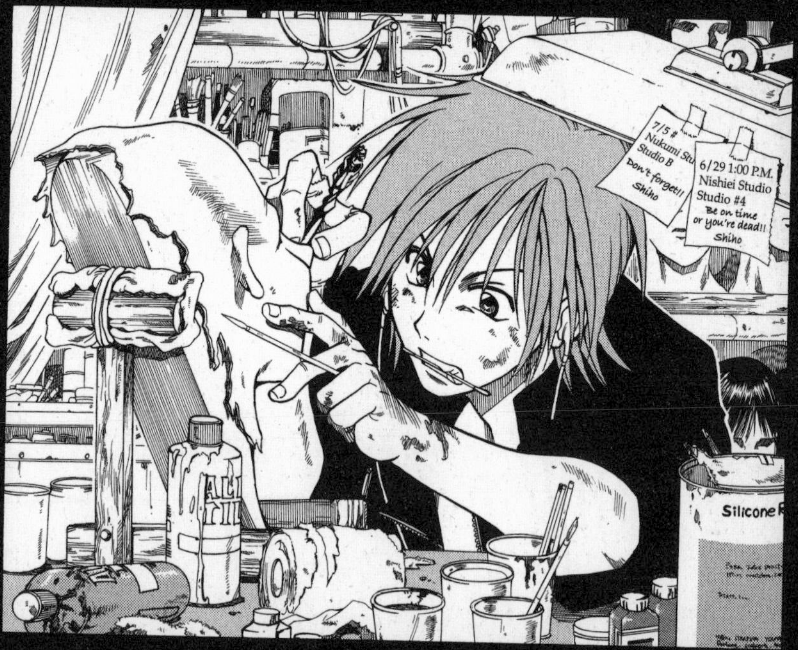

7/5 #
Nukumi Stu
Studio B
Don't forget!!
Shiho
6/29 1:00 P.M.
Nishiei Studio
Studio #4
Be on time
or you're dead!!
Shiho
Silicone R

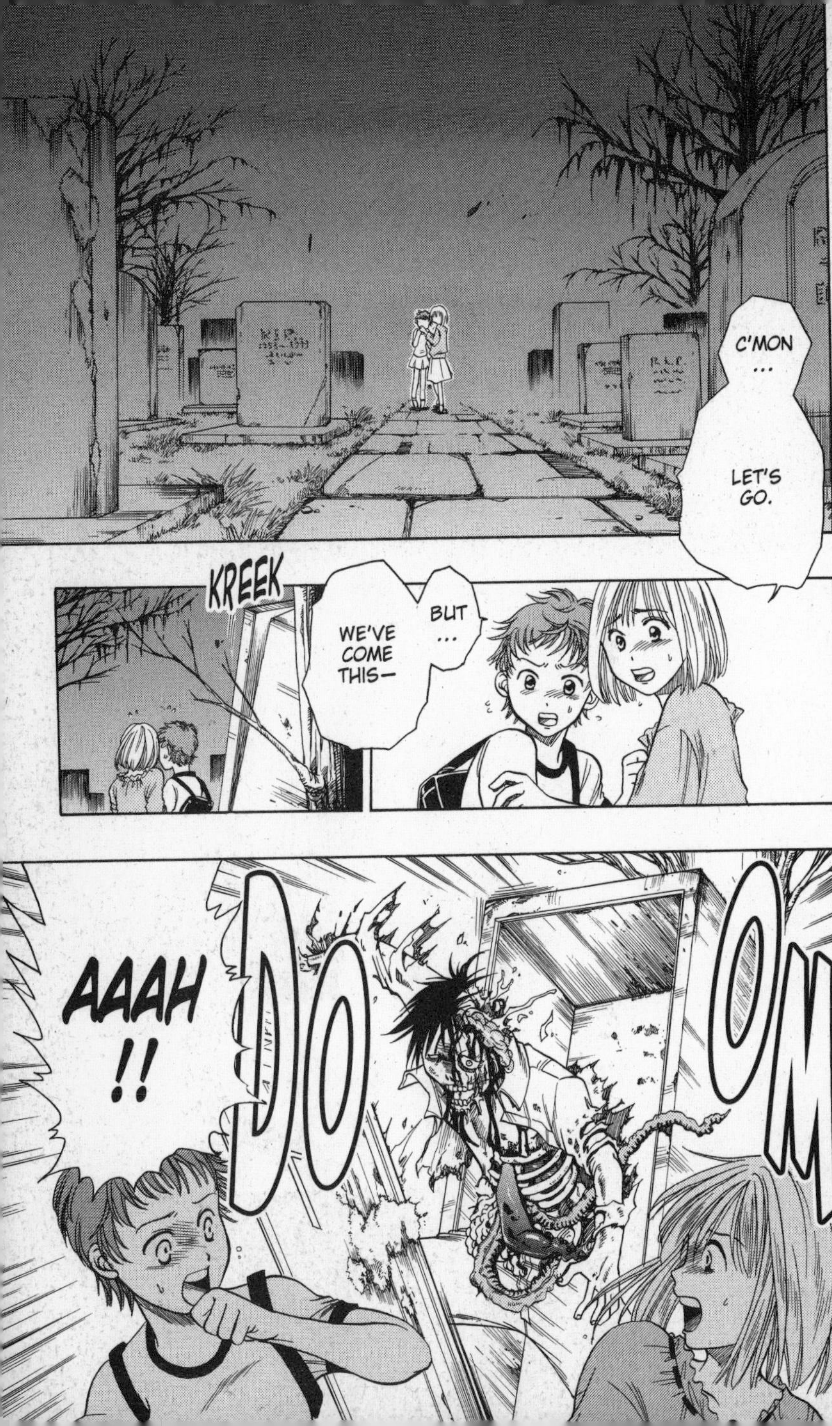
C'MON ...
LET'S GO.
BUT ...
WE'VE COME THIS—
KREEK
DOOM
AAAH !!

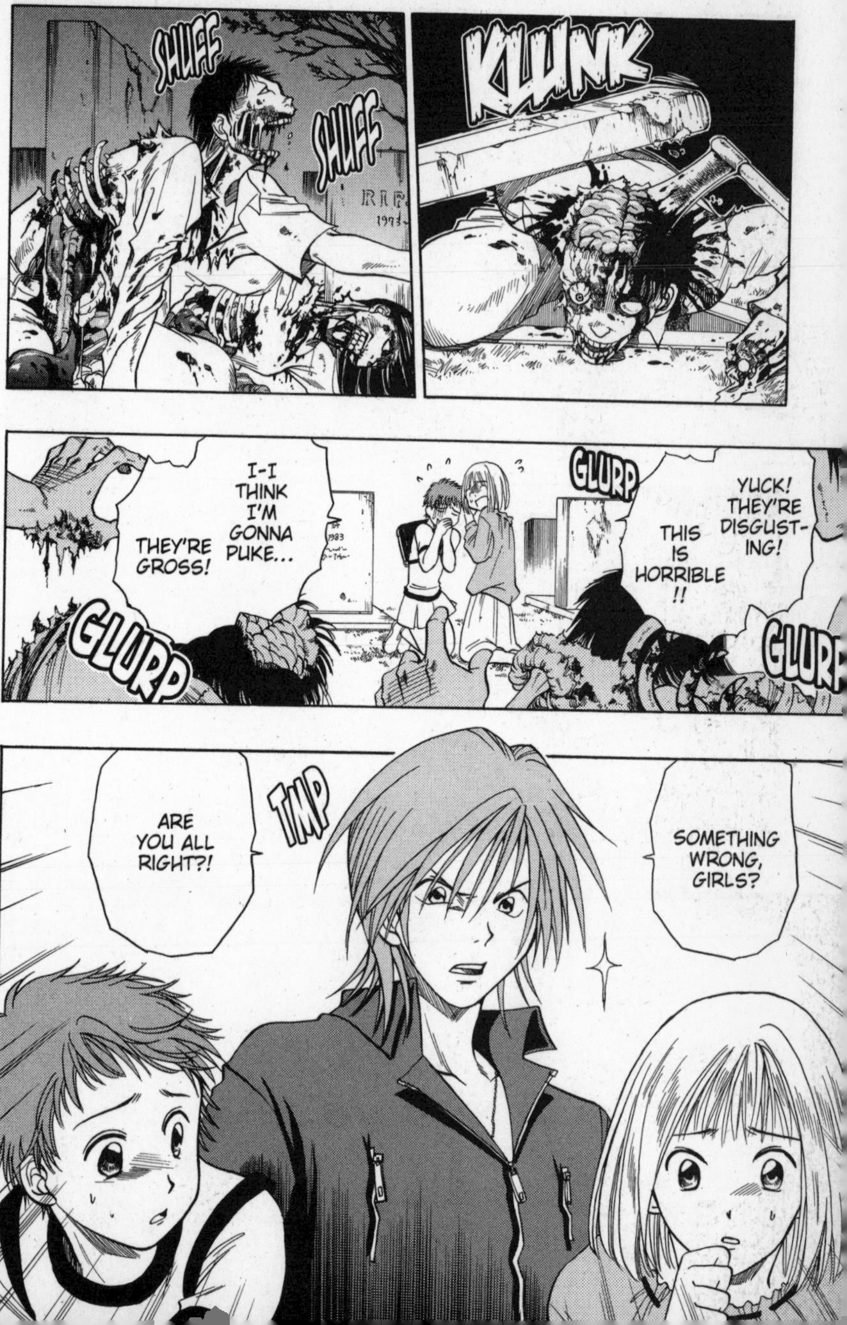
KLUNK
SHUFF
SHUFF
RIP
1973
GLURP
YUCK! THEY'RE DISGUSTING!
THIS IS HORRIBLE!!
I-I THINK I'M GONNA PUKE...
THEY'RE GROSS!
GLURP
GLURP
1983
SOMETHING WRONG, GIRLS?
TMP
ARE YOU ALL RIGHT?!

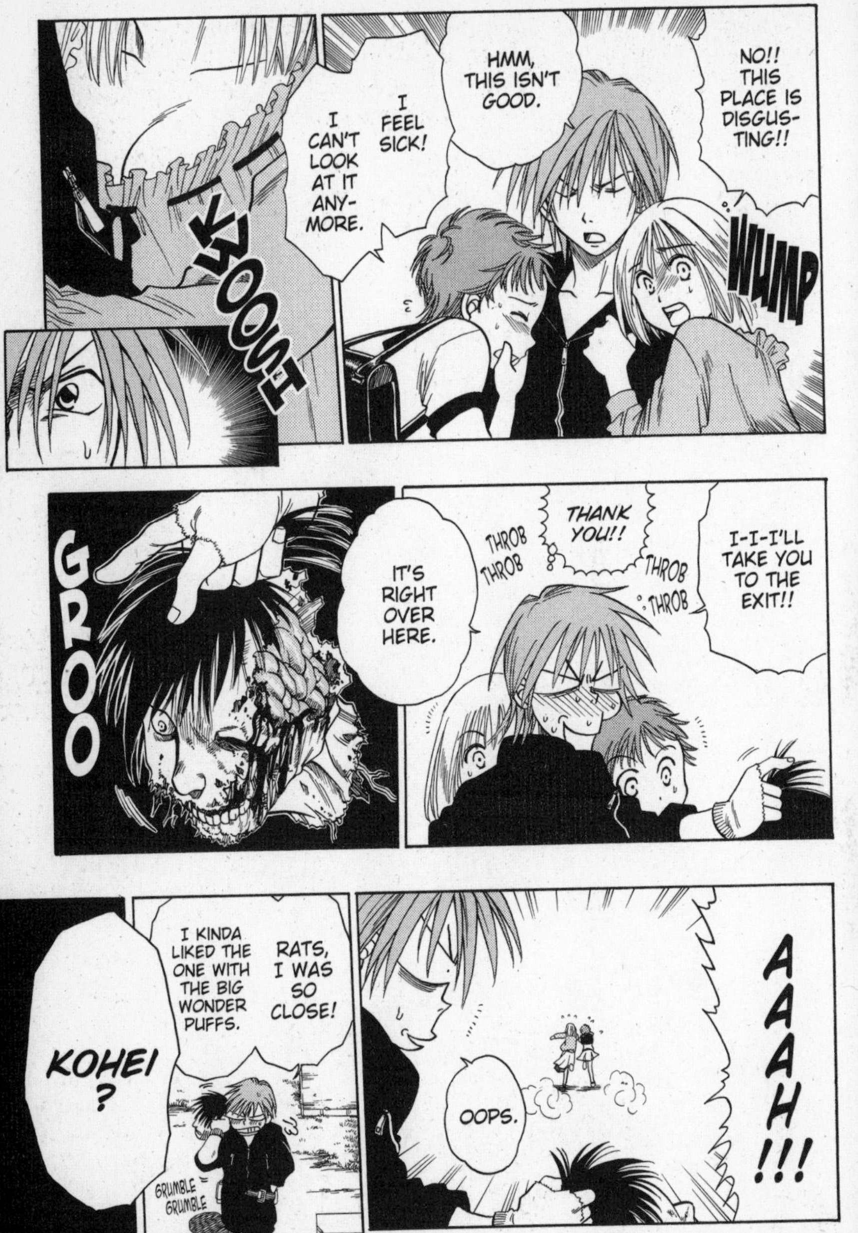
NO!! THIS PLACE IS DISGUSTING!!
HMM, THIS ISN'T GOOD.
I FEEL SICK!
I CAN'T LOOK AT IT ANYMORE.
WUMP
KWOOSH!
I-I-I'LL TAKE YOU TO THE EXIT!!
THROB THROB
THANK YOU!!
THROB THROB
IT'S RIGHT OVER HERE.
GROO
AAAAH!!!
OOPS.
RATS, I WAS SO CLOSE!
I KINDA LIKED THE ONE WITH THE BIG WONDER PUFFS.
KOHEI?
GRUMBLE GRUMBLE
R.I.P.

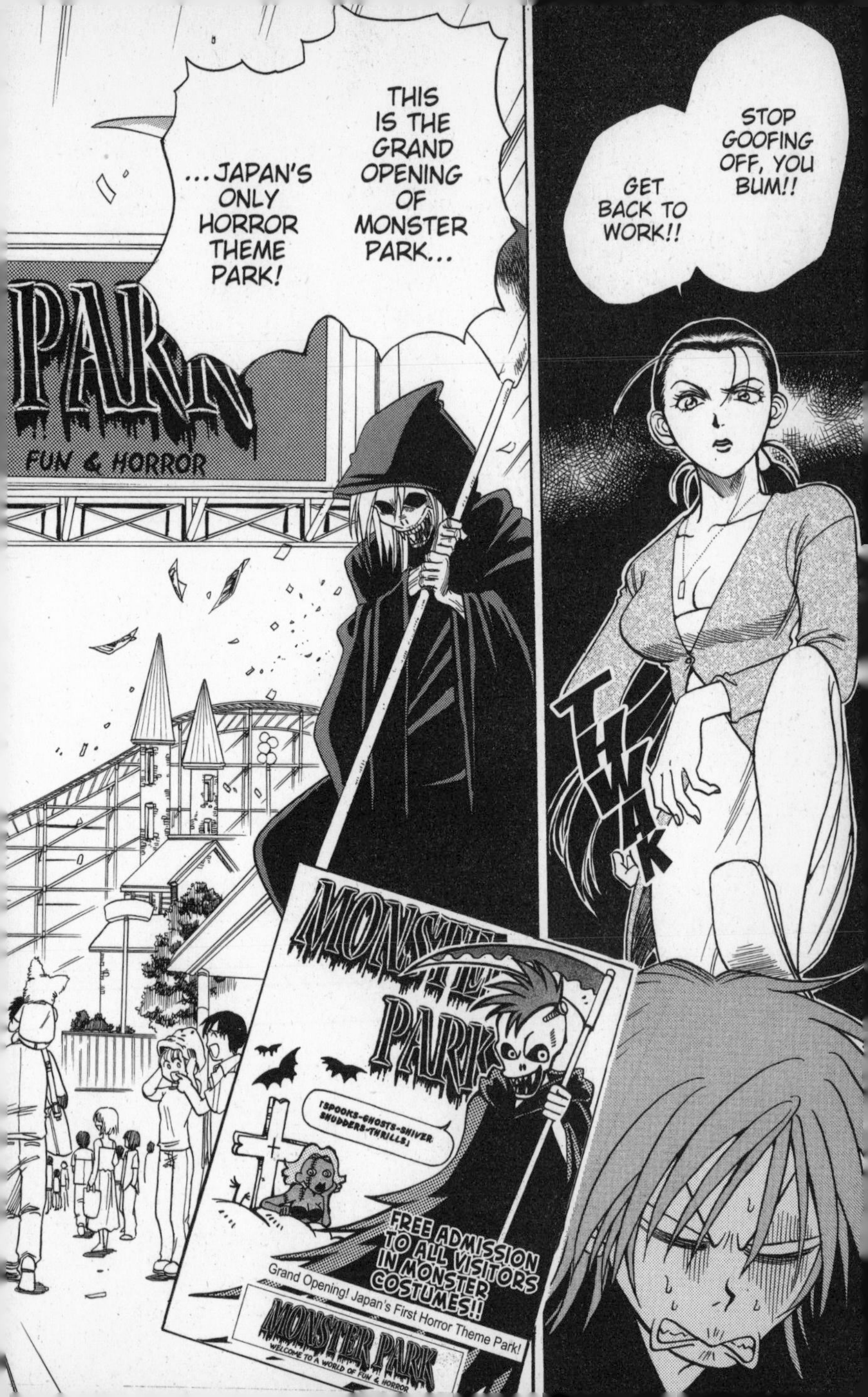
STOP GOOFING OFF, YOU BUM!!
GET BACK TO WORK!!
THWAK
THIS IS THE GRAND OPENING OF MONSTER PARK...
...JAPAN'S ONLY HORROR THEME PARK!
PARK
FUN & HORROR
MONSTER PARK
「SPOOKS-GHOSTS-SHIVER SHUDDERS-THRILLS」
FREE ADMISSION TO ALL VISITORS IN MONSTER COSTUMES!!
Grand Opening! Japan's First Horror Theme Park!
MONSTER PARK
WELCOME TO A WORLD OF FUN & HORROR

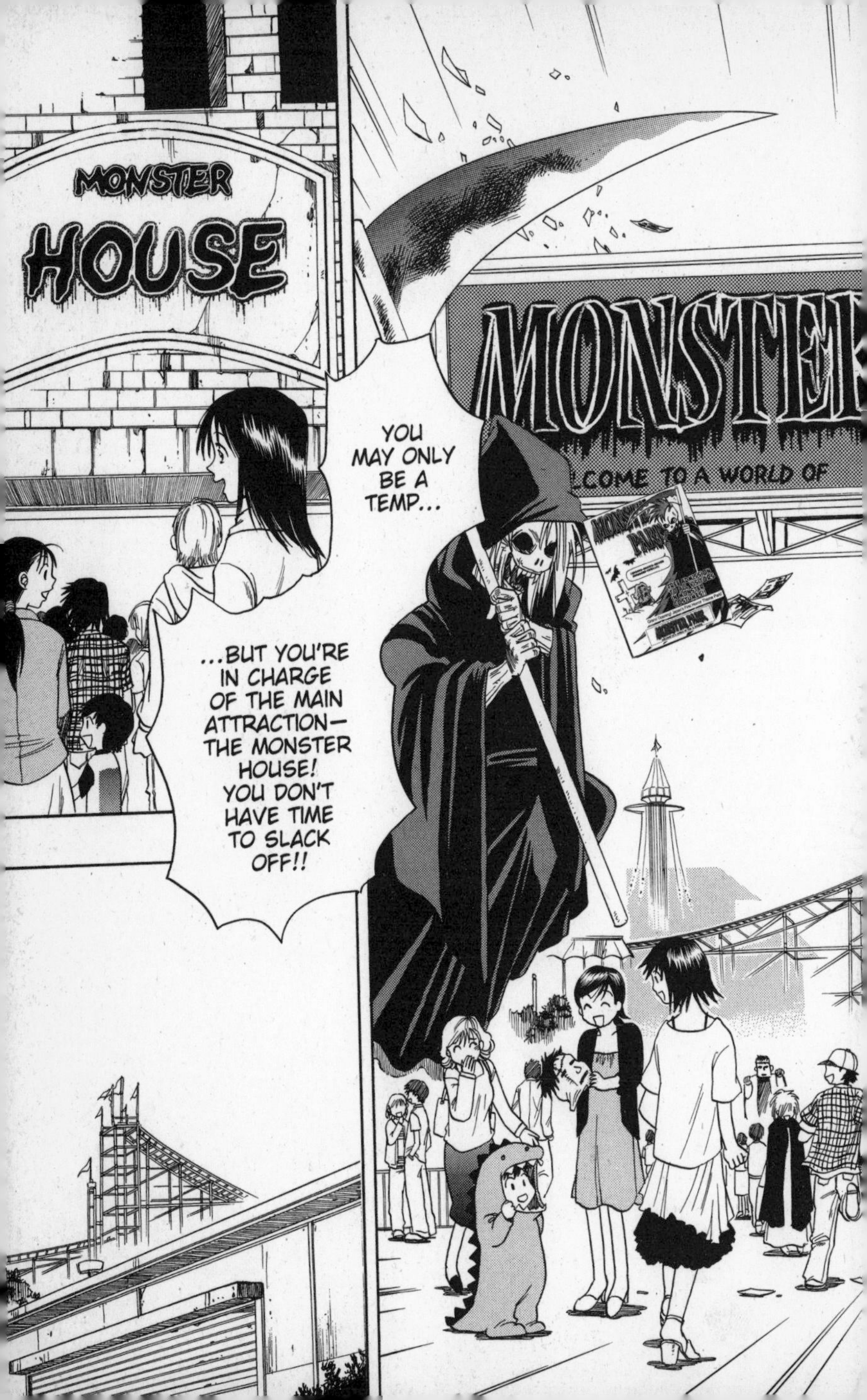
LCOME TO A WORLD OF
YOU MAY ONLY BE A TEMP...
MONSTER HOUSE
...BUT YOU'RE IN CHARGE OF THE MAIN ATTRACTION—THE MONSTER HOUSE! YOU DON'T HAVE TIME TO SLACK OFF!!

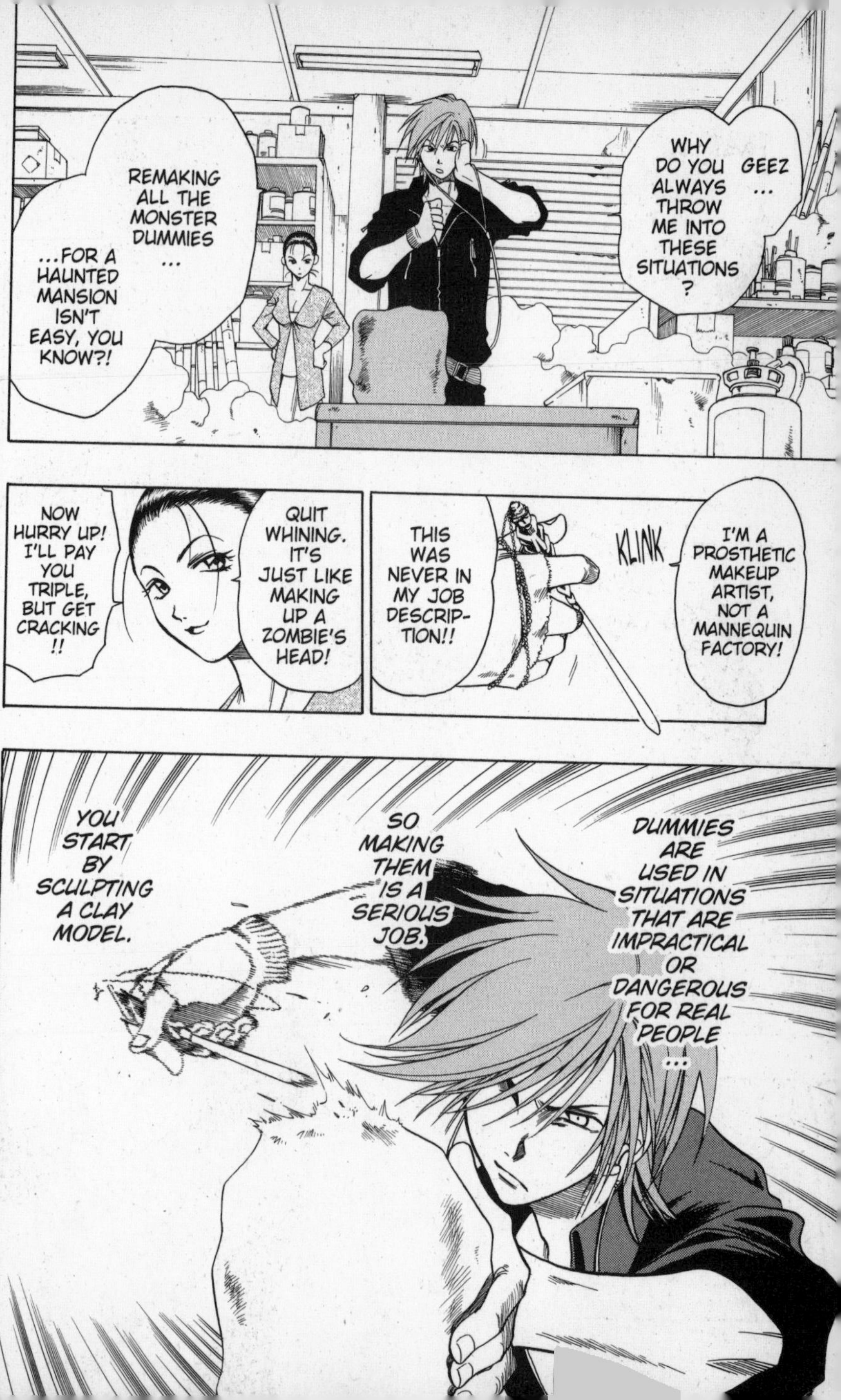
GEEZ...
WHY DO YOU ALWAYS THROW ME INTO THESE SITUATIONS?
REMAKING ALL THE MONSTER DUMMIES...
...FOR A HAUNTED MANSION ISN'T EASY, YOU KNOW?!
I'M A PROSTHETIC MAKEUP ARTIST, NOT A MANNEQUIN FACTORY!
KLINK
THIS WAS NEVER IN MY JOB DESCRIPTION!!
QUIT WHINING. IT'S JUST LIKE MAKING UP A ZOMBIE'S HEAD!
NOW HURRY UP! I'LL PAY YOU TRIPLE, BUT GET CRACKING!!
DUMMIES ARE USED IN SITUATIONS THAT ARE IMPRACTICAL OR DANGEROUS FOR REAL PEOPLE...
SO MAKING THEM IS A SERIOUS JOB.
YOU START BY SCULPTING A CLAY MODEL.

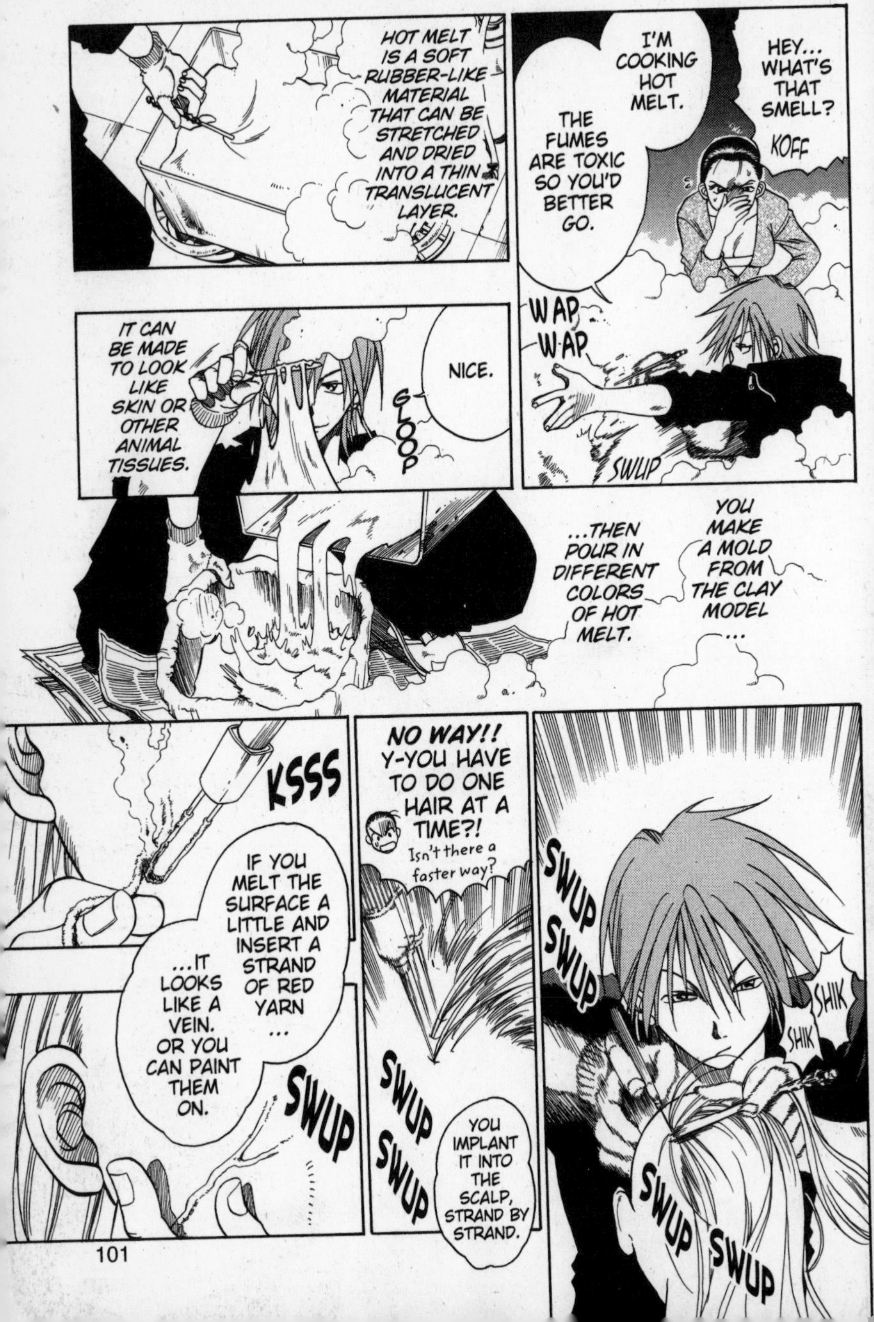
HEY... WHAT'S THAT SMELL?
KOFF
I'M COOKING HOT MELT.
THE FUMES ARE TOXIC SO YOU'D BETTER GO.
WAP WAP
SWUP
HOT MELT IS A SOFT RUBBER-LIKE MATERIAL THAT CAN BE STRETCHED AND DRIED INTO A THIN TRANSLUCENT LAYER.
NICE.
GLOOP
IT CAN BE MADE TO LOOK LIKE SKIN OR OTHER ANIMAL TISSUES.
YOU MAKE A MOLD FROM THE CLAY MODEL ...
...THEN POUR IN DIFFERENT COLORS OF HOT MELT.
SWUP SWUP SWUP
SHIK SHIK
SWUP SWUP
NO WAY!! Y-YOU HAVE TO DO ONE HAIR AT A TIME?!
Isn't there a faster way?
SWUP SWUP
YOU IMPLANT IT INTO THE SCALP, STRAND BY STRAND.
KSSS
IF YOU MELT THE SURFACE A LITTLE AND INSERT A STRAND OF RED YARN ...
...IT LOOKS LIKE A VEIN. OR YOU CAN PAINT THEM ON.
SWUP

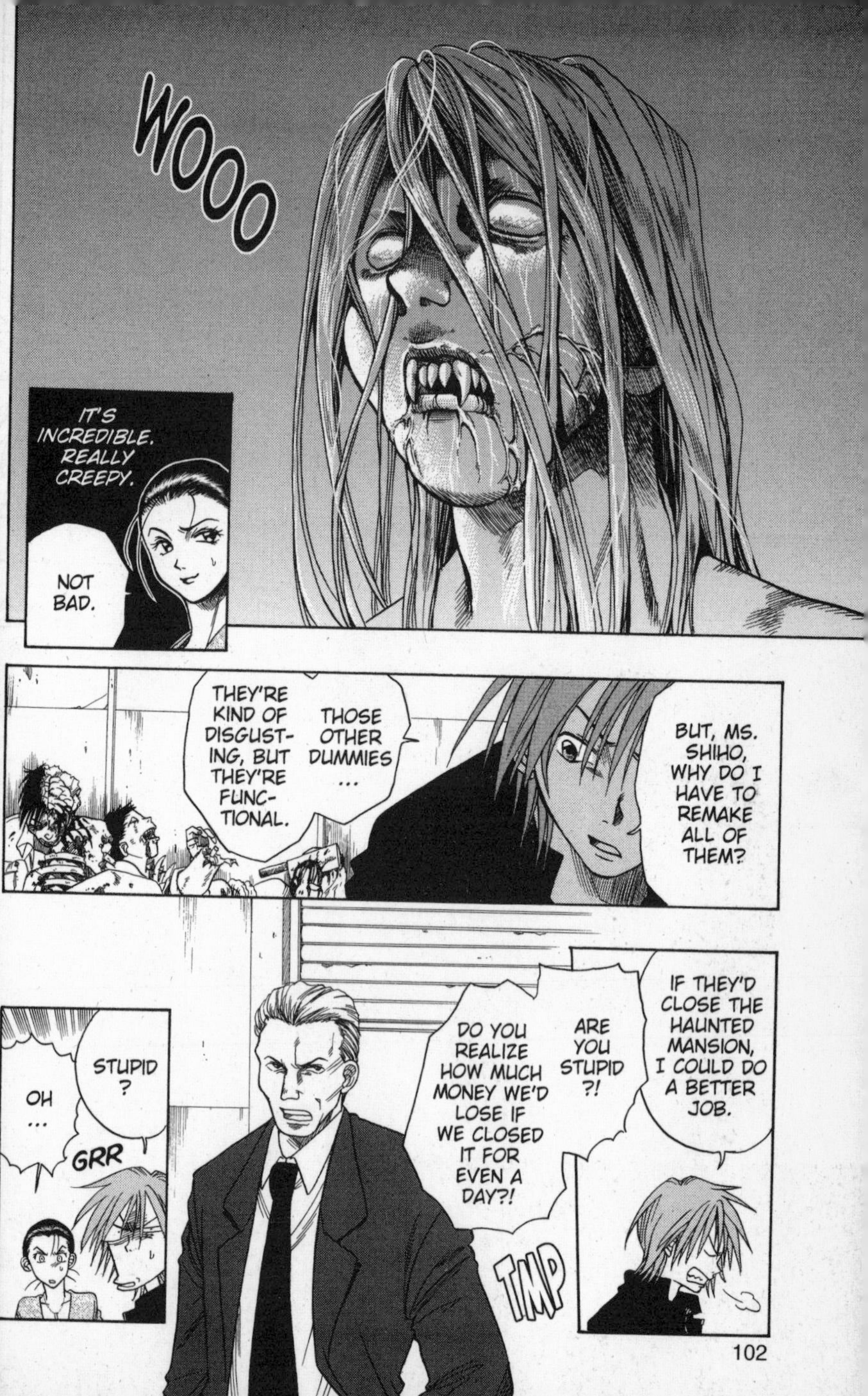
WOOO
IT'S INCREDIBLE. REALLY CREEPY.
NOT BAD.
BUT, MS. SHIHO, WHY DO I HAVE TO REMAKE ALL OF THEM?
THOSE OTHER DUMMIES...
THEY'RE KIND OF DISGUSTING, BUT THEY'RE FUNCTIONAL.
IF THEY'D CLOSE THE HAUNTED MANSION, I COULD DO A BETTER JOB.
ARE YOU STUPID?!
DO YOU REALIZE HOW MUCH MONEY WE'D LOSE IF WE CLOSED IT FOR EVEN A DAY?!
TMP
STUPID?
OH...
GRR

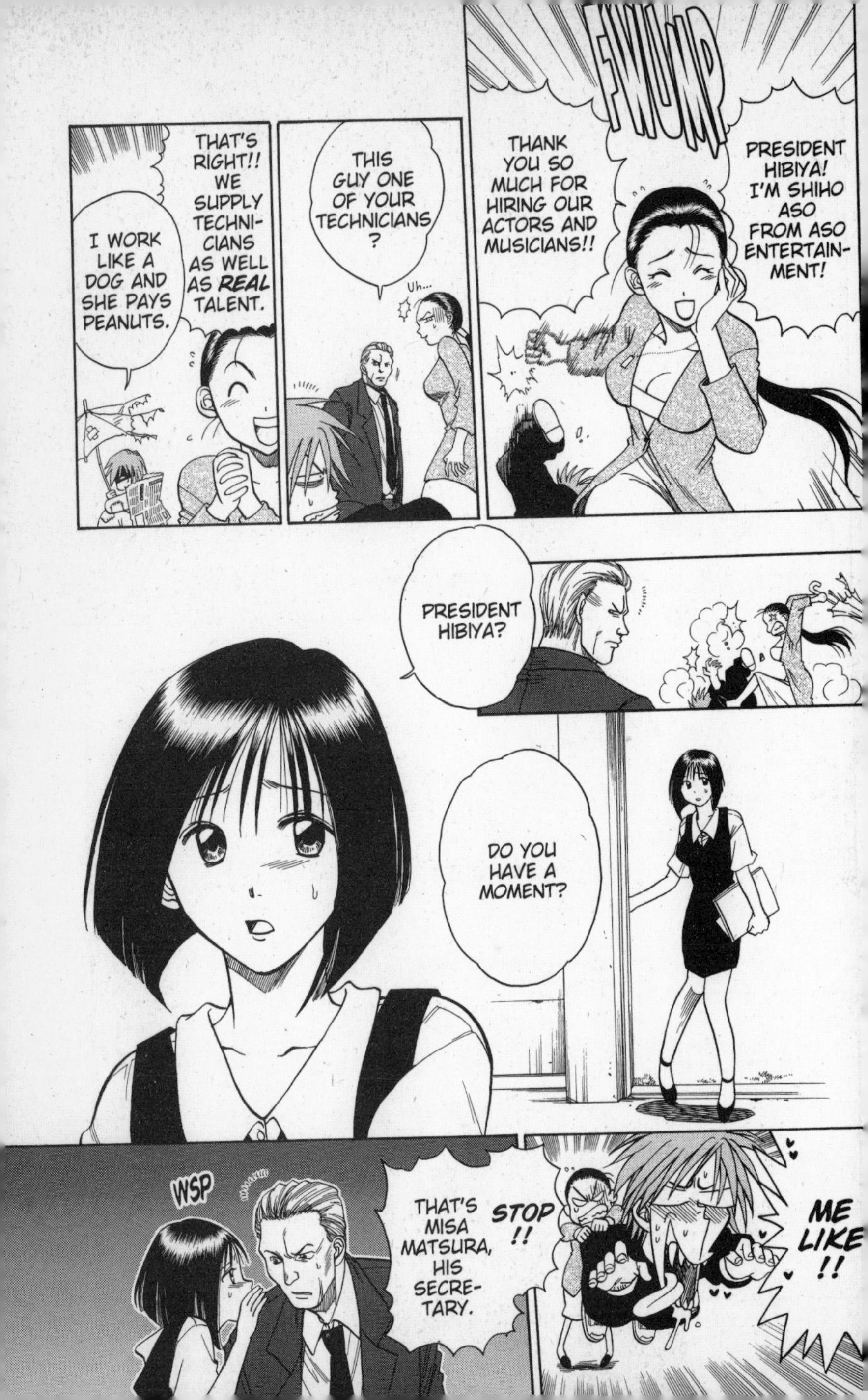
FWUMP
PRESIDENT HIBIYA! I'M SHIHO ASO FROM ASO ENTERTAINMENT!
THANK YOU SO MUCH FOR HIRING OUR ACTORS AND MUSICIANS!!
THIS GUY ONE OF YOUR TECHNICIANS?
Uh...
THAT'S RIGHT!! WE SUPPLY TECHNICIANS AS WELL AS *REAL* TALENT.
I WORK LIKE A DOG AND SHE PAYS PEANUTS.
PRESIDENT HIBIYA?
DO YOU HAVE A MOMENT?
ME LIKE!!
STOP!!
THAT'S MISA MATSURA, HIS SECRETARY.
WSP

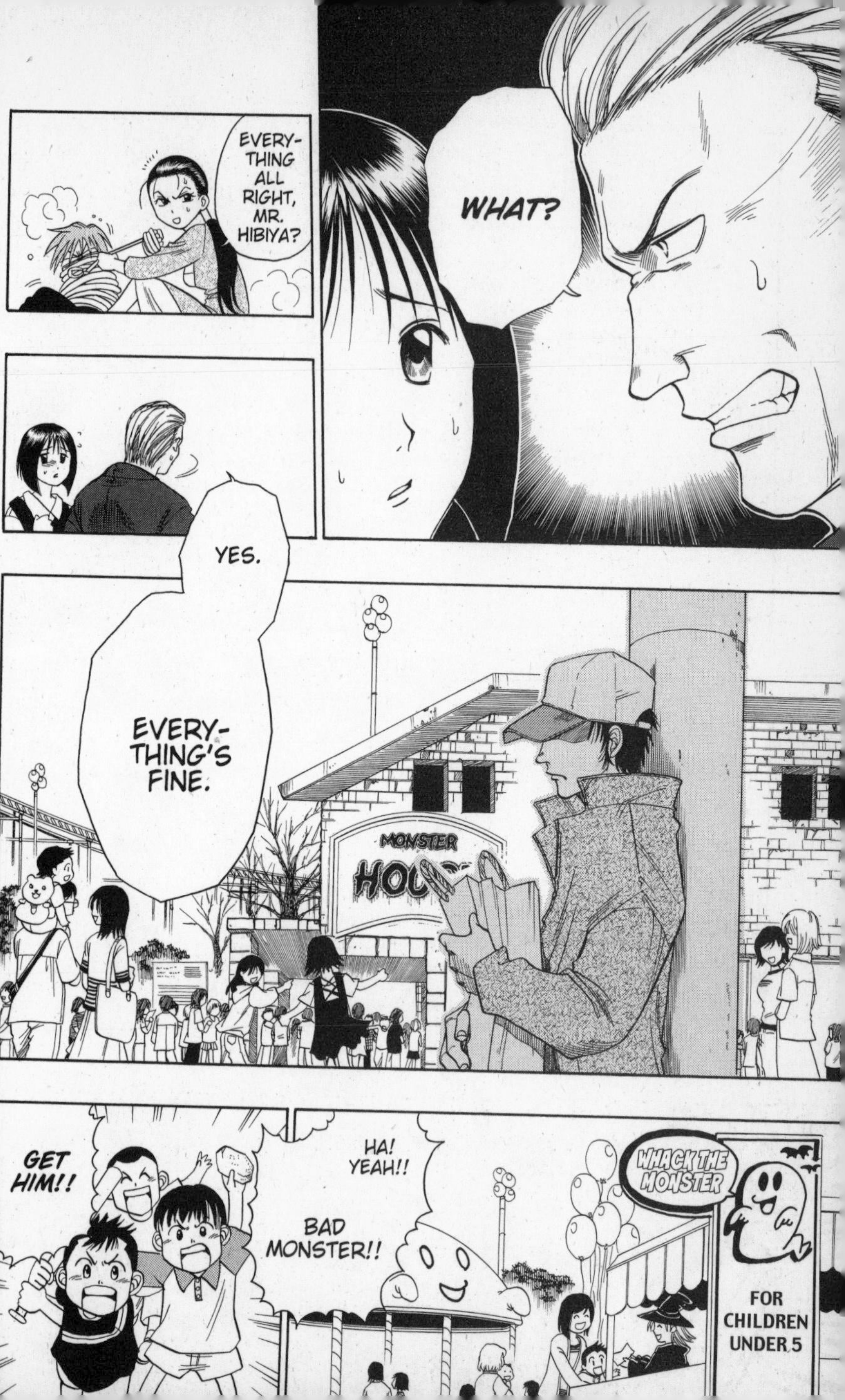
WHAT?
EVERY-THING ALL RIGHT, MR. HIBIYA?
YES.
EVERY-THING'S FINE.
MONSTER
WHACK THE MONSTER
FOR CHILDREN UNDER 5
HA! YEAH!!
BAD MONSTER!!
GET HIM!!

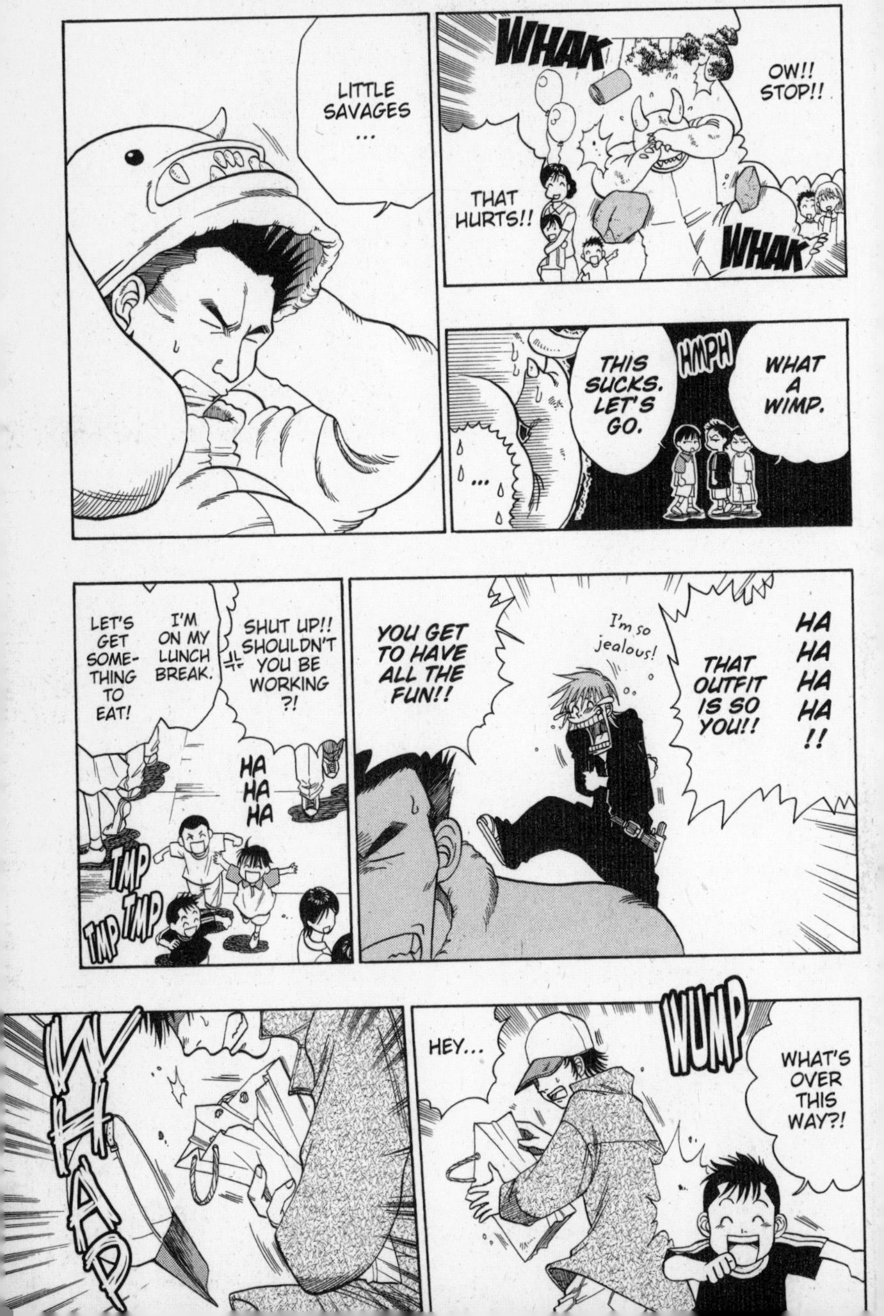

WHAK
OW!! STOP!!
THAT HURTS!!
WHAK
WHAT A WIMP.
HMPH
THIS SUCKS. LET'S GO.
...
LITTLE SAVAGES ...
HA HA HA HA !!
THAT OUTFIT IS SO YOU!!
I'm so jealous!
YOU GET TO HAVE ALL THE FUN!!
SHUT UP!! SHOULDN'T YOU BE WORKING ?!
I'M ON MY LUNCH BREAK.
LET'S GET SOME-THING TO EAT!
HA HA HA
TMP TMP TMP
WUMP
WHAT'S OVER THIS WAY?!
HEY...
WHAP

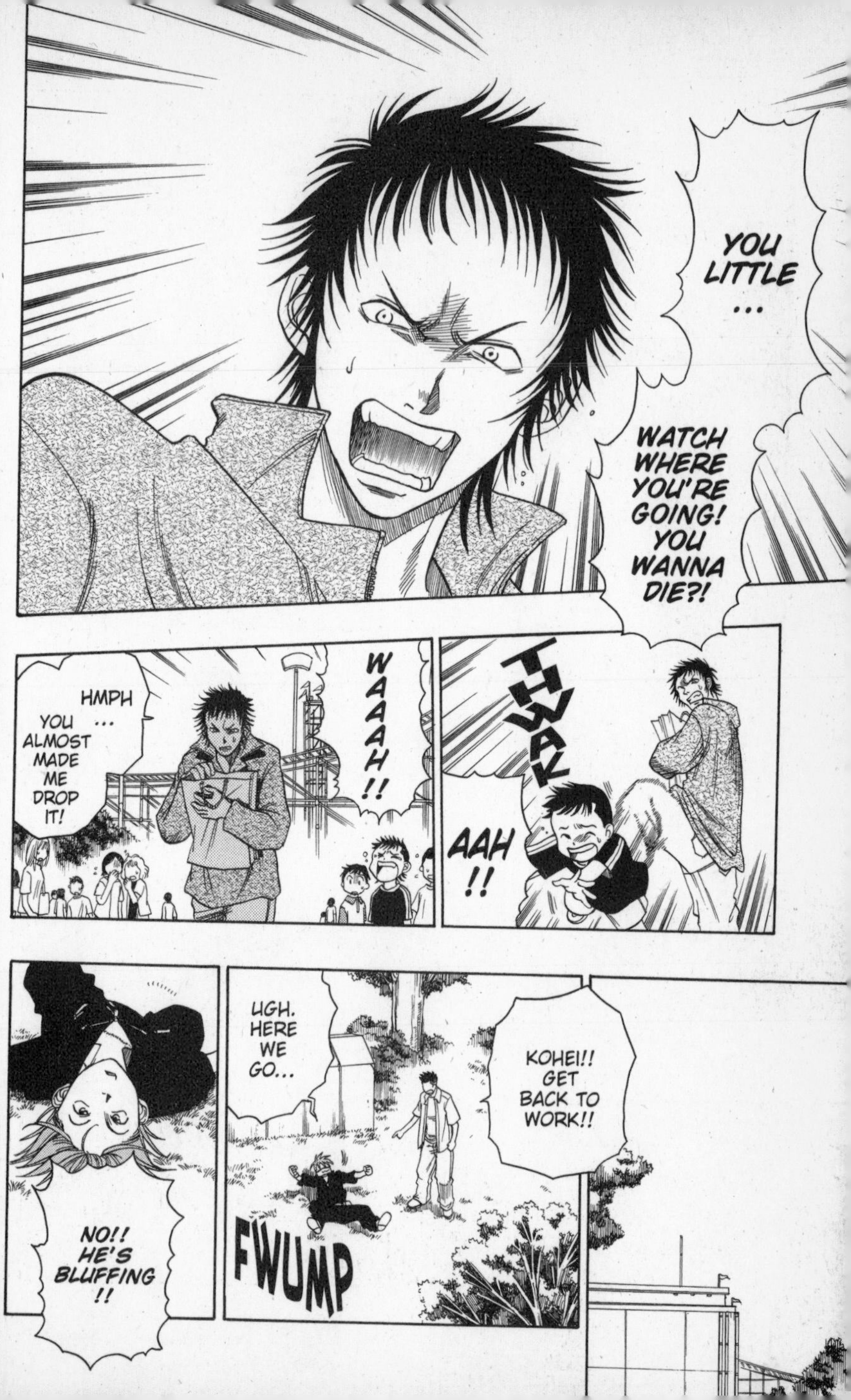
YOU LITTLE ...
WATCH WHERE YOU'RE GOING! YOU WANNA DIE?!
THWAK
AAH!!
WAAAAH!!
HMPH ... YOU ALMOST MADE ME DROP IT!
KOHEI!! GET BACK TO WORK!!
UGH. HERE WE GO...
FWUMP
NO!! HE'S BLUFFING!!

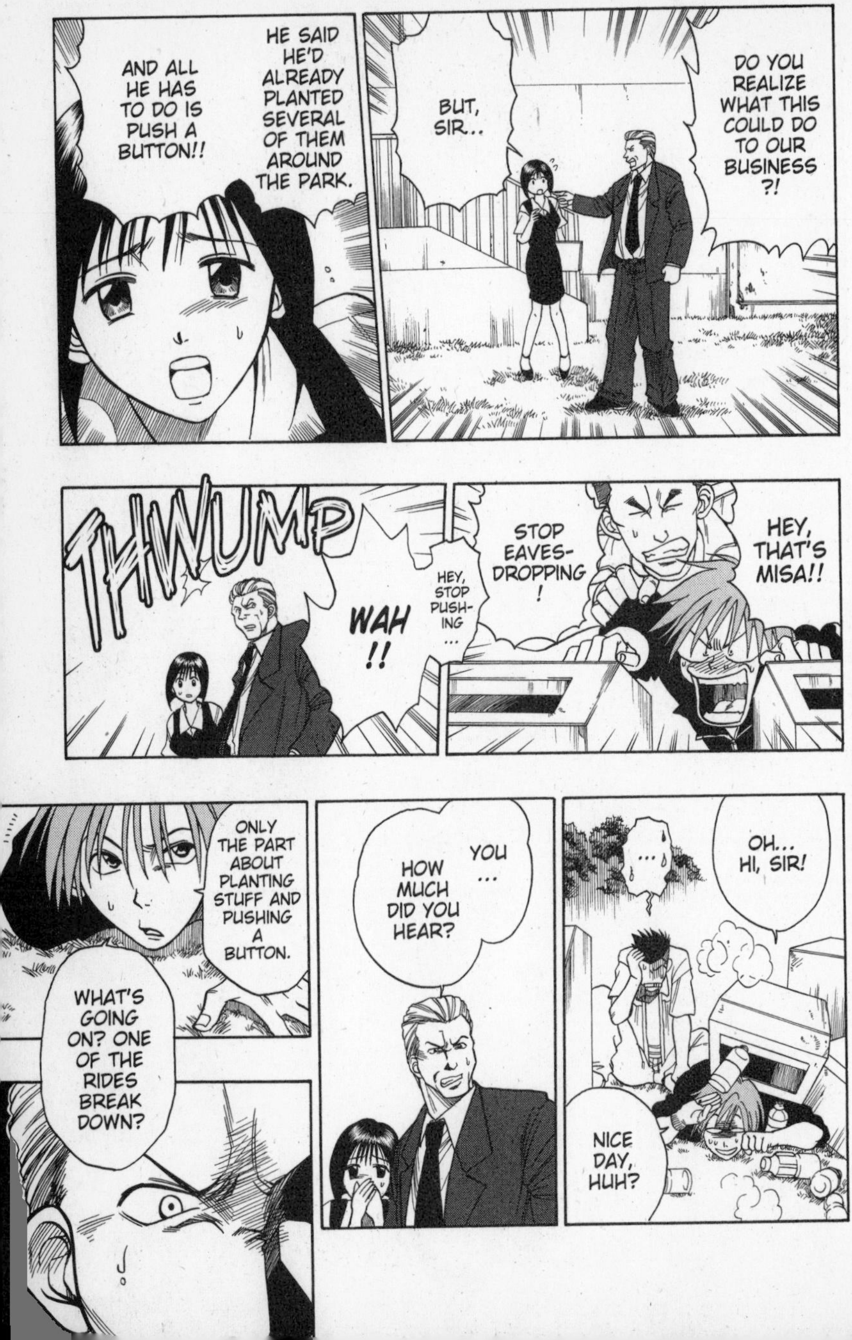
DO YOU REALIZE WHAT THIS COULD DO TO OUR BUSINESS ?!
BUT, SIR...
HE SAID HE'D ALREADY PLANTED SEVERAL OF THEM AROUND THE PARK.
AND ALL HE HAS TO DO IS PUSH A BUTTON!!
HEY, THAT'S MISA!!
STOP EAVES-DROPPING!
HEY, STOP PUSH-ING...
WAH!!
THWUMP
OH... HI, SIR!
...
NICE DAY, HUH?
YOU...
HOW MUCH DID YOU HEAR?
ONLY THE PART ABOUT PLANTING STUFF AND PUSHING A BUTTON.
WHAT'S GOING ON? ONE OF THE RIDES BREAK DOWN?

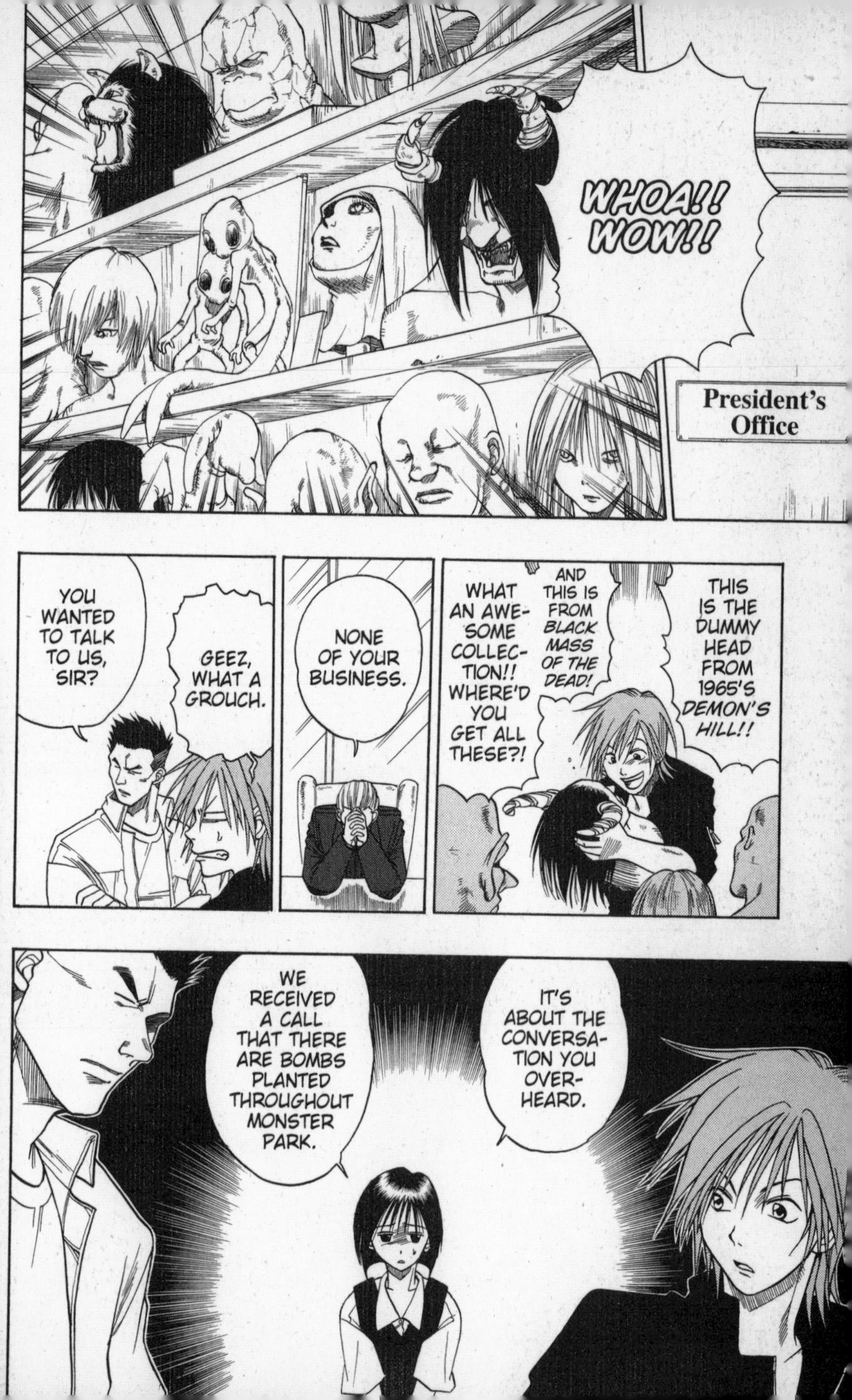
WHOA!! WOW!!
President's Office
THIS IS THE DUMMY HEAD FROM 1965'S DEMON'S HILL!!
AND THIS IS FROM BLACK MASS OF THE DEAD!
WHAT AN AWE-SOME COLLEC-TION!! WHERE'D YOU GET ALL THESE?!
NONE OF YOUR BUSINESS.
GEEZ, WHAT A GROUCH.
YOU WANTED TO TALK TO US, SIR?
IT'S ABOUT THE CONVERSA-TION YOU OVER-HEARD.
WE RECEIVED A CALL THAT THERE ARE BOMBS PLANTED THROUGHOUT MONSTER PARK.

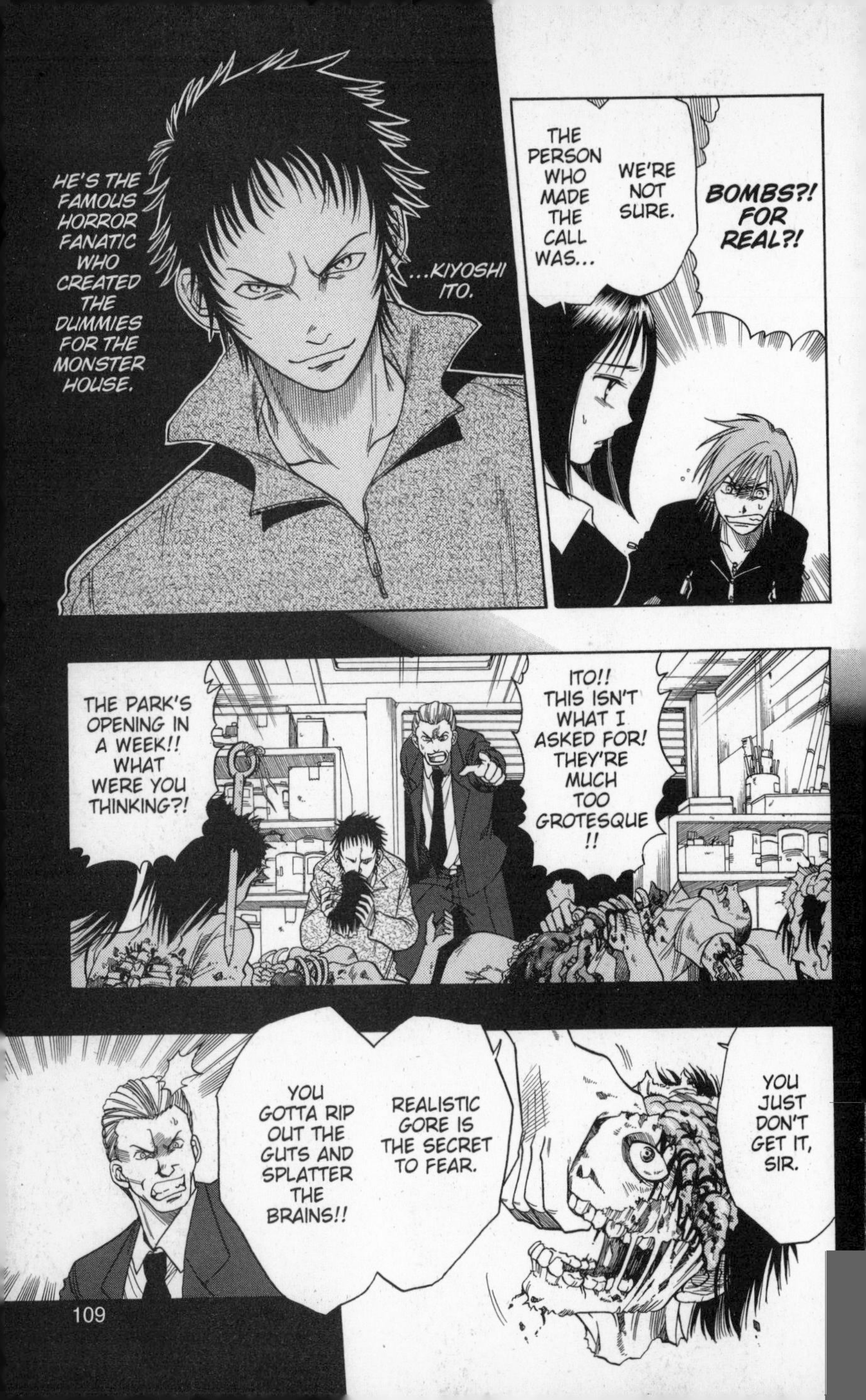
BOMBS?! FOR REAL?!
WE'RE NOT SURE.
THE PERSON WHO MADE THE CALL WAS...
...KIYOSHI ITO.
HE'S THE FAMOUS HORROR FANATIC WHO CREATED THE DUMMIES FOR THE MONSTER HOUSE.
ITO!! THIS ISN'T WHAT I ASKED FOR! THEY'RE MUCH TOO GROTESQUE!!
THE PARK'S OPENING IN A WEEK!! WHAT WERE YOU THINKING?!
YOU JUST DON'T GET IT, SIR.
REALISTIC GORE IS THE SECRET TO FEAR.
YOU GOTTA RIP OUT THE GUTS AND SPLATTER THE BRAINS!!

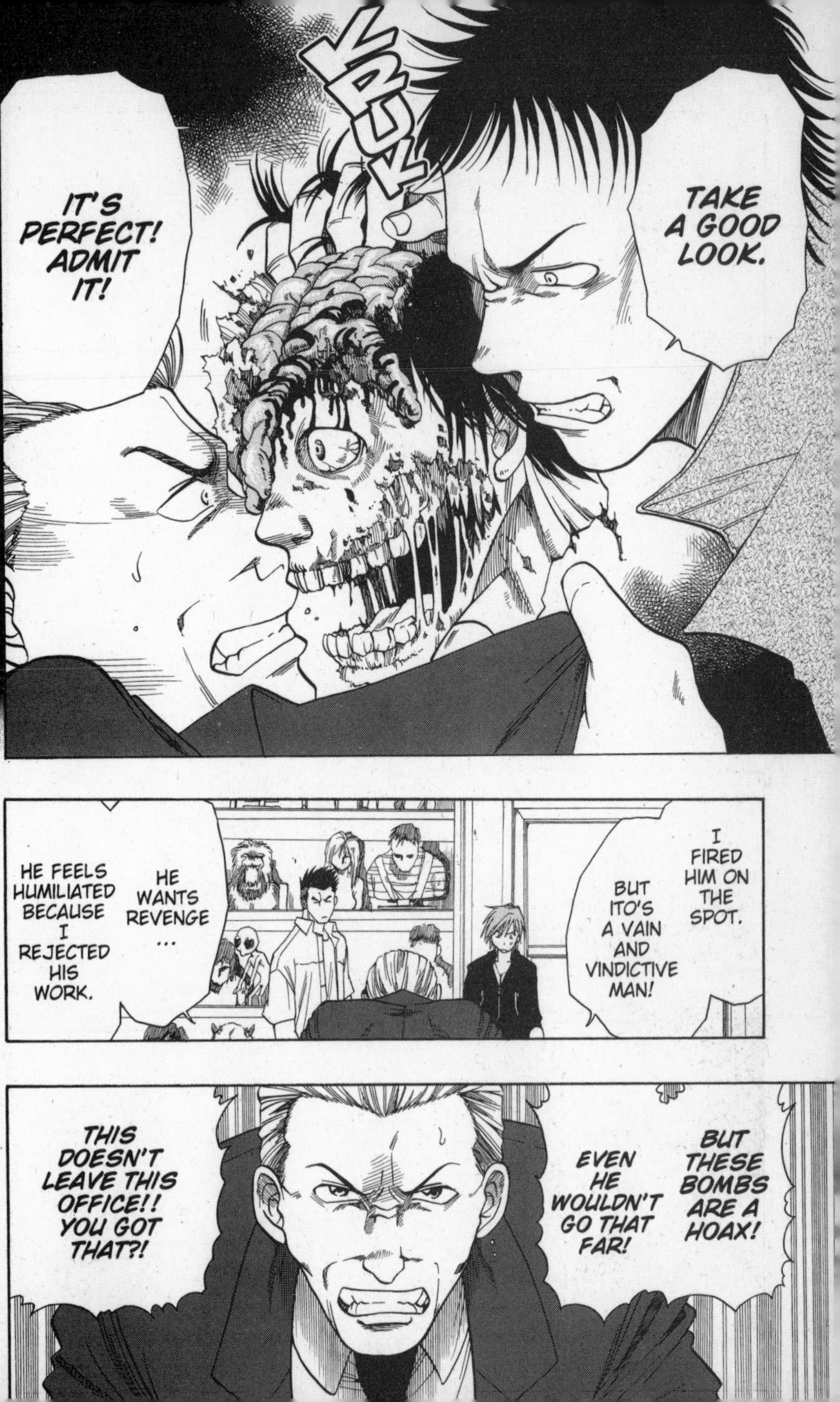
YANK
TAKE A GOOD LOOK.
IT'S PERFECT! ADMIT IT!
I FIRED HIM ON THE SPOT.
BUT ITO'S A VAIN AND VINDICTIVE MAN!
HE WANTS REVENGE ...
HE FEELS HUMILIATED BECAUSE I REJECTED HIS WORK.
BUT THESE BOMBS ARE A HOAX!
EVEN HE WOULDN'T GO THAT FAR!
THIS DOESN'T LEAVE THIS OFFICE!! YOU GOT THAT?!

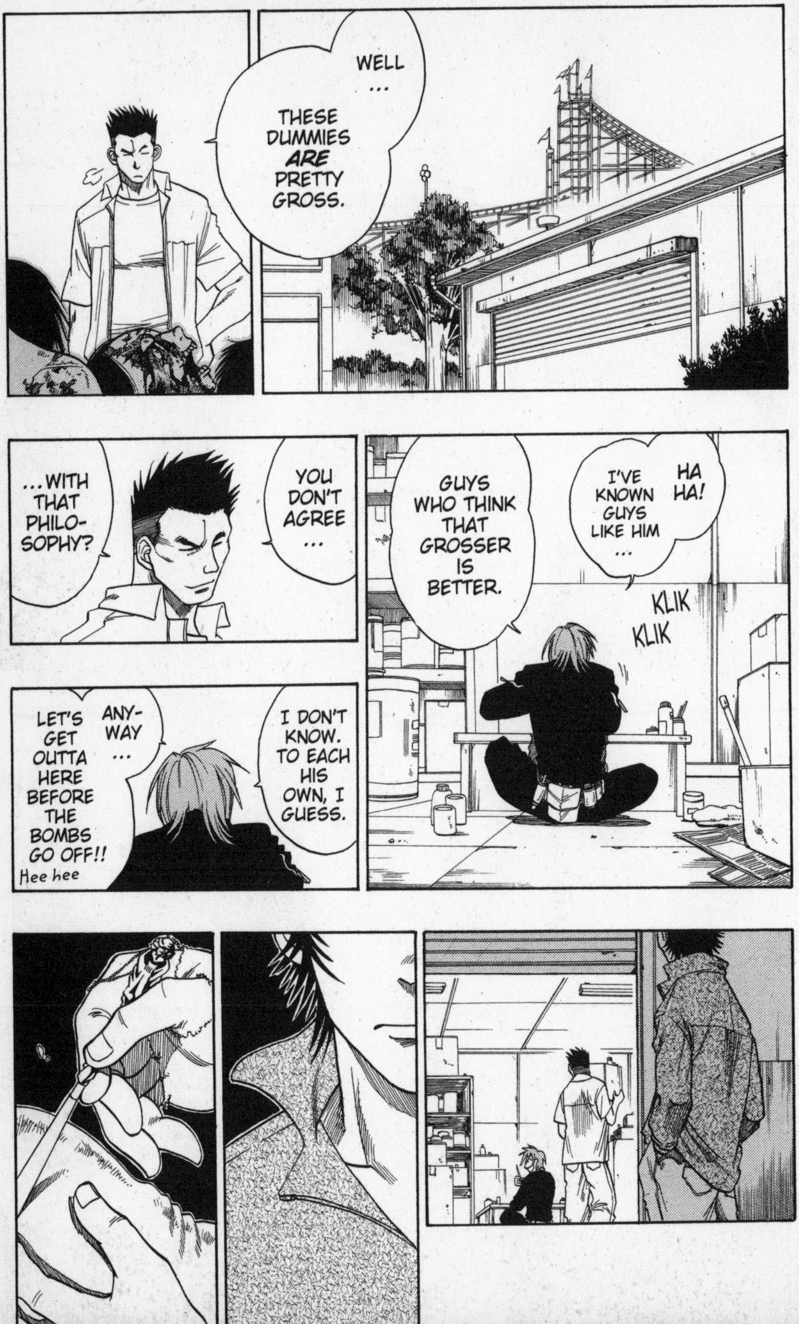
WELL ... THESE DUMMIES *ARE* PRETTY GROSS.
HA HA!
I'VE KNOWN GUYS LIKE HIM ...
GUYS WHO THINK THAT GROSSER IS BETTER.
KLIK KLIK
YOU DON'T AGREE ...
...WITH THAT PHILOSOPHY?
I DON'T KNOW. TO EACH HIS OWN, I GUESS.
ANYWAY ...
LET'S GET OUTTA HERE BEFORE THE BOMBS GO OFF!!
Hee hee

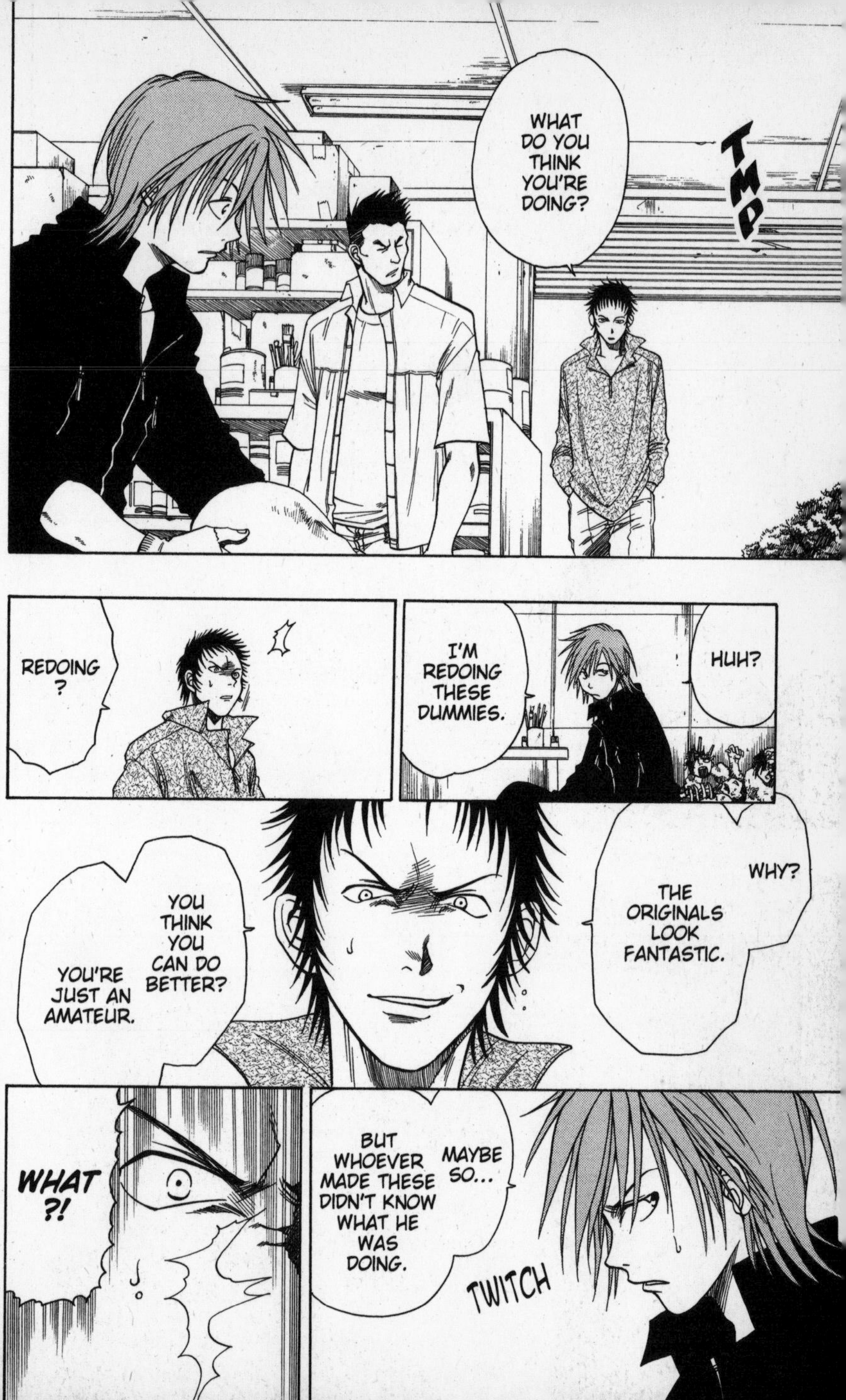
TMP
WHAT DO YOU THINK YOU'RE DOING?
HUH?
I'M REDOING THESE DUMMIES.
REDOING?
WHY? THE ORIGINALS LOOK FANTASTIC.
YOU THINK YOU CAN DO BETTER? YOU'RE JUST AN AMATEUR.
MAYBE SO... BUT WHOEVER MADE THESE DIDN'T KNOW WHAT HE WAS DOING.
TWITCH
WHAT?!

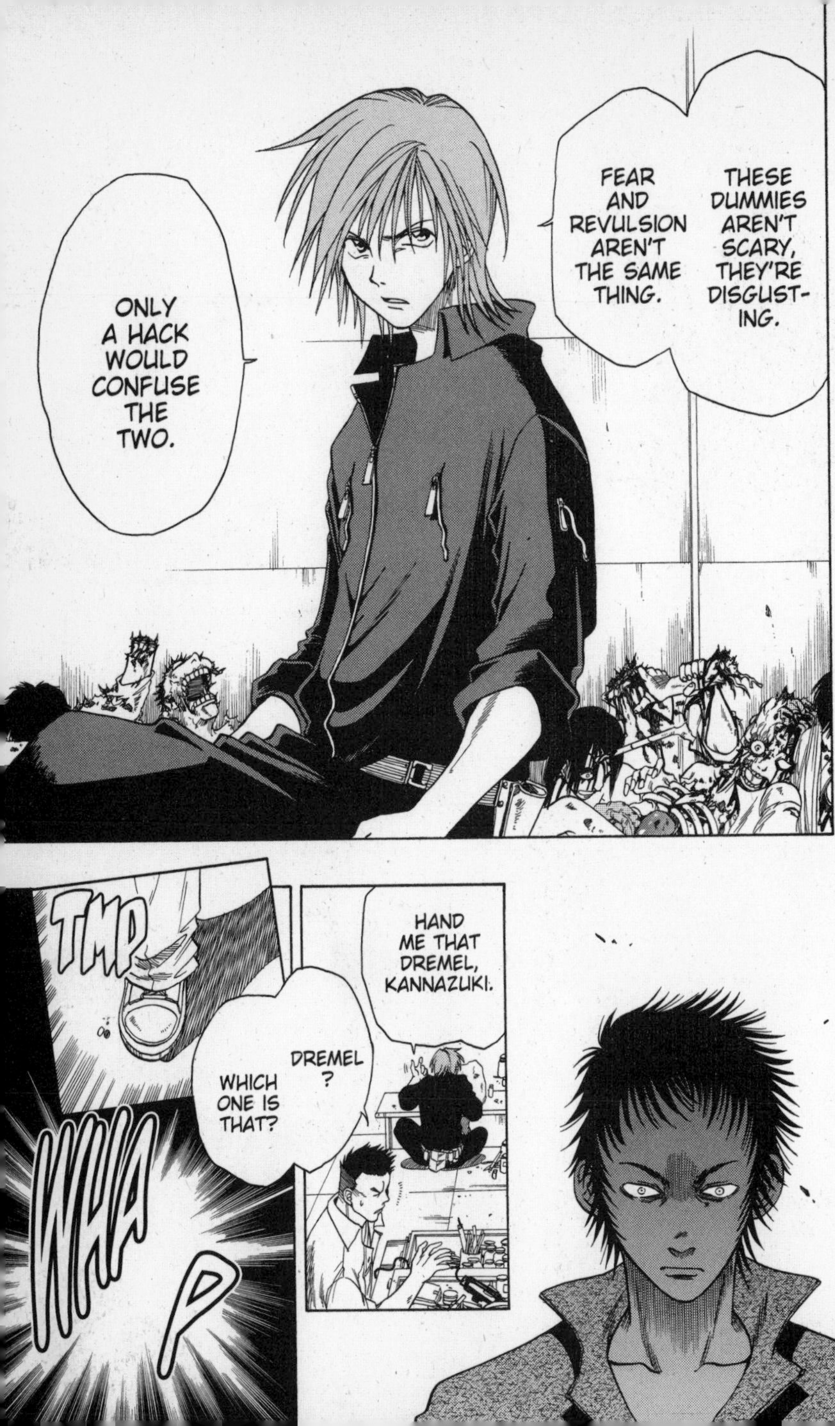
THESE DUMMIES AREN'T SCARY, THEY'RE DISGUST-ING.
FEAR AND REVULSION AREN'T THE SAME THING.
ONLY A HACK WOULD CONFUSE THE TWO.
HAND ME THAT DREMEL, KANNAZUKI.
DREMEL? WHICH ONE IS THAT?
TMP
WHAP

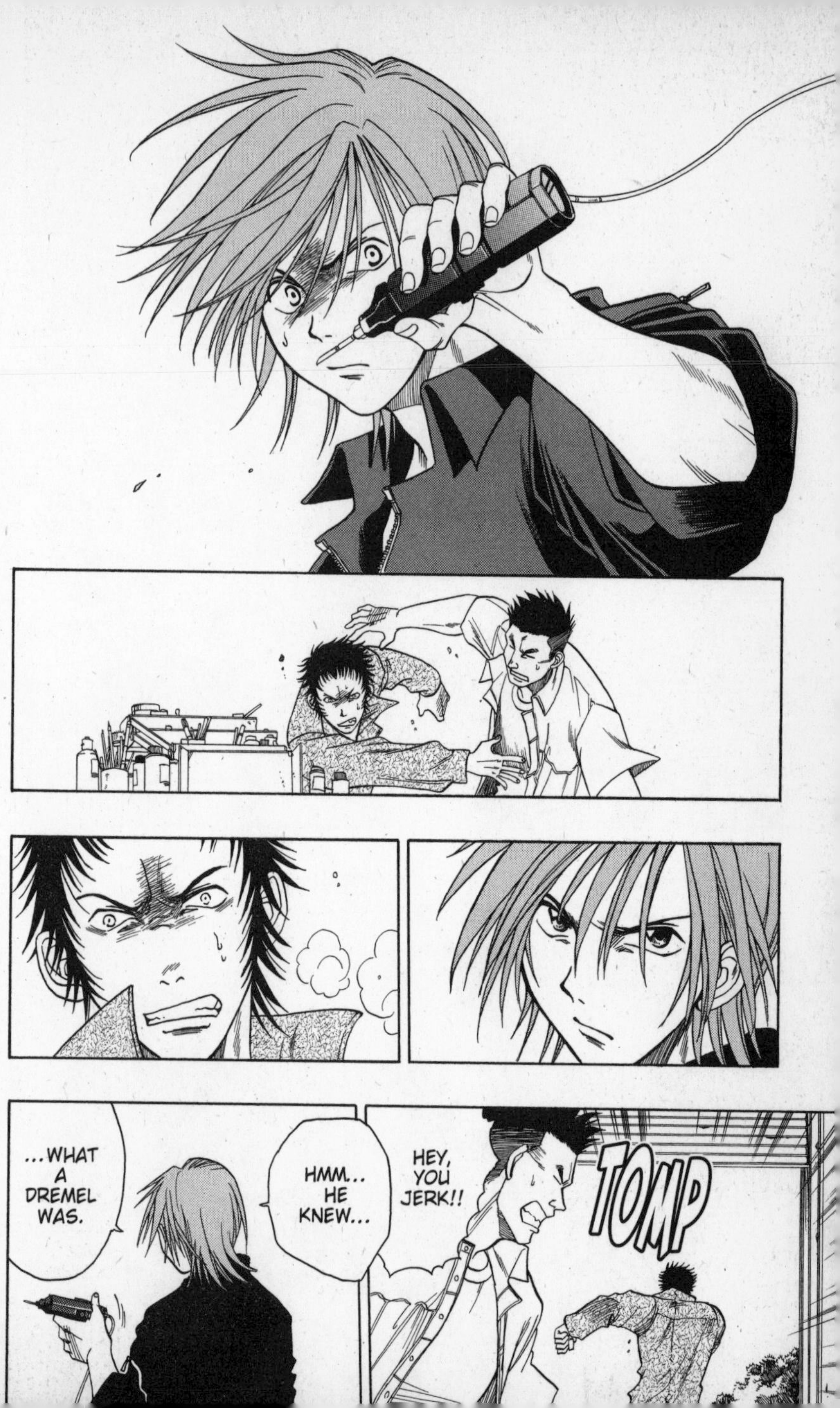
TOMP
HEY, YOU JERK!!
HMM... HE KNEW...
...WHAT A DREMEL WAS.

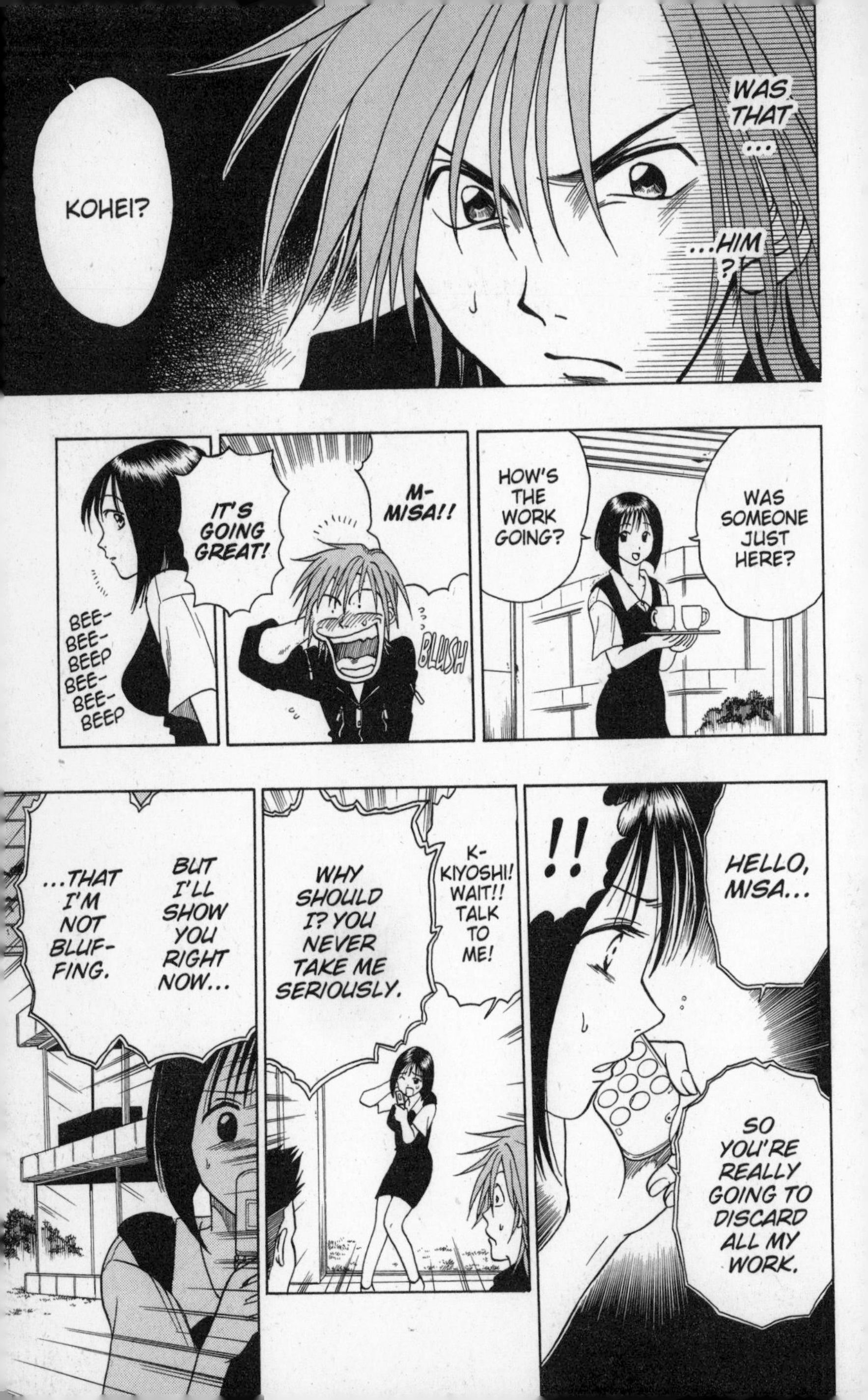
WAS THAT ...
...HIM ?
KOHEI?
WAS SOMEONE JUST HERE?
HOW'S THE WORK GOING?
M-MISA!!
IT'S GOING GREAT!
BLUSH
BEE-BEE-BEEP BEE-BEE-BEEP
!!
HELLO, MISA...
SO YOU'RE REALLY GOING TO DISCARD ALL MY WORK.
K-KIYOSHI! WAIT!! TALK TO ME!
WHY SHOULD I? YOU NEVER TAKE ME SERIOUSLY.
BUT I'LL SHOW YOU RIGHT NOW...
...THAT I'M NOT BLUF-FING.

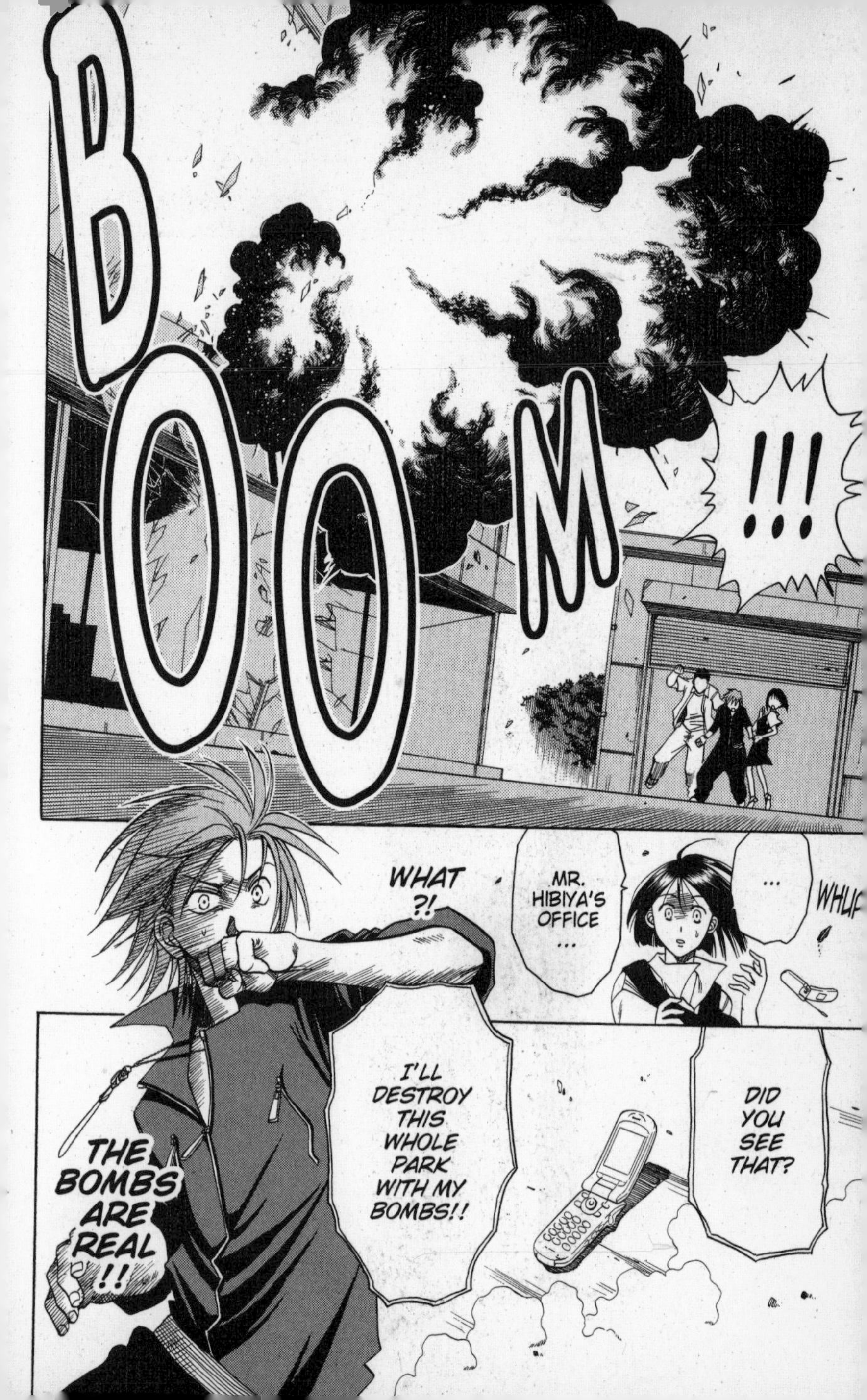
BOOOM!!!
...
WHUP
MR. HIBIYA'S OFFICE ...
WHAT ?!
DID YOU SEE THAT?
I'LL DESTROY THIS WHOLE PARK WITH MY BOMBS!!
THE BOMBS ARE REAL!!

Scene 4:

Monster House of Terror (Part 2)

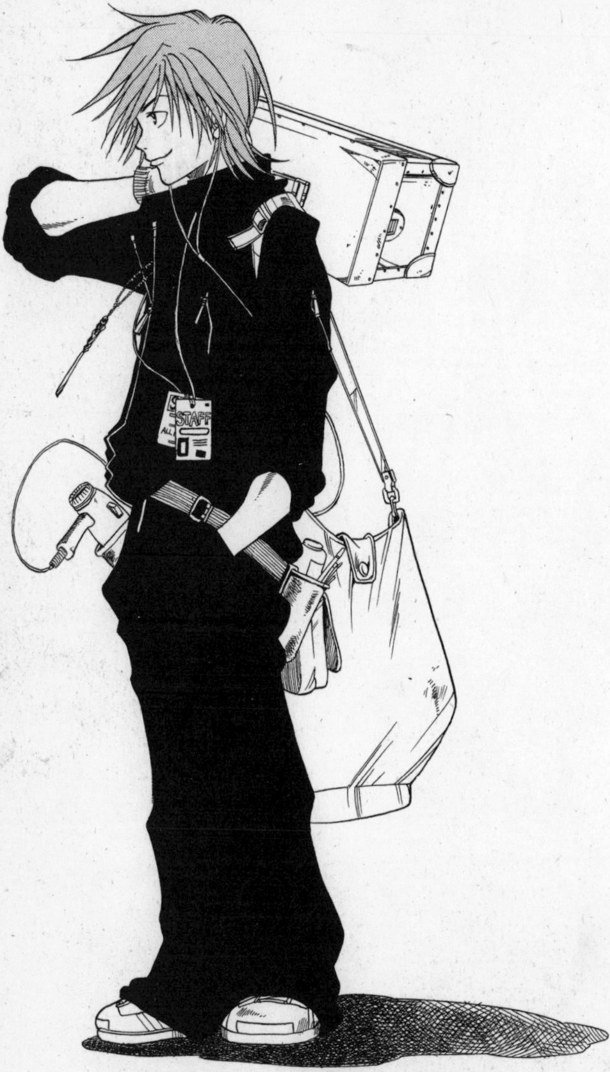
STAFF

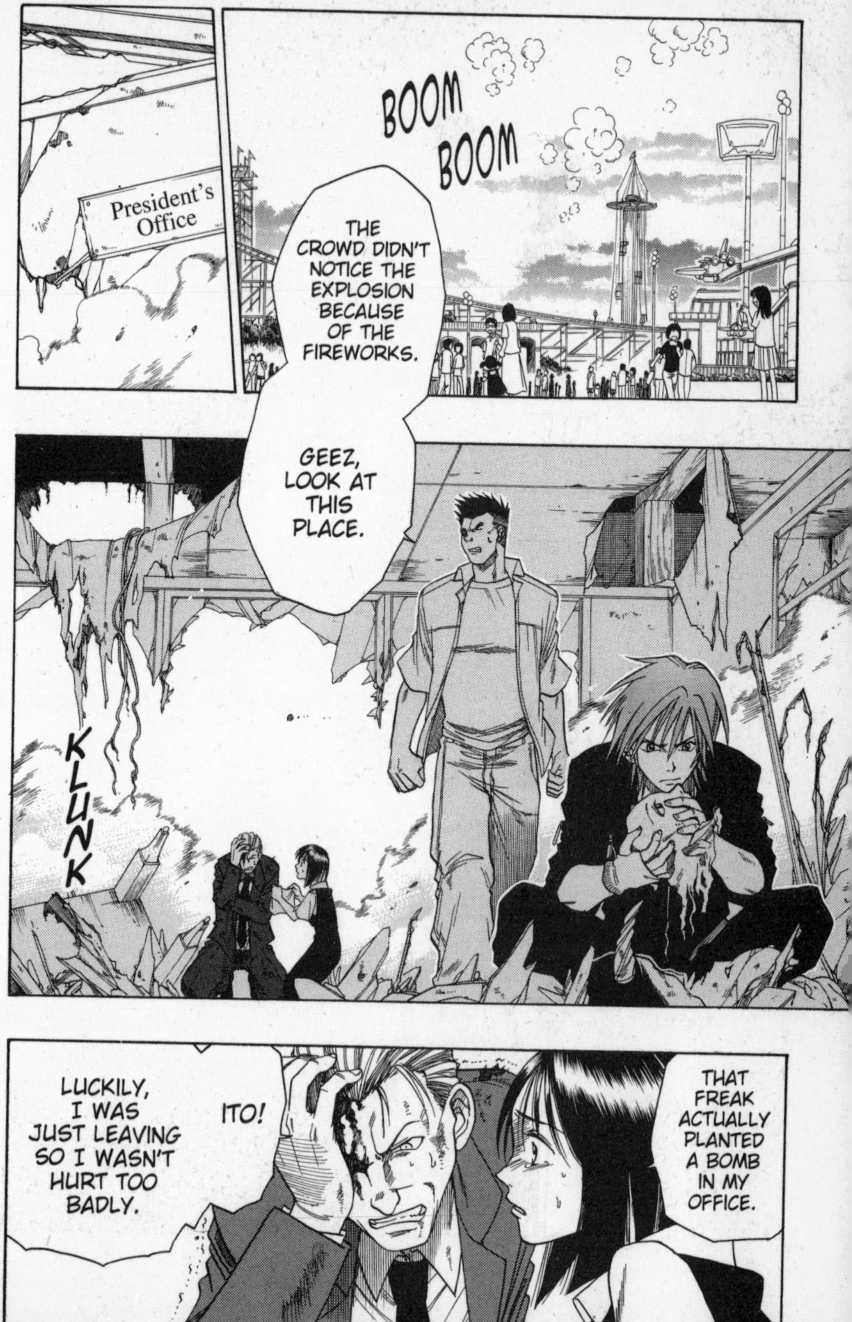
BOOM
BOOM
THE CROWD DIDN'T NOTICE THE EXPLOSION BECAUSE OF THE FIREWORKS.
President's Office
GEEZ, LOOK AT THIS PLACE.
...
KLUNK
THAT FREAK ACTUALLY PLANTED A BOMB IN MY OFFICE.
ITO!
LUCKILY, I WAS JUST LEAVING SO I WASN'T HURT TOO BADLY.

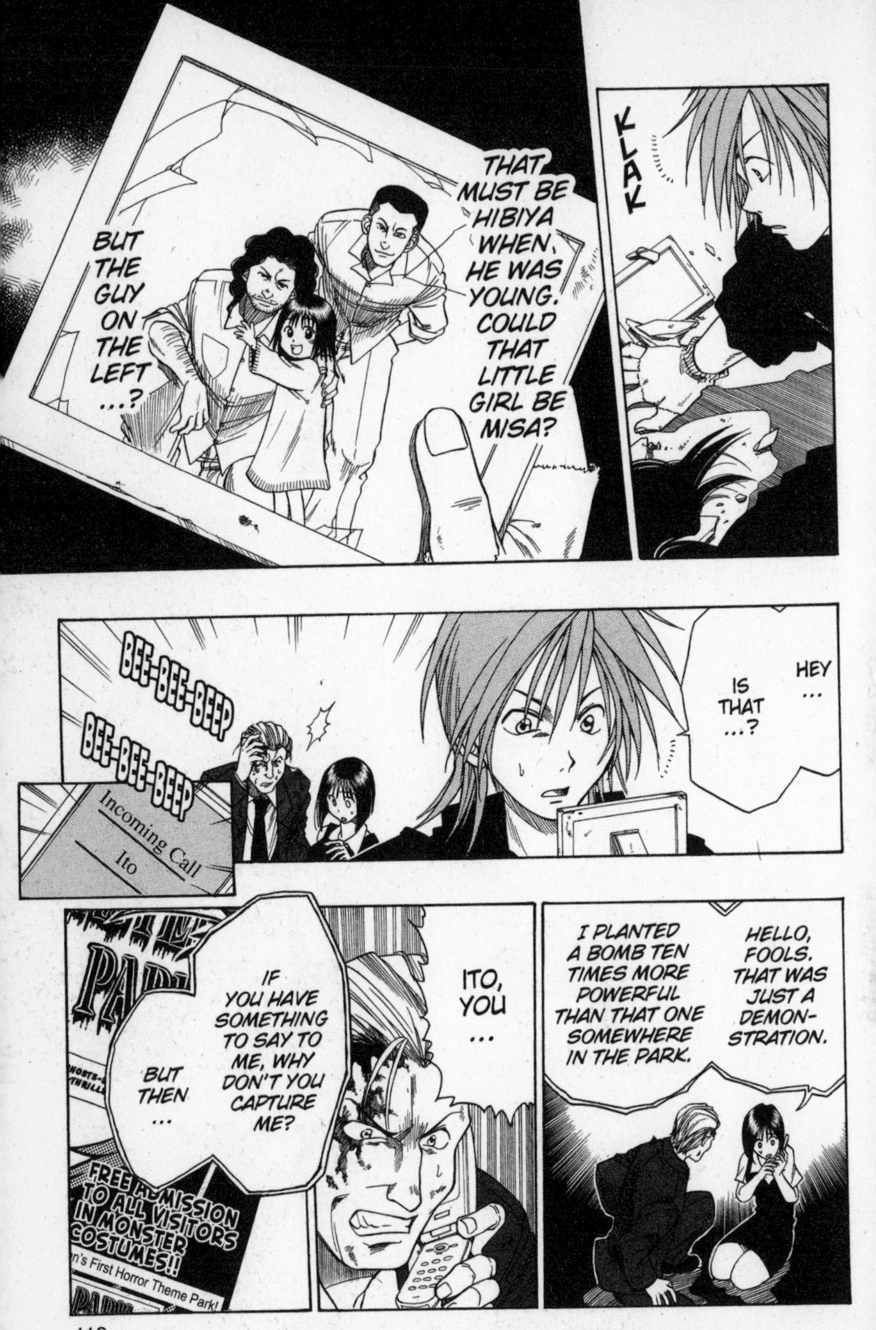
KLAK
THAT MUST BE HIBIYA WHEN HE WAS YOUNG. COULD THAT LITTLE GIRL BE MISA?
BUT THE GUY ON THE LEFT ...?
HEY ...
IS THAT ...?
BEE-BEE-BEEP
BEE-BEE-BEEP
Incoming Call
Ito
HELLO, FOOLS. THAT WAS JUST A DEMONSTRATION.
I PLANTED A BOMB TEN TIMES MORE POWERFUL THAN THAT ONE SOMEWHERE IN THE PARK.
ITO, YOU ...
IF YOU HAVE SOMETHING TO SAY TO ME, WHY DON'T YOU CAPTURE ME?
BUT THEN ...
FREE ADMISSION TO ALL VISITORS IN MONSTER COSTUMES!!
First Horror Theme Park!

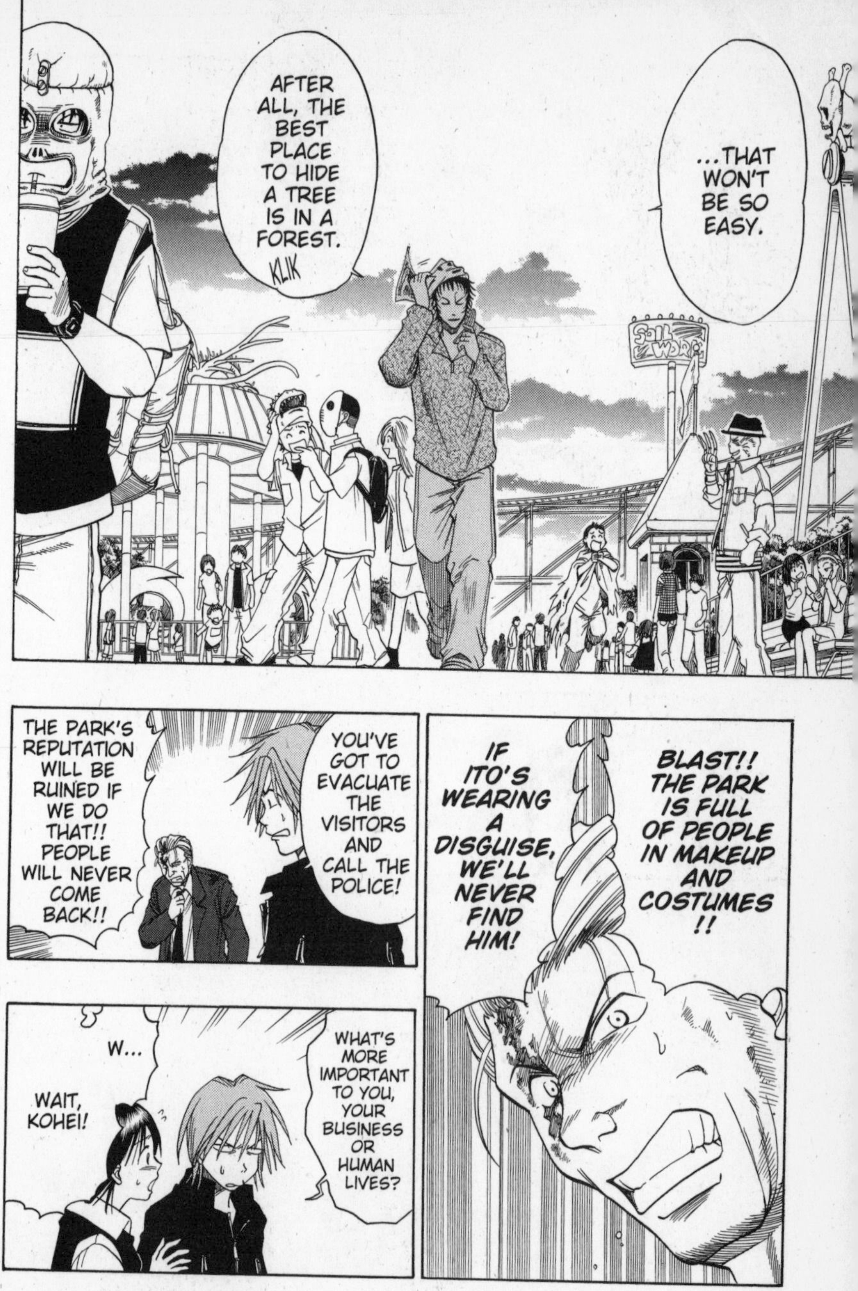
...THAT WON'T BE SO EASY.
AFTER ALL, THE BEST PLACE TO HIDE A TREE IS IN A FOREST.
KLIK
BLAST!! THE PARK IS FULL OF PEOPLE IN MAKEUP AND COSTUMES!!
IF ITO'S WEARING A DISGUISE, WE'LL NEVER FIND HIM!
YOU'VE GOT TO EVACUATE THE VISITORS AND CALL THE POLICE!
THE PARK'S REPUTATION WILL BE RUINED IF WE DO THAT!! PEOPLE WILL NEVER COME BACK!!
WHAT'S MORE IMPORTANT TO YOU, YOUR BUSINESS OR HUMAN LIVES?
W...
WAIT, KOHEI!

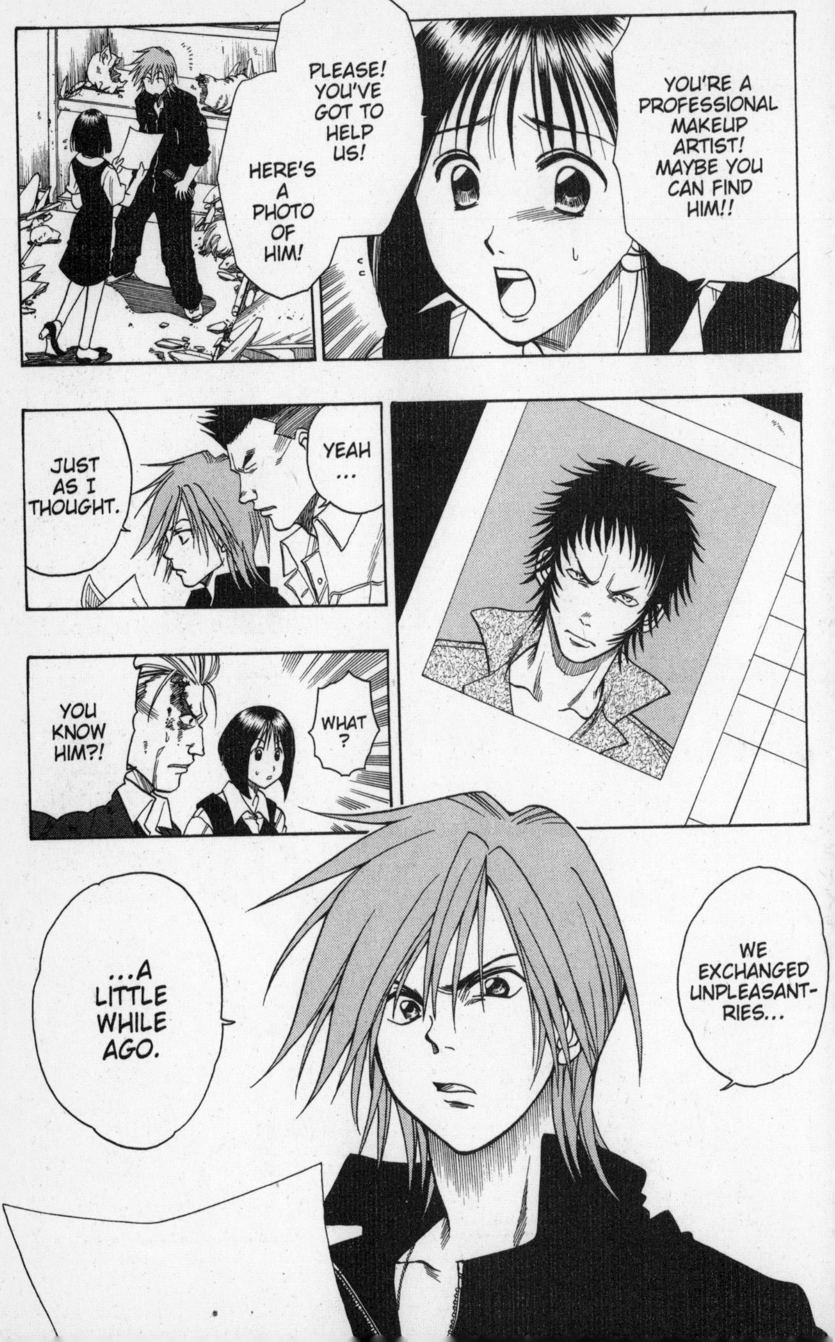
YOU'RE A PROFESSIONAL MAKEUP ARTIST! MAYBE YOU CAN FIND HIM!!
PLEASE! YOU'VE GOT TO HELP US!
HERE'S A PHOTO OF HIM!
YEAH...
JUST AS I THOUGHT.
WHAT?
YOU KNOW HIM?!
WE EXCHANGED UNPLEASANT-RIES...
...A LITTLE WHILE AGO.

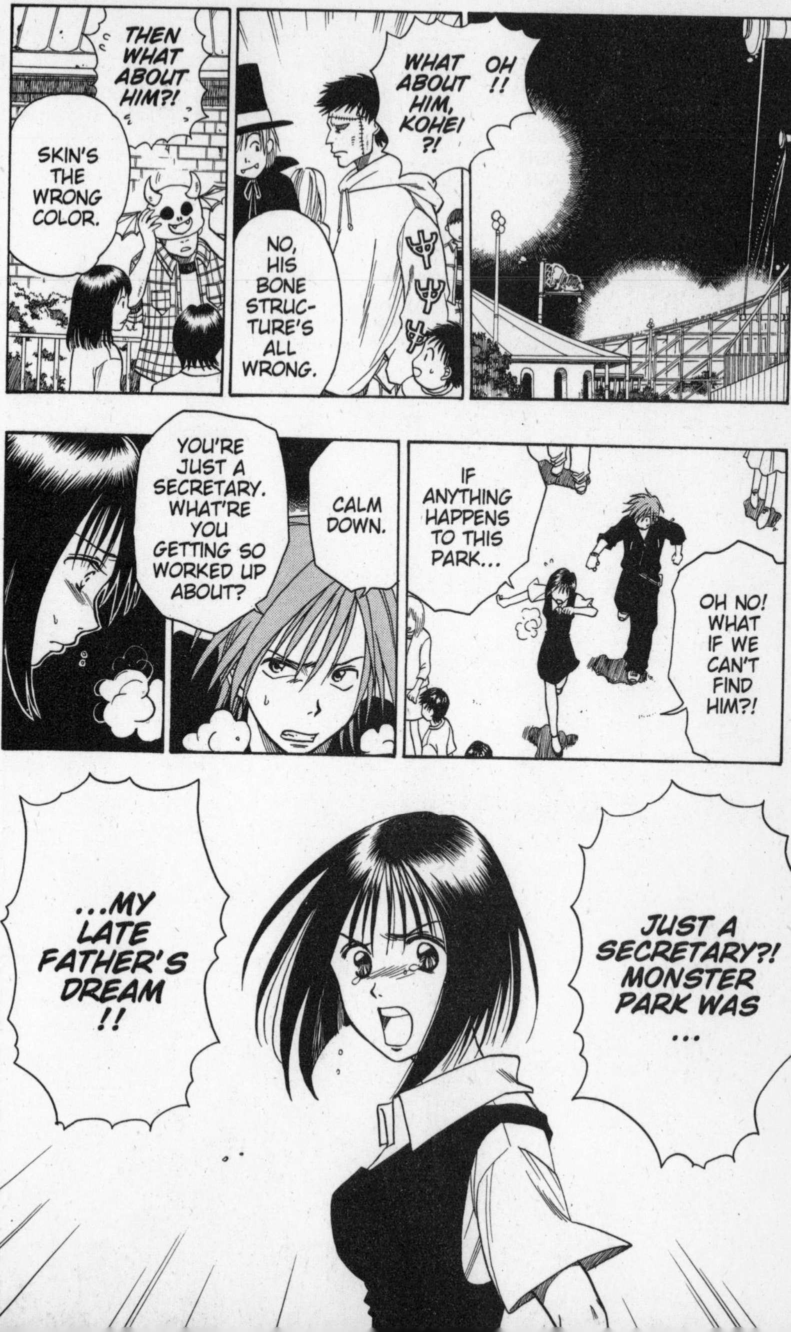
OH!!
WHAT ABOUT HIM, KOHEI?!
NO, HIS BONE STRUCTURE'S ALL WRONG.
THEN WHAT ABOUT HIM?!
SKIN'S THE WRONG COLOR.
OH NO! WHAT IF WE CAN'T FIND HIM?!
IF ANYTHING HAPPENS TO THIS PARK...
CALM DOWN.
YOU'RE JUST A SECRETARY. WHAT'RE YOU GETTING SO WORKED UP ABOUT?
JUST A SECRETARY?! MONSTER PARK WAS ...
...MY LATE FATHER'S DREAM!!

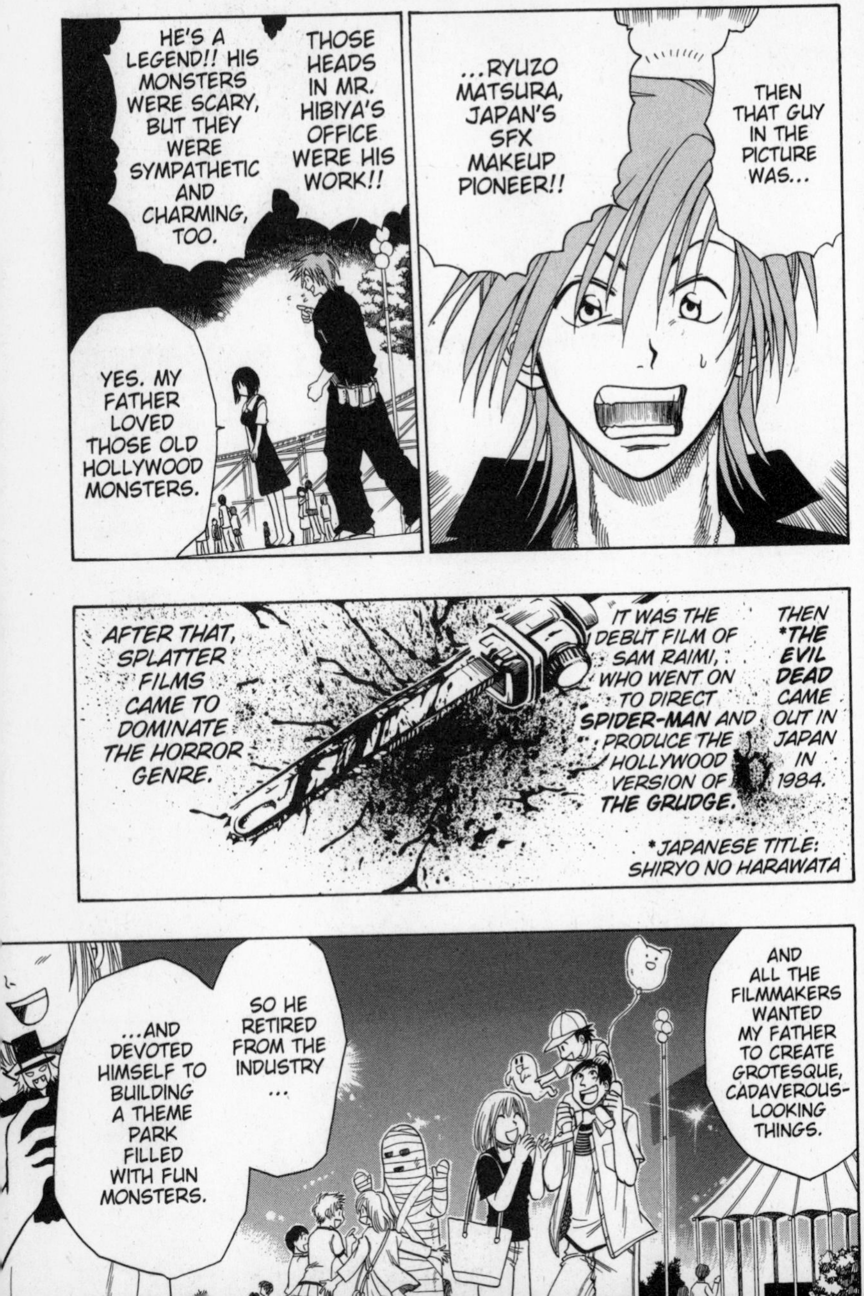
THEN THAT GUY IN THE PICTURE WAS...
...RYUZO MATSURA, JAPAN'S SFX MAKEUP PIONEER!!
THOSE HEADS IN MR. HIBIYA'S OFFICE WERE HIS WORK!!
HE'S A LEGEND!! HIS MONSTERS WERE SCARY, BUT THEY WERE SYMPATHETIC AND CHARMING, TOO.
YES. MY FATHER LOVED THOSE OLD HOLLYWOOD MONSTERS.
THEN *THE EVIL DEAD CAME OUT IN JAPAN IN 1984.
IT WAS THE DEBUT FILM OF SAM RAIMI, WHO WENT ON TO DIRECT SPIDER-MAN AND PRODUCE THE HOLLYWOOD VERSION OF THE GRUDGE.
AFTER THAT, SPLATTER FILMS CAME TO DOMINATE THE HORROR GENRE.
*JAPANESE TITLE: SHIRYO NO HARAWATA
AND ALL THE FILMMAKERS WANTED MY FATHER TO CREATE GROTESQUE, CADAVEROUS-LOOKING THINGS.
SO HE RETIRED FROM THE INDUSTRY...
...AND DEVOTED HIMSELF TO BUILDING A THEME PARK FILLED WITH FUN MONSTERS.

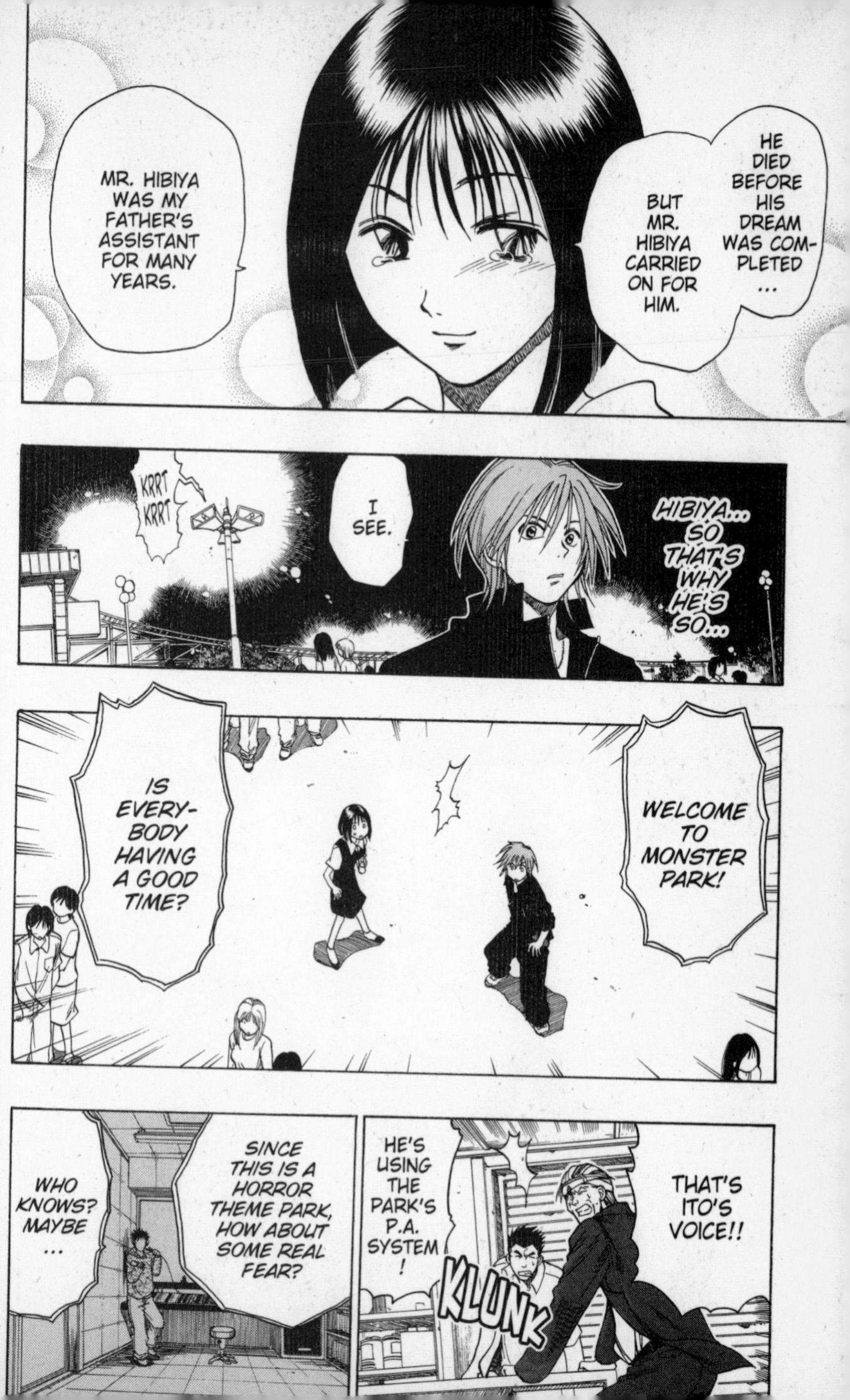
HE DIED BEFORE HIS DREAM WAS COMPLETED ...
BUT MR. HIBIYA CARRIED ON FOR HIM.
MR. HIBIYA WAS MY FATHER'S ASSISTANT FOR MANY YEARS.
HIBIYA... SO THAT'S WHY HE'S SO...
I SEE.
KRRT KRRT
WELCOME TO MONSTER PARK!
IS EVERYBODY HAVING A GOOD TIME?
THAT'S ITO'S VOICE!!
KLUNK
HE'S USING THE PARK'S P.A. SYSTEM!
SINCE THIS IS A HORROR THEME PARK, HOW ABOUT SOME REAL FEAR?
WHO KNOWS? MAYBE ...

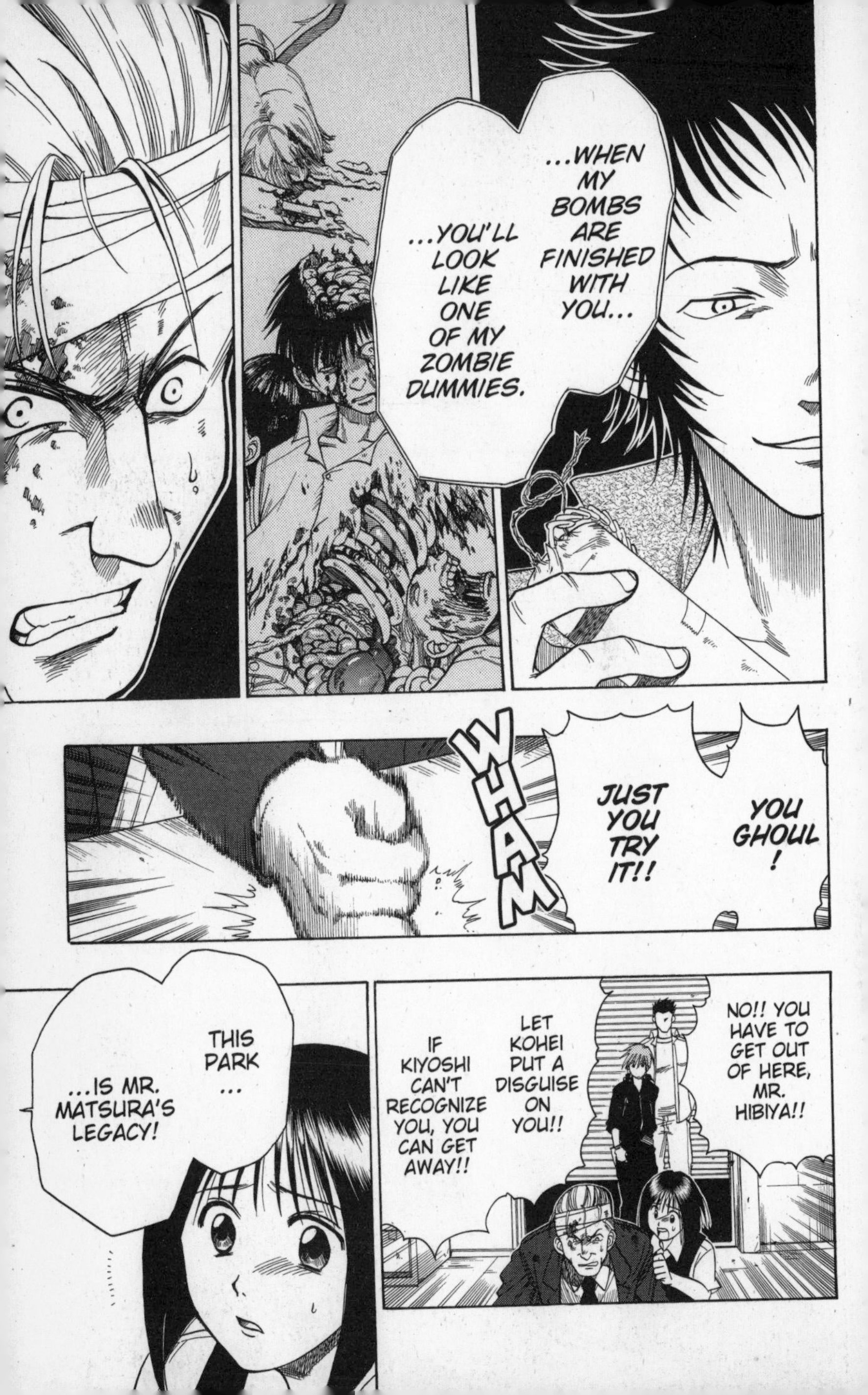
...WHEN MY BOMBS ARE FINISHED WITH YOU...
...YOU'LL LOOK LIKE ONE OF MY ZOMBIE DUMMIES.
YOU GHOUL!
JUST YOU TRY IT!!
WHAM
NO!! YOU HAVE TO GET OUT OF HERE, MR. HIBIYA!!
LET KOHEI PUT A DISGUISE ON YOU!!
IF KIYOSHI CAN'T RECOGNIZE YOU, YOU CAN GET AWAY!!
THIS PARK...
...IS MR. MATSURA'S LEGACY!

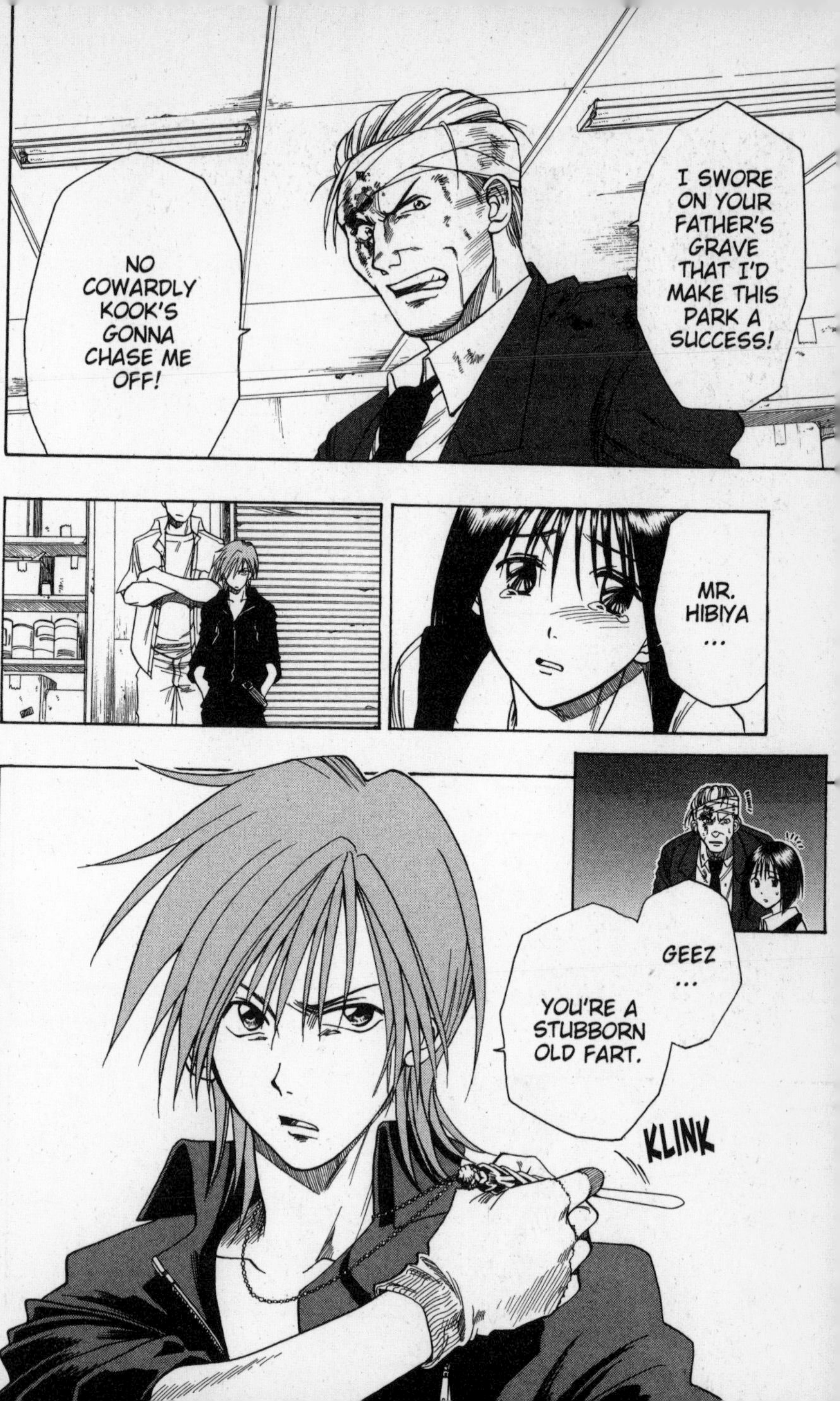
I SWORE ON YOUR FATHER'S GRAVE THAT I'D MAKE THIS PARK A SUCCESS!
NO COWARDLY KOOK'S GONNA CHASE ME OFF!
MR. HIBIYA ...
GEEZ ...
YOU'RE A STUBBORN OLD FART.
KLINK

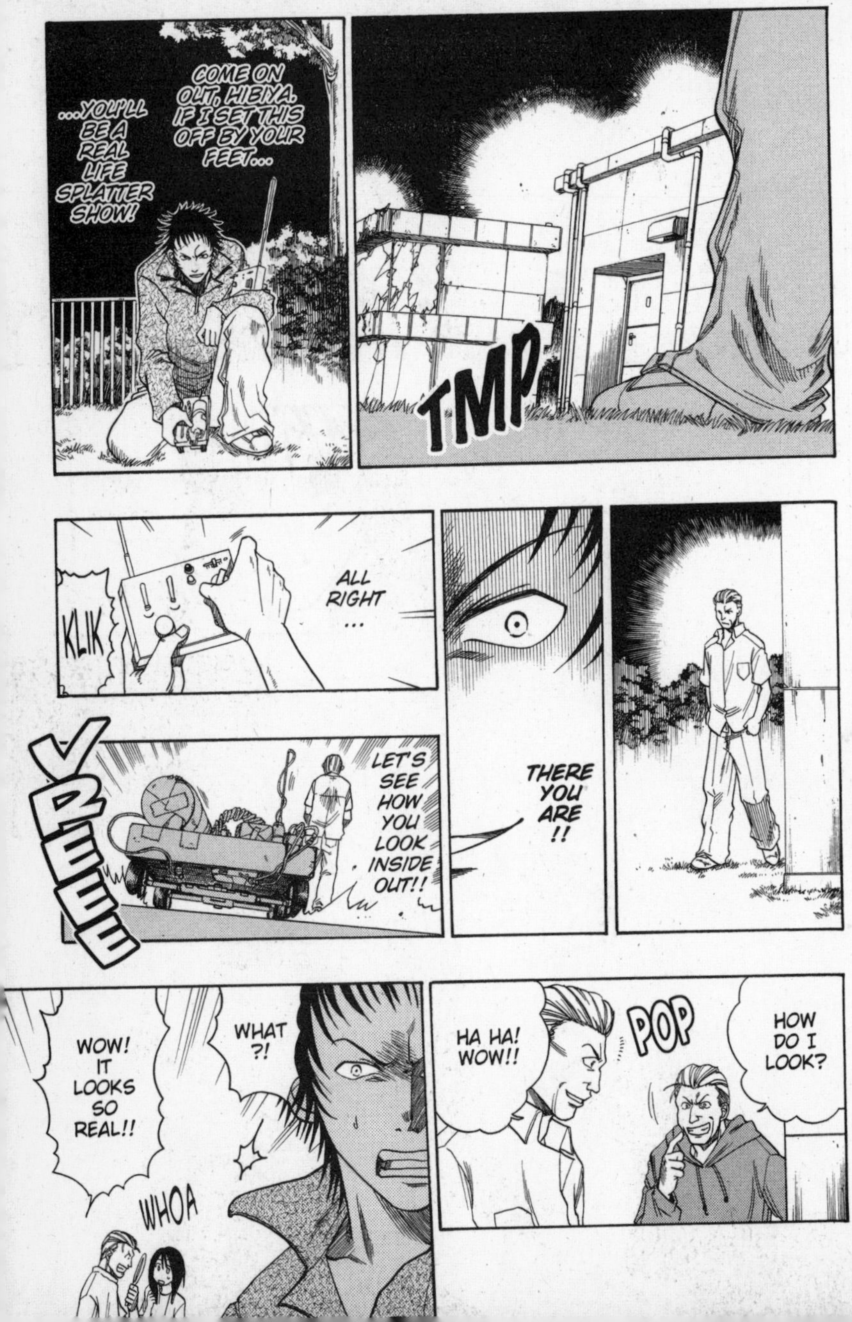
TMP
COME ON OUT, HIBIYA. IF I SET THIS OFF BY YOUR FEET...
...YOU'LL BE A REAL LIFE SPLATTER SHOW!
THERE YOU ARE!!
ALL RIGHT...
KLIK
LET'S SEE HOW YOU LOOK INSIDE OUT!!
VREEE
HOW DO I LOOK?
POP
HA HA! WOW!!
WHAT?!
WOW! IT LOOKS SO REAL!!
WHOA

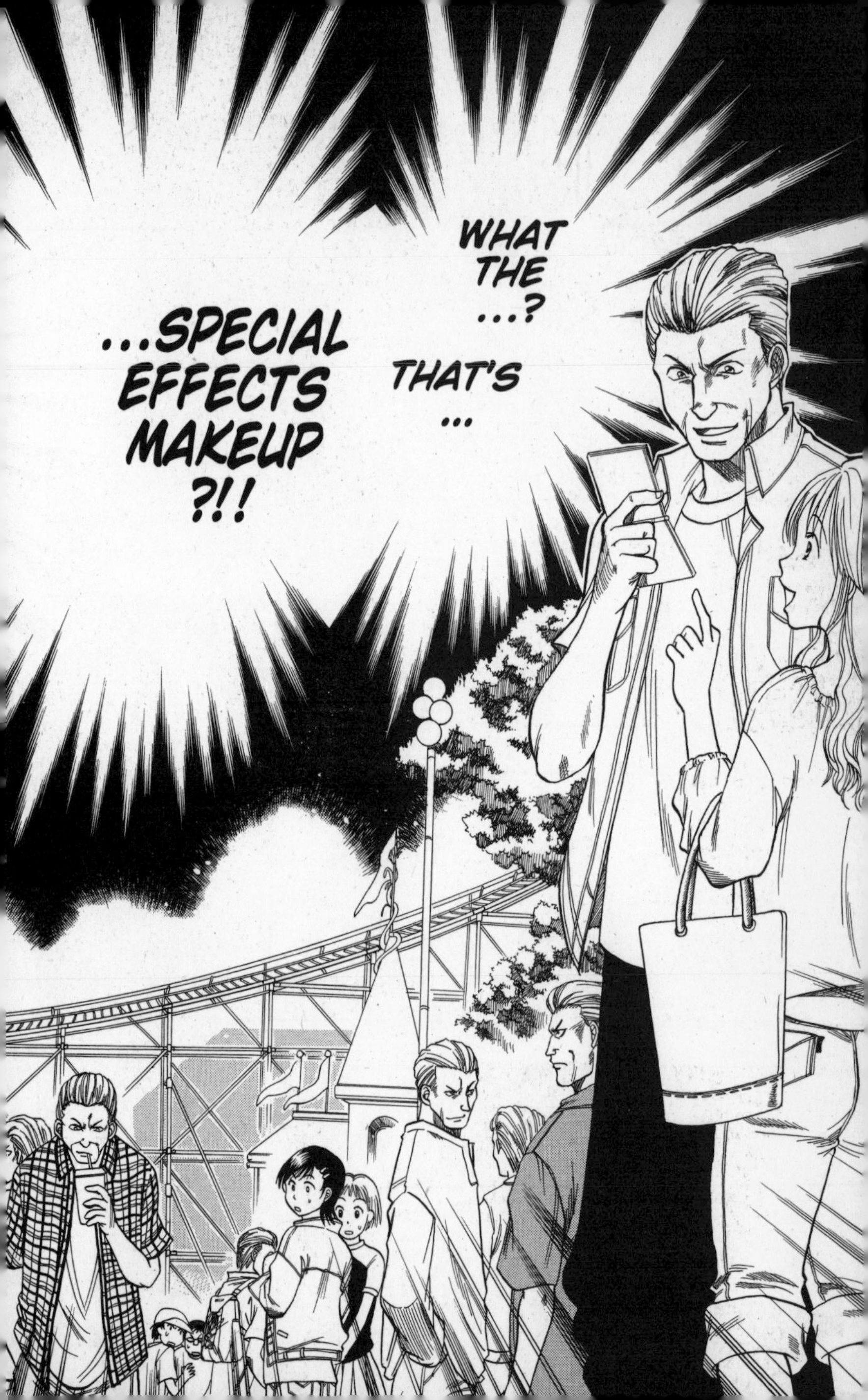
WHAT THE ...?
THAT'S ...
...SPECIAL EFFECTS MAKEUP ?!!

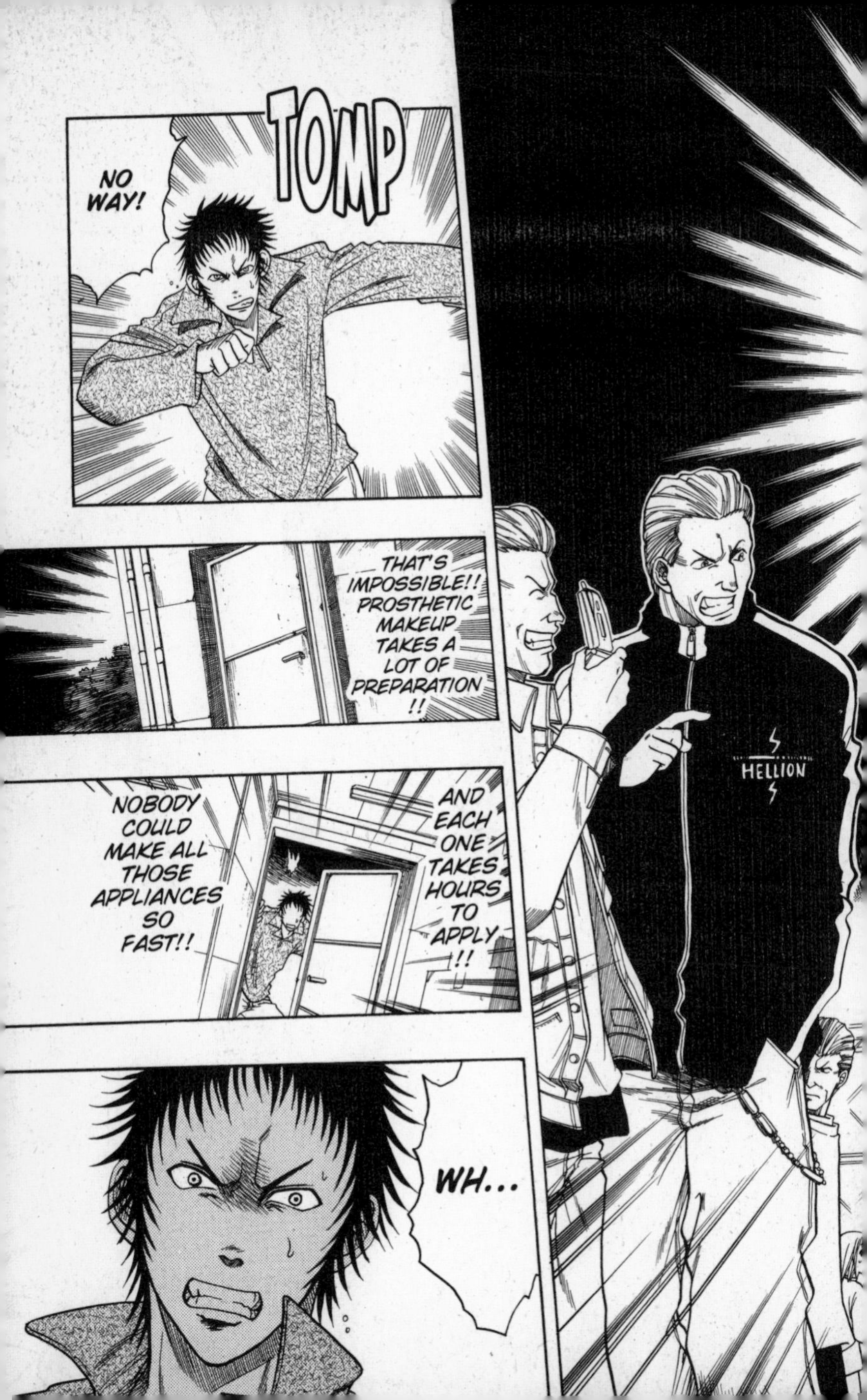
HELLION
TOMP
NO WAY!
THAT'S IMPOSSIBLE!! PROSTHETIC MAKEUP TAKES A LOT OF PREPARATION!!
AND EACH ONE TAKES HOURS TO APPLY!!
NOBODY COULD MAKE ALL THOSE APPLIANCES SO FAST!!
WH...

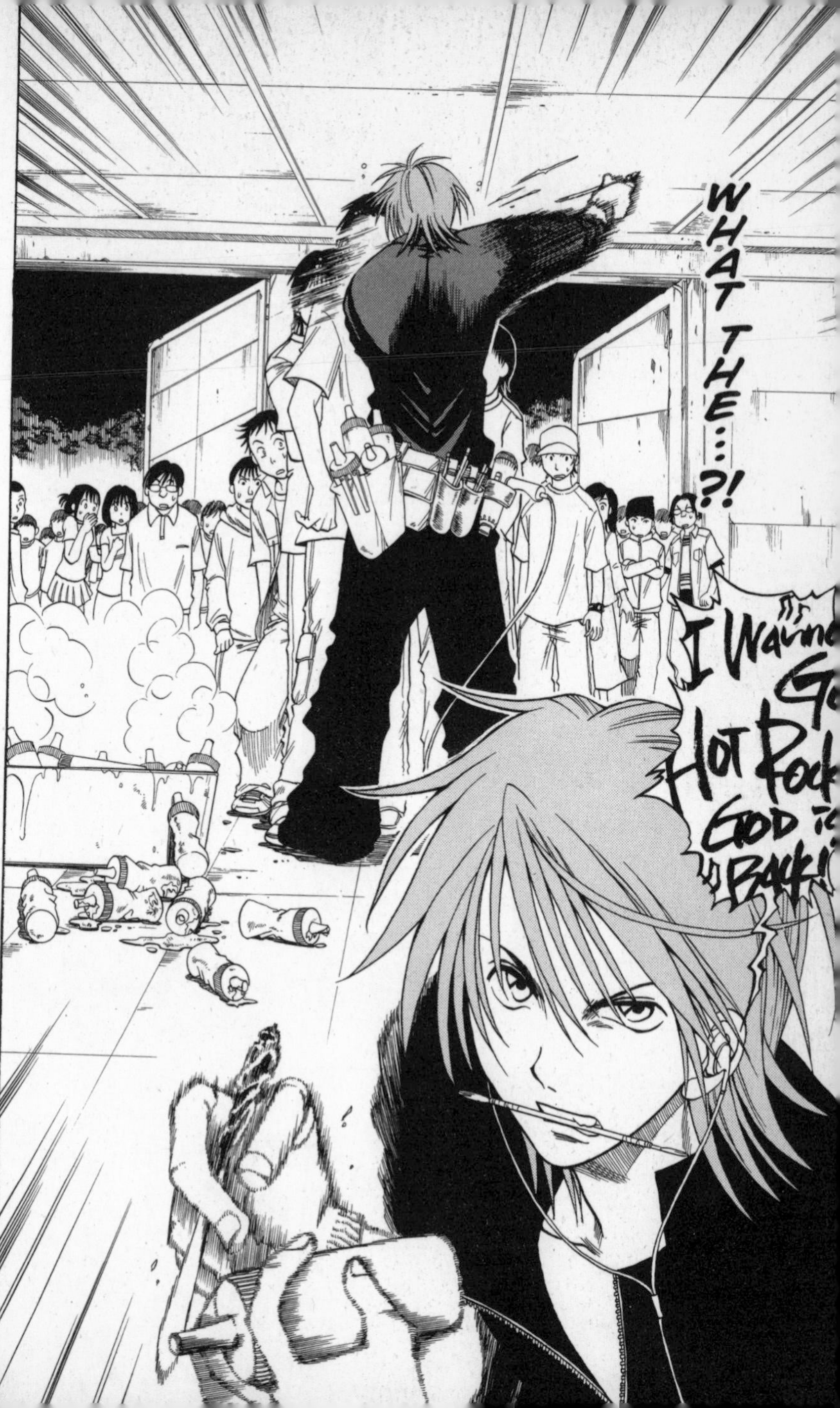
WHAT THE...?!
I Wanna Go Hot Rock GOD is BACK!

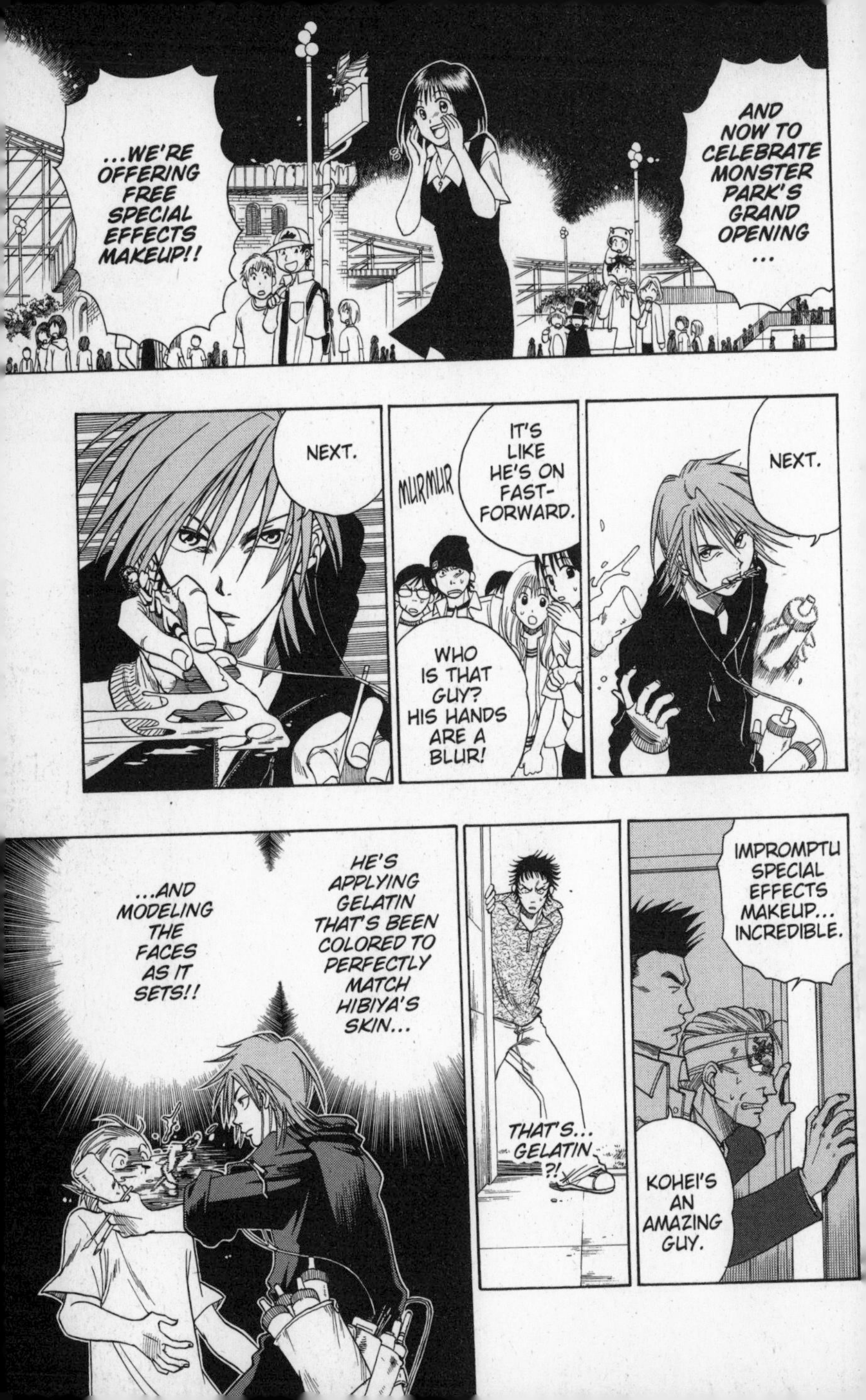
AND NOW TO CELEBRATE MONSTER PARK'S GRAND OPENING...
...WE'RE OFFERING FREE SPECIAL EFFECTS MAKEUP!!
NEXT.
IT'S LIKE HE'S ON FAST-FORWARD.
MURMUR
WHO IS THAT GUY? HIS HANDS ARE A BLUR!
NEXT.
IMPROMPTU SPECIAL EFFECTS MAKEUP... INCREDIBLE.
KOHEI'S AN AMAZING GUY.
THAT'S... GELATIN?!
HE'S APPLYING GELATIN THAT'S BEEN COLORED TO PERFECTLY MATCH HIBIYA'S SKIN...
...AND MODELING THE FACES AS IT SETS!!

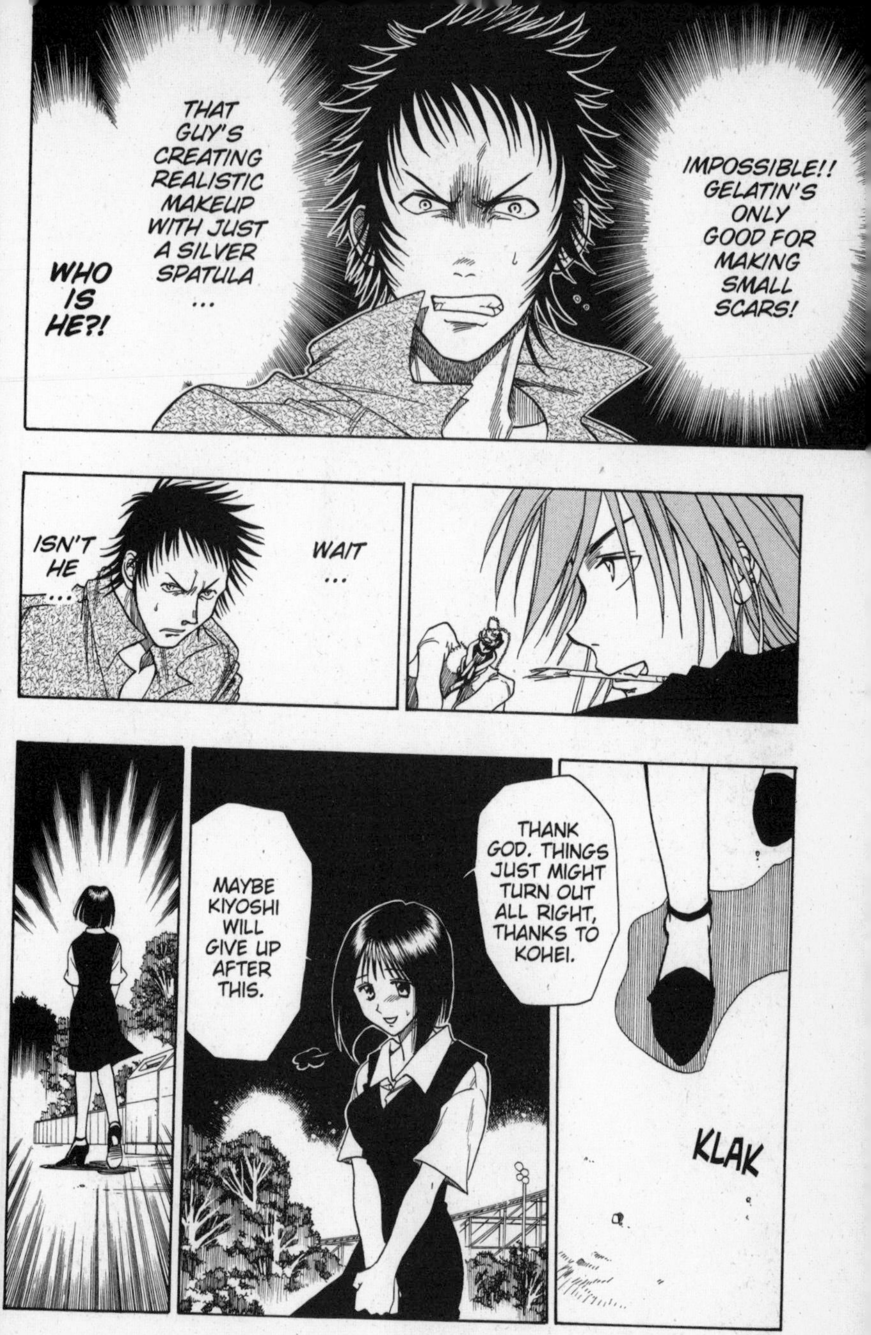
IMPOSSIBLE!! GELATIN'S ONLY GOOD FOR MAKING SMALL SCARS!
THAT GUY'S CREATING REALISTIC MAKEUP WITH JUST A SILVER SPATULA ...
WHO IS HE?!
WAIT ...
ISN'T HE ...
KLAK
THANK GOD. THINGS JUST MIGHT TURN OUT ALL RIGHT, THANKS TO KOHEI.
MAYBE KIYOSHI WILL GIVE UP AFTER THIS.

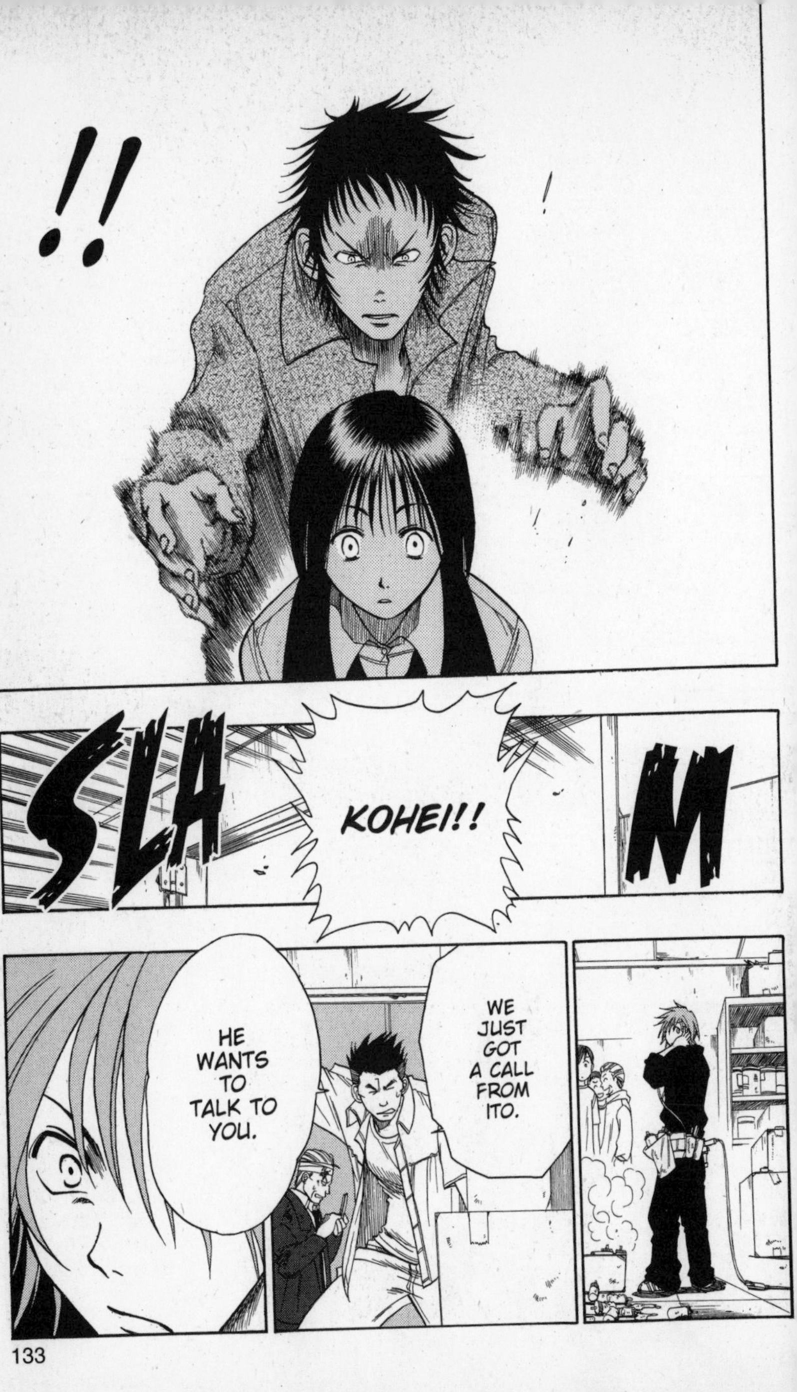
!!
SLAM
KOHEI!!
WE JUST GOT A CALL FROM ITO.
HE WANTS TO TALK TO YOU.

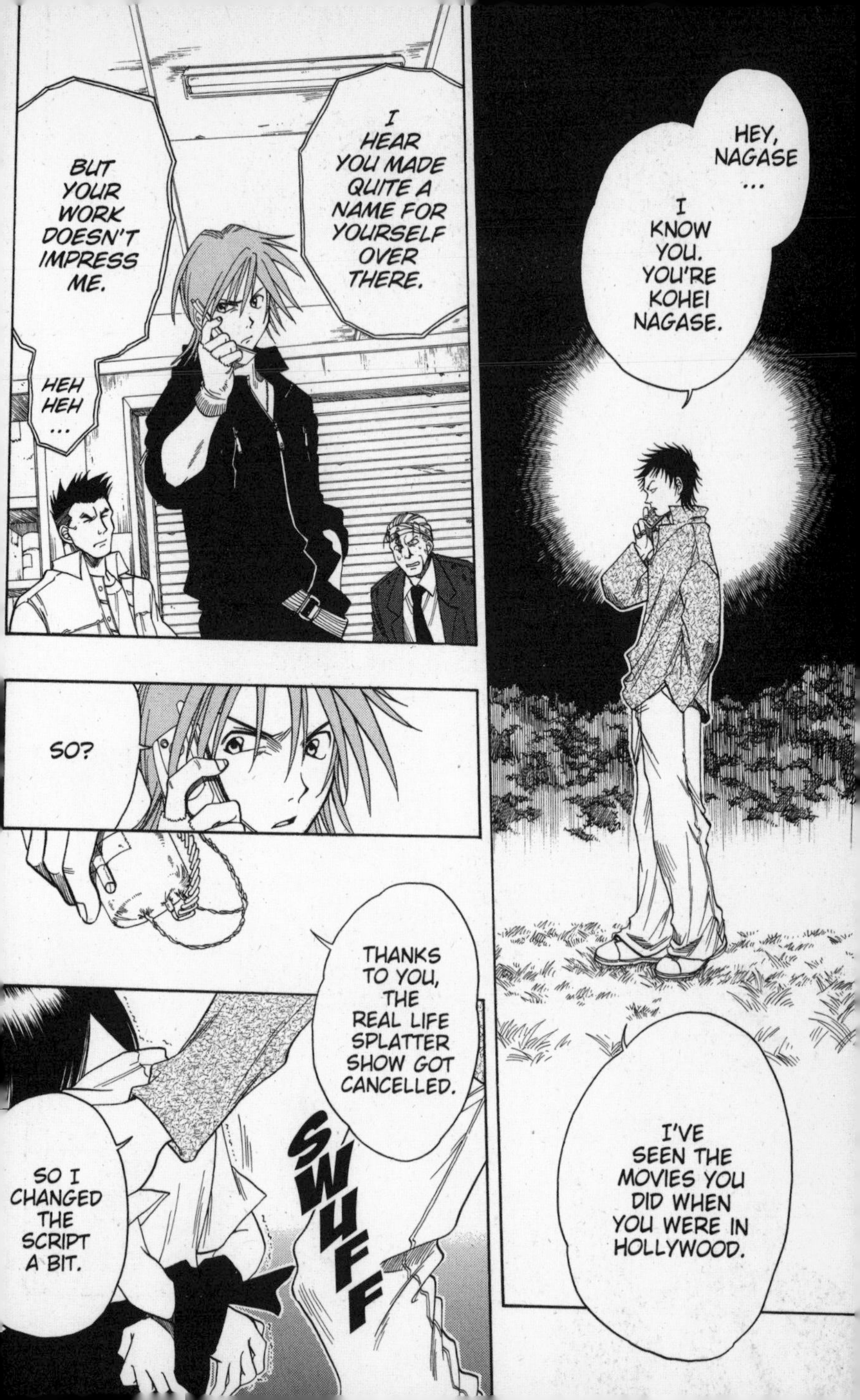
HEY, NAGASE ...
I KNOW YOU. YOU'RE KOHEI NAGASE.
I'VE SEEN THE MOVIES YOU DID WHEN YOU WERE IN HOLLYWOOD.
I HEAR YOU MADE QUITE A NAME FOR YOURSELF OVER THERE.
BUT YOUR WORK DOESN'T IMPRESS ME.
HEH HEH ...
SO?
THANKS TO YOU, THE REAL LIFE SPLATTER SHOW GOT CANCELLED.
SWUFF
SO I CHANGED THE SCRIPT A BIT.

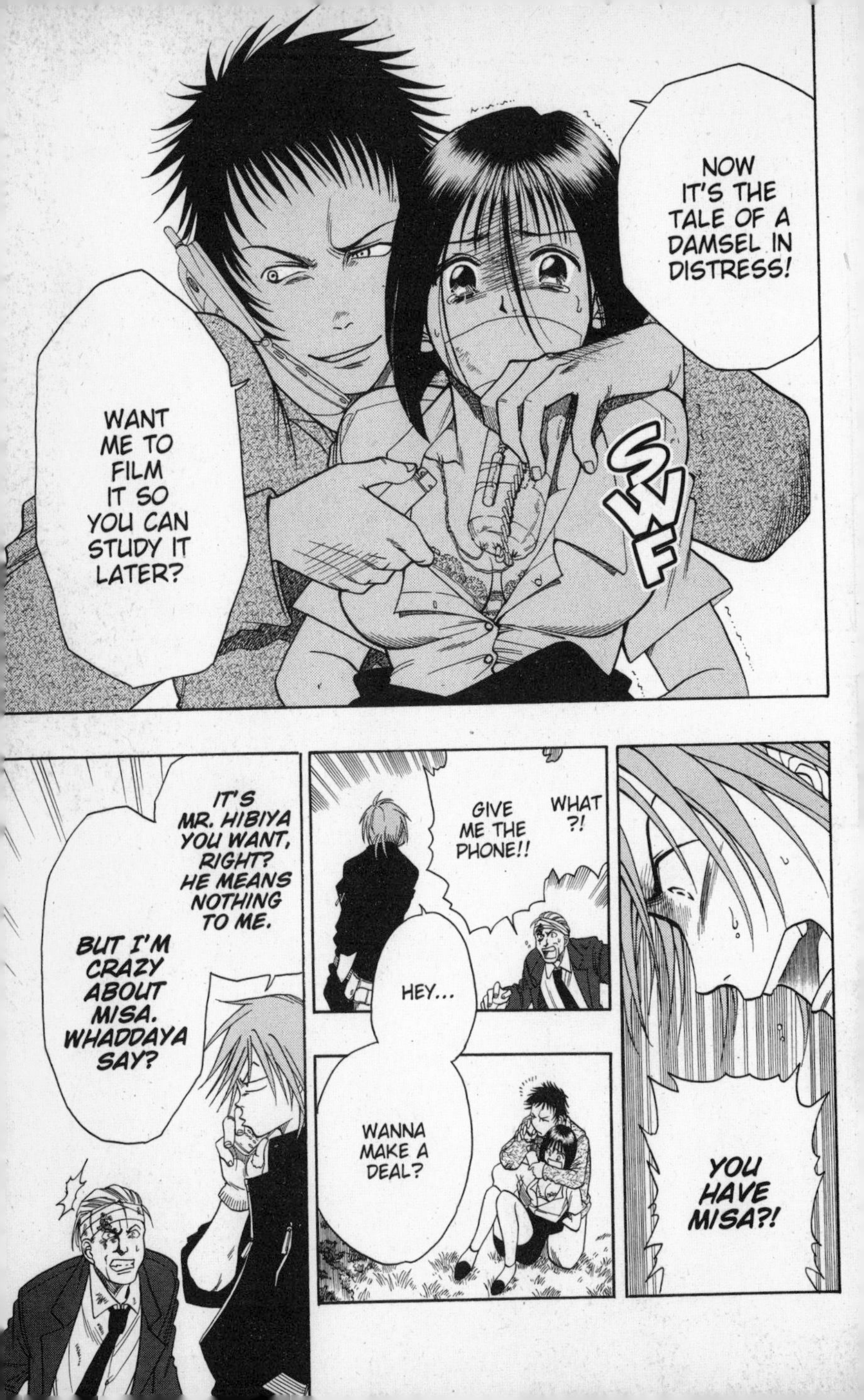
NOW IT'S THE TALE OF A DAMSEL IN DISTRESS!
SWF
WANT ME TO FILM IT SO YOU CAN STUDY IT LATER?
YOU HAVE MISA?!
WHAT?!
GIVE ME THE PHONE!!
HEY...
WANNA MAKE A DEAL?
IT'S MR. HIBIYA YOU WANT, RIGHT? HE MEANS NOTHING TO ME.
BUT I'M CRAZY ABOUT MISA. WHADDAYA SAY?

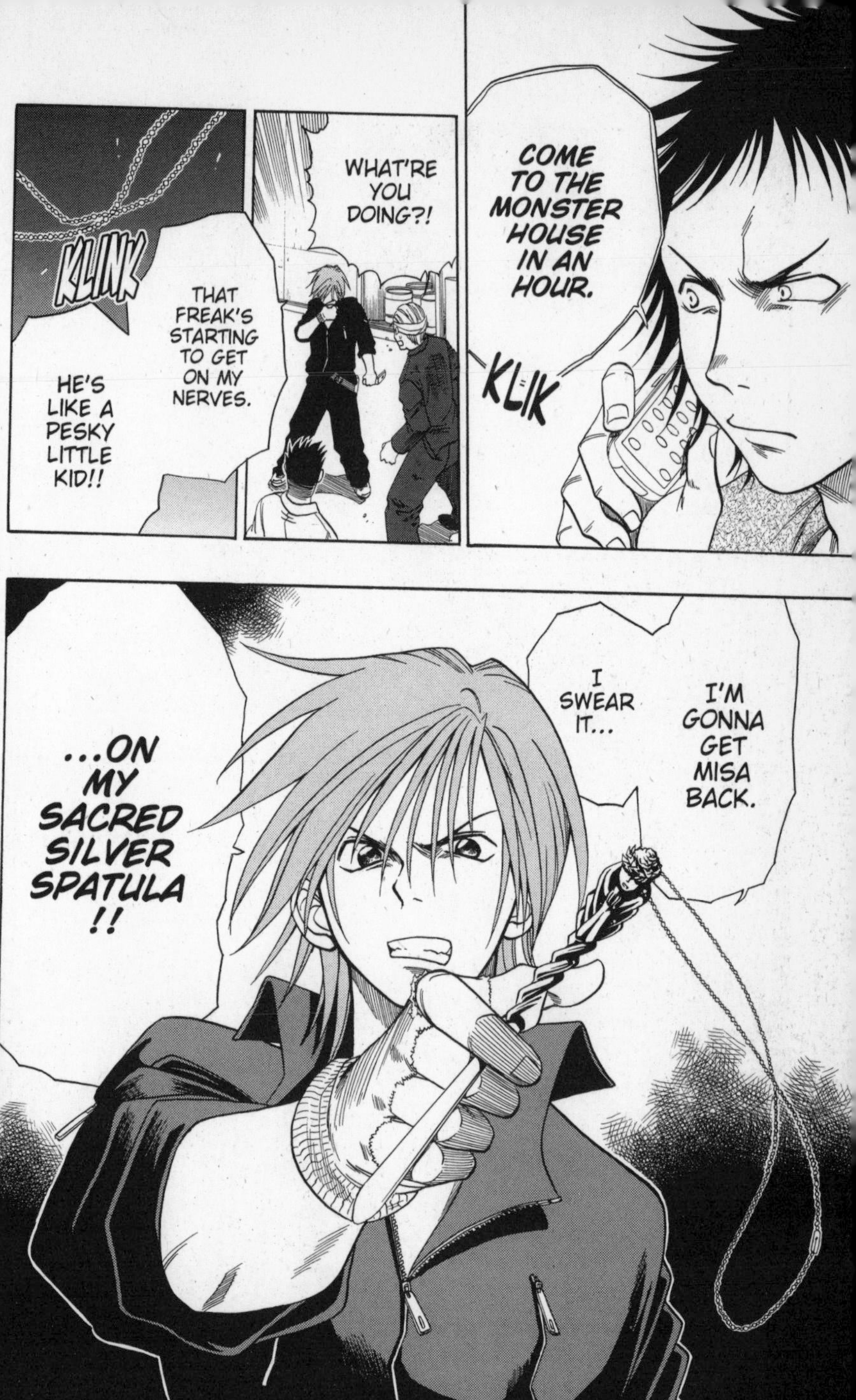
COME TO THE MONSTER HOUSE IN AN HOUR.
KLIK
WHAT'RE YOU DOING?!
THAT FREAK'S STARTING TO GET ON MY NERVES.
KLINK
HE'S LIKE A PESKY LITTLE KID!!
I'M GONNA GET MISA BACK.
I SWEAR IT...
...ON MY SACRED SILVER SPATULA!!

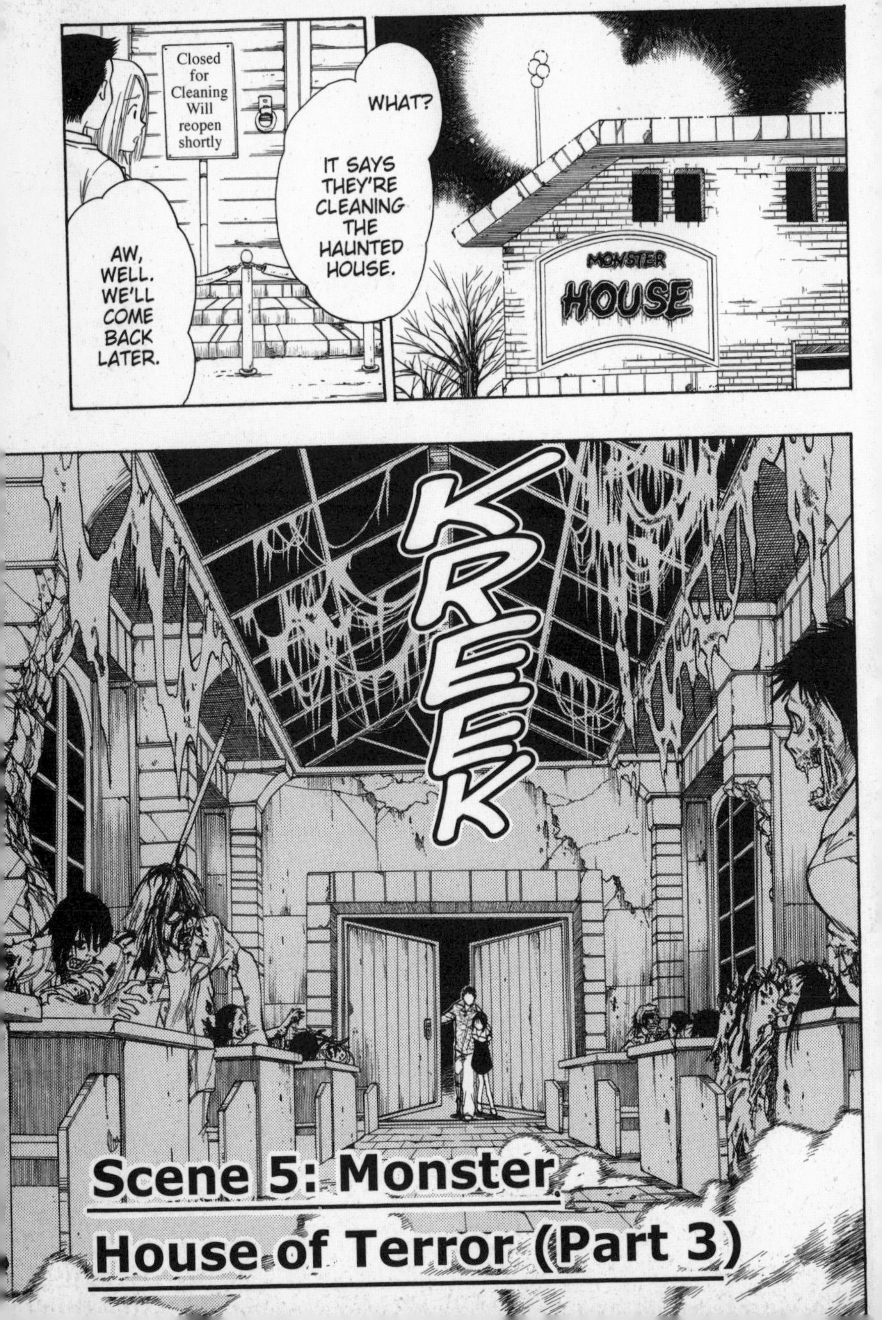
MONSTER HOUSE
Closed for Cleaning Will reopen shortly
WHAT?
IT SAYS THEY'RE CLEANING THE HAUNTED HOUSE.
AW, WELL. WE'LL COME BACK LATER.
KREEK

Scene 5: Monster House of Terror (Part 3)

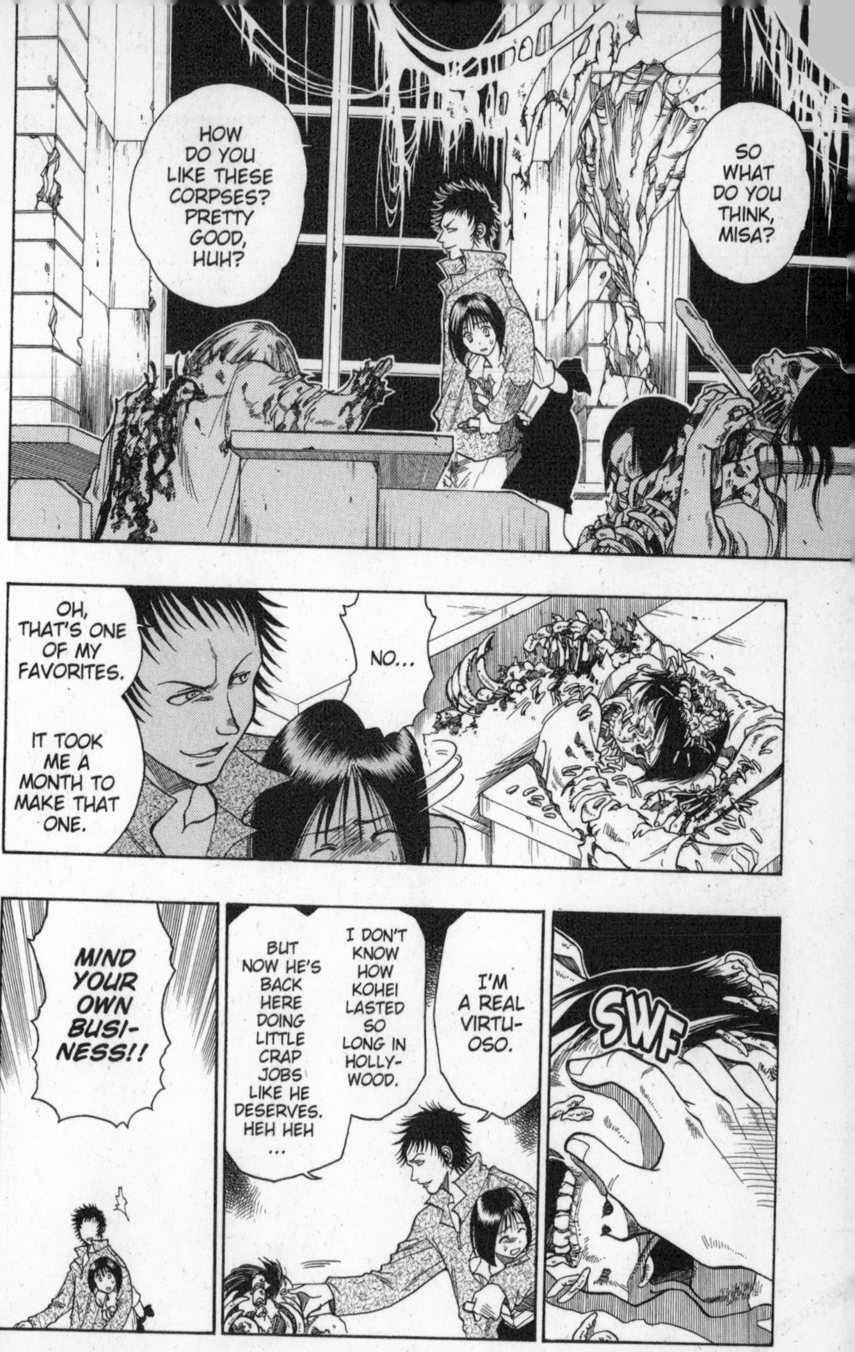
SO WHAT DO YOU THINK, MISA?
HOW DO YOU LIKE THESE CORPSES? PRETTY GOOD, HUH?
NO...
OH, THAT'S ONE OF MY FAVORITES.
IT TOOK ME A MONTH TO MAKE THAT ONE.
SWF
I'M A REAL VIRTUOSO.
I DON'T KNOW HOW KOHEI LASTED SO LONG IN HOLLYWOOD.
BUT NOW HE'S BACK HERE DOING LITTLE CRAP JOBS LIKE HE DESERVES. HEH HEH ...
MIND YOUR OWN BUSINESS!!

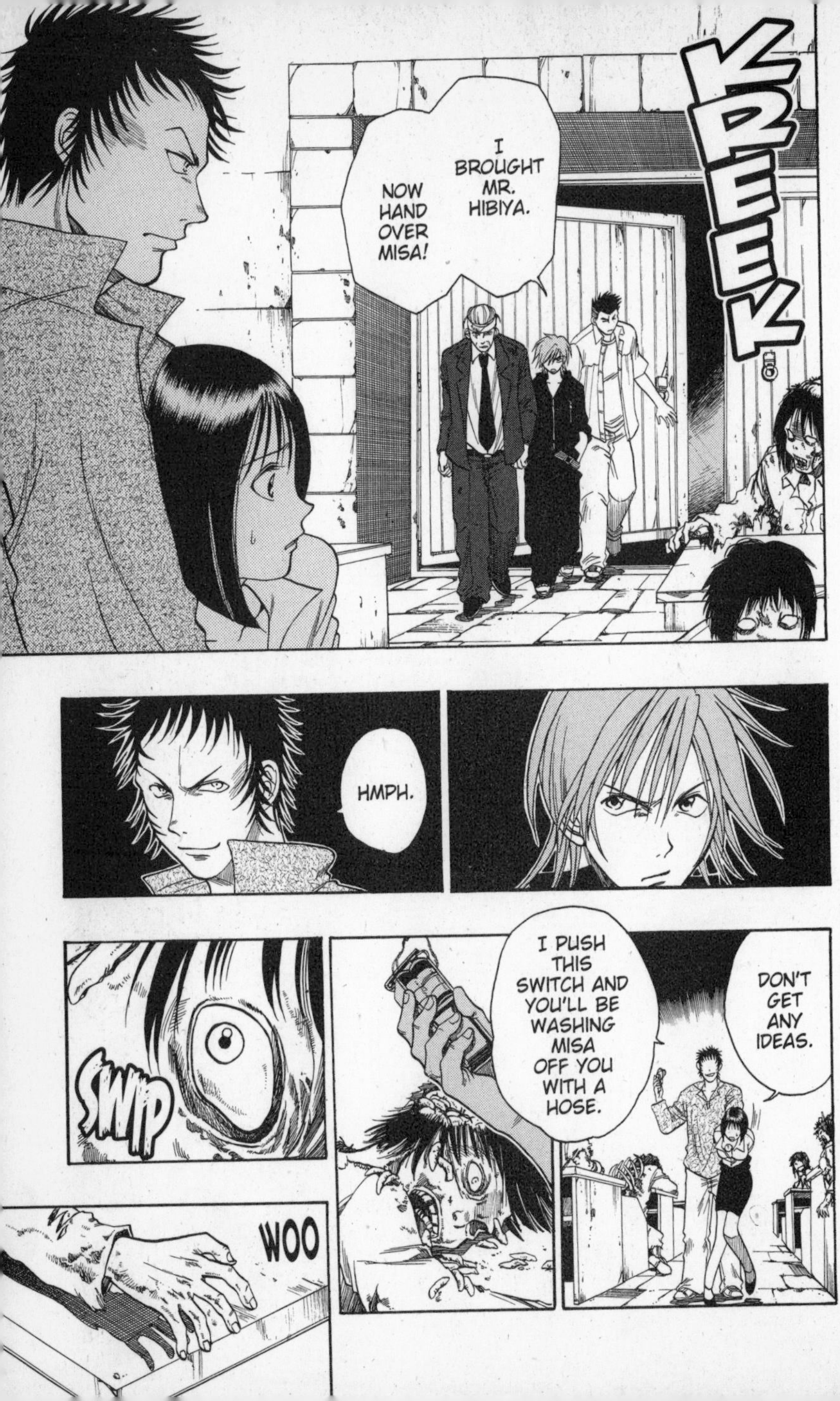
KREEK
I BROUGHT MR. HIBIYA.
NOW HAND OVER MISA!
HMPH.
DON'T GET ANY IDEAS.
I PUSH THIS SWITCH AND YOU'LL BE WASHING MISA OFF YOU WITH A HOSE.
SWIP
WOO

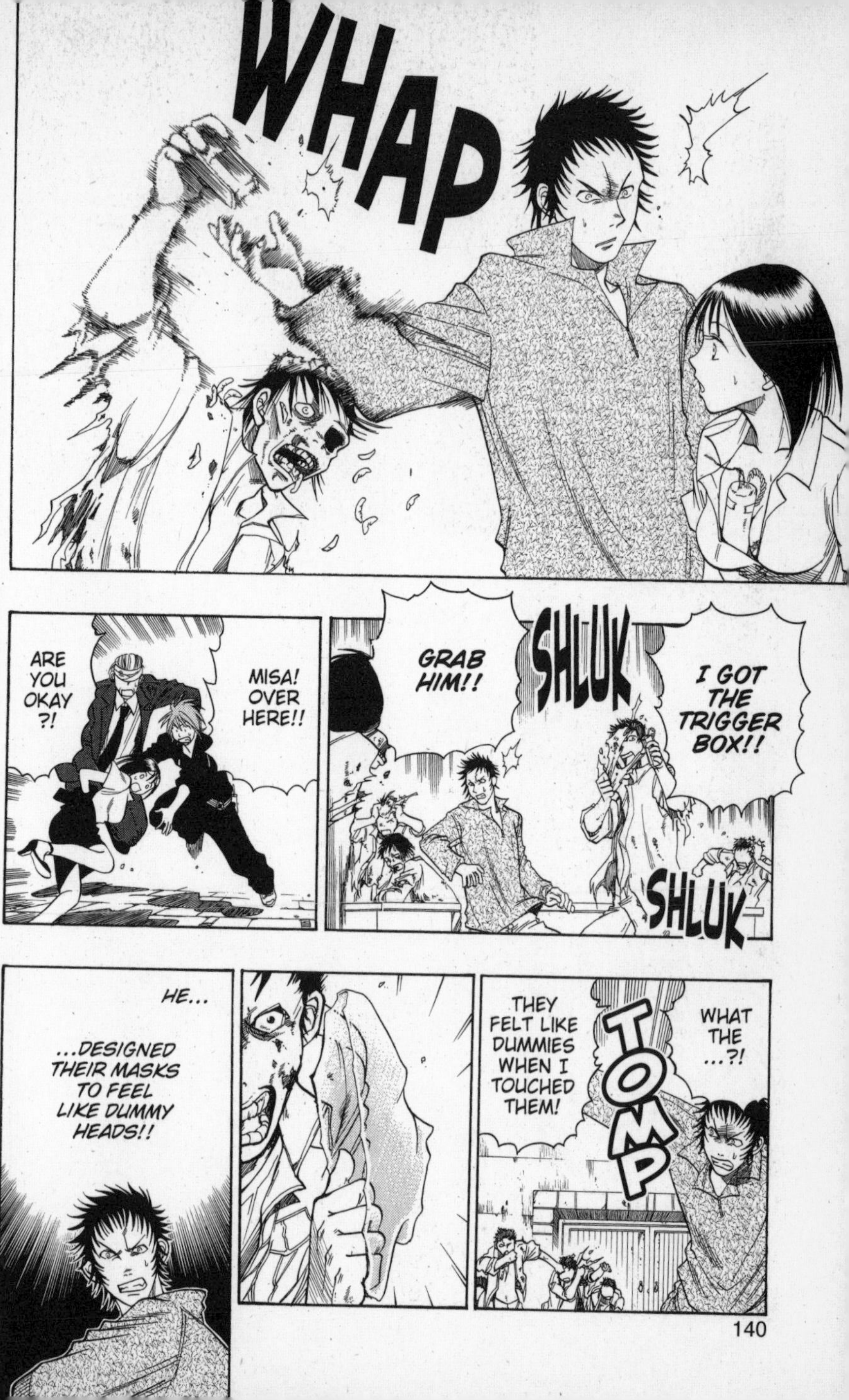
WHAP
I GOT THE TRIGGER BOX!!
SHLUK
GRAB HIM!!
SHLUK
MISA! OVER HERE!!
ARE YOU OKAY ?!
WHAT THE ...?!
TOMP
THEY FELT LIKE DUMMIES WHEN I TOUCHED THEM!
HE...
...DESIGNED THEIR MASKS TO FEEL LIKE DUMMY HEADS!!

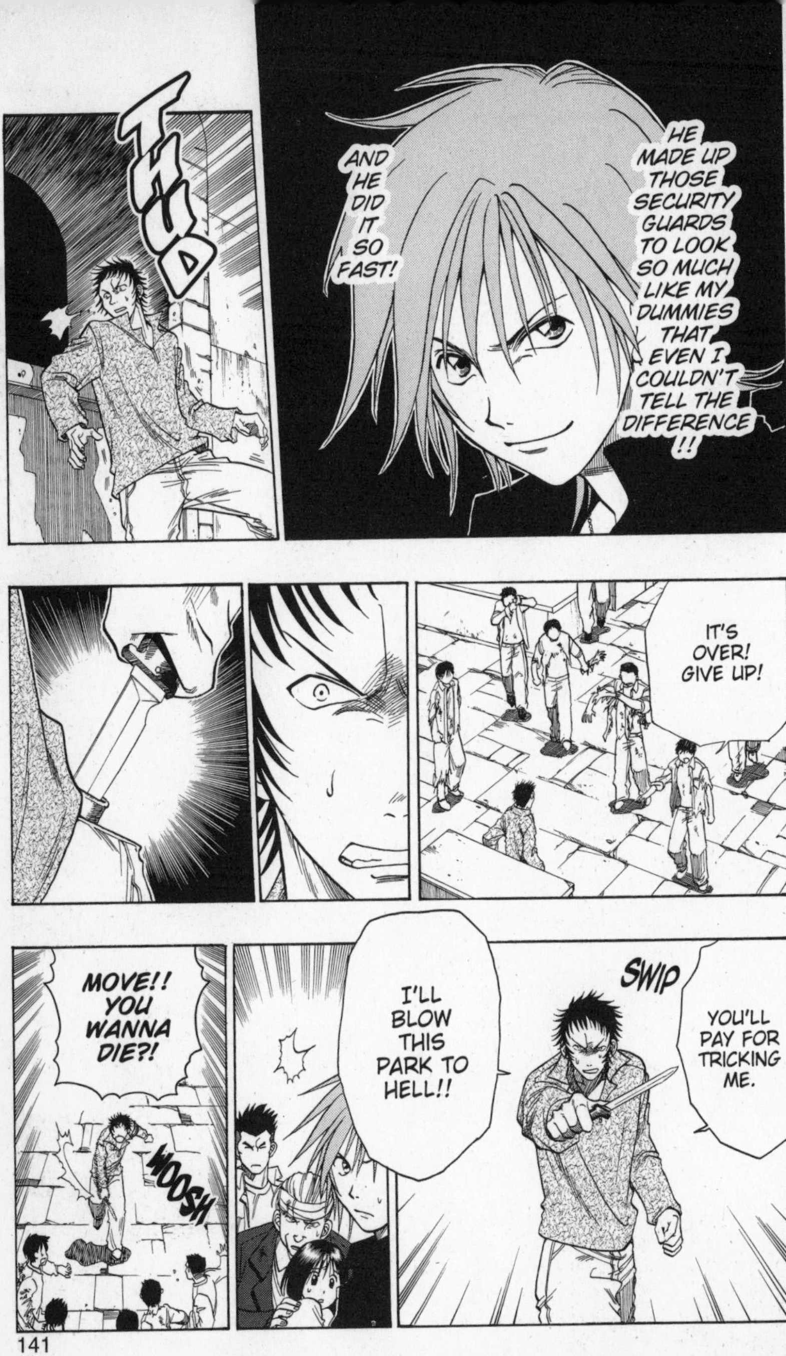
HE MADE UP THOSE SECURITY GUARDS TO LOOK SO MUCH LIKE MY DUMMIES THAT EVEN I COULDN'T TELL THE DIFFERENCE!!
AND HE DID IT SO FAST!
THUD
IT'S OVER! GIVE UP!
SWIP
YOU'LL PAY FOR TRICKING ME.
I'LL BLOW THIS PARK TO HELL!!
MOVE!! YOU WANNA DIE?!
WOOSH

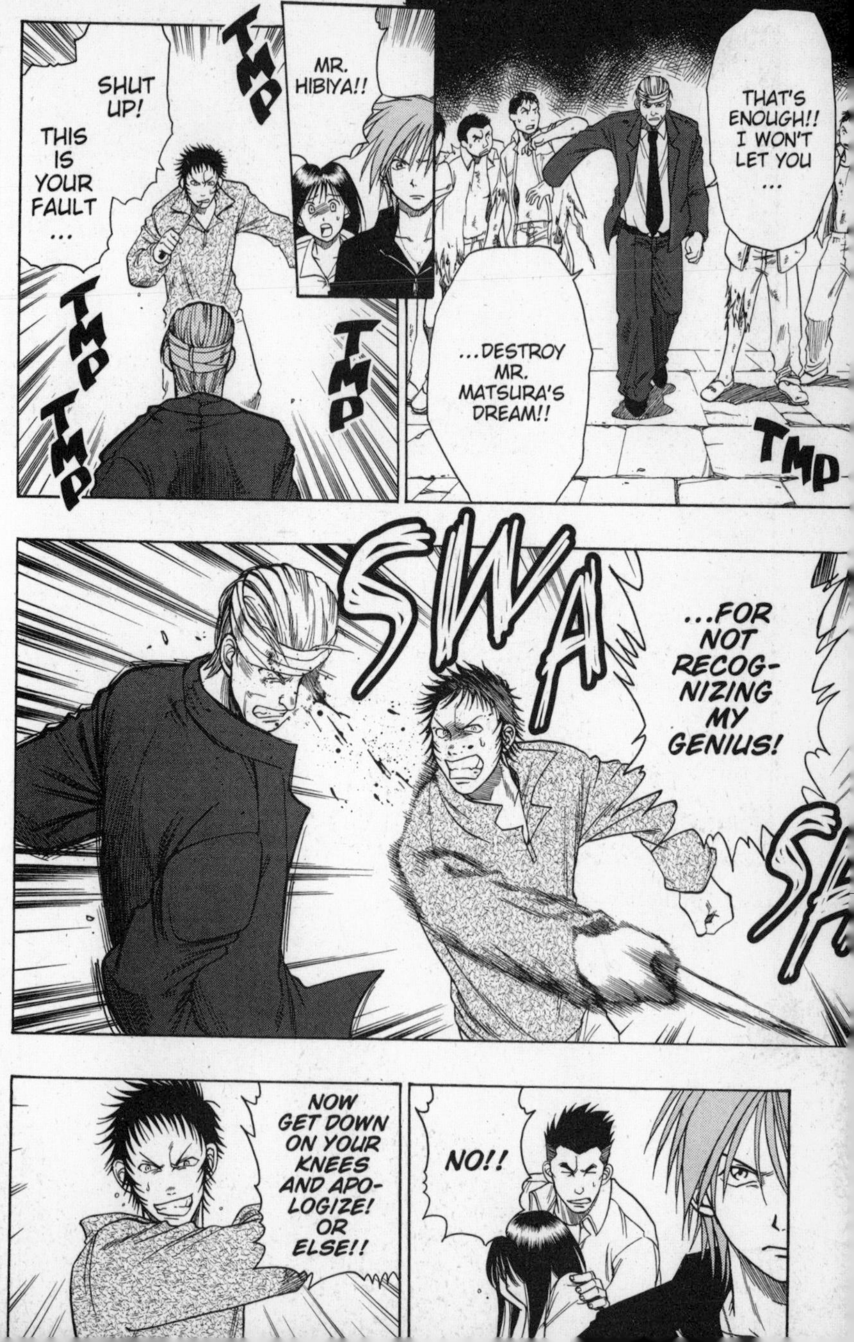
THAT'S ENOUGH!! I WON'T LET YOU ...
...DESTROY MR. MATSURA'S DREAM!!
TMP
MR. HIBIYA!!
TMP
SHUT UP!
THIS IS YOUR FAULT ...
TMP
TMP
TMP
SWA
...FOR NOT RECOGNIZING MY GENIUS!
NO!!
NOW GET DOWN ON YOUR KNEES AND APOLOGIZE! OR ELSE!!

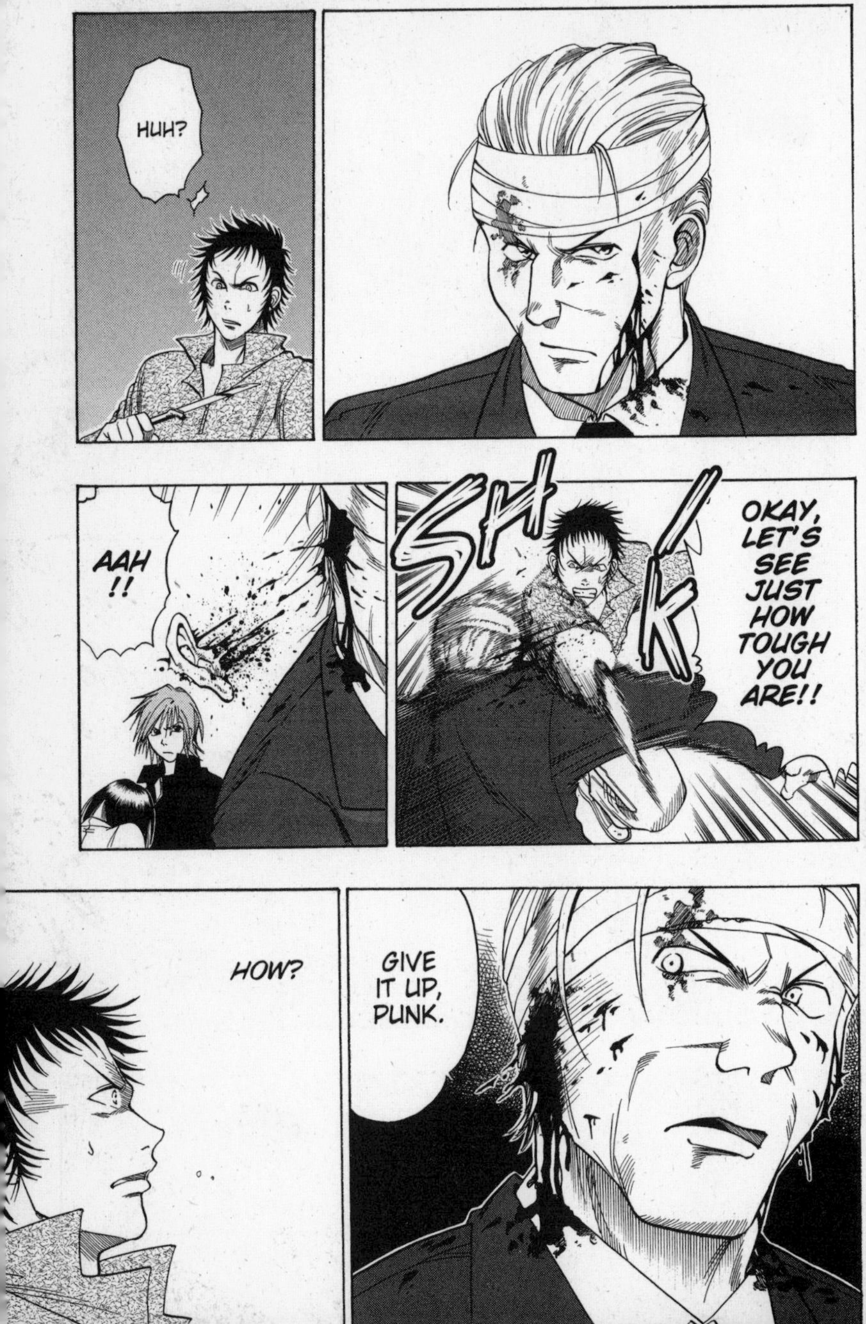
HUH?
SHIK
OKAY, LET'S SEE JUST HOW TOUGH YOU ARE!!
AAH!!
GIVE IT UP, PUNK.
HOW?

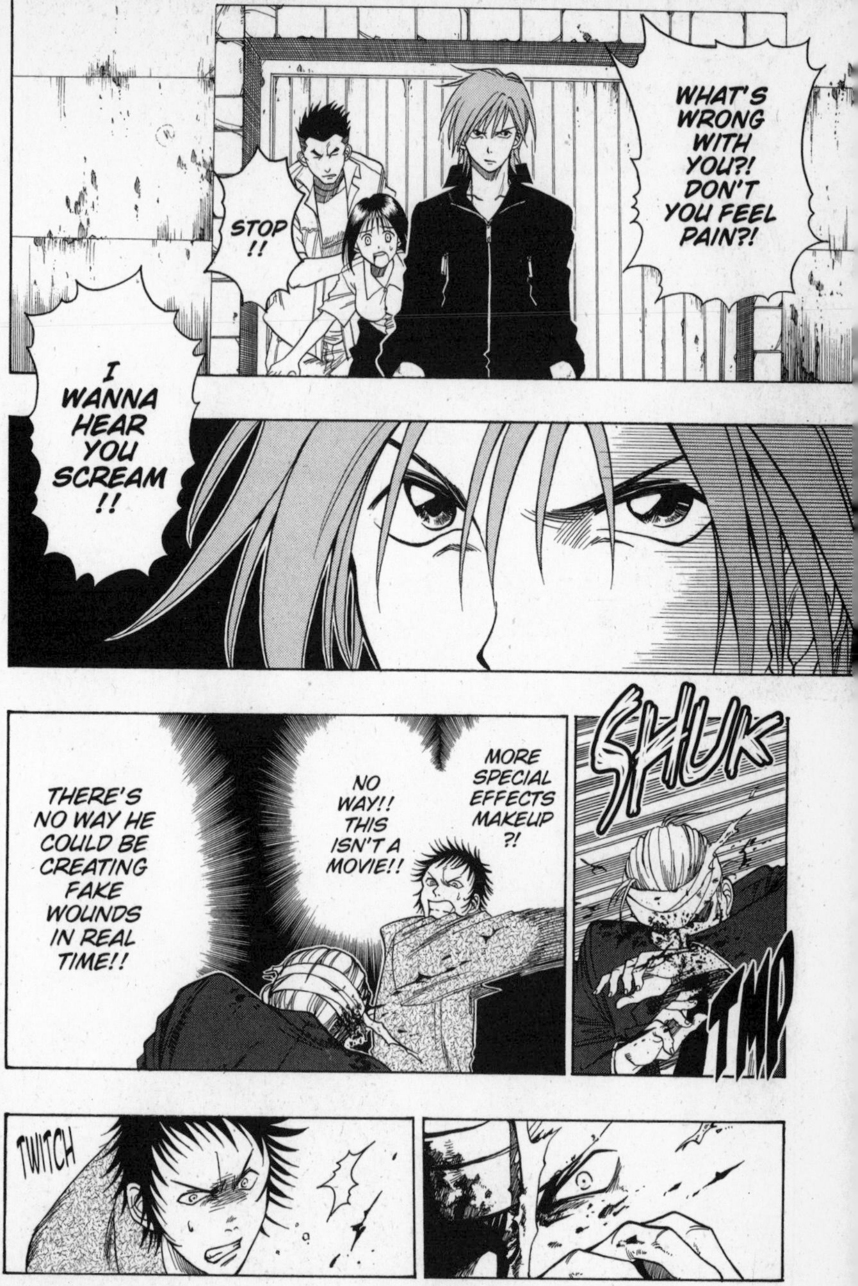
WHAT'S WRONG WITH YOU?! DON'T YOU FEEL PAIN?!
STOP !!
I WANNA HEAR YOU SCREAM !!
SHUK
THD
MORE SPECIAL EFFECTS MAKEUP ?!
NO WAY!! THIS ISN'T A MOVIE!!
THERE'S NO WAY HE COULD BE CREATING FAKE WOUNDS IN REAL TIME!!
TWITCH

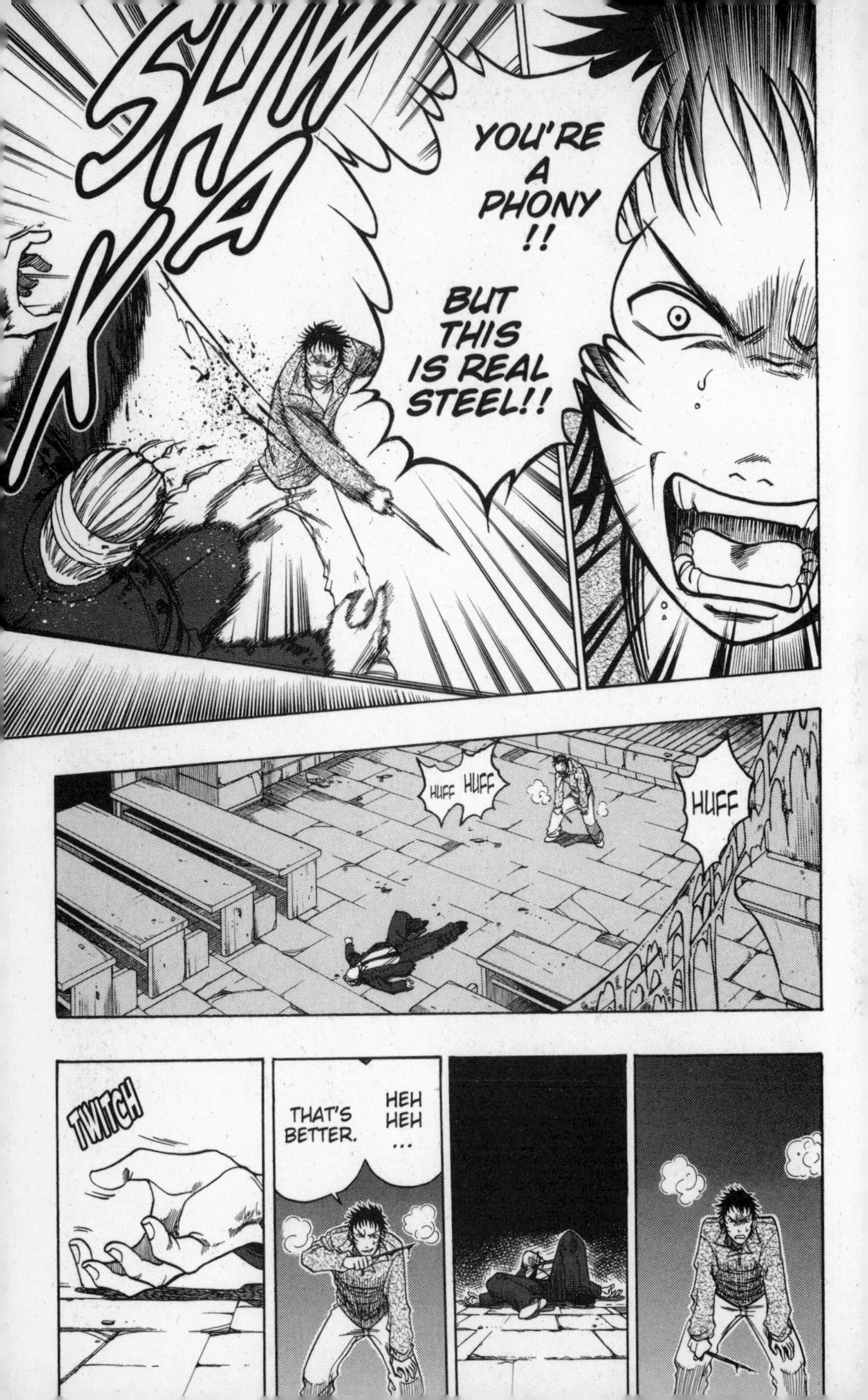
YOU'RE A PHONY!!
BUT THIS IS REAL STEEL!!
SHWAK
HUFF
HUFF HUFF
HEH HEH...
THAT'S BETTER.
TWITCH

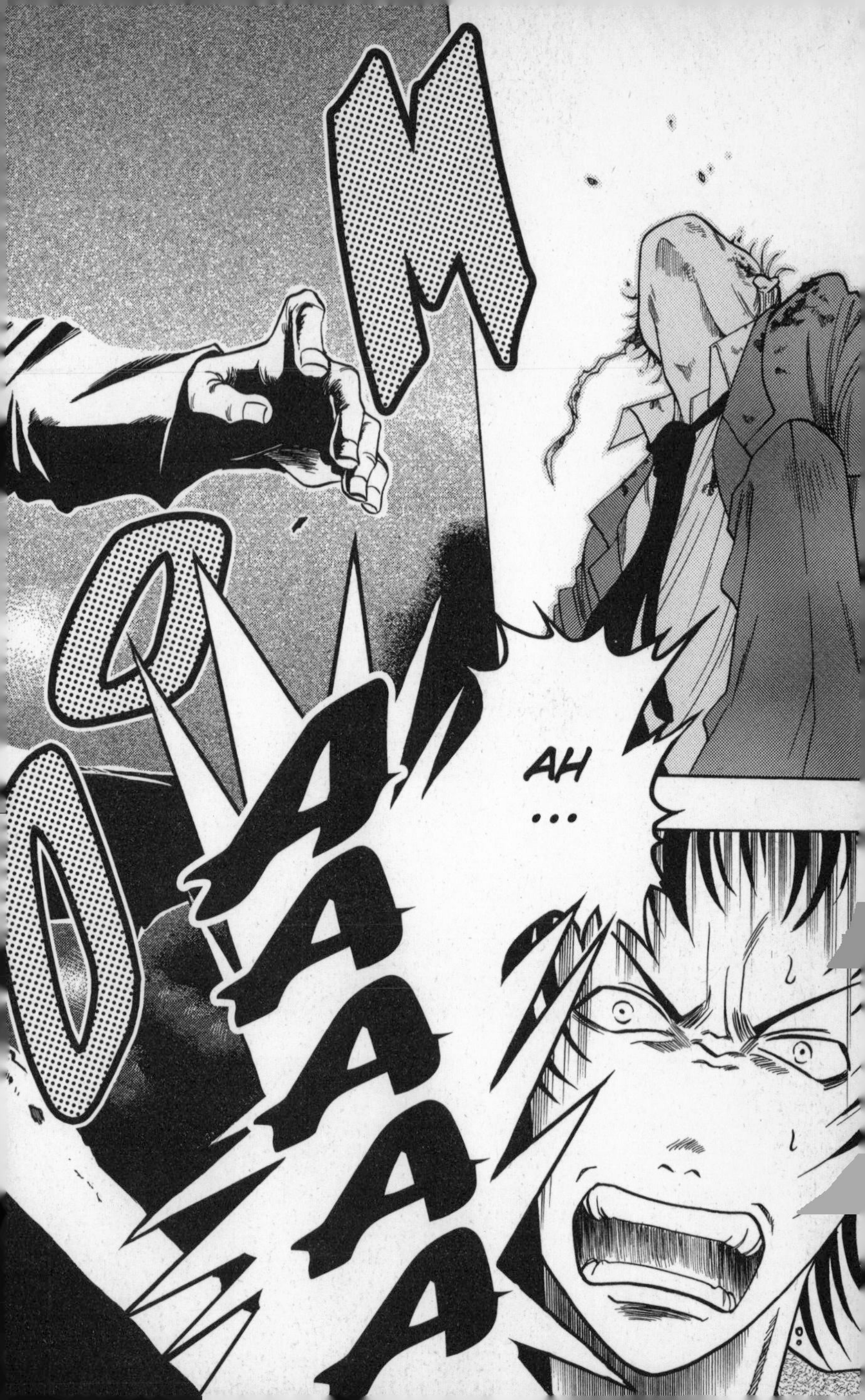
AH ...

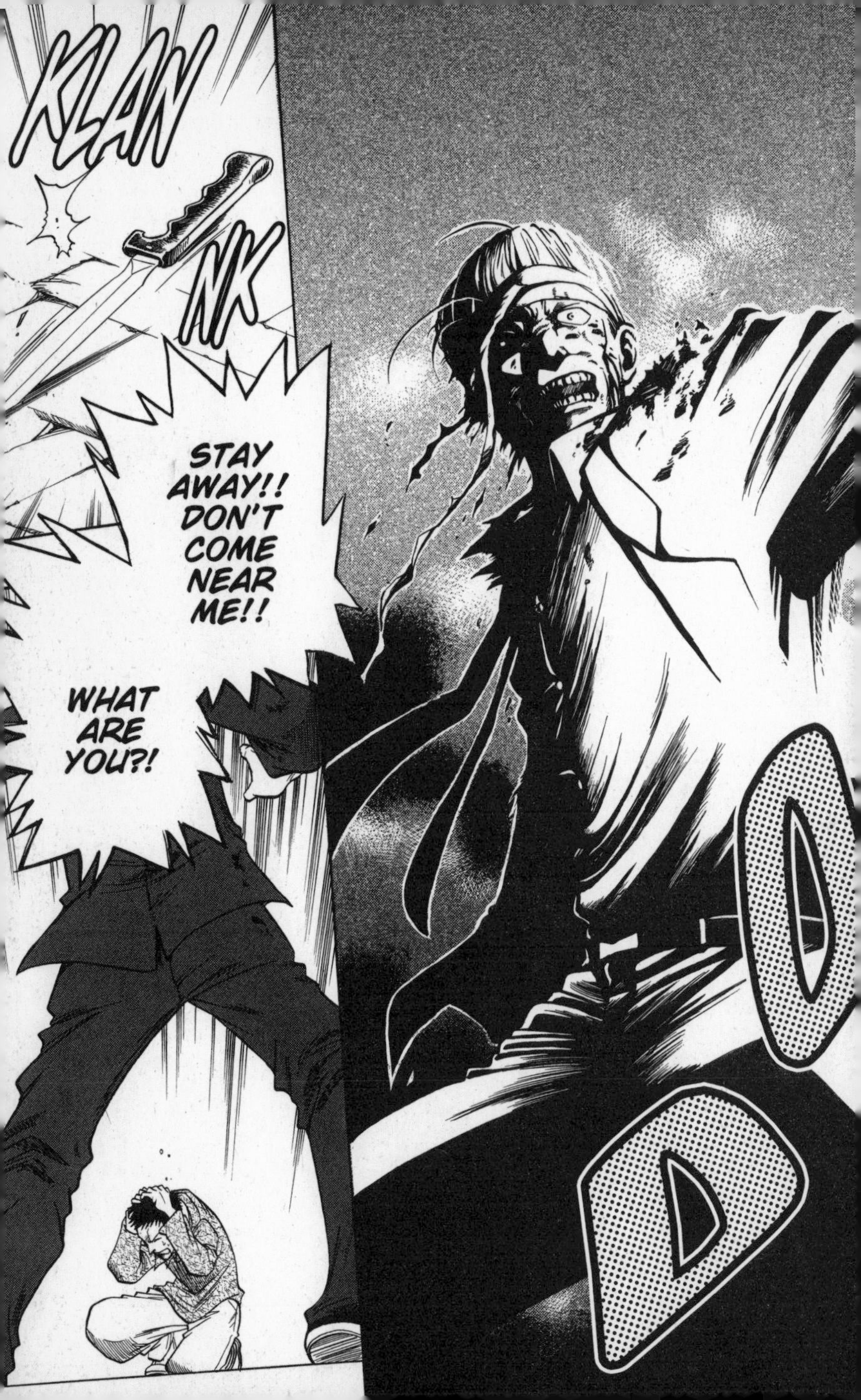
DOOM
KLANNK
STAY AWAY!! DON'T COME NEAR ME!!
WHAT ARE YOU?!

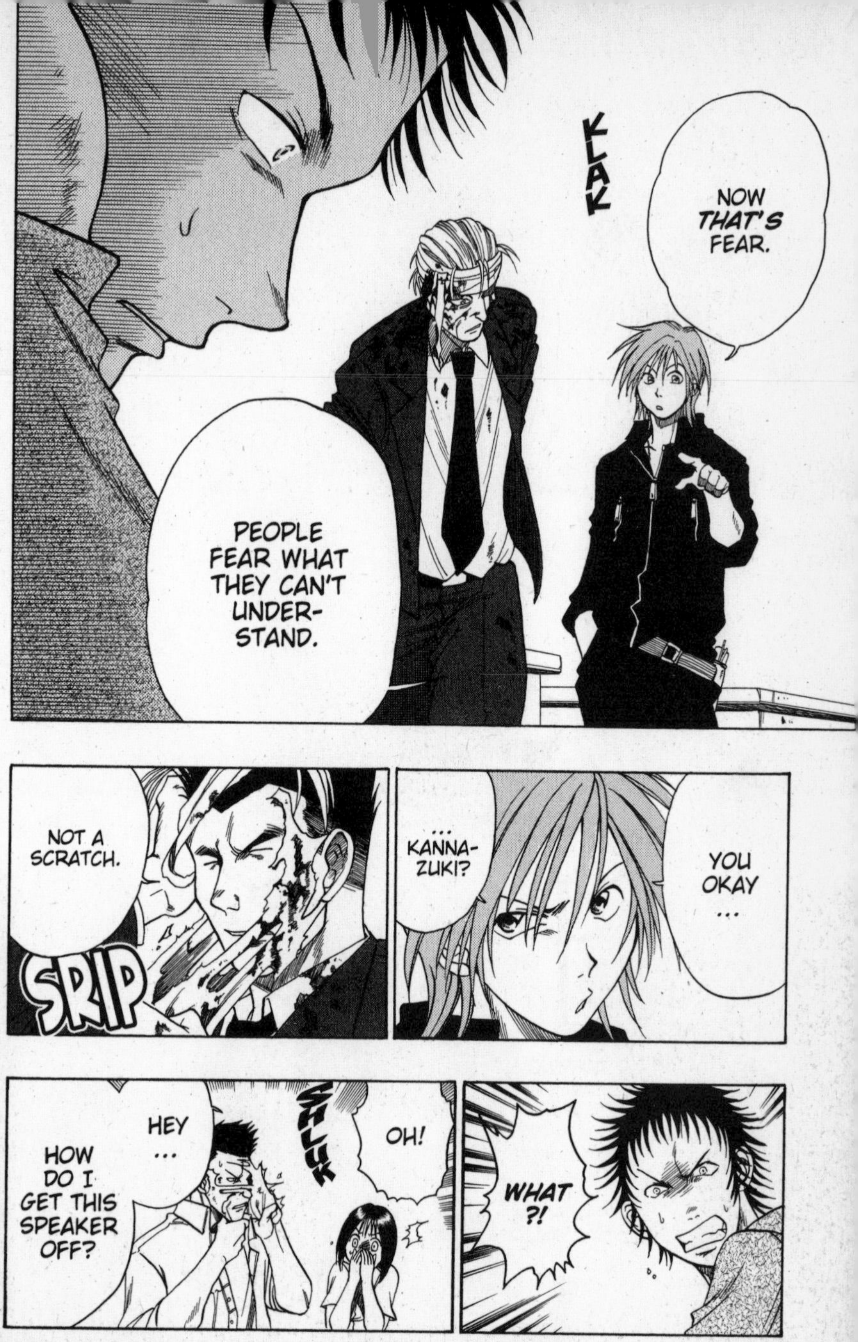
NOW THAT'S FEAR.
KLAK
PEOPLE FEAR WHAT THEY CAN'T UNDER-STAND.
YOU OKAY ...
... KANNA-ZUKI?
NOT A SCRATCH.
SRIP
WHAT ?!
OH!
SHLUK
HEY ...
HOW DO I GET THIS SPEAKER OFF?

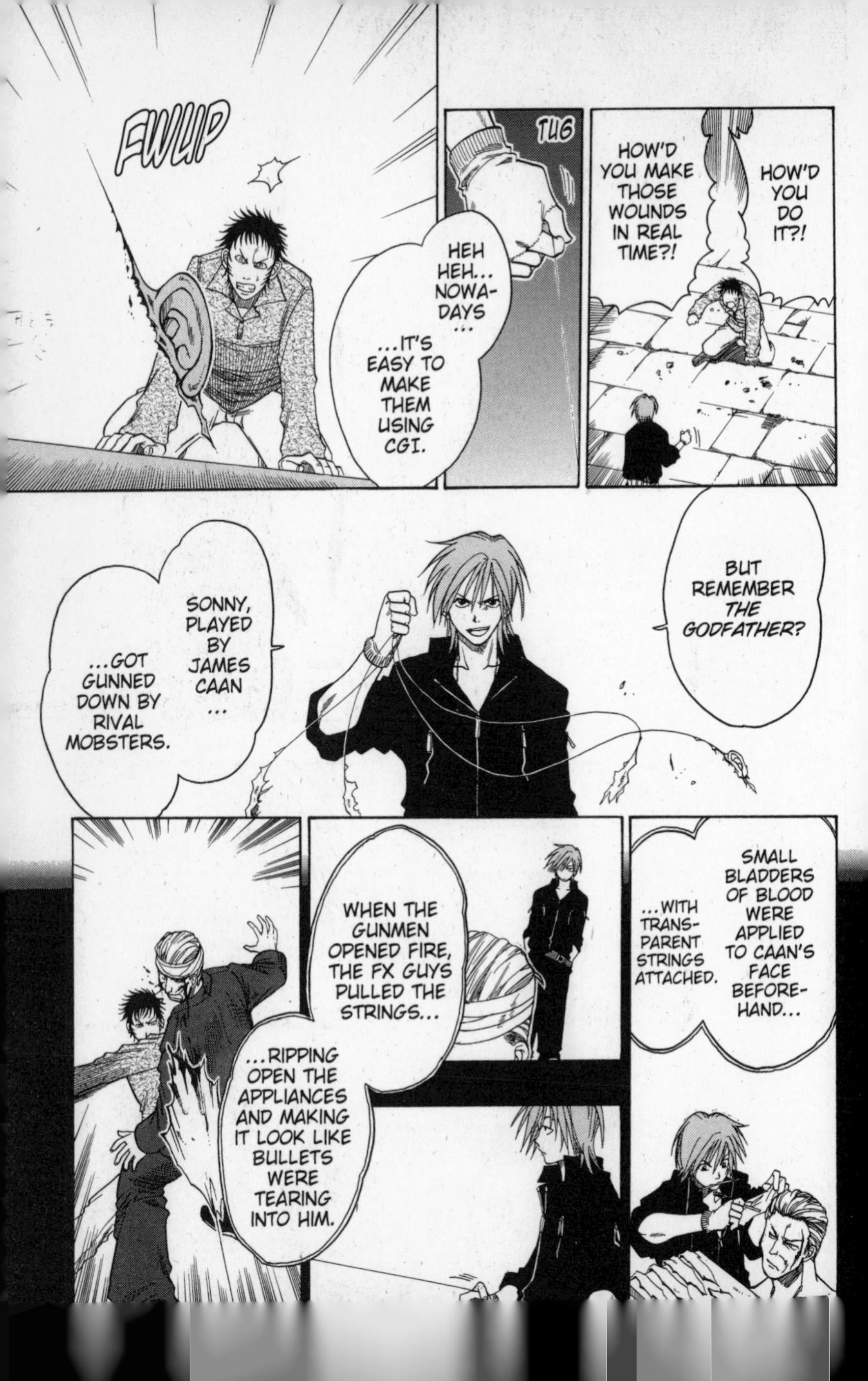
HOW'D YOU DO IT?!
HOW'D YOU MAKE THOSE WOUNDS IN REAL TIME?!
TUG
HEH HEH... NOWA-DAYS...
...IT'S EASY TO MAKE THEM USING CGI.
FWLIP
BUT REMEMBER *THE GODFATHER?*
SONNY, PLAYED BY JAMES CAAN...
...GOT GUNNED DOWN BY RIVAL MOBSTERS.
SMALL BLADDERS OF BLOOD WERE APPLIED TO CAAN'S FACE BEFORE-HAND...
...WITH TRANS-PARENT STRINGS ATTACHED.
WHEN THE GUNMEN OPENED FIRE, THE FX GUYS PULLED THE STRINGS...
...RIPPING OPEN THE APPLIANCES AND MAKING IT LOOK LIKE BULLETS WERE TEARING INTO HIM.

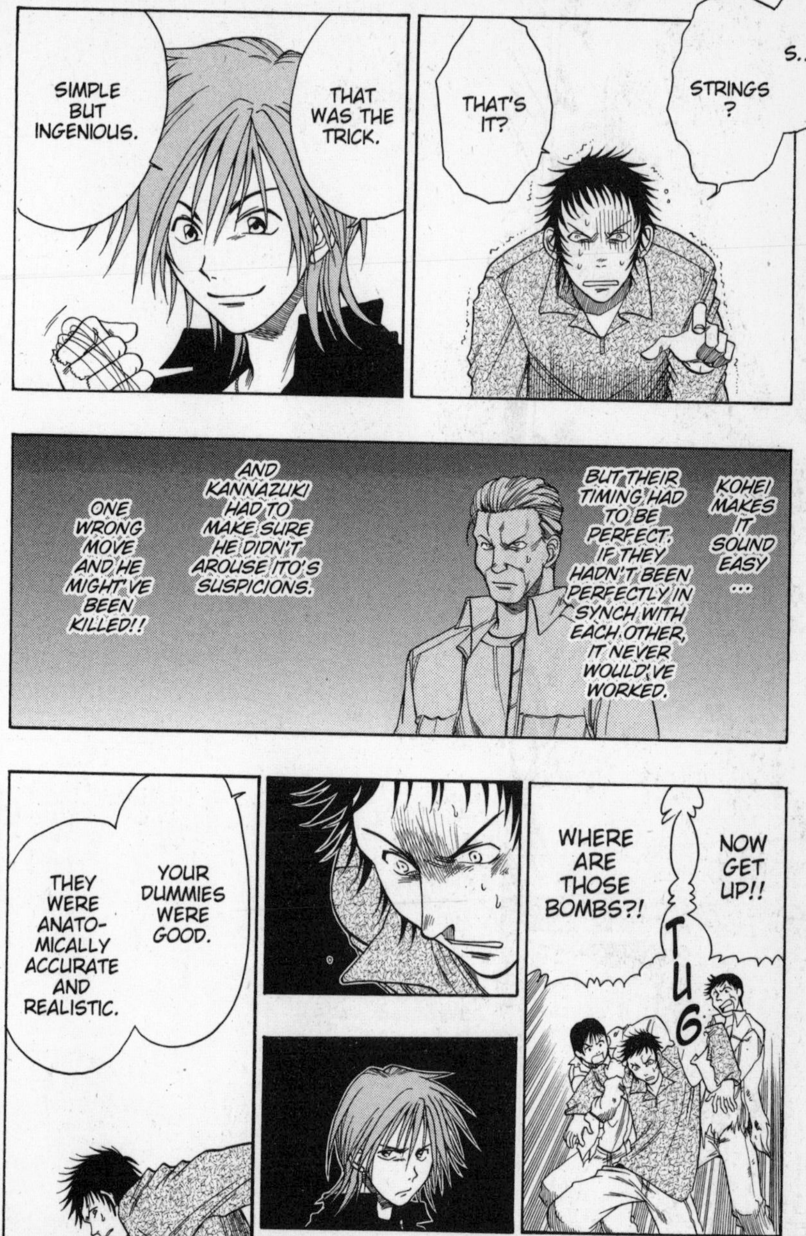
S...
STRINGS?
THAT'S IT?
THAT WAS THE TRICK.
SIMPLE BUT INGENIOUS.
KOHEI MAKES IT SOUND EASY...
BUT THEIR TIMING HAD TO BE PERFECT. IF THEY HADN'T BEEN PERFECTLY IN SYNCH WITH EACH OTHER, IT NEVER WOULD'VE WORKED.
AND KANNAZUKI HAD TO MAKE SURE HE DIDN'T AROUSE ITO'S SUSPICIONS.
ONE WRONG MOVE AND HE MIGHT'VE BEEN KILLED!!
NOW GET UP!!
TUG
WHERE ARE THOSE BOMBS?!
YOUR DUMMIES WERE GOOD.
THEY WERE ANATO-MICALLY ACCURATE AND REALISTIC.

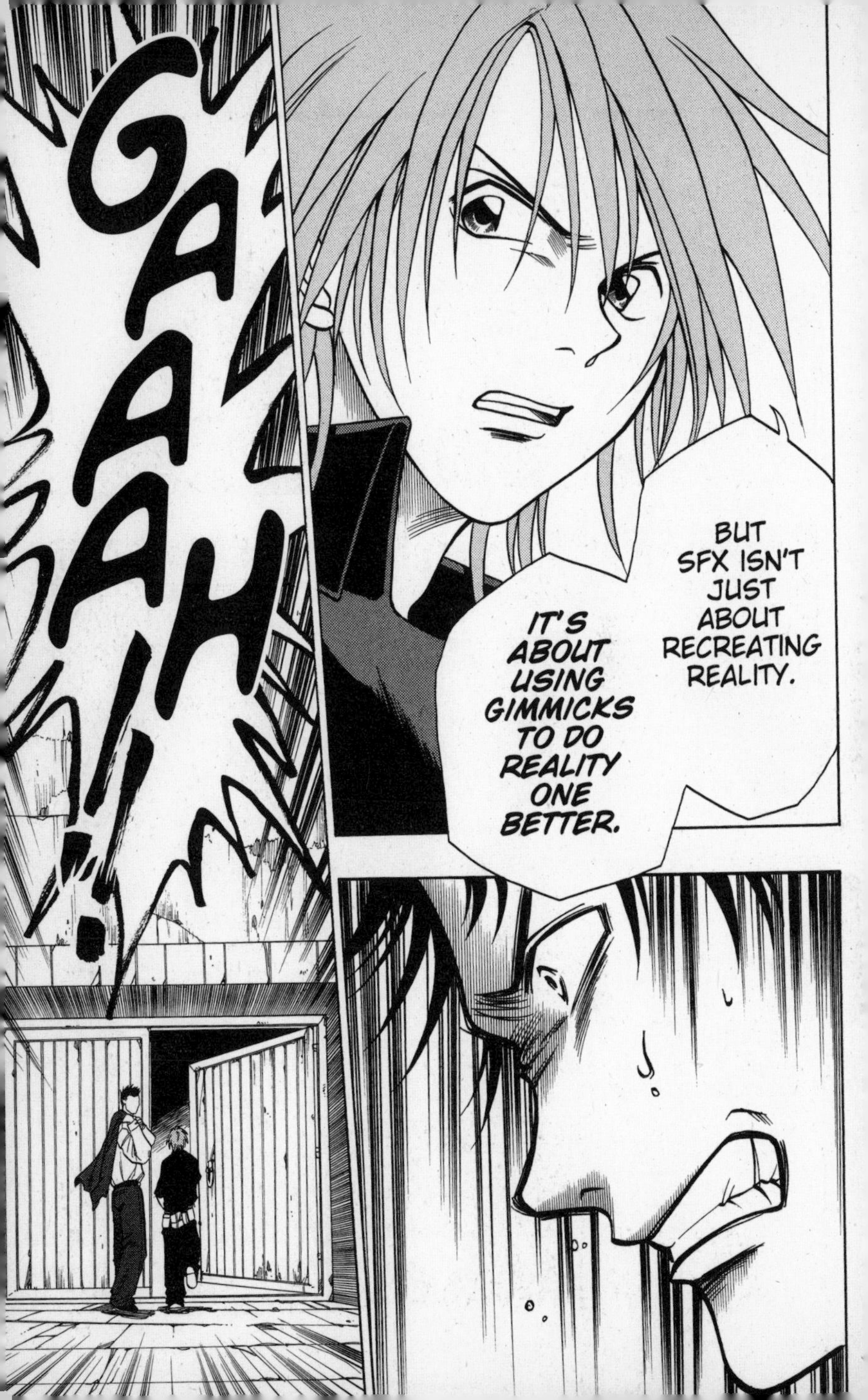
BUT SFX ISN'T JUST ABOUT RECREATING REALITY.
IT'S ABOUT USING GIMMICKS TO DO REALITY ONE BETTER.
GAAAH!!

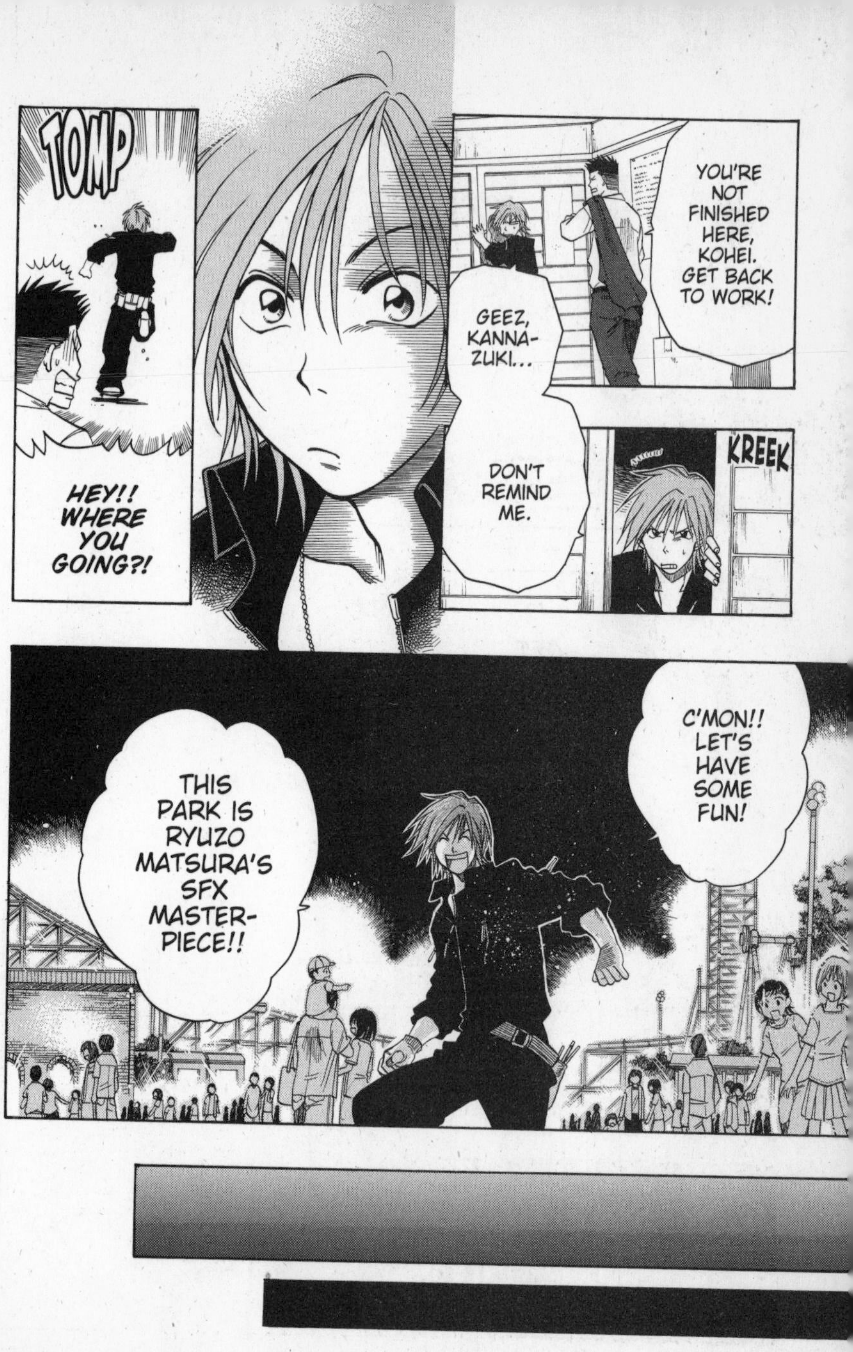
YOU'RE NOT FINISHED HERE, KOHEI. GET BACK TO WORK!
GEEZ, KANNA-ZUKI...
KREEK
DON'T REMIND ME.
TOMP
HEY!! WHERE YOU GOING?!
C'MON!! LET'S HAVE SOME FUN!
THIS PARK IS RYUZO MATSURA'S SFX MASTER-PIECE!!

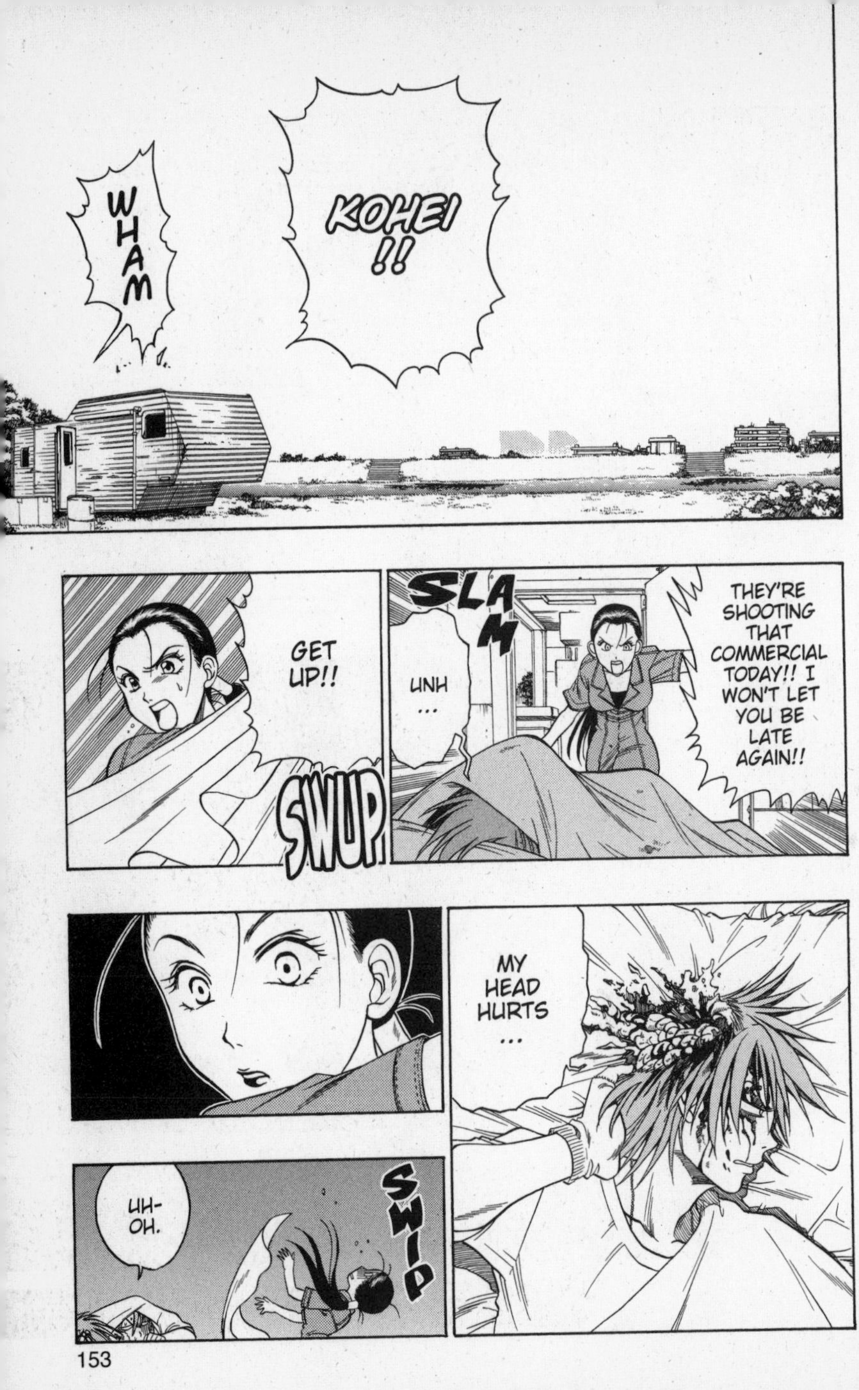
KOHEI !!
WHAM
THEY'RE SHOOTING THAT COMMERCIAL TODAY!! I WON'T LET YOU BE LATE AGAIN!!
SLAM
UNH ...
GET UP!!
SWUP
MY HEAD HURTS ...
SWIP
UH-OH.

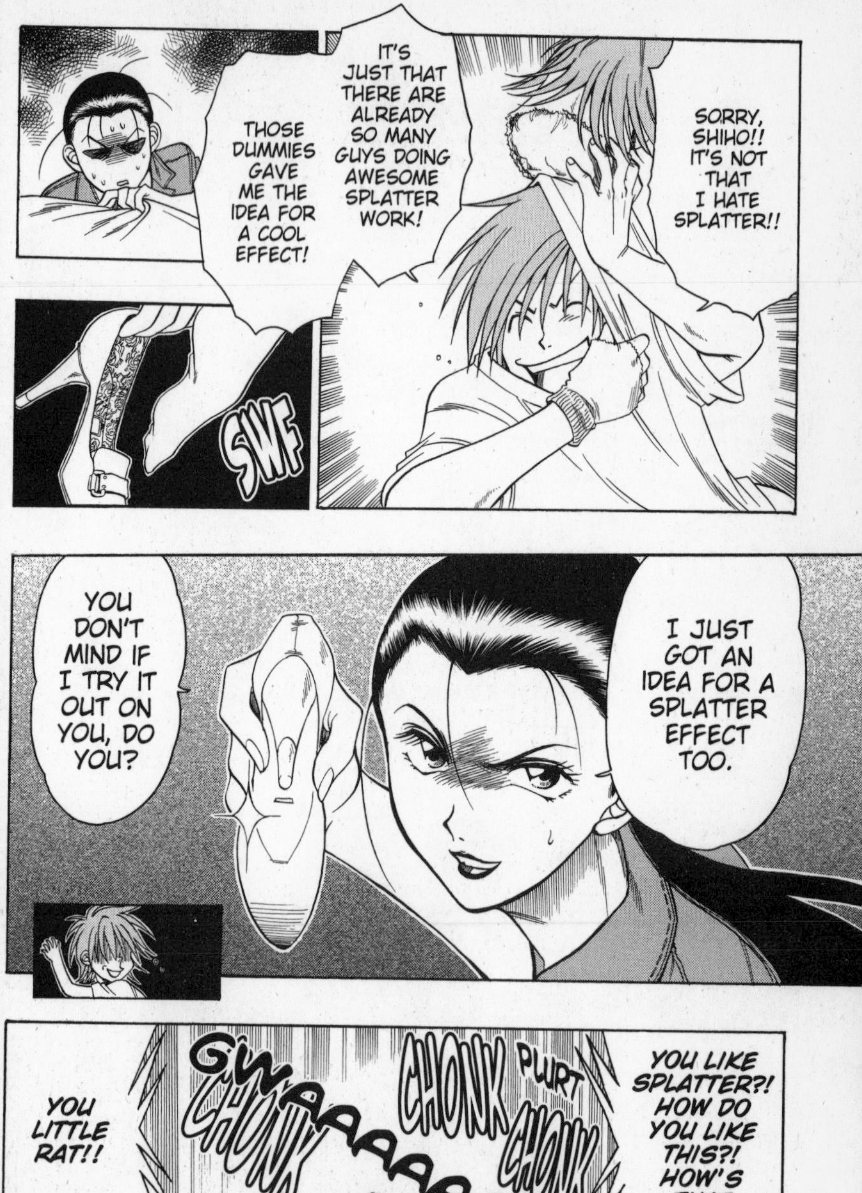

SORRY, SHIHO!! IT'S NOT THAT I HATE SPLATTER!!
IT'S JUST THAT THERE ARE ALREADY SO MANY GUYS DOING AWESOME SPLATTER WORK!
THOSE DUMMIES GAVE ME THE IDEA FOR A COOL EFFECT!
SWF
I JUST GOT AN IDEA FOR A SPLATTER EFFECT TOO.
YOU DON'T MIND IF I TRY IT OUT ON YOU, DO YOU?
YOU LIKE SPLATTER?! HOW DO YOU LIKE THIS?! HOW'S THAT FEEL?!
CHONK
PLURT
CHONK
GWAAAAAAAA
CHONK
YOU LITTLE RAT!!

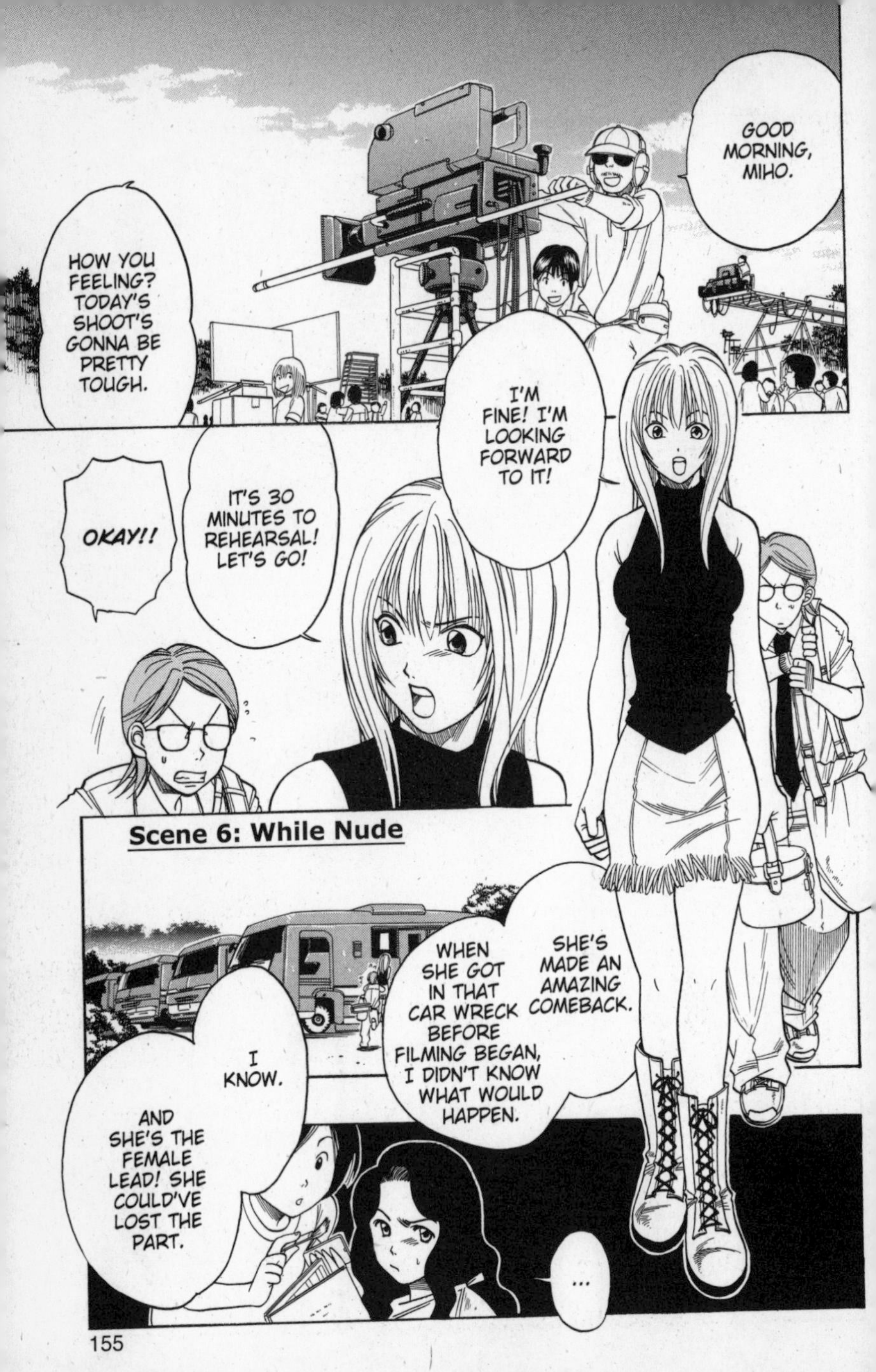
GOOD MORNING, MIHO.
HOW YOU FEELING? TODAY'S SHOOT'S GONNA BE PRETTY TOUGH.
I'M FINE! I'M LOOKING FORWARD TO IT!
IT'S 30 MINUTES TO REHEARSAL! LET'S GO!
OKAY!!
Scene 6: While Nude
SHE'S MADE AN AMAZING COMEBACK.
WHEN SHE GOT IN THAT CAR WRECK BEFORE FILMING BEGAN, I DIDN'T KNOW WHAT WOULD HAPPEN.
I KNOW.
AND SHE'S THE FEMALE LEAD! SHE COULD'VE LOST THE PART.
...

Scene 6: While Nude

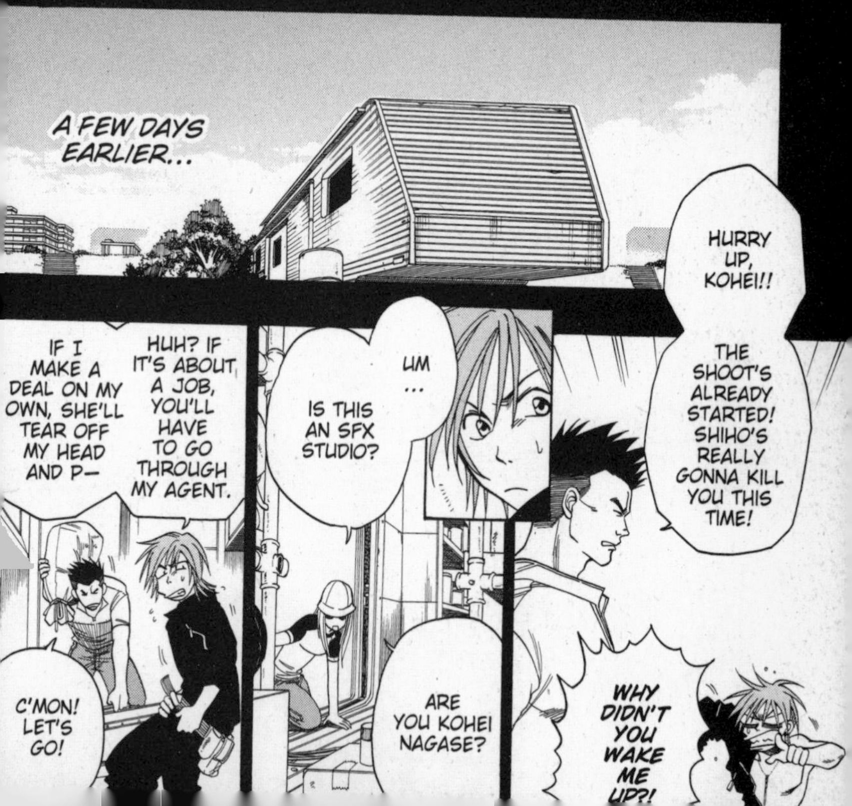
A FEW DAYS EARLIER...
HURRY UP, KOHEI!!
THE SHOOT'S ALREADY STARTED! SHIHO'S REALLY GONNA KILL YOU THIS TIME!
WHY DIDN'T YOU WAKE ME UP?!
UM ...
IS THIS AN SFX STUDIO?
ARE YOU KOHEI NAGASE?
HUH? IF IT'S ABOUT A JOB, YOU'LL HAVE TO GO THROUGH MY AGENT.
IF I MAKE A DEAL ON MY OWN, SHE'LL TEAR OFF MY HEAD AND P—
C'MON! LET'S GO!

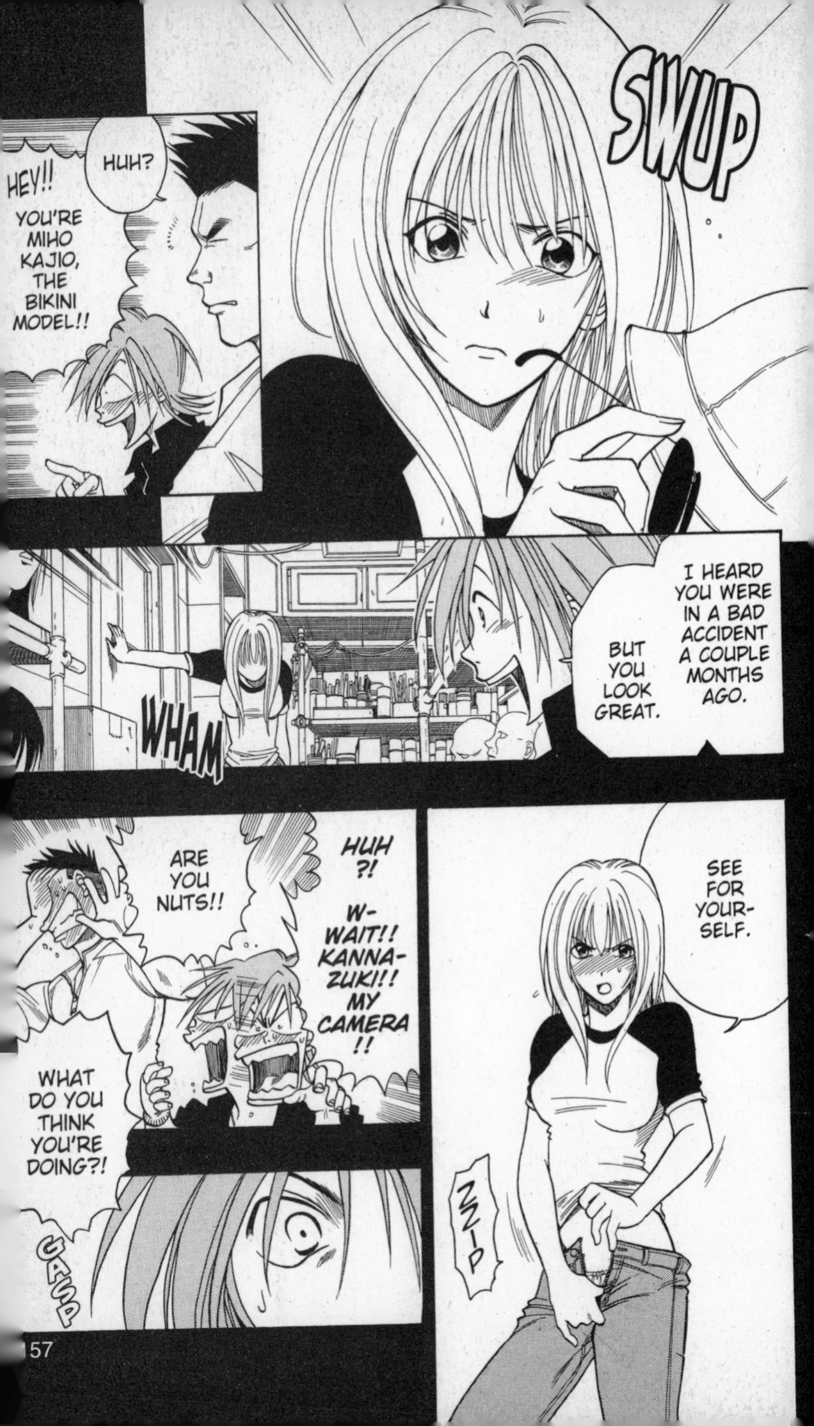
SWUP
HUH?
HEY!!
YOU'RE MIHO KAJIO, THE BIKINI MODEL!!
I HEARD YOU WERE IN A BAD ACCIDENT A COUPLE MONTHS AGO.
BUT YOU LOOK GREAT.
WHAM
SEE FOR YOURSELF.
ZZIP
HUH?!
W-WAIT!! KANNAZUKI!! MY CAMERA!!
ARE YOU NUTS!!
WHAT DO YOU THINK YOU'RE DOING?!
GASP

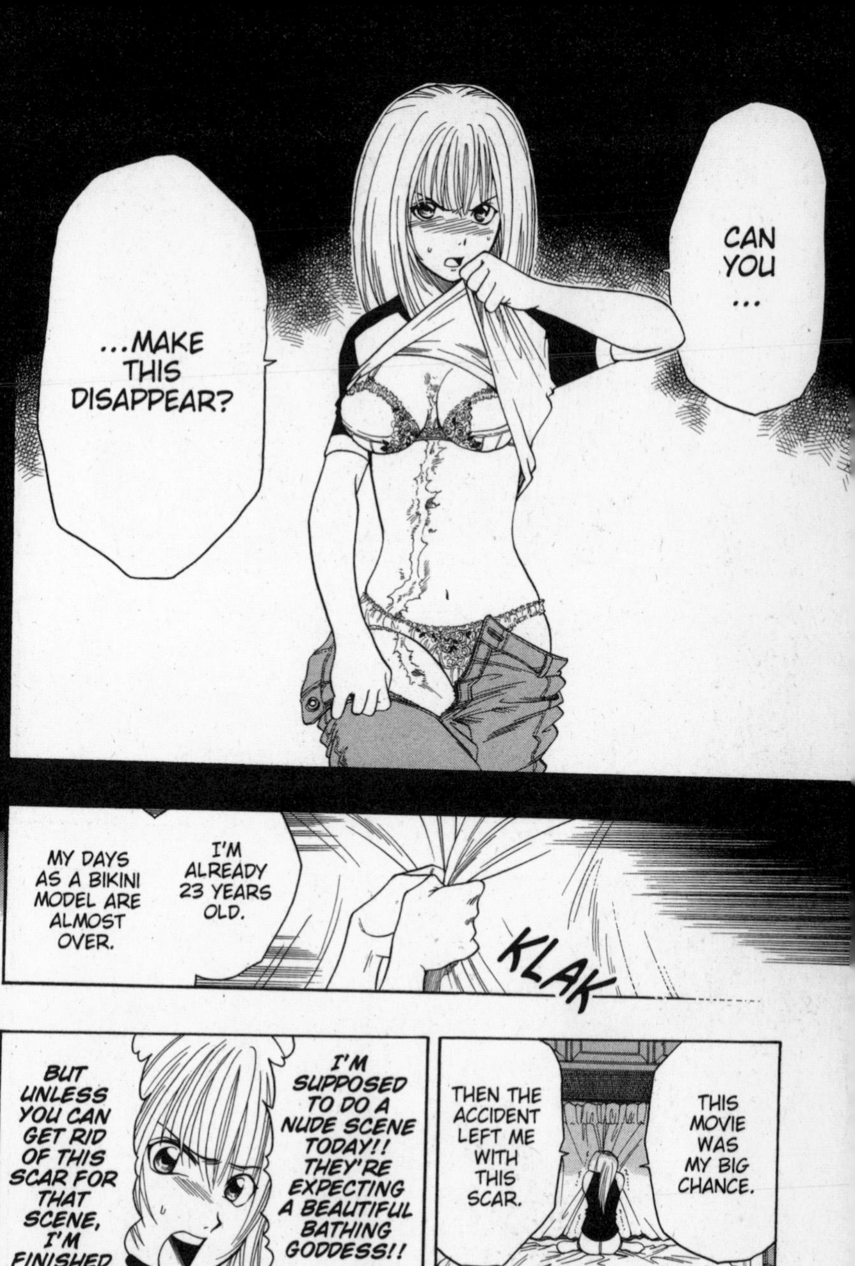
CAN YOU ...
...MAKE THIS DISAPPEAR?
I'M ALREADY 23 YEARS OLD.
MY DAYS AS A BIKINI MODEL ARE ALMOST OVER.
KLAK
THIS MOVIE WAS MY BIG CHANCE.
THEN THE ACCIDENT LEFT ME WITH THIS SCAR.
I'M SUPPOSED TO DO A NUDE SCENE TODAY!! THEY'RE EXPECTING A BEAUTIFUL BATHING GODDESS!!
BUT UNLESS YOU CAN GET RID OF THIS SCAR FOR THAT SCENE, I'M FINISHED!!

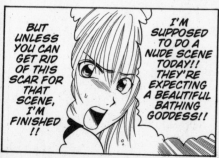

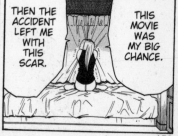

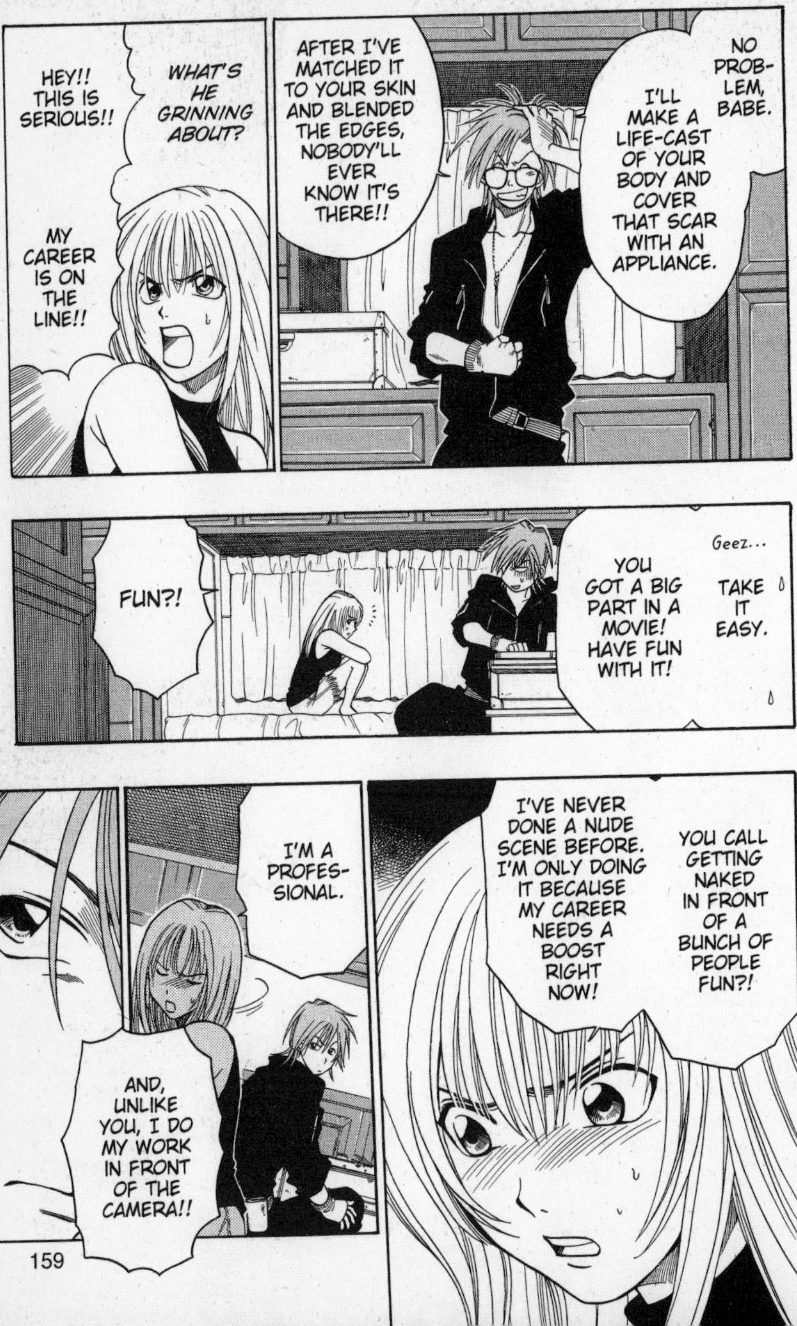
NO PROBLEM, BABE.
I'LL MAKE A LIFE-CAST OF YOUR BODY AND COVER THAT SCAR WITH AN APPLIANCE.
AFTER I'VE MATCHED IT TO YOUR SKIN AND BLENDED THE EDGES, NOBODY'LL EVER KNOW IT'S THERE!!
WHAT'S HE GRINNING ABOUT?
HEY!! THIS IS SERIOUS!!
MY CAREER IS ON THE LINE!!
Geez...
TAKE IT EASY.
YOU GOT A BIG PART IN A MOVIE! HAVE FUN WITH IT!
FUN?!
YOU CALL GETTING NAKED IN FRONT OF A BUNCH OF PEOPLE FUN?!
I'VE NEVER DONE A NUDE SCENE BEFORE. I'M ONLY DOING IT BECAUSE MY CAREER NEEDS A BOOST RIGHT NOW!
I'M A PROFESSIONAL.
AND, UNLIKE YOU, I DO MY WORK IN FRONT OF THE CAMERA!!

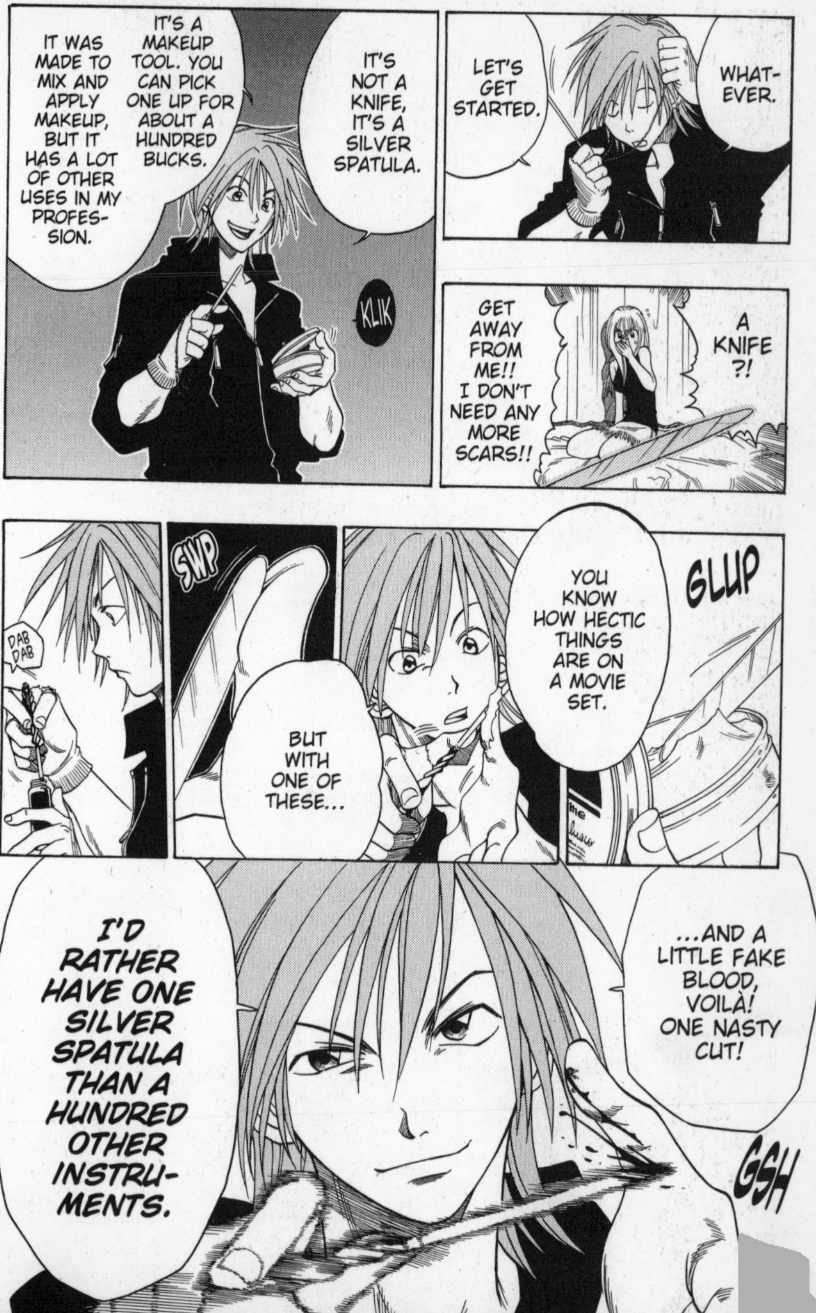
WHAT-EVER.
LET'S GET STARTED.
A KNIFE?!
GET AWAY FROM ME!! I DON'T NEED ANY MORE SCARS!!
IT'S NOT A KNIFE, IT'S A SILVER SPATULA.
IT'S A MAKEUP TOOL. YOU CAN PICK ONE UP FOR ABOUT A HUNDRED BUCKS.
IT WAS MADE TO MIX AND APPLY MAKEUP, BUT IT HAS A LOT OF OTHER USES IN MY PROFES-SION.
KLIK
GLUP
YOU KNOW HOW HECTIC THINGS ARE ON A MOVIE SET.
SWP
BUT WITH ONE OF THESE...
DAB DAB
...AND A LITTLE FAKE BLOOD, VOILÀ! ONE NASTY CUT!
GSH
I'D RATHER HAVE ONE SILVER SPATULA THAN A HUNDRED OTHER INSTRU-MENTS.

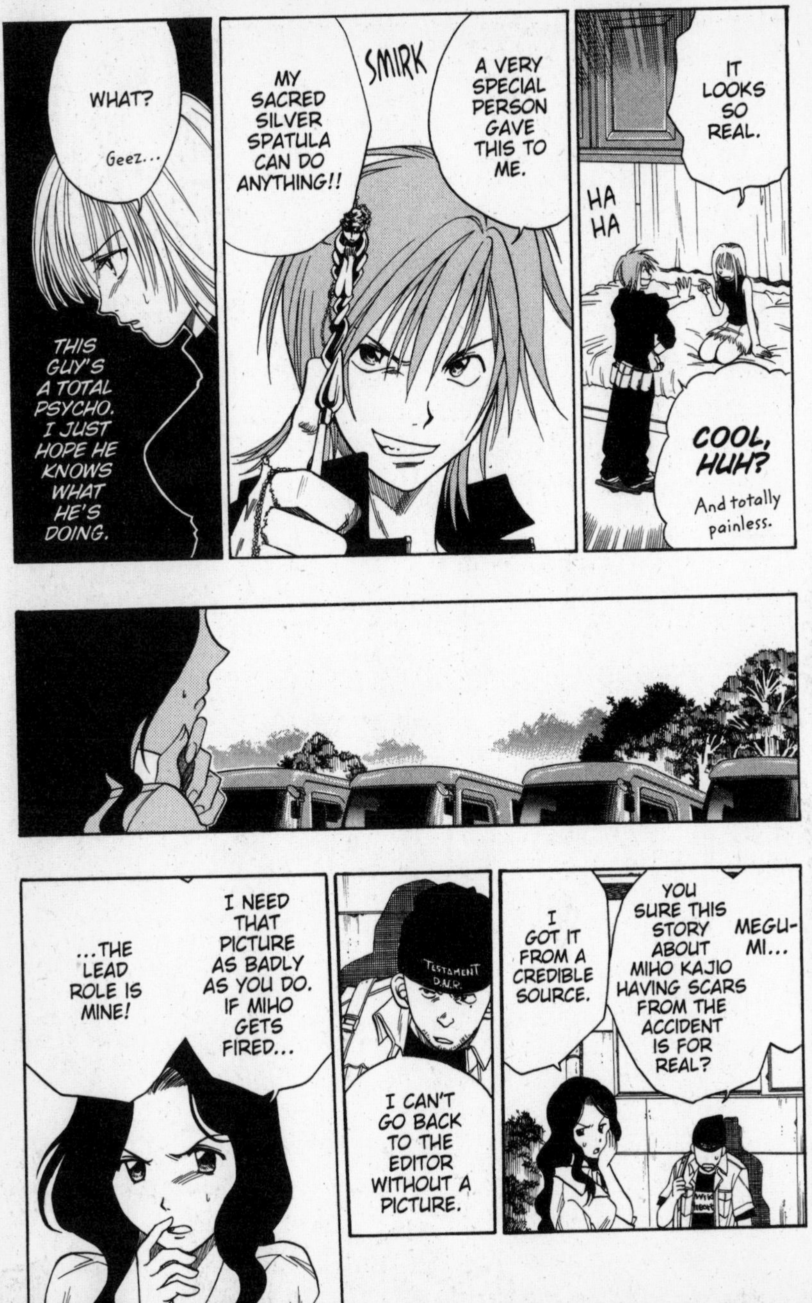
IT LOOKS SO REAL.
HA HA
COOL, HUH?
And totally painless.
A VERY SPECIAL PERSON GAVE THIS TO ME.
SMIRK
MY SACRED SILVER SPATULA CAN DO ANYTHING!!
WHAT?
Geez...
THIS GUY'S A TOTAL PSYCHO. I JUST HOPE HE KNOWS WHAT HE'S DOING.
MEGUMI...
YOU SURE THIS STORY ABOUT MIHO KAJIO HAVING SCARS FROM THE ACCIDENT IS FOR REAL?
I GOT IT FROM A CREDIBLE SOURCE.
TESTAMENT D.N.R.
I CAN'T GO BACK TO THE EDITOR WITHOUT A PICTURE.
I NEED THAT PICTURE AS BADLY AS YOU DO. IF MIHO GETS FIRED...
...THE LEAD ROLE IS MINE!

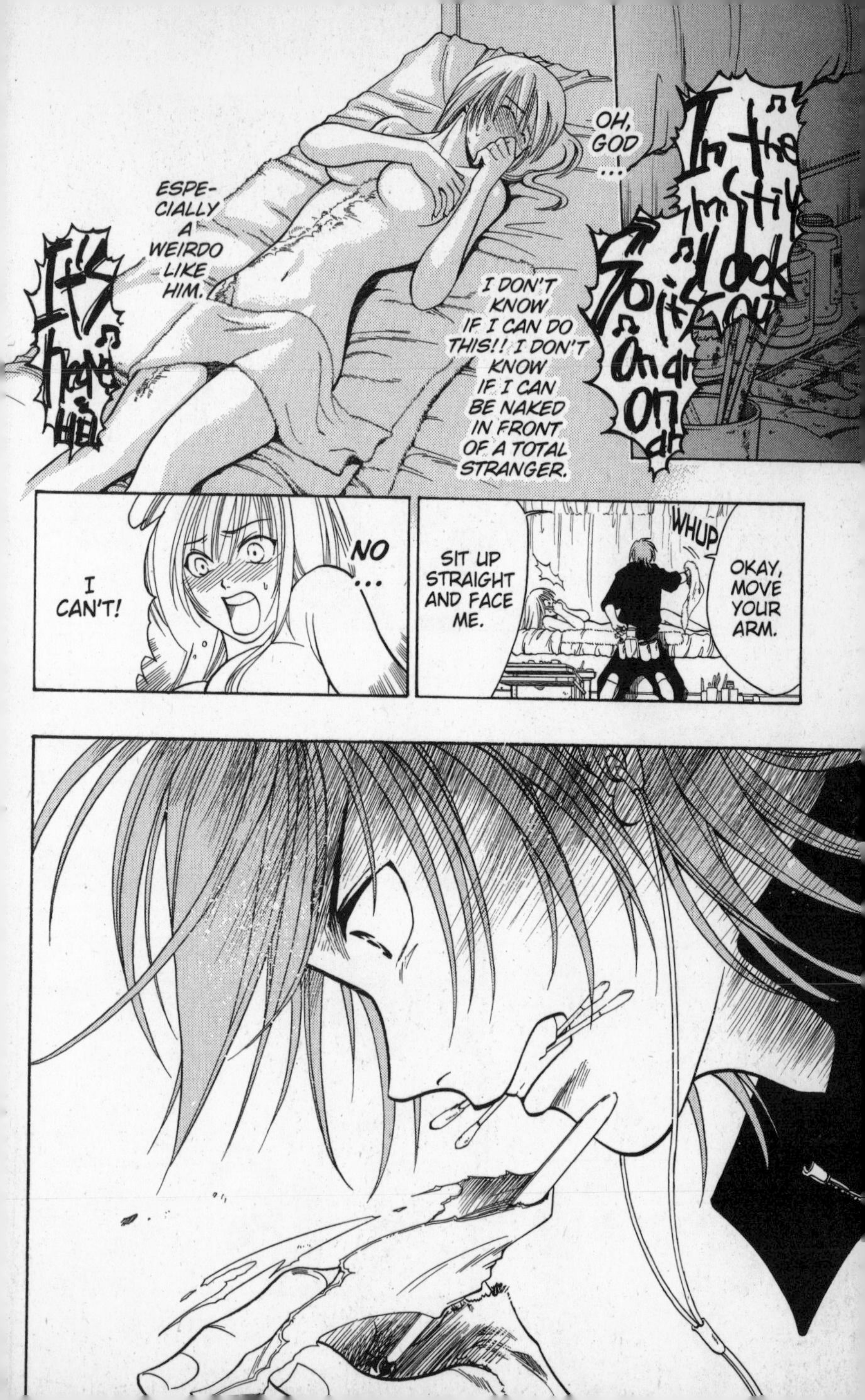
OH, GOD ...
I DON'T KNOW IF I CAN DO THIS!! I DON'T KNOW IF I CAN BE NAKED IN FRONT OF A TOTAL STRANGER.
ESPECIALLY A WEIRDO LIKE HIM.
OKAY, MOVE YOUR ARM.
WHUP
SIT UP STRAIGHT AND FACE ME.
NO ...
I CAN'T!

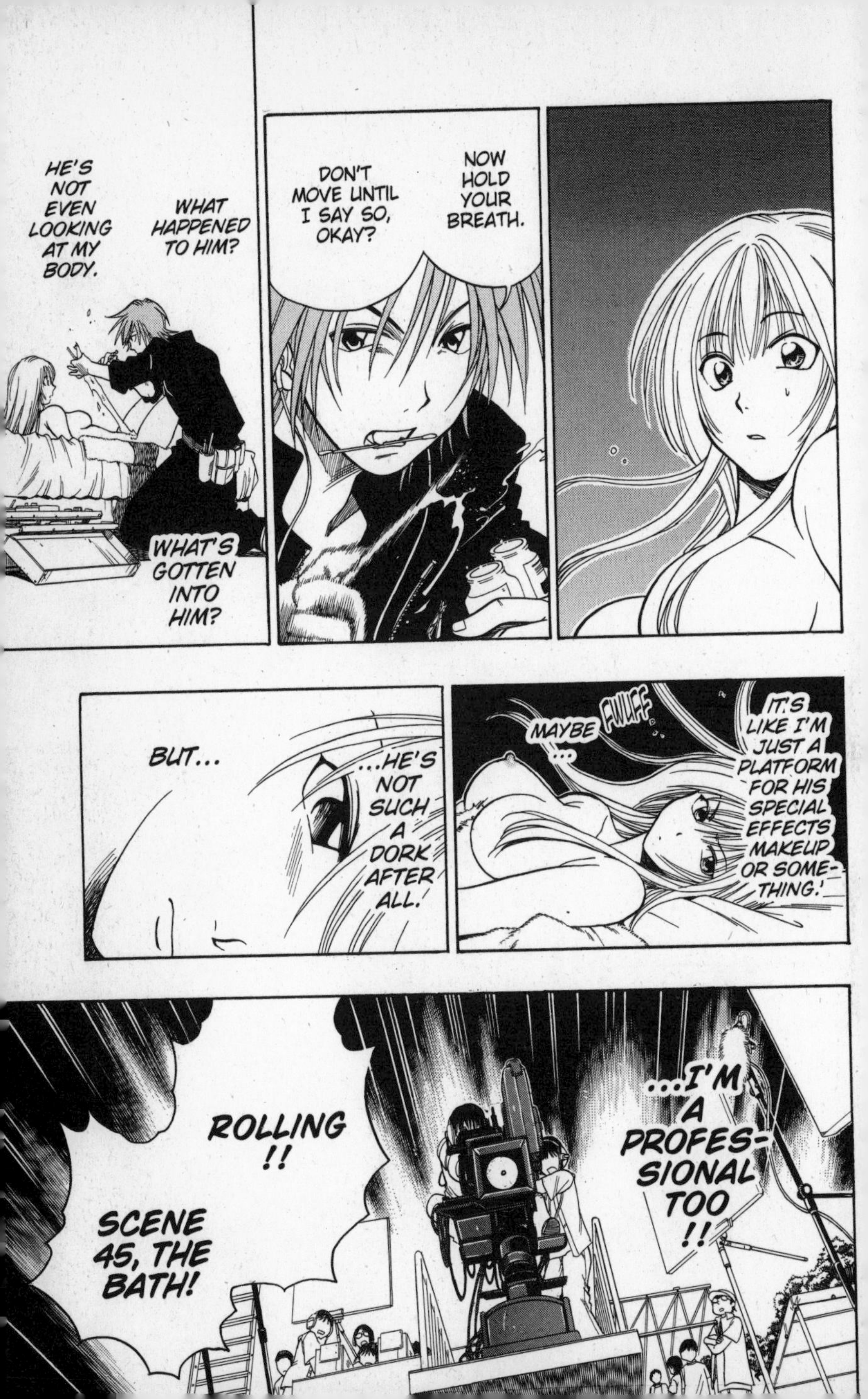
NOW HOLD YOUR BREATH.
DON'T MOVE UNTIL I SAY SO, OKAY?
WHAT HAPPENED TO HIM?
HE'S NOT EVEN LOOKING AT MY BODY.
WHAT'S GOTTEN INTO HIM?
IT'S LIKE I'M JUST A PLATFORM FOR HIS SPECIAL EFFECTS MAKEUP OR SOMETHING.
FWUFF
MAYBE...
BUT...
...HE'S NOT SUCH A DORK AFTER ALL.
...I'M A PROFESSIONAL TOO!!
ROLLING!!
SCENE 45, THE BATH!

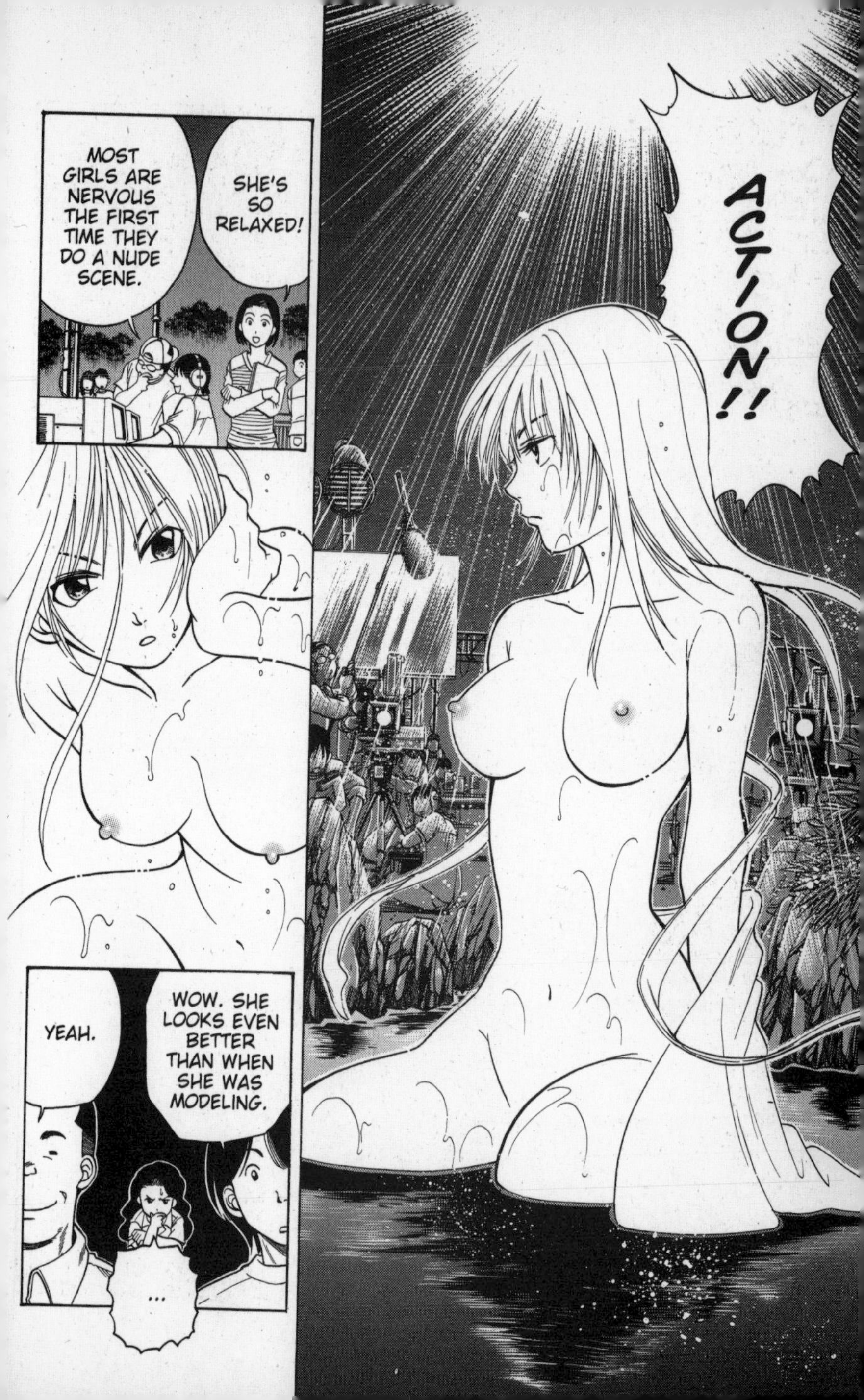
ACTION!!
SHE'S SO RELAXED!
MOST GIRLS ARE NERVOUS THE FIRST TIME THEY DO A NUDE SCENE.
WOW. SHE LOOKS EVEN BETTER THAN WHEN SHE WAS MODELING.
YEAH.
...

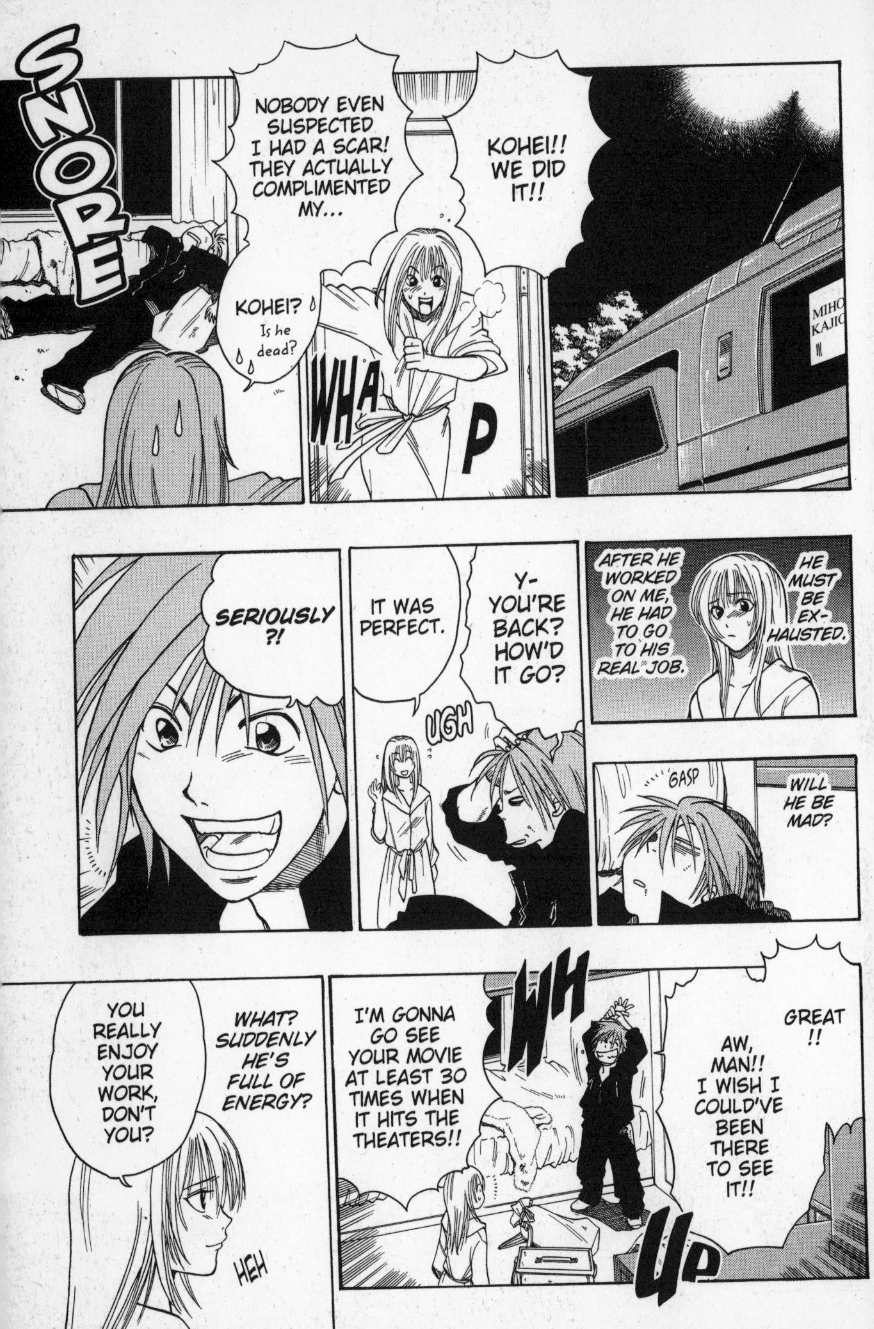
MIHO KAJIO
KOHEI!! WE DID IT!!
NOBODY EVEN SUSPECTED I HAD A SCAR! THEY ACTUALLY COMPLIMENTED MY...
WHAP
SNORE
KOHEI? Is he dead?
HE MUST BE EX-HAUSTED.
AFTER HE WORKED ON ME, HE HAD TO GO TO HIS REAL* JOB.
WILL HE BE MAD?
GASP
Y- YOU'RE BACK? HOW'D IT GO?
IT WAS PERFECT.
UGH
SERIOUSLY?!
GREAT!!
AW, MAN!! I WISH I COULD'VE BEEN THERE TO SEE IT!!
WHUP
I'M GONNA GO SEE YOUR MOVIE AT LEAST 30 TIMES WHEN IT HITS THE THEATERS!!
WHAT? SUDDENLY HE'S FULL OF ENERGY?
YOU REALLY ENJOY YOUR WORK, DON'T YOU?
HEH

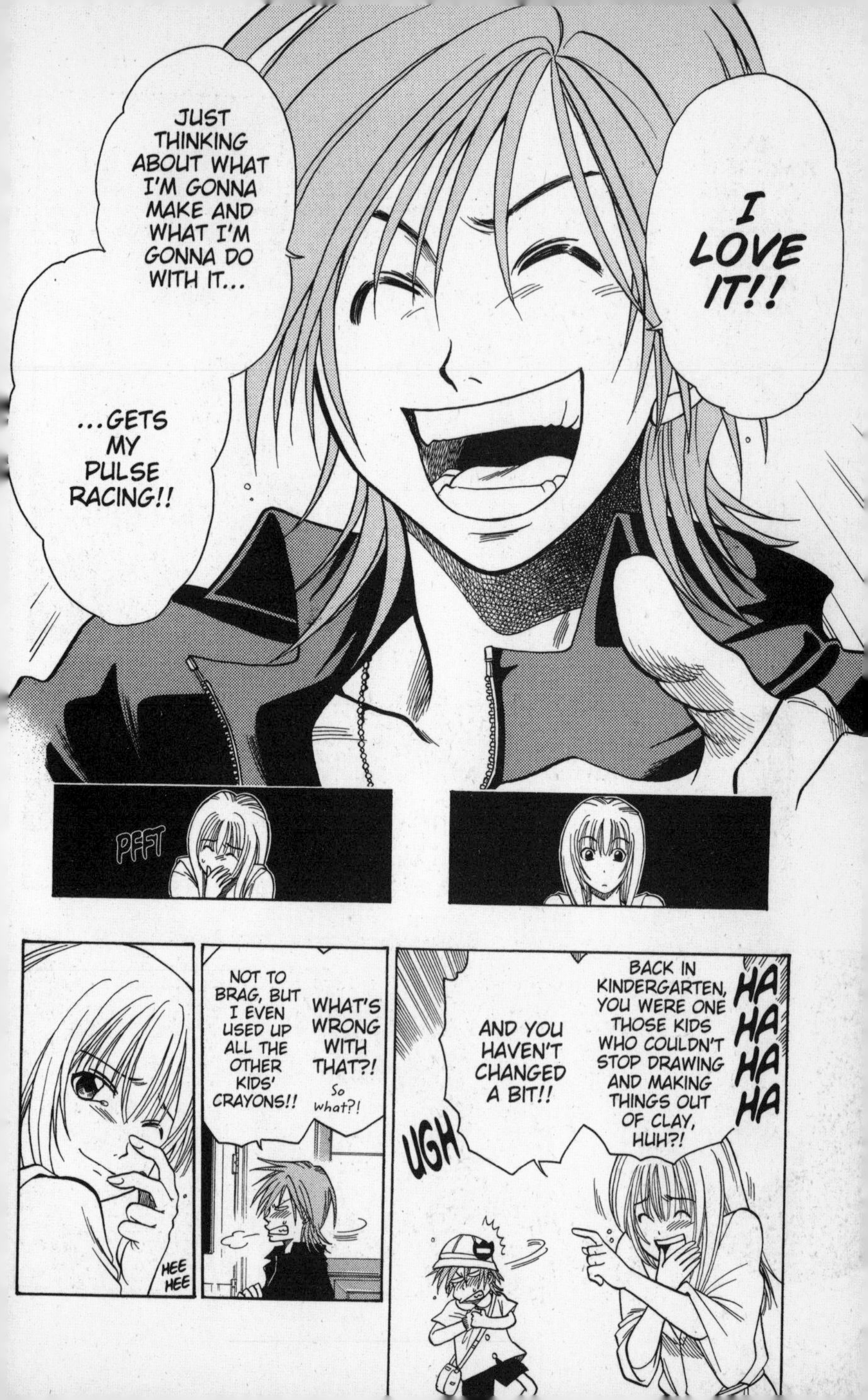
I LOVE IT!!
JUST THINKING ABOUT WHAT I'M GONNA MAKE AND WHAT I'M GONNA DO WITH IT...
...GETS MY PULSE RACING!!
PFFT
HA HA HA HA
BACK IN KINDERGARTEN, YOU WERE ONE THOSE KIDS WHO COULDN'T STOP DRAWING AND MAKING THINGS OUT OF CLAY, HUH?!
AND YOU HAVEN'T CHANGED A BIT!!
UGH
WHAT'S WRONG WITH THAT?!
NOT TO BRAG, BUT I EVEN USED UP ALL THE OTHER KIDS' CRAYONS!!
So what?!
HEE HEE

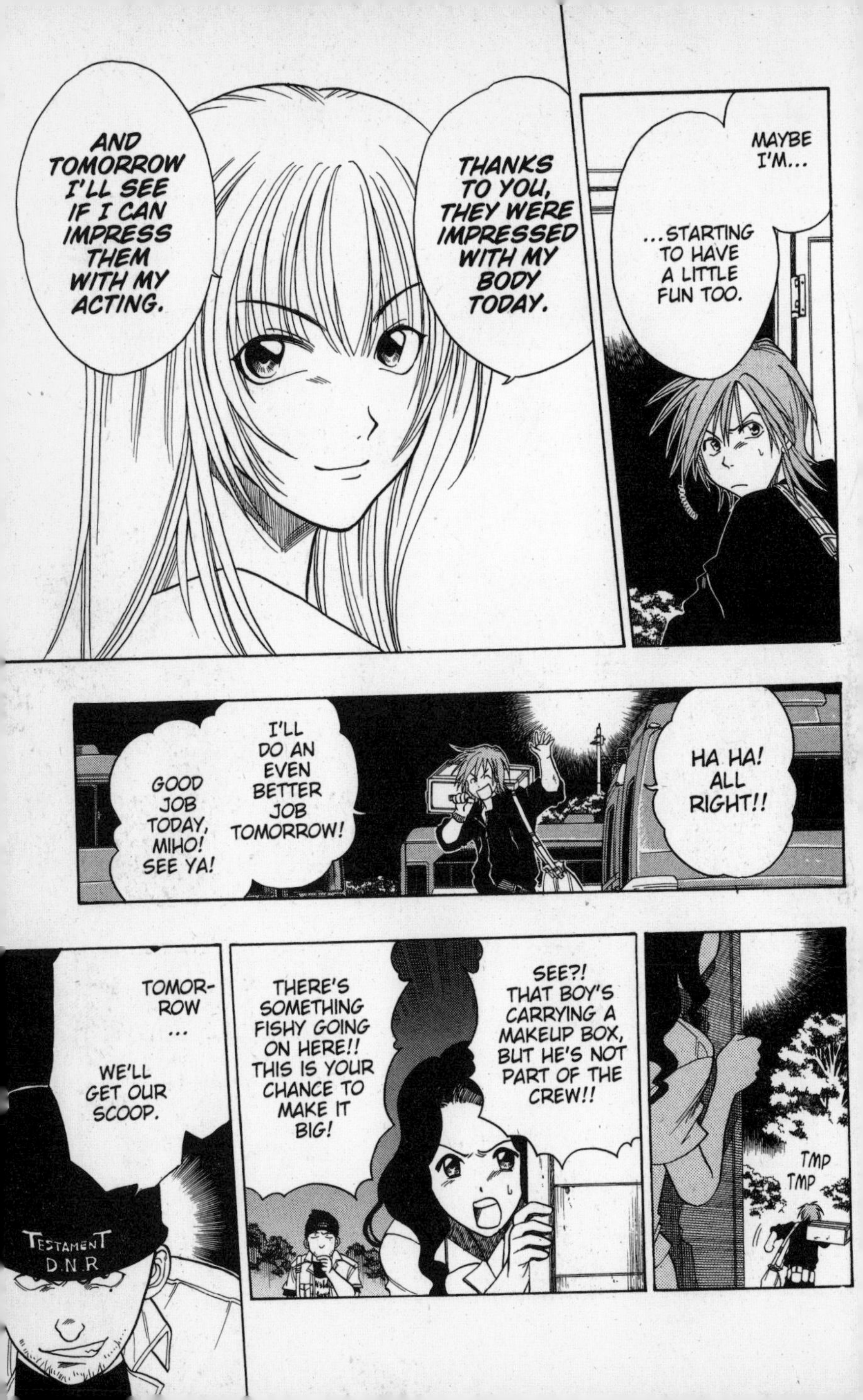
MAYBE I'M...
...STARTING TO HAVE A LITTLE FUN TOO.
THANKS TO YOU, THEY WERE IMPRESSED WITH MY BODY TODAY.
AND TOMORROW I'LL SEE IF I CAN IMPRESS THEM WITH MY ACTING.
HA HA! ALL RIGHT!!
I'LL DO AN EVEN BETTER JOB TOMORROW!
GOOD JOB TODAY, MIHO! SEE YA!
TMP TMP
SEE?! THAT BOY'S CARRYING A MAKEUP BOX, BUT HE'S NOT PART OF THE CREW!!
THERE'S SOMETHING FISHY GOING ON HERE!! THIS IS YOUR CHANCE TO MAKE IT BIG!
TOMOR-ROW...
WE'LL GET OUR SCOOP.
TESTAMENT D.N.R

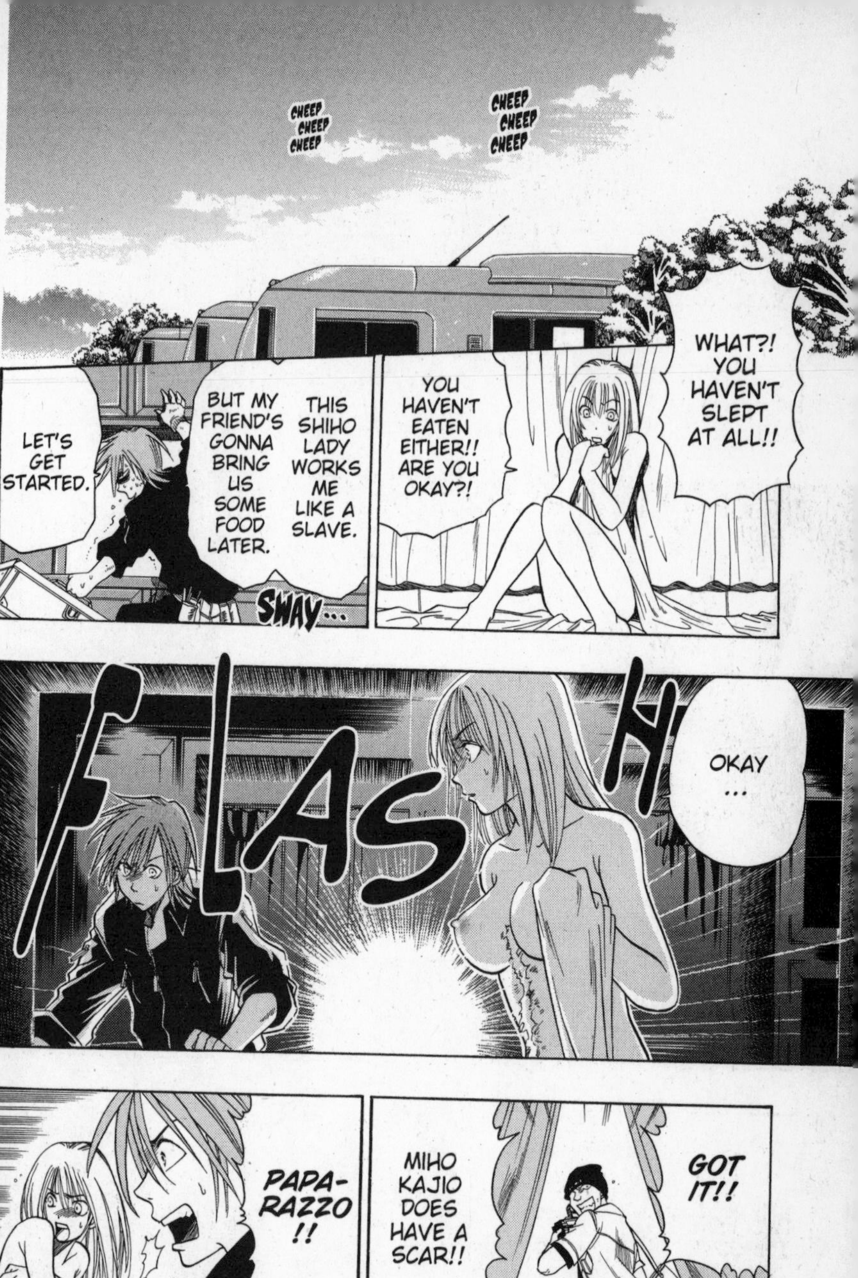
CHEEP CHEEP CHEEP
CHEEP CHEEP CHEEP
WHAT?! YOU HAVEN'T SLEPT AT ALL!!
YOU HAVEN'T EATEN EITHER!! ARE YOU OKAY?!
THIS SHIHO LADY WORKS ME LIKE A SLAVE.
BUT MY FRIEND'S GONNA BRING US SOME FOOD LATER.
SWAY...
LET'S GET STARTED.
OKAY ...
FLASH
GOT IT!!
MIHO KAJIO DOES HAVE A SCAR!!
PAPA-RAZZO!!

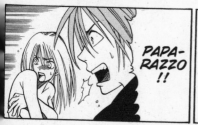

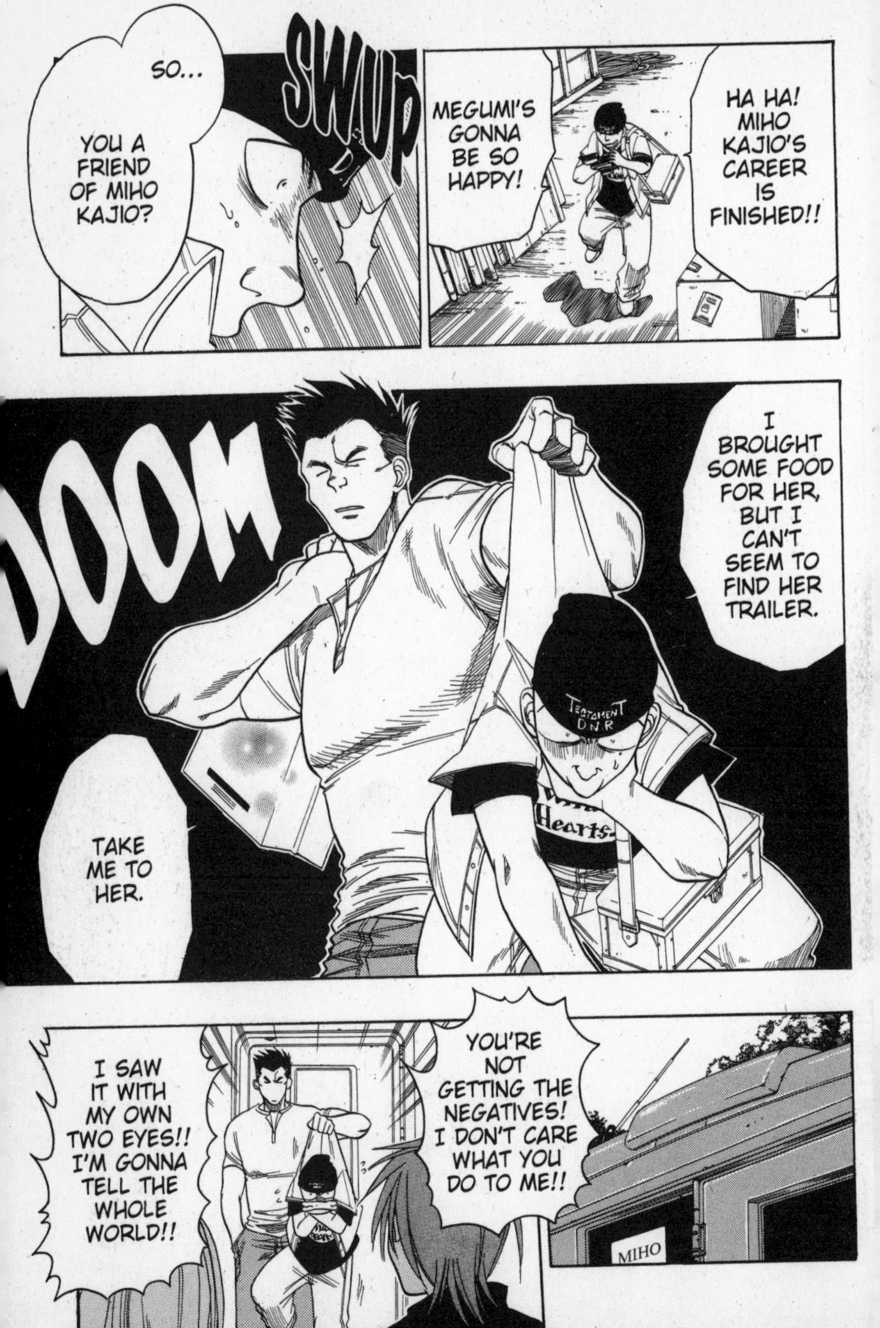
HA HA! MIHO KAJIO'S CAREER IS FINISHED!!
MEGUMI'S GONNA BE SO HAPPY!
SWUP
SO...
YOU A FRIEND OF MIHO KAJIO?
I BROUGHT SOME FOOD FOR HER, BUT I CAN'T SEEM TO FIND HER TRAILER.
DOOM
TEATAMENT D.N.R
Hearts
TAKE ME TO HER.
MIHO
YOU'RE NOT GETTING THE NEGATIVES! I DON'T CARE WHAT YOU DO TO ME!!
I SAW IT WITH MY OWN TWO EYES!! I'M GONNA TELL THE WHOLE WORLD!!

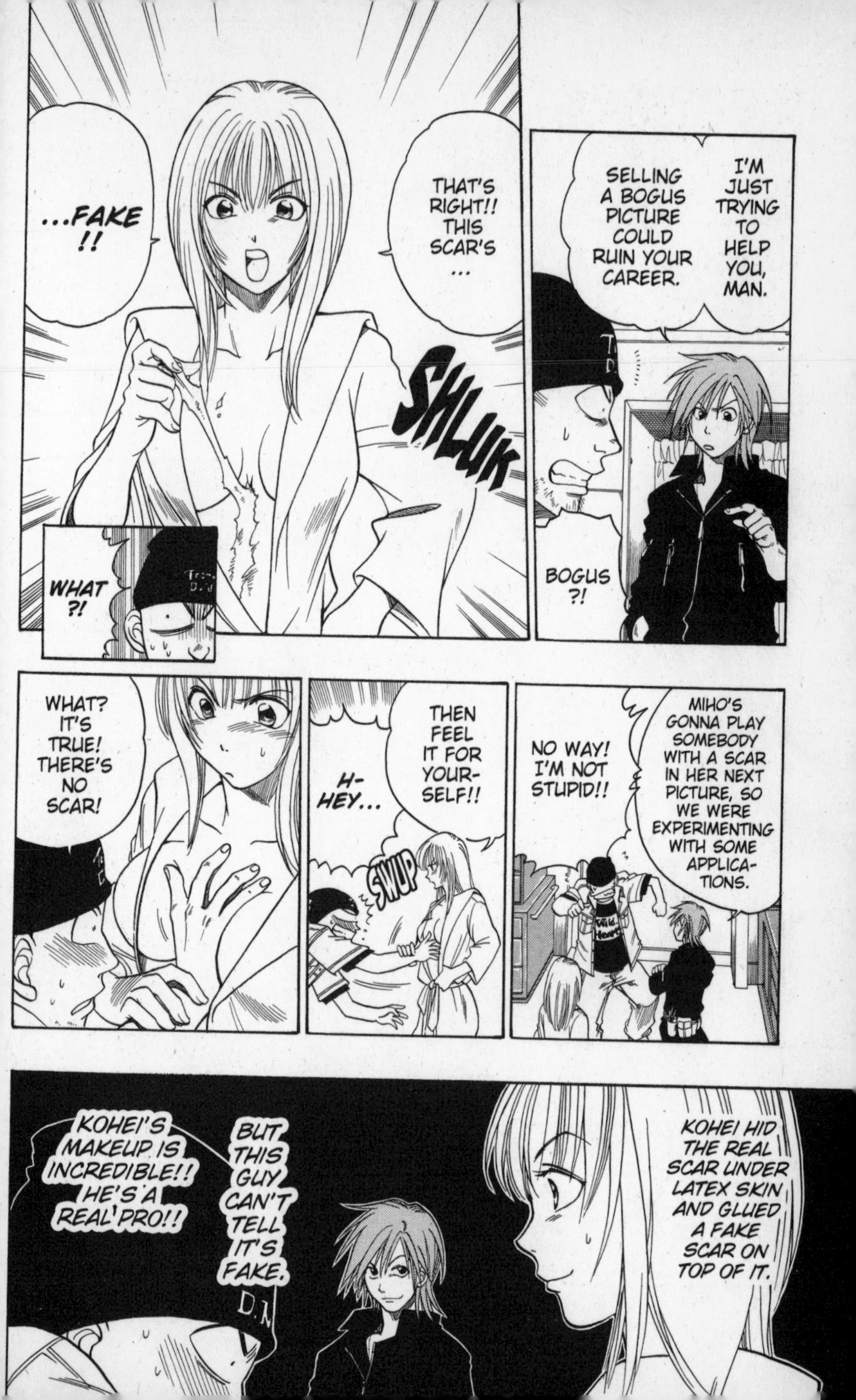
I'M JUST TRYING TO HELP YOU, MAN.
SELLING A BOGUS PICTURE COULD RUIN YOUR CAREER.
BOGUS ?!
THAT'S RIGHT!! THIS SCAR'S ...
...FAKE !!
SHLUK
WHAT ?!
MIHO'S GONNA PLAY SOMEBODY WITH A SCAR IN HER NEXT PICTURE, SO WE WERE EXPERIMENTING WITH SOME APPLICATIONS.
NO WAY! I'M NOT STUPID!!
THEN FEEL IT FOR YOURSELF!!
H- HEY...
SWUP
WHAT? IT'S TRUE! THERE'S NO SCAR!
KOHEI HID THE REAL SCAR UNDER LATEX SKIN AND GLUED A FAKE SCAR ON TOP OF IT.
BUT THIS GUY CAN'T TELL IT'S FAKE.
KOHEI'S MAKEUP IS INCREDIBLE!! HE'S A REAL PRO!!

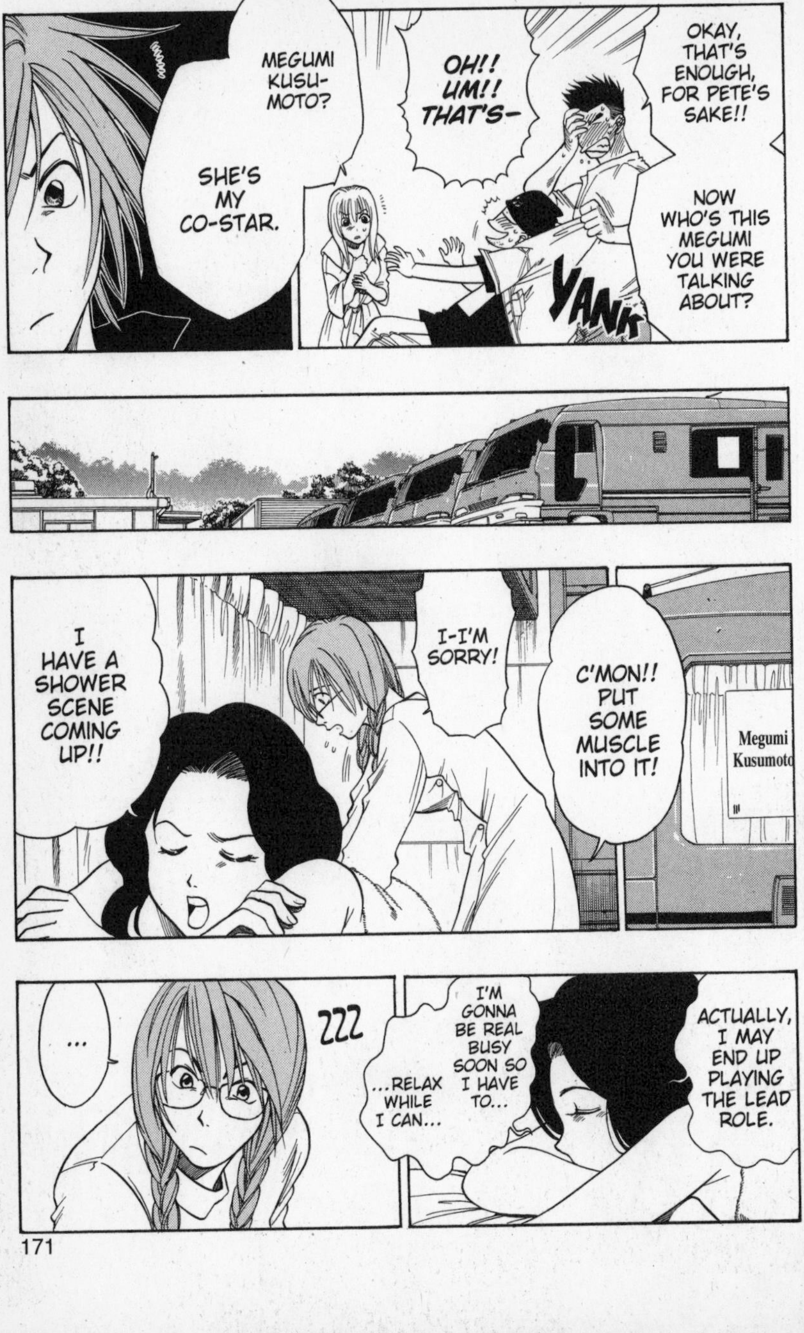
OKAY, THAT'S ENOUGH, FOR PETE'S SAKE!!
NOW WHO'S THIS MEGUMI YOU WERE TALKING ABOUT?
YANK
OH!! UM!! THAT'S–
MEGUMI KUSU-MOTO?
SHE'S MY CO-STAR.
Megumi Kusumoto
C'MON!! PUT SOME MUSCLE INTO IT!
I-I'M SORRY!
I HAVE A SHOWER SCENE COMING UP!!
ACTUALLY, I MAY END UP PLAYING THE LEAD ROLE.
I'M GONNA BE REAL BUSY SOON SO I HAVE TO...
...RELAX WHILE I CAN...
ZZZ
...

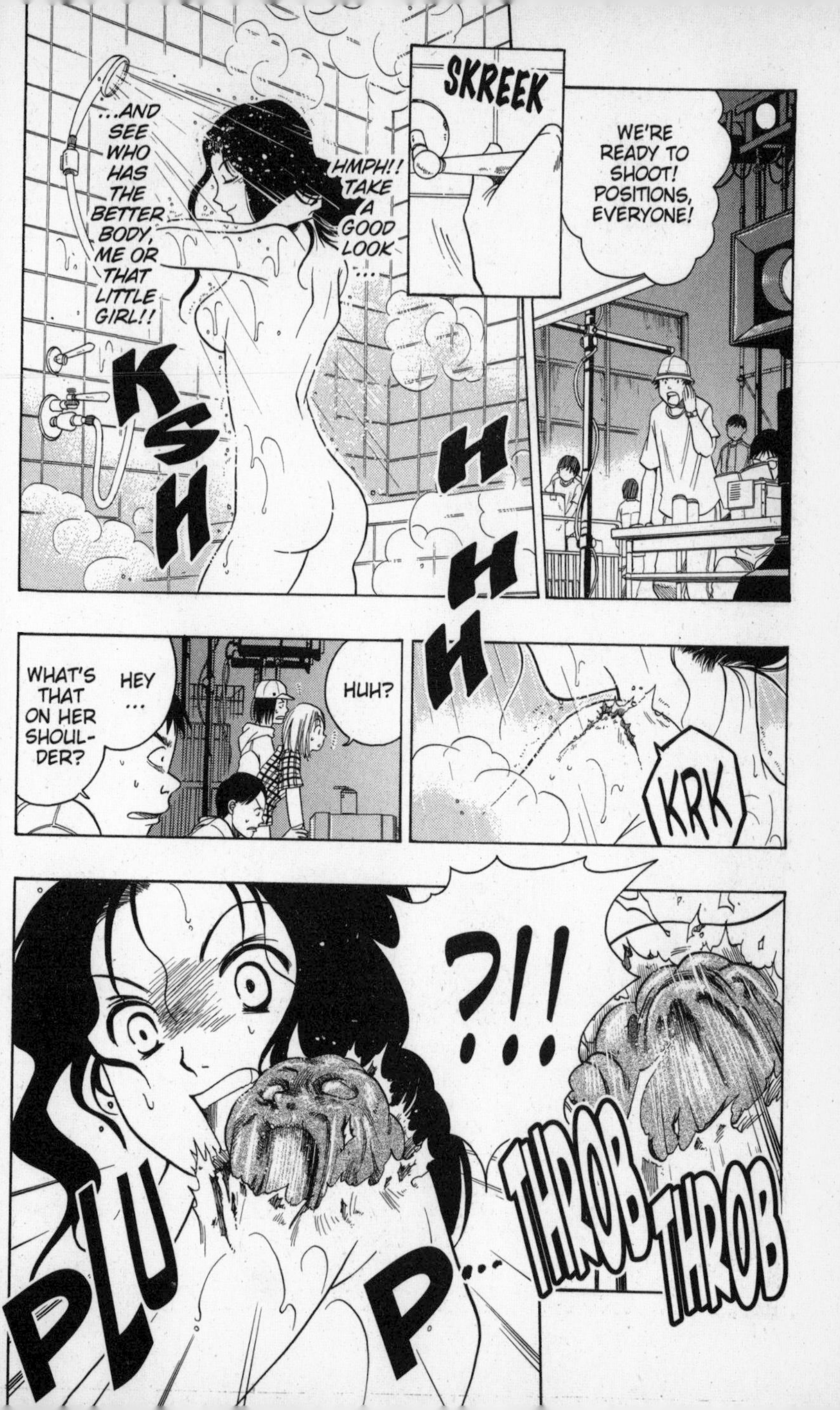
WE'RE READY TO SHOOT! POSITIONS, EVERYONE!
SKREEK
HMPH!! TAKE A GOOD LOOK...
...AND SEE WHO HAS THE BETTER BODY, ME OR THAT LITTLE GIRL!!
KSHHHHH
KRK
HUH?
HEY...
WHAT'S THAT ON HER SHOULDER?
?!!
THROB THROB
PLUP...

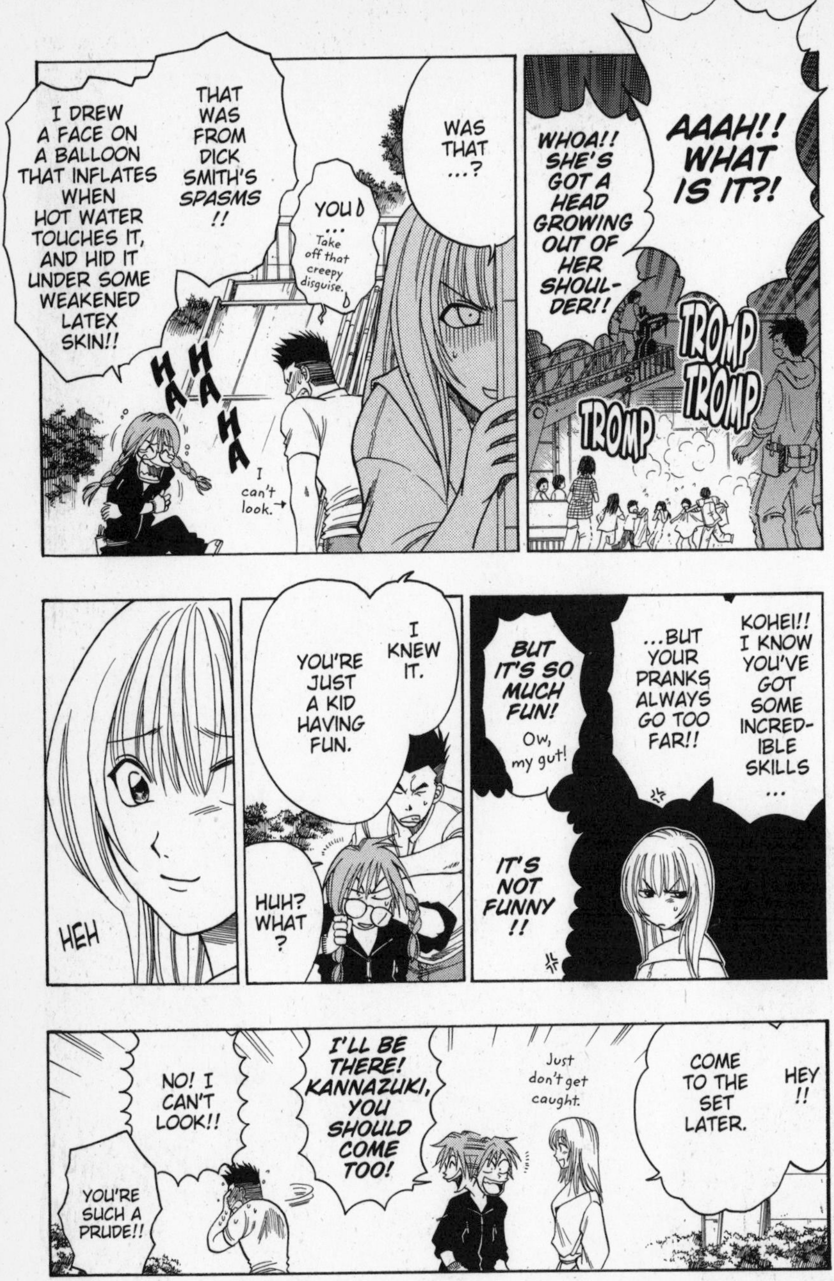

AAAH!! WHAT IS IT?!
WHOA!! SHE'S GOT A HEAD GROWING OUT OF HER SHOULDER!!
TROMP TROMP
TROMP
WAS THAT ...?
YOU ...
Take off that creepy disguise.
THAT WAS FROM DICK SMITH'S SPASMS!!
I DREW A FACE ON A BALLOON THAT INFLATES WHEN HOT WATER TOUCHES IT, AND HID IT UNDER SOME WEAKENED LATEX SKIN!!
HA HA HA HA
I can't look.
KOHEI!! I KNOW YOU'VE GOT SOME INCREDIBLE SKILLS...
...BUT YOUR PRANKS ALWAYS GO TOO FAR!!
BUT IT'S SO MUCH FUN!
Ow, my gut!
IT'S NOT FUNNY!!
I KNEW IT.
YOU'RE JUST A KID HAVING FUN.
HUH? WHAT?
HEH
HEY!!
COME TO THE SET LATER.
Just don't get caught.
I'LL BE THERE! KANNAZUKI, YOU SHOULD COME TOO!
NO! I CAN'T LOOK!!
YOU'RE SUCH A PRUDE!!

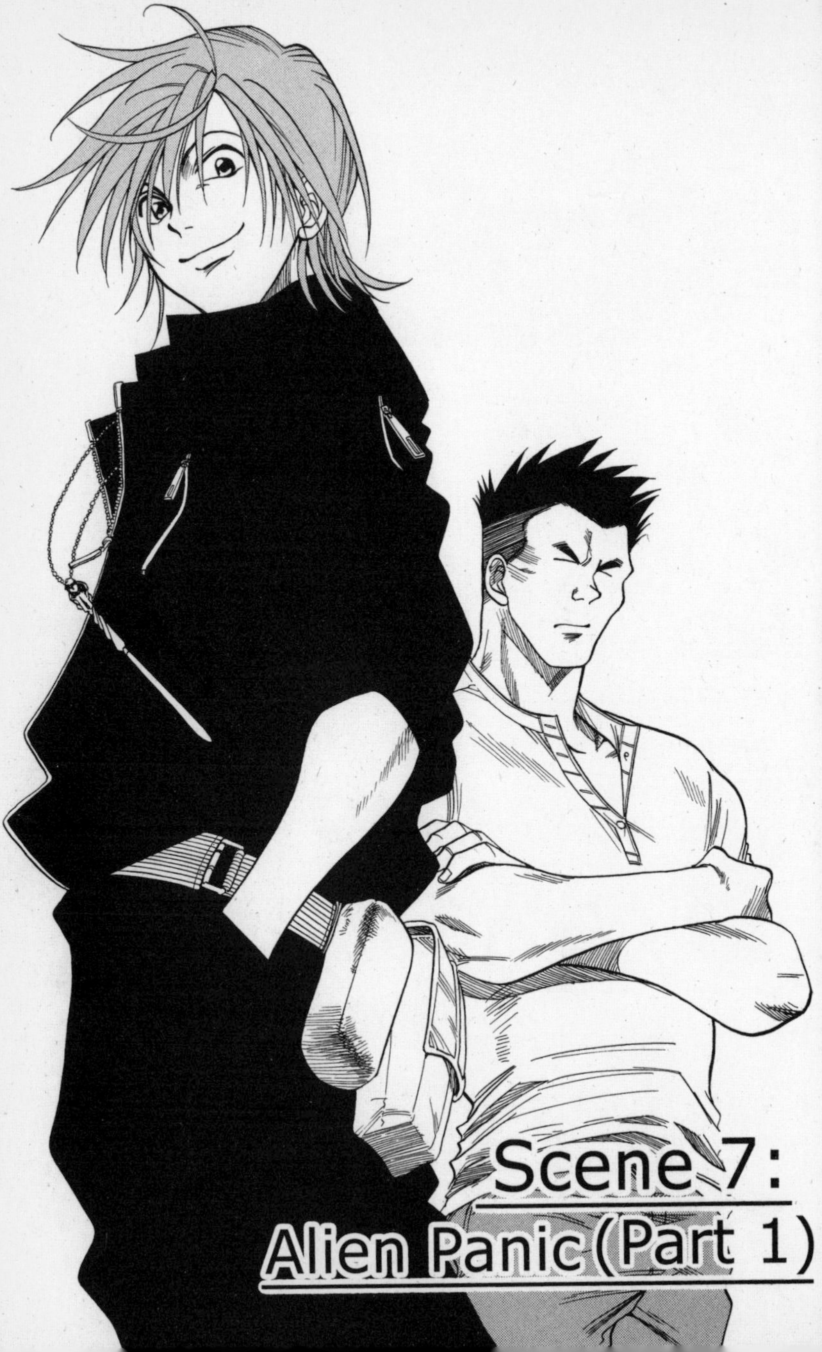
Scene 7:
Alien Panic (Part 1)

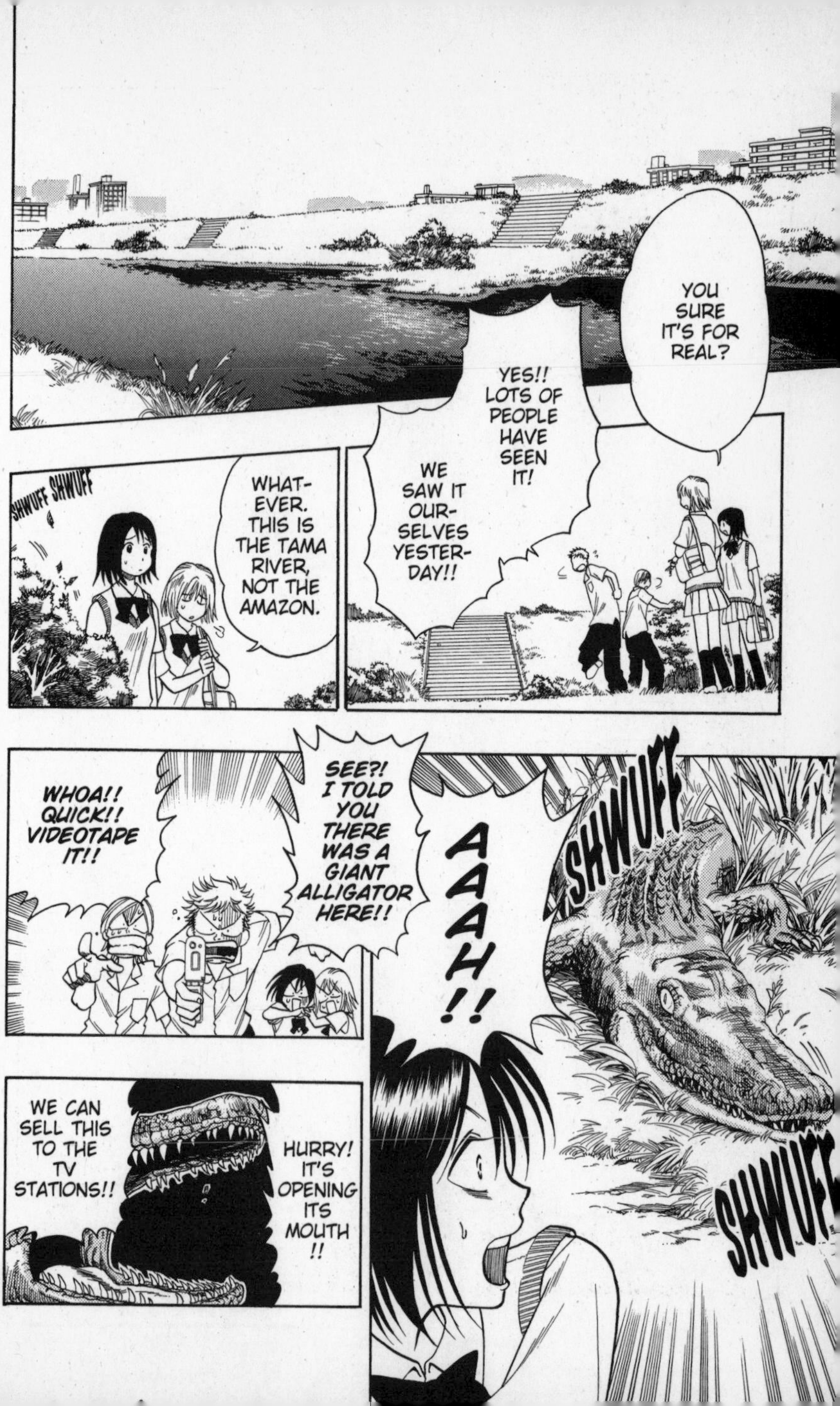
YOU SURE IT'S FOR REAL?
YES!! LOTS OF PEOPLE HAVE SEEN IT!
WE SAW IT OURSELVES YESTERDAY!!
SHWUFF SHWUFF
WHATEVER. THIS IS THE TAMA RIVER, NOT THE AMAZON.
SHWUFF
AAAAH!!
SHWUFF
SEE?! I TOLD YOU THERE WAS A GIANT ALLIGATOR HERE!!
WHOA!! QUICK!! VIDEOTAPE IT!!
HURRY! IT'S OPENING ITS MOUTH!!
WE CAN SELL THIS TO THE TV STATIONS!!

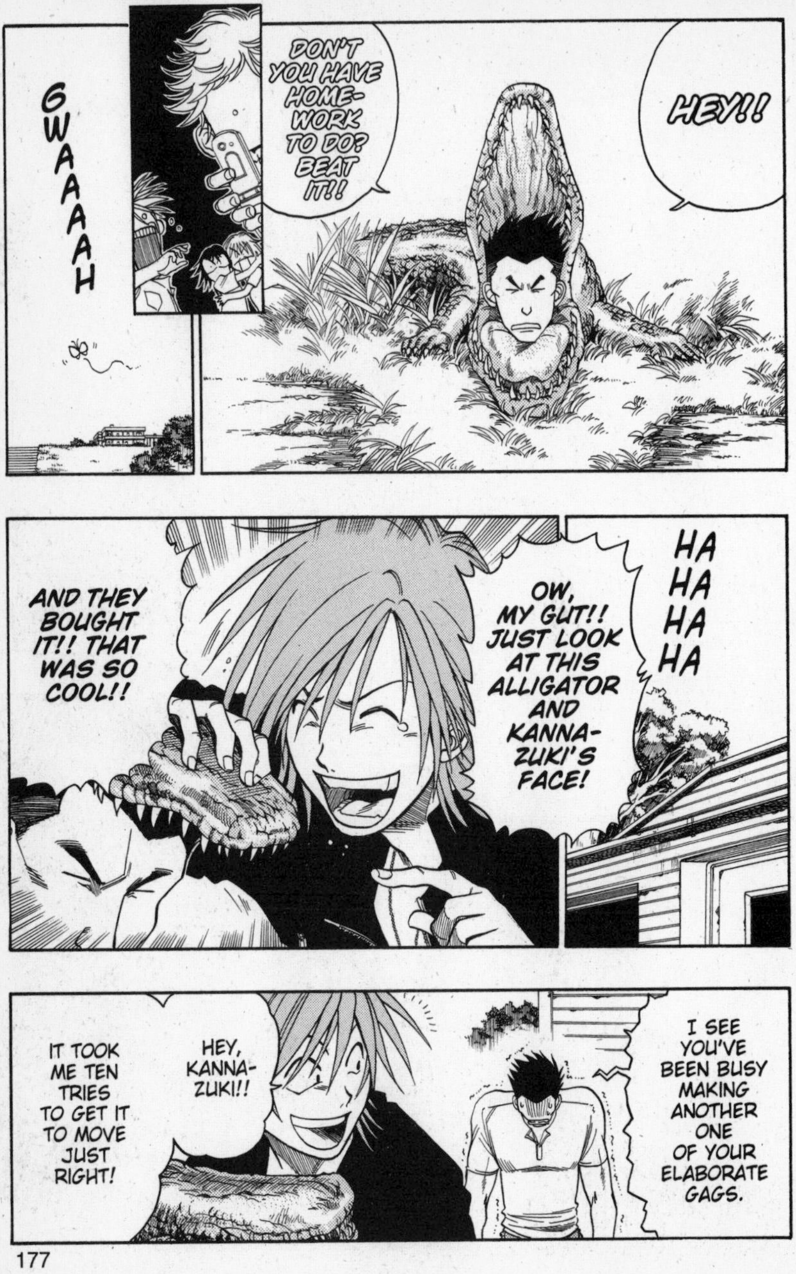
HEY!!
DON'T YOU HAVE HOME-WORK TO DO? BEAT IT!!
GWAAAAAH
HA HA HA HA
OW, MY GUT!! JUST LOOK AT THIS ALLIGATOR AND KANNA-ZUKI'S FACE!
AND THEY BOUGHT IT!! THAT WAS SO COOL!!
I SEE YOU'VE BEEN BUSY MAKING ANOTHER ONE OF YOUR ELABORATE GAGS.
HEY, KANNA-ZUKI!!
IT TOOK ME TEN TRIES TO GET IT TO MOVE JUST RIGHT!

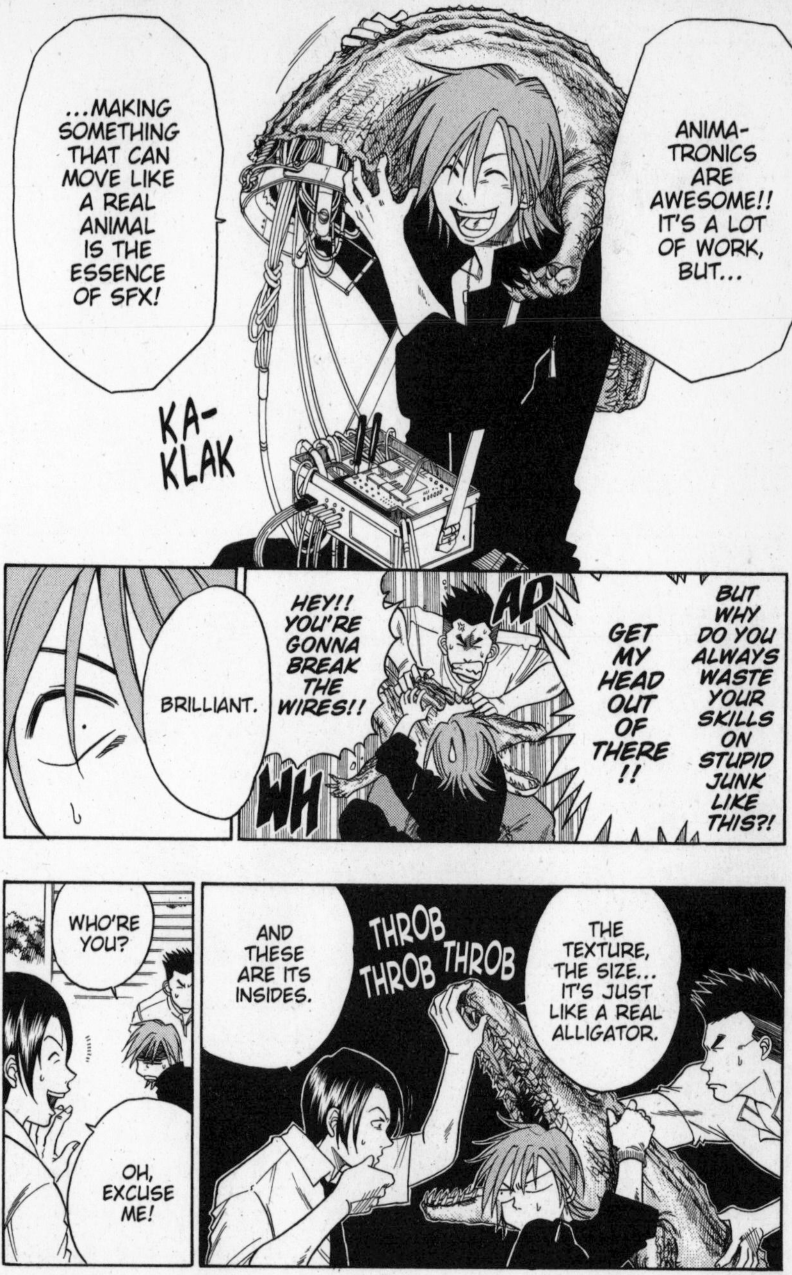
ANIMA-TRONICS ARE AWESOME!! IT'S A LOT OF WORK, BUT...
...MAKING SOMETHING THAT CAN MOVE LIKE A REAL ANIMAL IS THE ESSENCE OF SFX!
KA-KLAK
BUT WHY DO YOU ALWAYS WASTE YOUR SKILLS ON STUPID JUNK LIKE THIS?!
GET MY HEAD OUT OF THERE!!
HEY!! YOU'RE GONNA BREAK THE WIRES!!
BRILLIANT.
THE TEXTURE, THE SIZE... IT'S JUST LIKE A REAL ALLIGATOR.
THROB THROB THROB
AND THESE ARE ITS INSIDES.
WHO'RE YOU?
OH, EXCUSE ME!

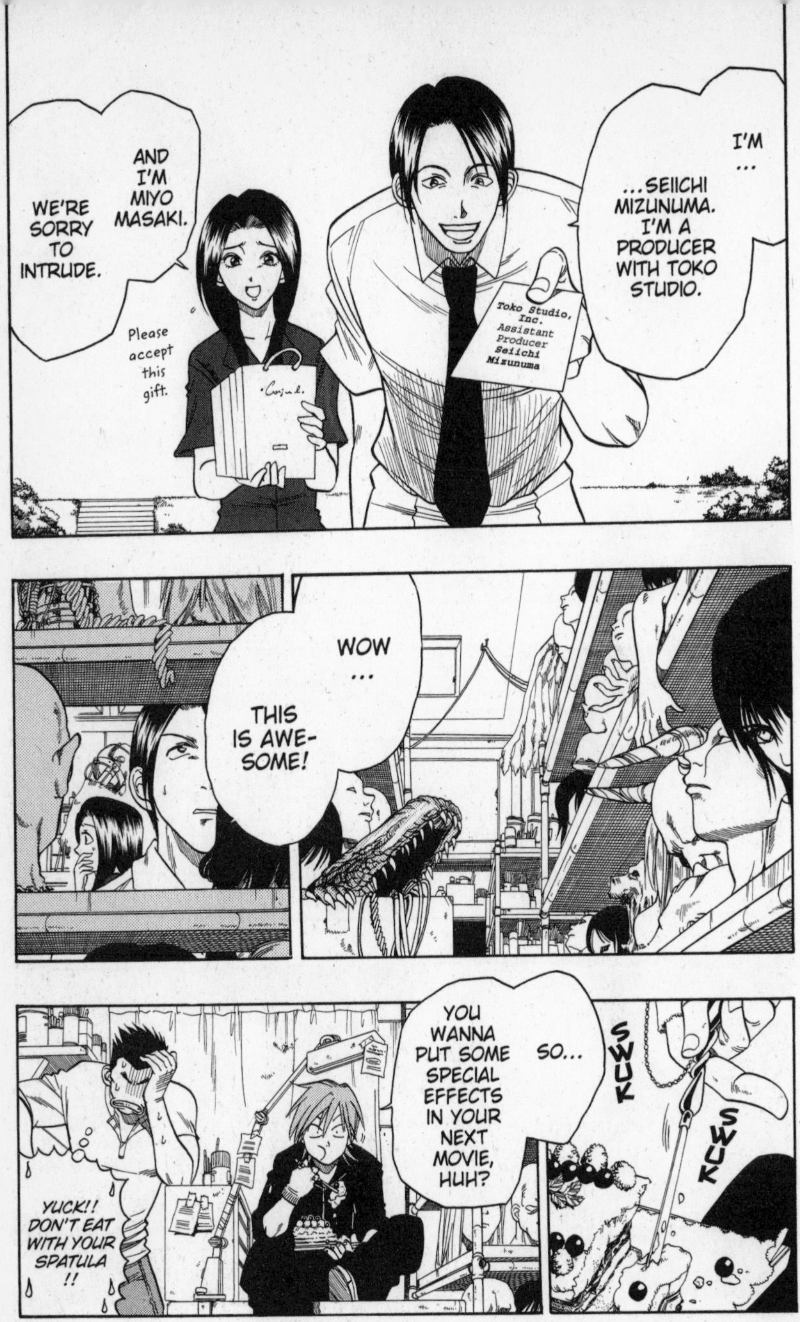
I'M ...
...SEIICHI MIZUNUMA. I'M A PRODUCER WITH TOKO STUDIO.
Toko Studio, Inc. Assistant Producer Seiichi Mizunuma
AND I'M MIYO MASAKI.
WE'RE SORRY TO INTRUDE.
Please accept this gift.
WOW ... THIS IS AWESOME!
SWUK
SWUK
SO...
YOU WANNA PUT SOME SPECIAL EFFECTS IN YOUR NEXT MOVIE, HUH?
YUCK!! DON'T EAT WITH YOUR SPATULA!!

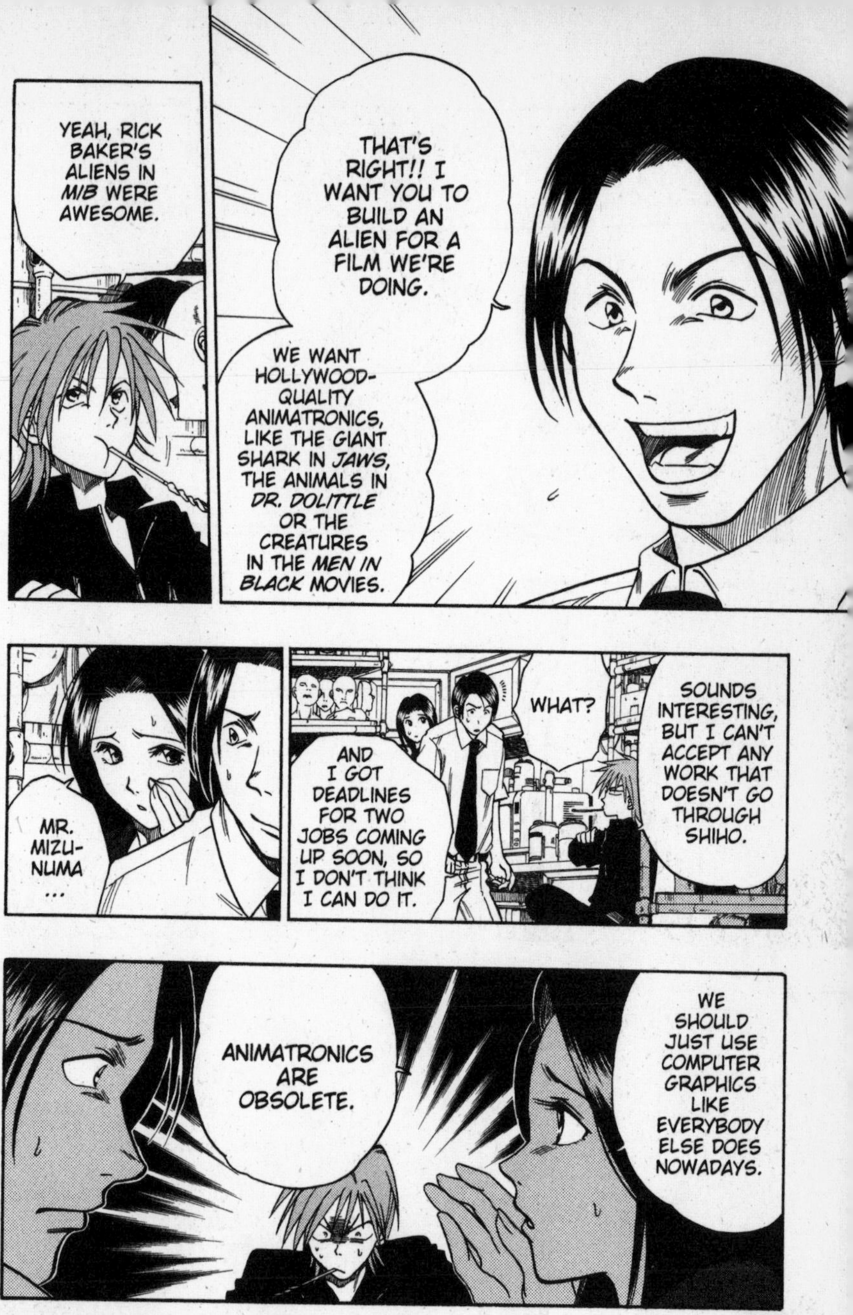
THAT'S RIGHT!! I WANT YOU TO BUILD AN ALIEN FOR A FILM WE'RE DOING.
WE WANT HOLLYWOOD-QUALITY ANIMATRONICS, LIKE THE GIANT SHARK IN *JAWS*, THE ANIMALS IN *DR. DOLITTLE* OR THE CREATURES IN THE *MEN IN BLACK* MOVIES.
YEAH, RICK BAKER'S ALIENS IN *MIB* WERE AWESOME.
SOUNDS INTERESTING, BUT I CAN'T ACCEPT ANY WORK THAT DOESN'T GO THROUGH SHIHO.
WHAT?
AND I GOT DEADLINES FOR TWO JOBS COMING UP SOON, SO I DON'T THINK I CAN DO IT.
MR. MIZUNUMA...
WE SHOULD JUST USE COMPUTER GRAPHICS LIKE EVERYBODY ELSE DOES NOWADAYS.
ANIMATRONICS ARE OBSOLETE.

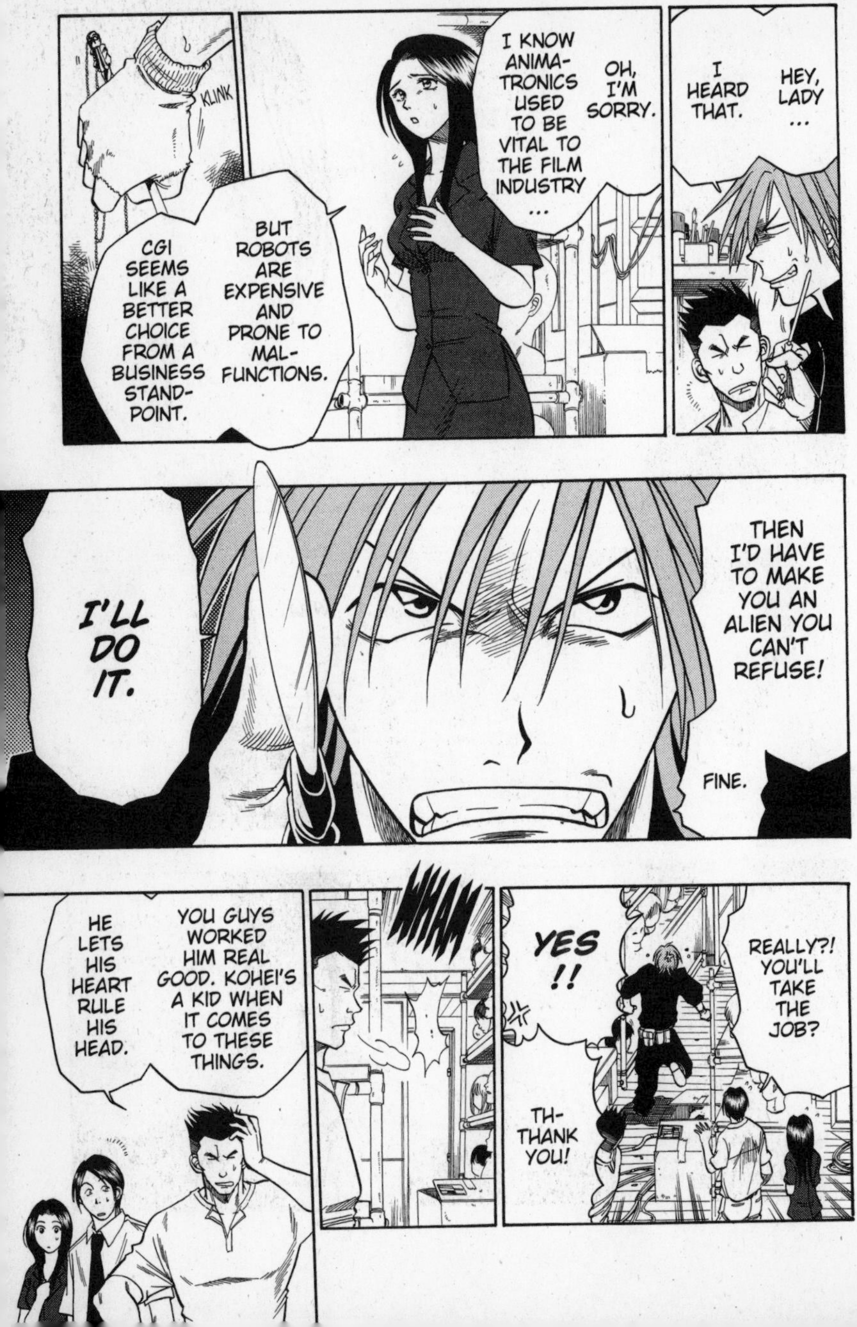
HEY, LADY ...
I HEARD THAT.
OH, I'M SORRY.
I KNOW ANIMA-TRONICS USED TO BE VITAL TO THE FILM INDUSTRY ...
KLINK
BUT ROBOTS ARE EXPENSIVE AND PRONE TO MAL-FUNCTIONS.
CGI SEEMS LIKE A BETTER CHOICE FROM A BUSINESS STAND-POINT.
THEN I'D HAVE TO MAKE YOU AN ALIEN YOU CAN'T REFUSE!
FINE.
I'LL DO IT.
REALLY?! YOU'LL TAKE THE JOB?
YES!!
TH-THANK YOU!
WHAM
YOU GUYS WORKED HIM REAL GOOD. KOHEI'S A KID WHEN IT COMES TO THESE THINGS.
HE LETS HIS HEART RULE HIS HEAD.

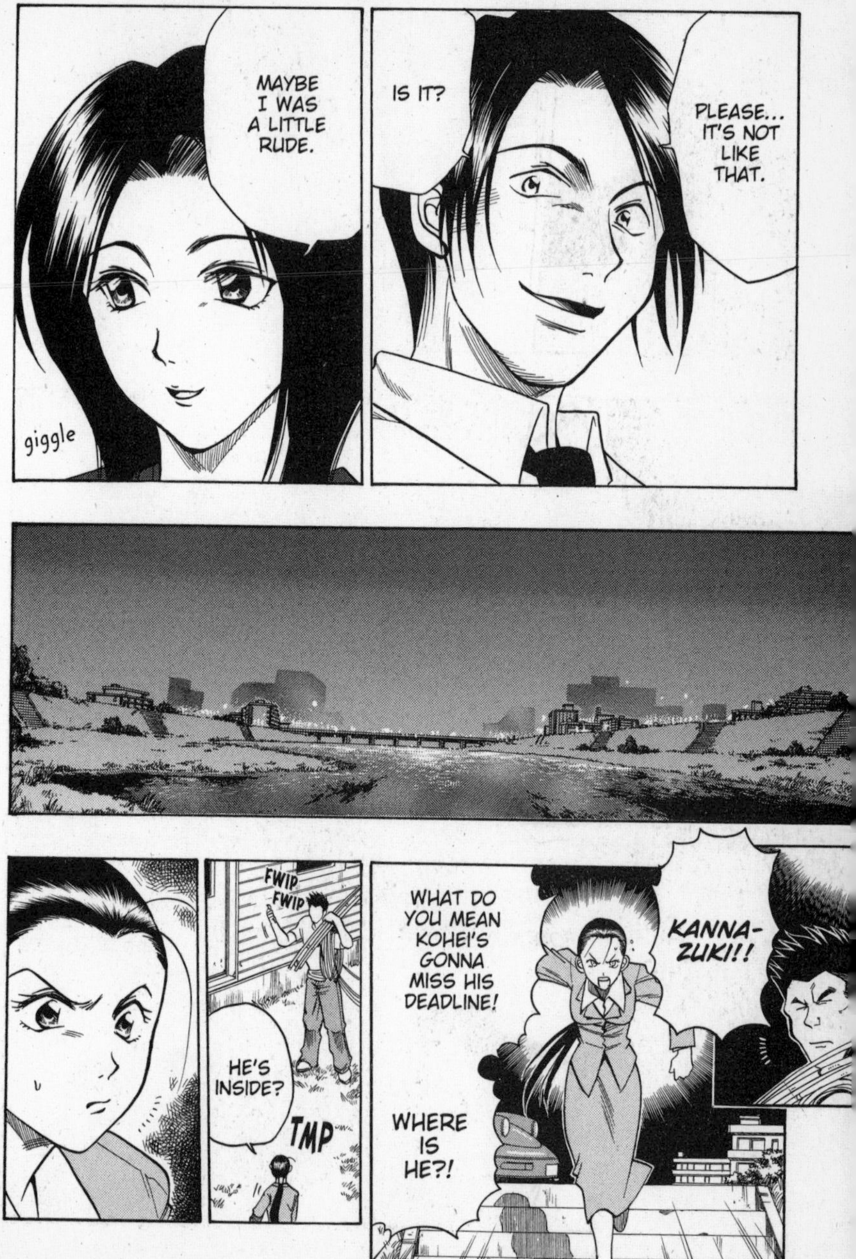
PLEASE... IT'S NOT LIKE THAT.
IS IT?
MAYBE I WAS A LITTLE RUDE.
giggle
KANNA-ZUKI!!
WHAT DO YOU MEAN KOHEI'S GONNA MISS HIS DEADLINE!
WHERE IS HE?!
FWIP FWIP
HE'S INSIDE?
TMP

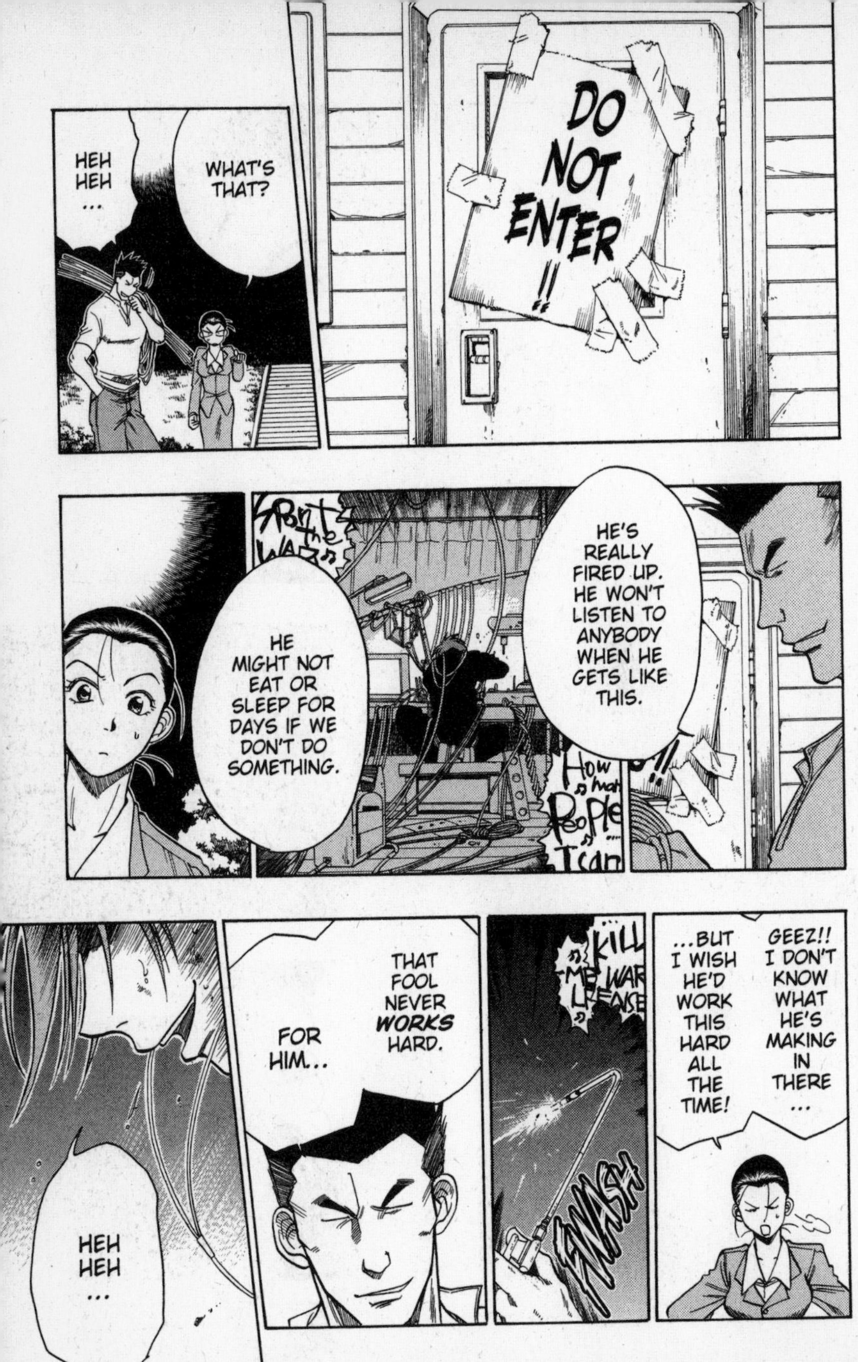
DO NOT ENTER !!
WHAT'S THAT?
HEH HEH ...
HE'S REALLY FIRED UP. HE WON'T LISTEN TO ANYBODY WHEN HE GETS LIKE THIS.
HE MIGHT NOT EAT OR SLEEP FOR DAYS IF WE DON'T DO SOMETHING.
GEEZ!! I DON'T KNOW WHAT HE'S MAKING IN THERE ...
...BUT I WISH HE'D WORK THIS HARD ALL THE TIME!
THAT FOOL NEVER *WORKS* HARD.
FOR HIM...
HEH HEH ...

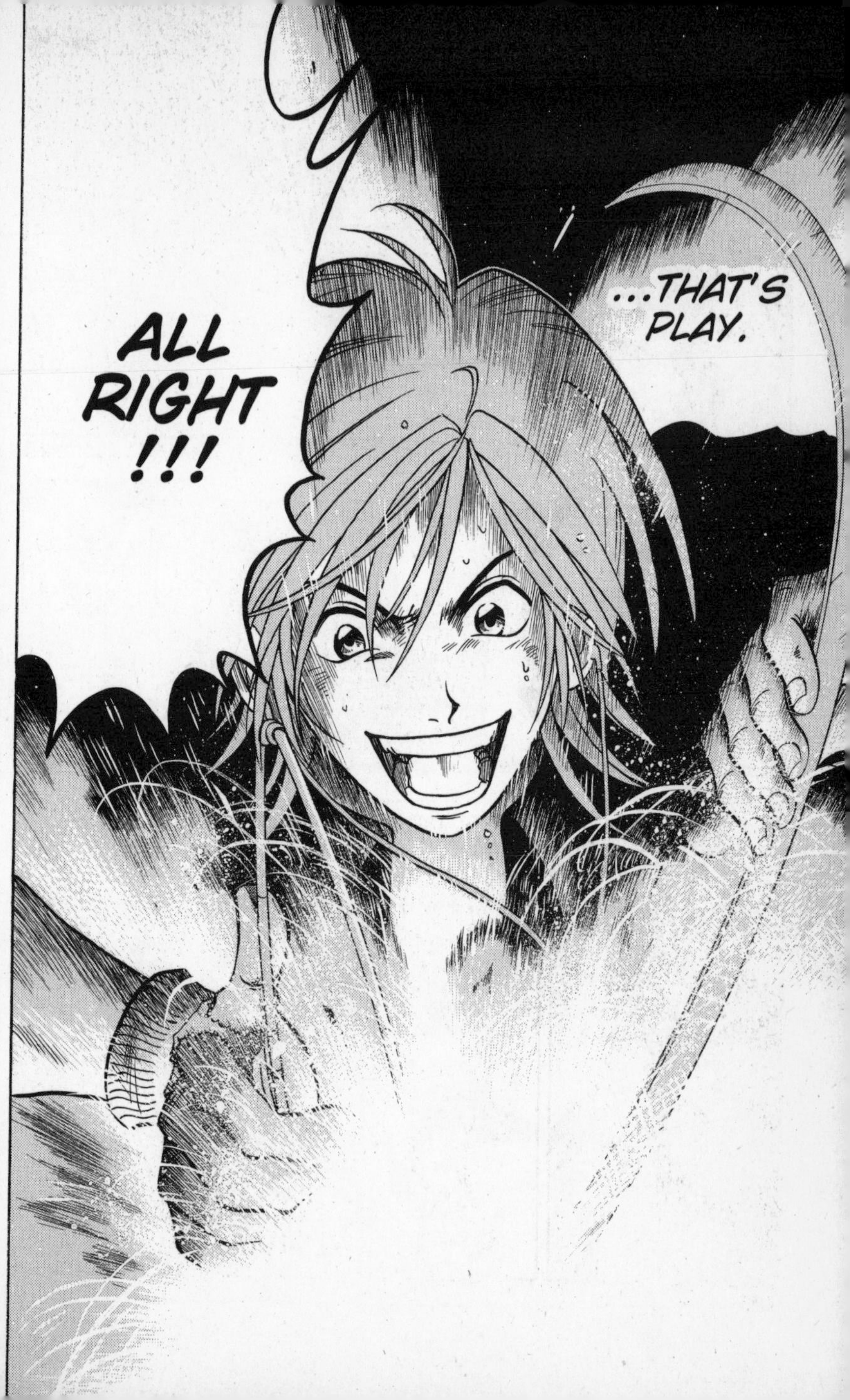
...THAT'S PLAY.
ALL RIGHT !!!

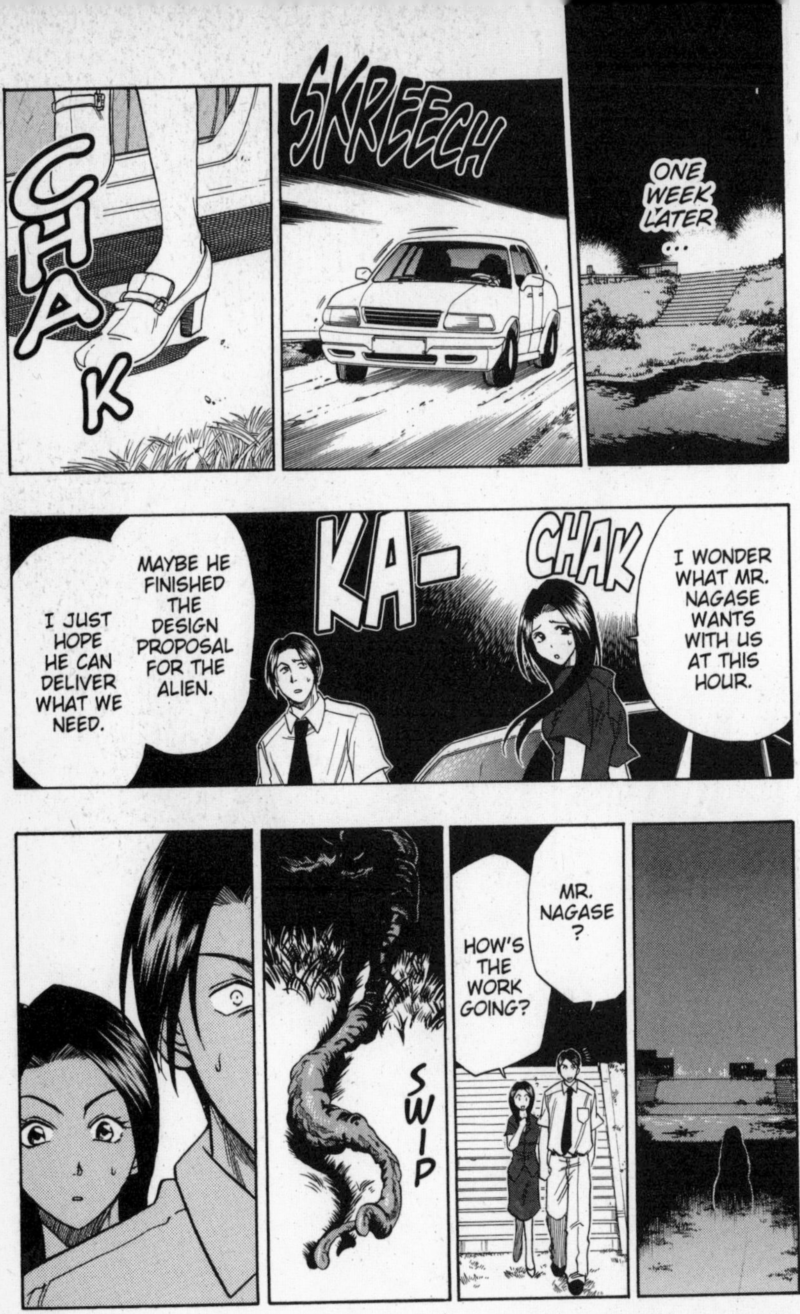
ONE WEEK LATER ...
SKREECH
CHAK
I WONDER WHAT MR. NAGASE WANTS WITH US AT THIS HOUR.
KA-CHAK
MAYBE HE FINISHED THE DESIGN PROPOSAL FOR THE ALIEN.
I JUST HOPE HE CAN DELIVER WHAT WE NEED.
MR. NAGASE?
HOW'S THE WORK GOING?
SWIP

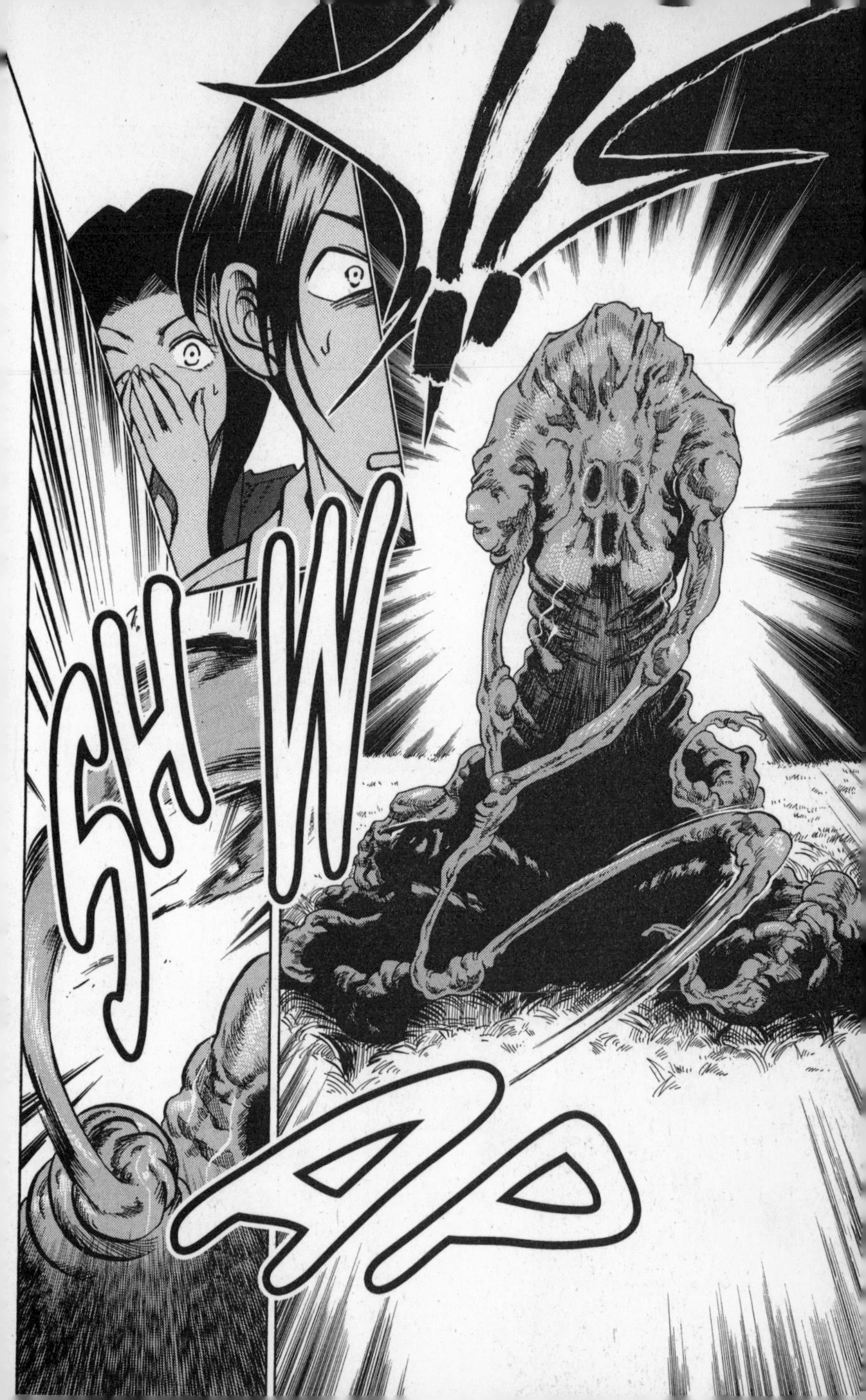
SHWAP

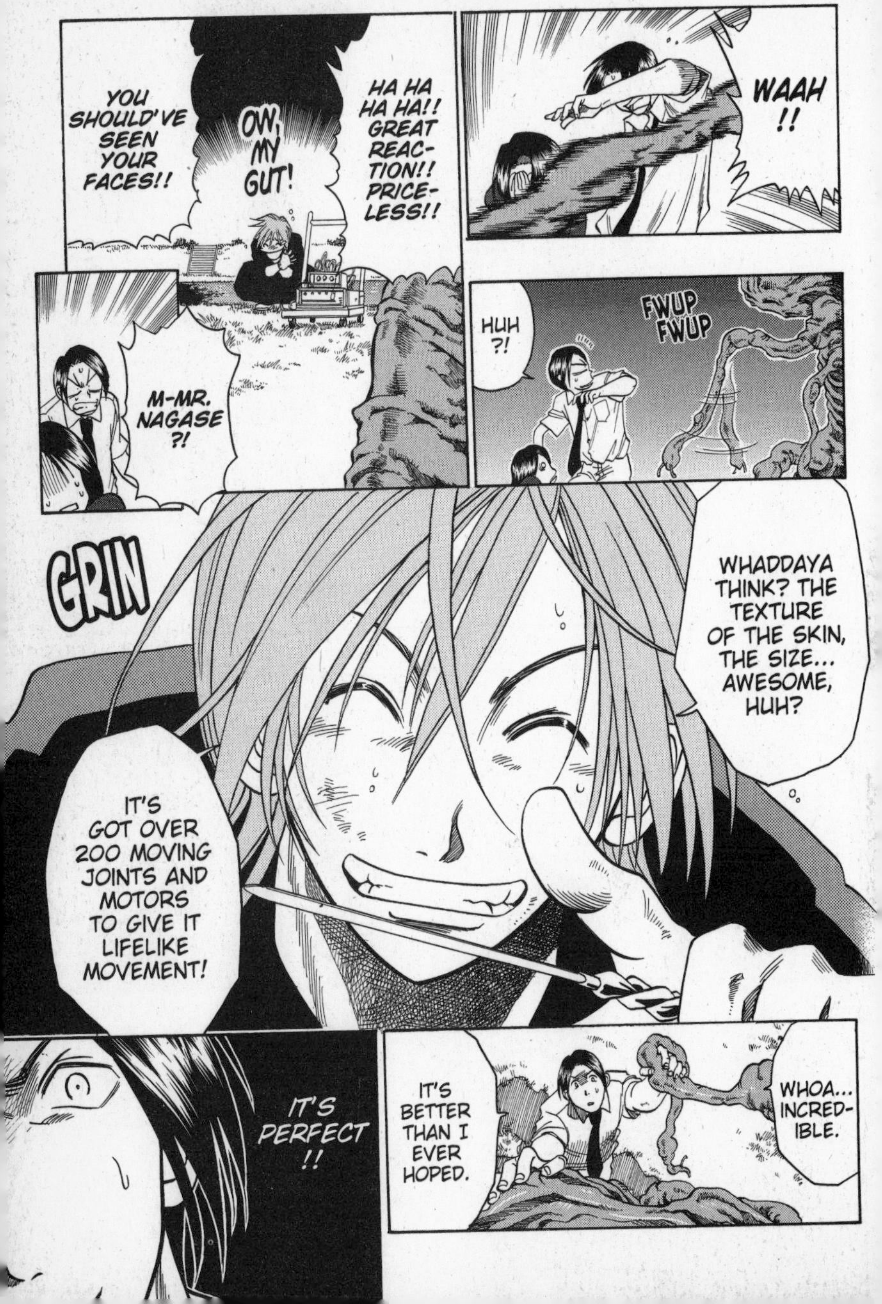
WAAH !!
HA HA HA HA!! GREAT REACTION!! PRICELESS!!
OW, MY GUT!
YOU SHOULD'VE SEEN YOUR FACES!!
FWUP FWUP
HUH ?!
M-MR. NAGASE ?!
WHADDAYA THINK? THE TEXTURE OF THE SKIN, THE SIZE... AWESOME, HUH?
IT'S GOT OVER 200 MOVING JOINTS AND MOTORS TO GIVE IT LIFELIKE MOVEMENT!
GRIN
WHOA... INCREDIBLE.
IT'S BETTER THAN I EVER HOPED.
IT'S PERFECT !!

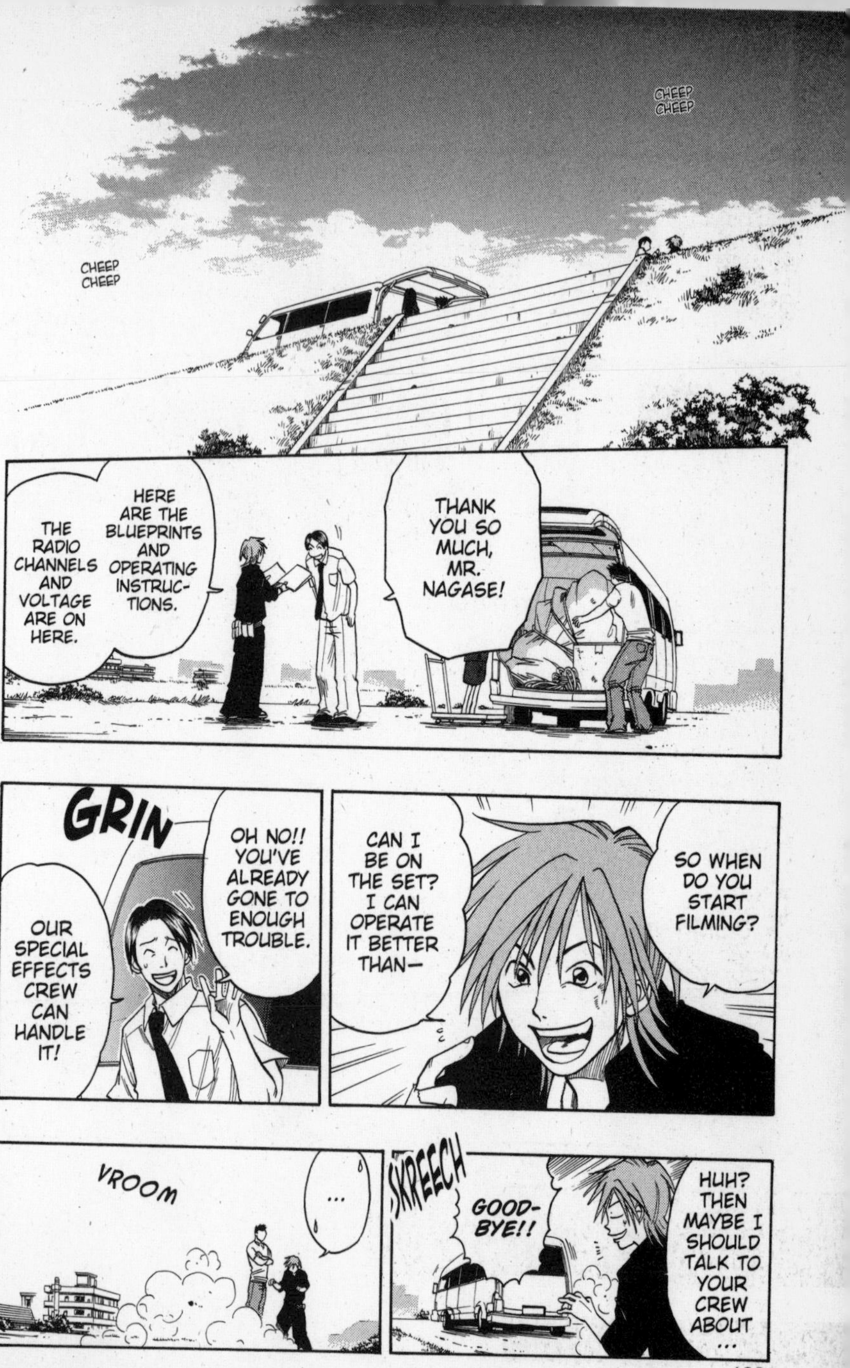
CHEEP CHEEP
CHEEP CHEEP
THANK YOU SO MUCH, MR. NAGASE!
HERE ARE THE BLUEPRINTS AND OPERATING INSTRUC-TIONS.
THE RADIO CHANNELS AND VOLTAGE ARE ON HERE.
SO WHEN DO YOU START FILMING?
CAN I BE ON THE SET? I CAN OPERATE IT BETTER THAN—
GRIN
OH NO!! YOU'VE ALREADY GONE TO ENOUGH TROUBLE.
OUR SPECIAL EFFECTS CREW CAN HANDLE IT!
HUH? THEN MAYBE I SHOULD TALK TO YOUR CREW ABOUT ...
GOOD-BYE!!
SKREECH
...
VROOM

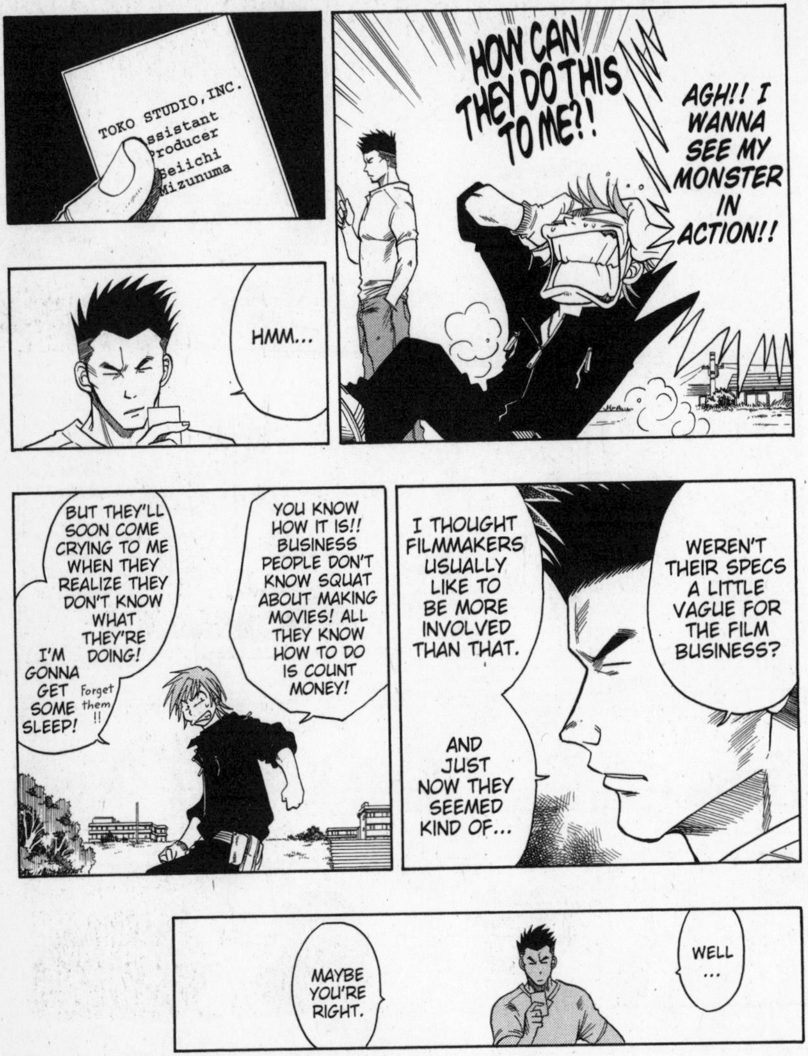
HOW CAN THEY DO THIS TO ME?!
AGH!! I WANNA SEE MY MONSTER IN ACTION!!
TOKO STUDIO,INC.
Assistant Producer
Seiichi Mizunuma
HMM...
WEREN'T THEIR SPECS A LITTLE VAGUE FOR THE FILM BUSINESS?
I THOUGHT FILMMAKERS USUALLY LIKE TO BE MORE INVOLVED THAN THAT.
AND JUST NOW THEY SEEMED KIND OF...
YOU KNOW HOW IT IS!! BUSINESS PEOPLE DON'T KNOW SQUAT ABOUT MAKING MOVIES! ALL THEY KNOW HOW TO DO IS COUNT MONEY!
BUT THEY'LL SOON COME CRYING TO ME WHEN THEY REALIZE THEY DON'T KNOW WHAT THEY'RE DOING!
I'M GONNA GET SOME SLEEP!
Forget them!!
WELL...
MAYBE YOU'RE RIGHT.

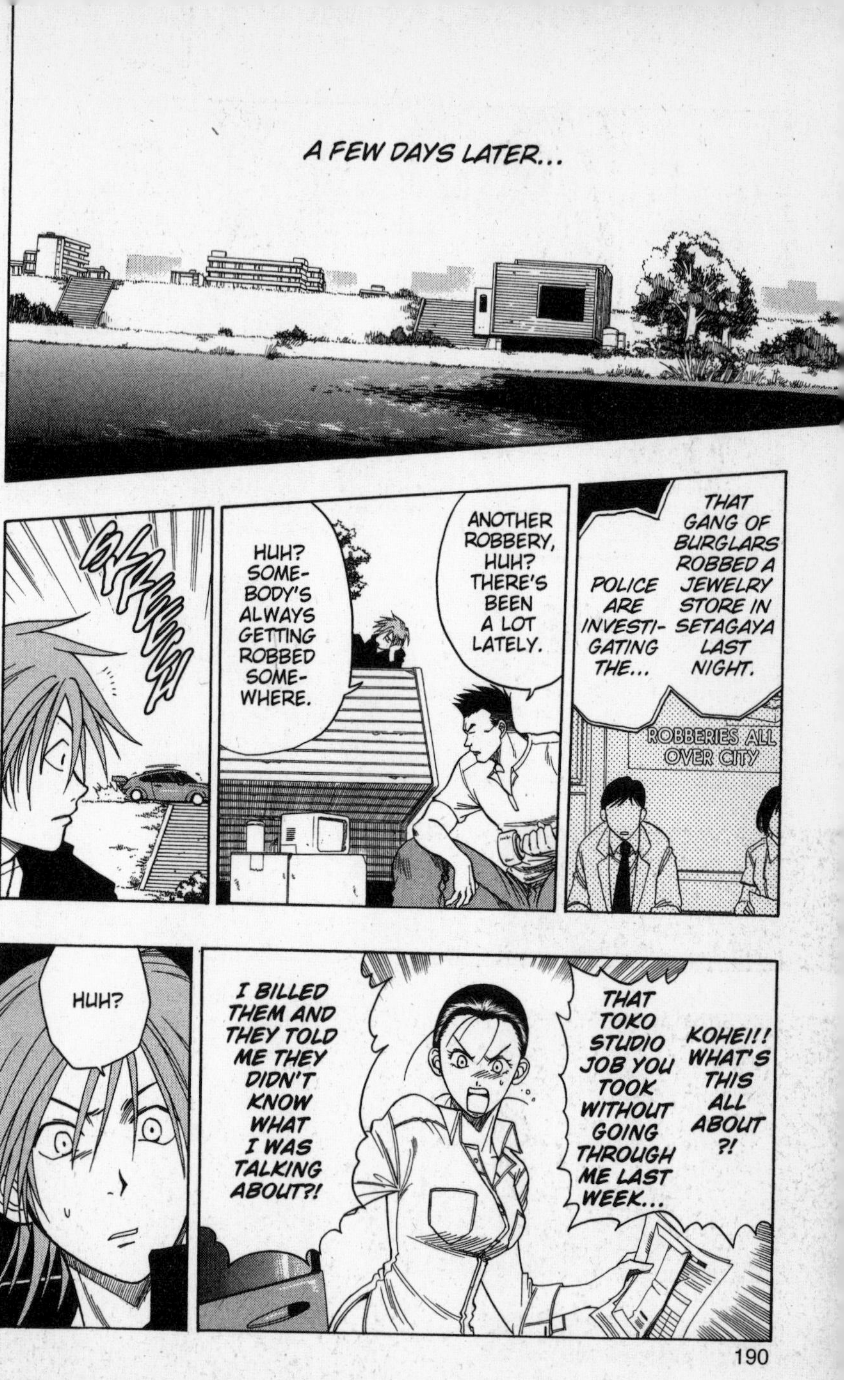
A FEW DAYS LATER...
THAT GANG OF BURGLARS ROBBED A JEWELRY STORE IN SETAGAYA LAST NIGHT.
POLICE ARE INVESTI-GATING THE...
ROBBERIES ALL OVER CITY
ANOTHER ROBBERY, HUH? THERE'S BEEN A LOT LATELY.
HUH? SOME-BODY'S ALWAYS GETTING ROBBED SOME-WHERE.
KOHEI!! WHAT'S THIS ALL ABOUT?!
THAT TOKO STUDIO JOB YOU TOOK WITHOUT GOING THROUGH ME LAST WEEK...
I BILLED THEM AND THEY TOLD ME THEY DIDN'T KNOW WHAT I WAS TALKING ABOUT?!
HUH?

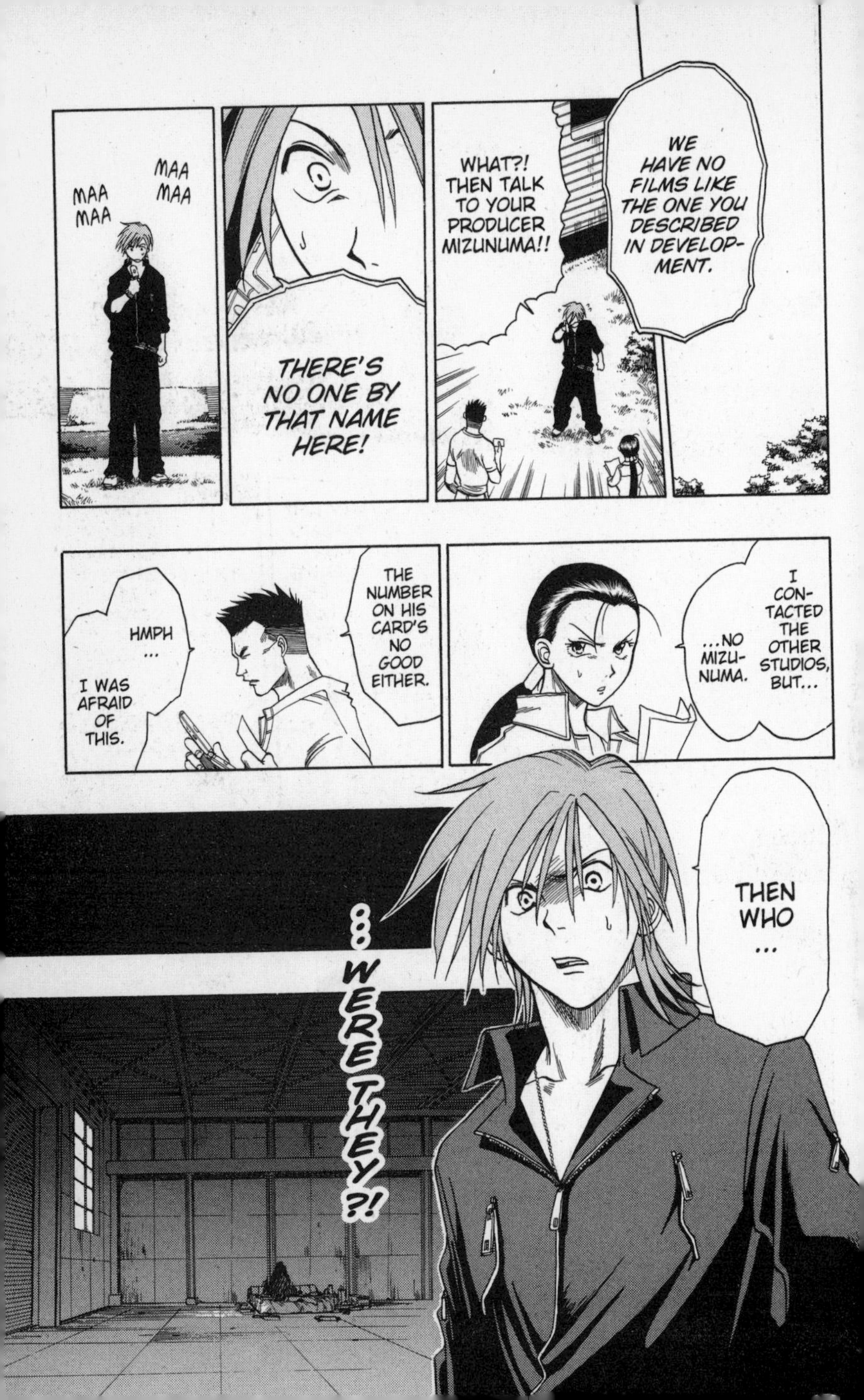
WE HAVE NO FILMS LIKE THE ONE YOU DESCRIBED IN DEVELOPMENT.
WHAT?! THEN TALK TO YOUR PRODUCER MIZUNUMA!!
THERE'S NO ONE BY THAT NAME HERE!
MAA MAA
MAA MAA
I CONTACTED THE OTHER STUDIOS, BUT...
...NO MIZUNUMA.
THE NUMBER ON HIS CARD'S NO GOOD EITHER.
HMPH...
I WAS AFRAID OF THIS.
THEN WHO...
...WERE THEY?!

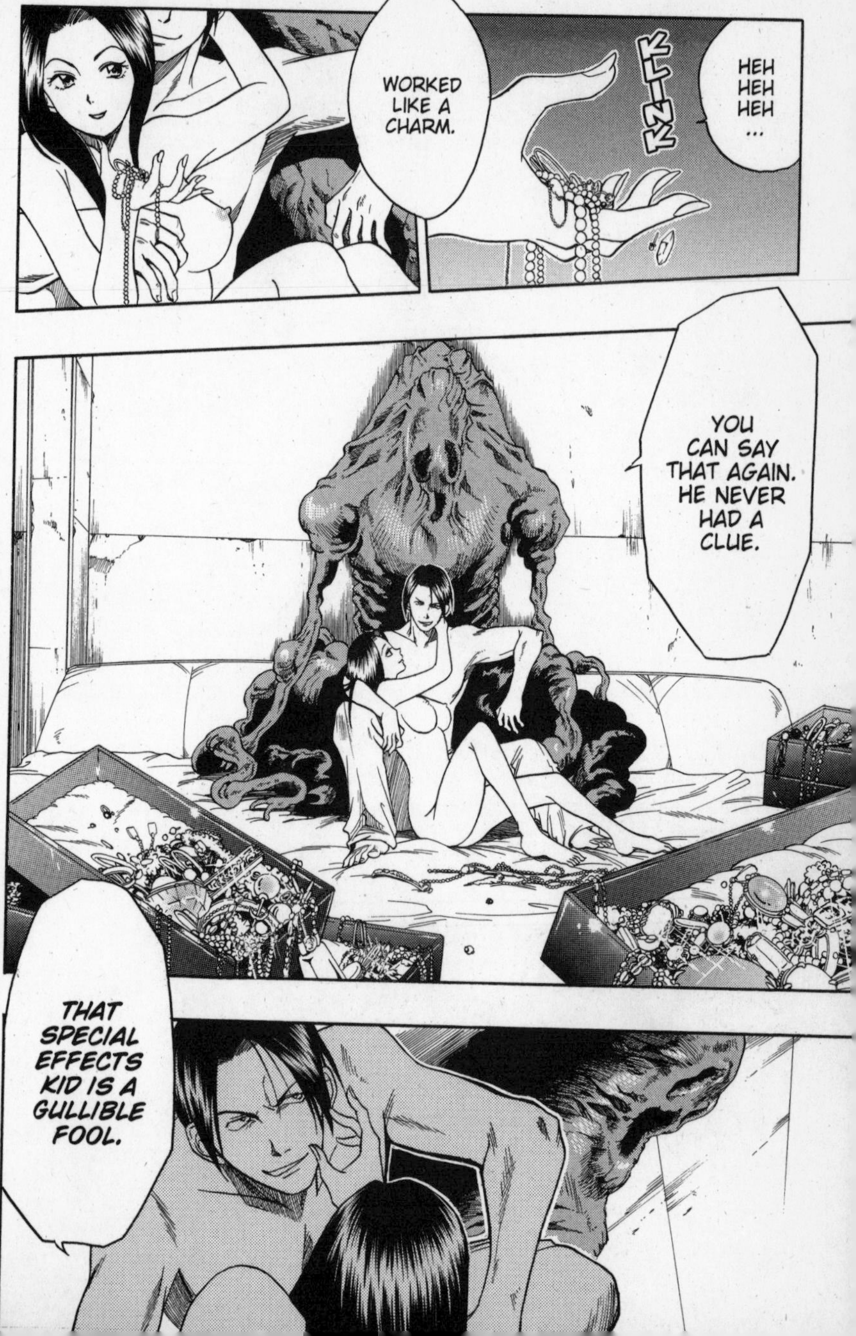
HEH HEH HEH ...
KLINK
WORKED LIKE A CHARM.
YOU CAN SAY THAT AGAIN. HE NEVER HAD A CLUE.
THAT SPECIAL EFFECTS KID IS A GULLIBLE FOOL.

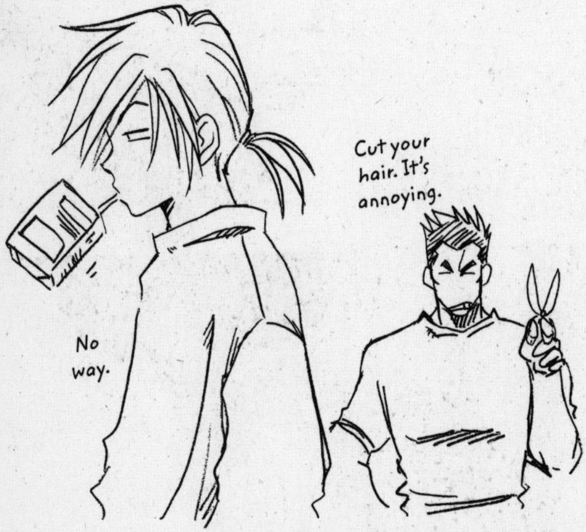
Cut your hair. It's annoying.
No way.

Scene 8:
Alien Panic (Part 2)

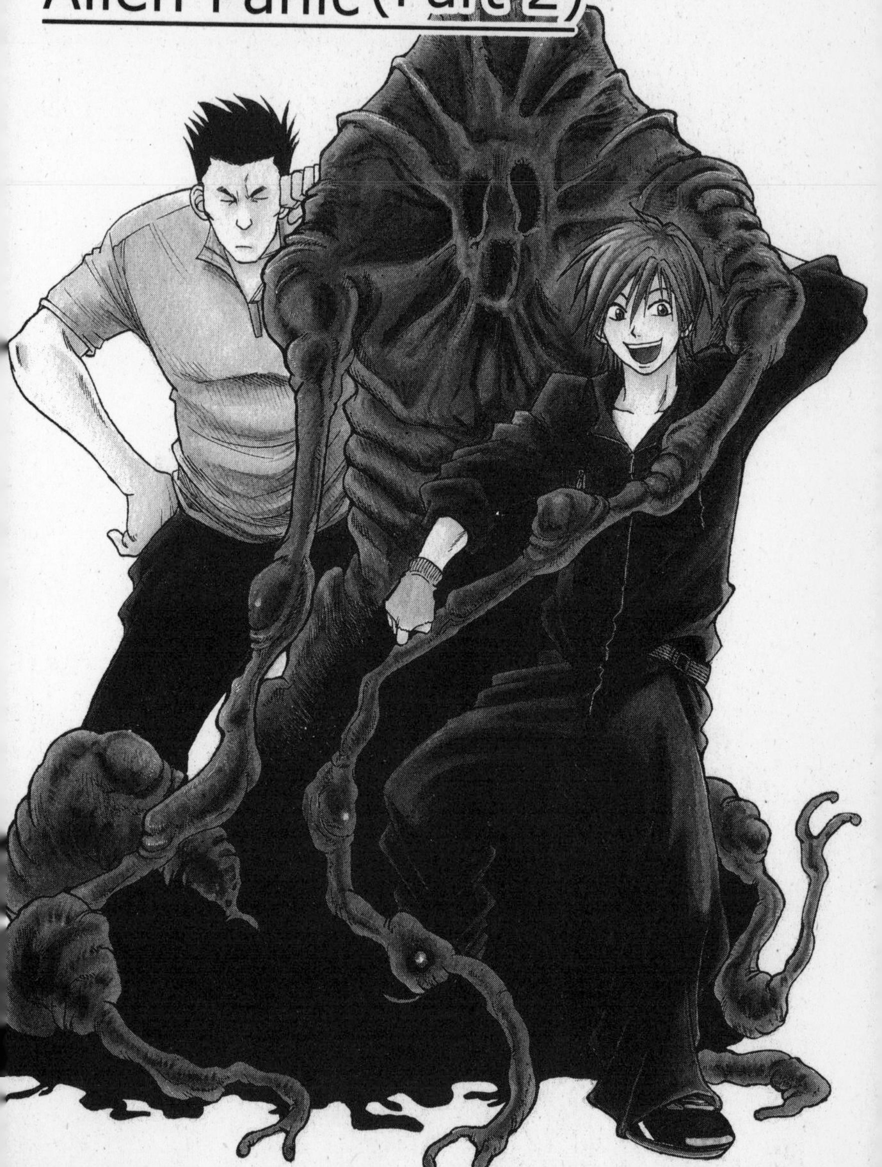

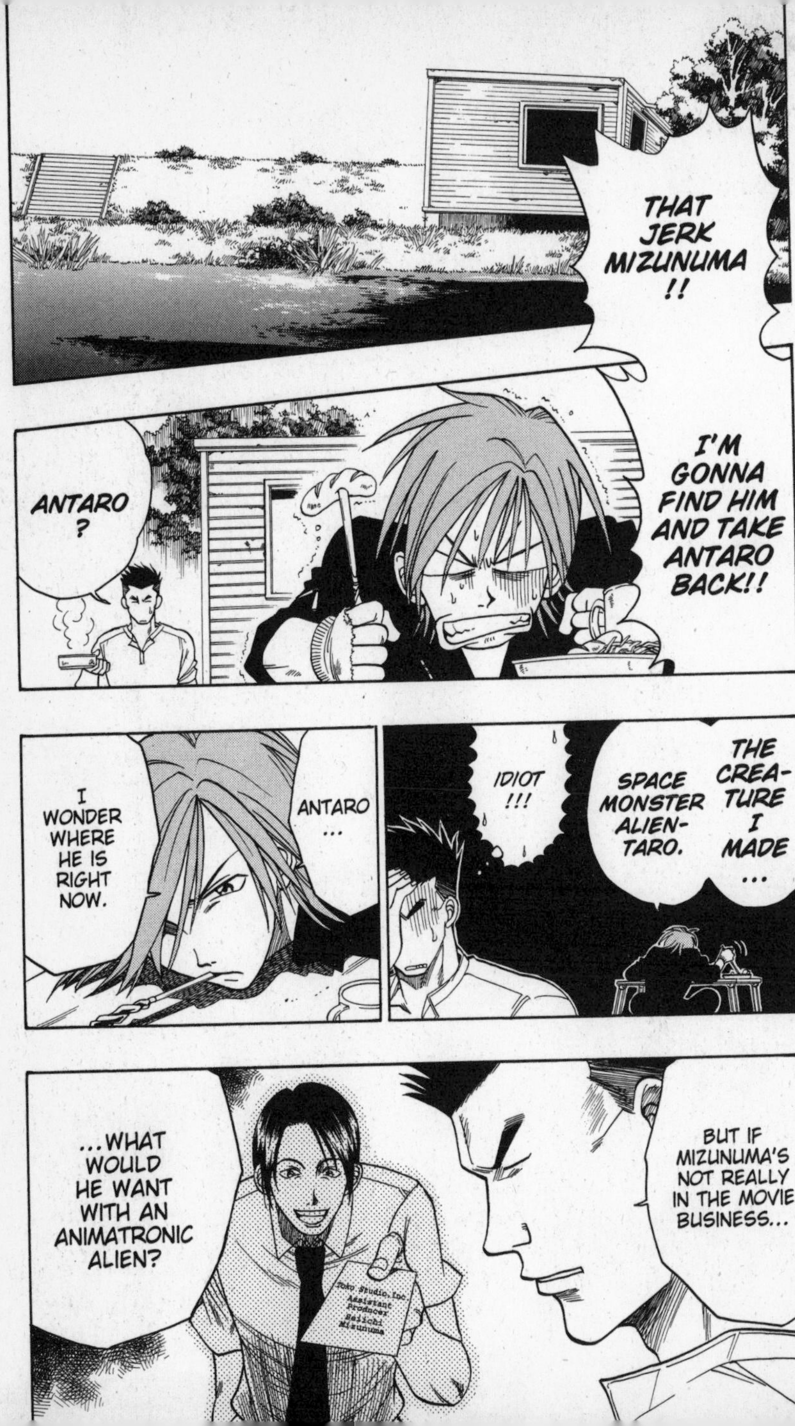
THAT JERK MIZUNUMA!!
I'M GONNA FIND HIM AND TAKE ANTARO BACK!!
ANTARO?
THE CREATURE I MADE...
SPACE MONSTER ALIEN-TARO.
IDIOT!!!
ANTARO...
I WONDER WHERE HE IS RIGHT NOW.
BUT IF MIZUNUMA'S NOT REALLY IN THE MOVIE BUSINESS...
...WHAT WOULD HE WANT WITH AN ANIMATRONIC ALIEN?
Toto Studio, Inc Assistant Producer Seiichi Mizunuma

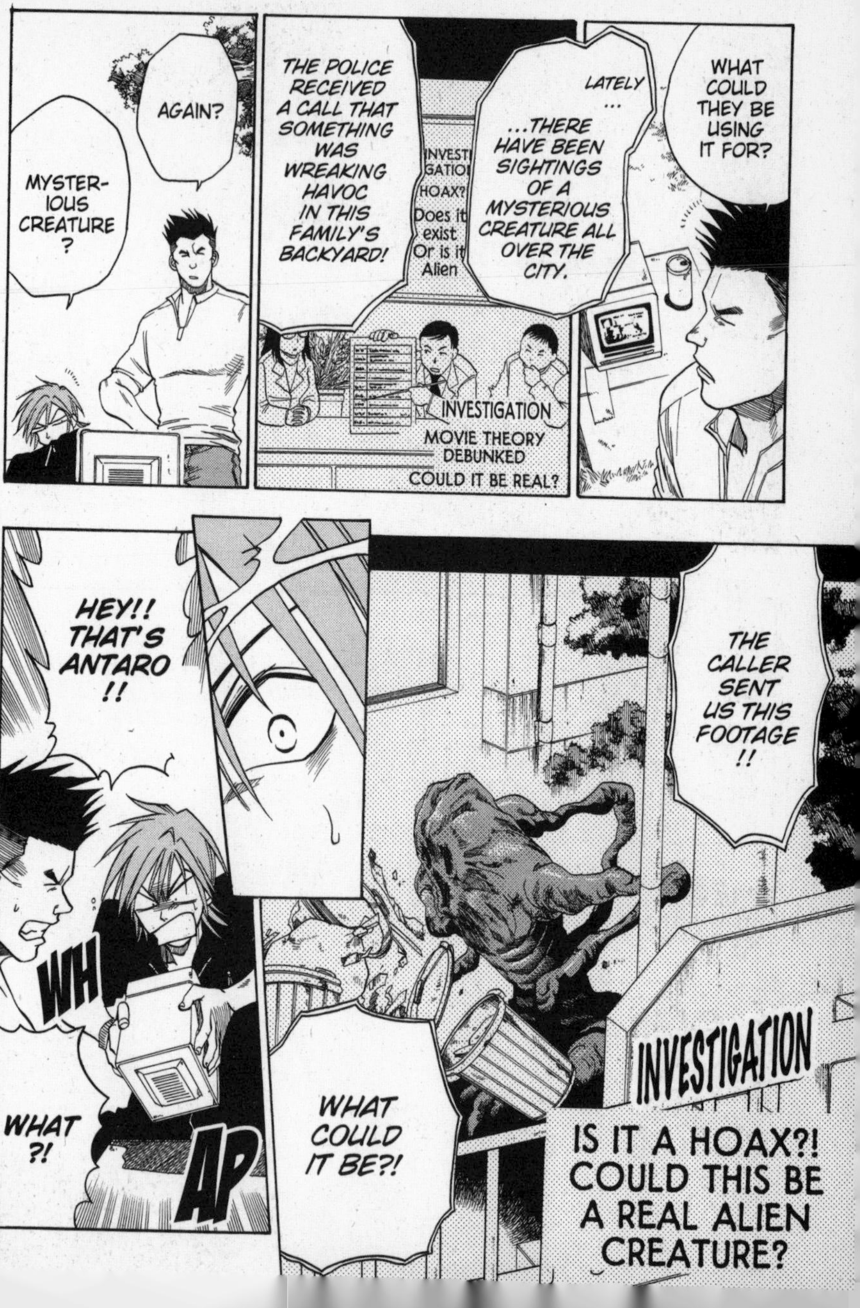
WHAT COULD THEY BE USING IT FOR?
LATELY ...
...THERE HAVE BEEN SIGHTINGS OF A MYSTERIOUS CREATURE ALL OVER THE CITY.
THE POLICE RECEIVED A CALL THAT SOMETHING WAS WREAKING HAVOC IN THIS FAMILY'S BACKYARD!
HOAX?!
Does it exist
Or is it
Alien
INVESTIGATION
MOVIE THEORY DEBUNKED
COULD IT BE REAL?
AGAIN?
MYSTER-IOUS CREATURE?
THE CALLER SENT US THIS FOOTAGE!!
INVESTIGATION
IS IT A HOAX?! COULD THIS BE A REAL ALIEN CREATURE?
WHAT COULD IT BE?!
HEY!! THAT'S ANTARO!!
WH
AP
WHAT?!

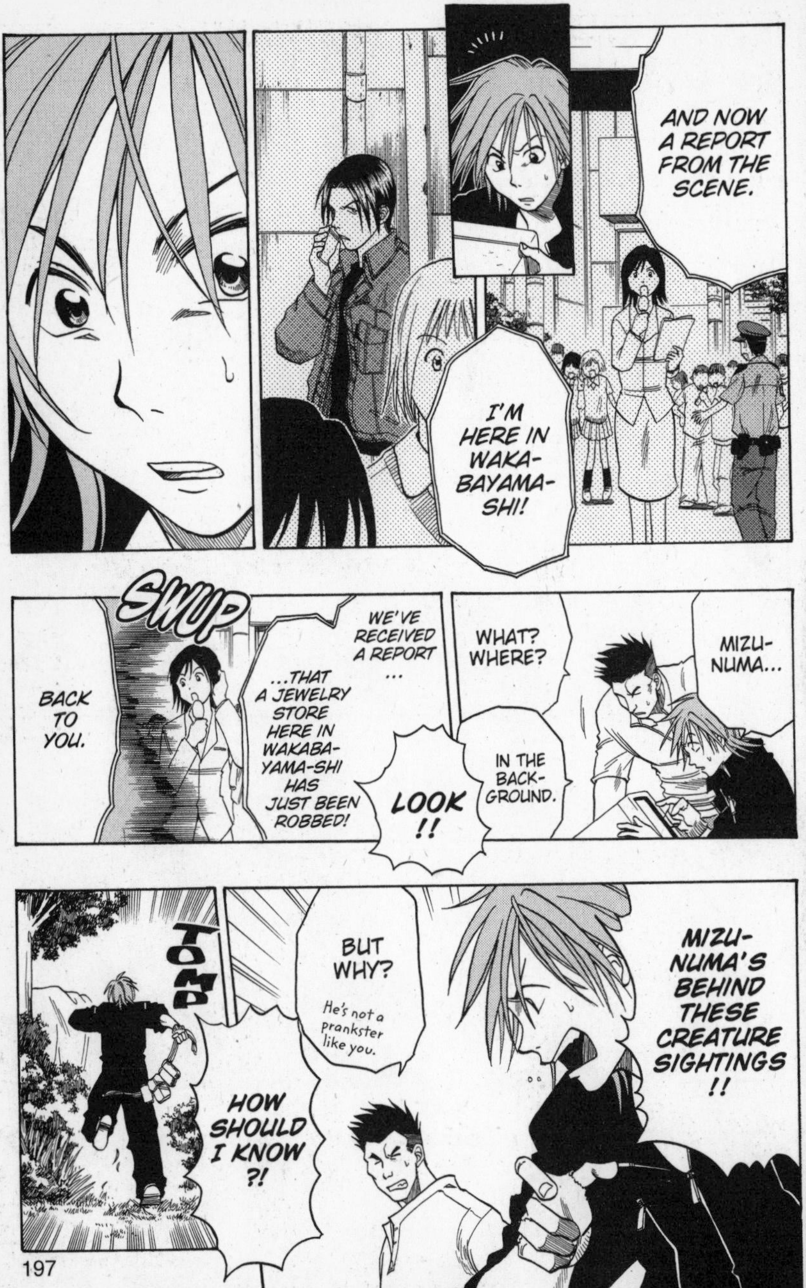
AND NOW A REPORT FROM THE SCENE.
I'M HERE IN WAKA-BAYAMA-SHI!
MIZU-NUMA...
WHAT? WHERE?
IN THE BACK-GROUND.
LOOK!!
WE'VE RECEIVED A REPORT ...
...THAT A JEWELRY STORE HERE IN WAKABA-YAMA-SHI HAS JUST BEEN ROBBED!
BACK TO YOU.
SWUP
MIZU-NUMA'S BEHIND THESE CREATURE SIGHTINGS!!
BUT WHY?
He's not a prankster like you.
HOW SHOULD I KNOW?!
TOMP

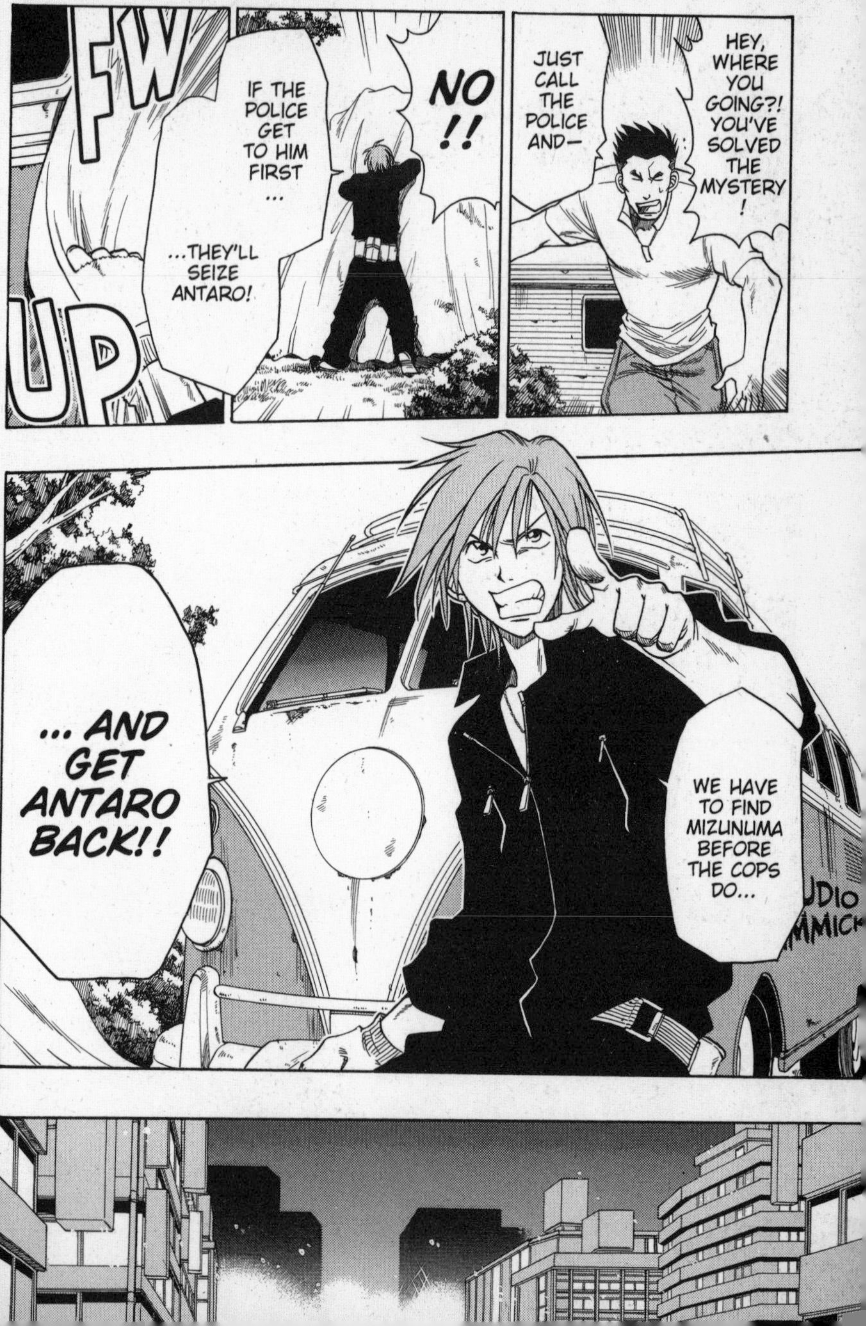
HEY, WHERE YOU GOING?! YOU'VE SOLVED THE MYSTERY!
JUST CALL THE POLICE AND—
NO!!
IF THE POLICE GET TO HIM FIRST...
...THEY'LL SEIZE ANTARO!
FWUP
WE HAVE TO FIND MIZUNUMA BEFORE THE COPS DO...
... AND GET ANTARO BACK!!

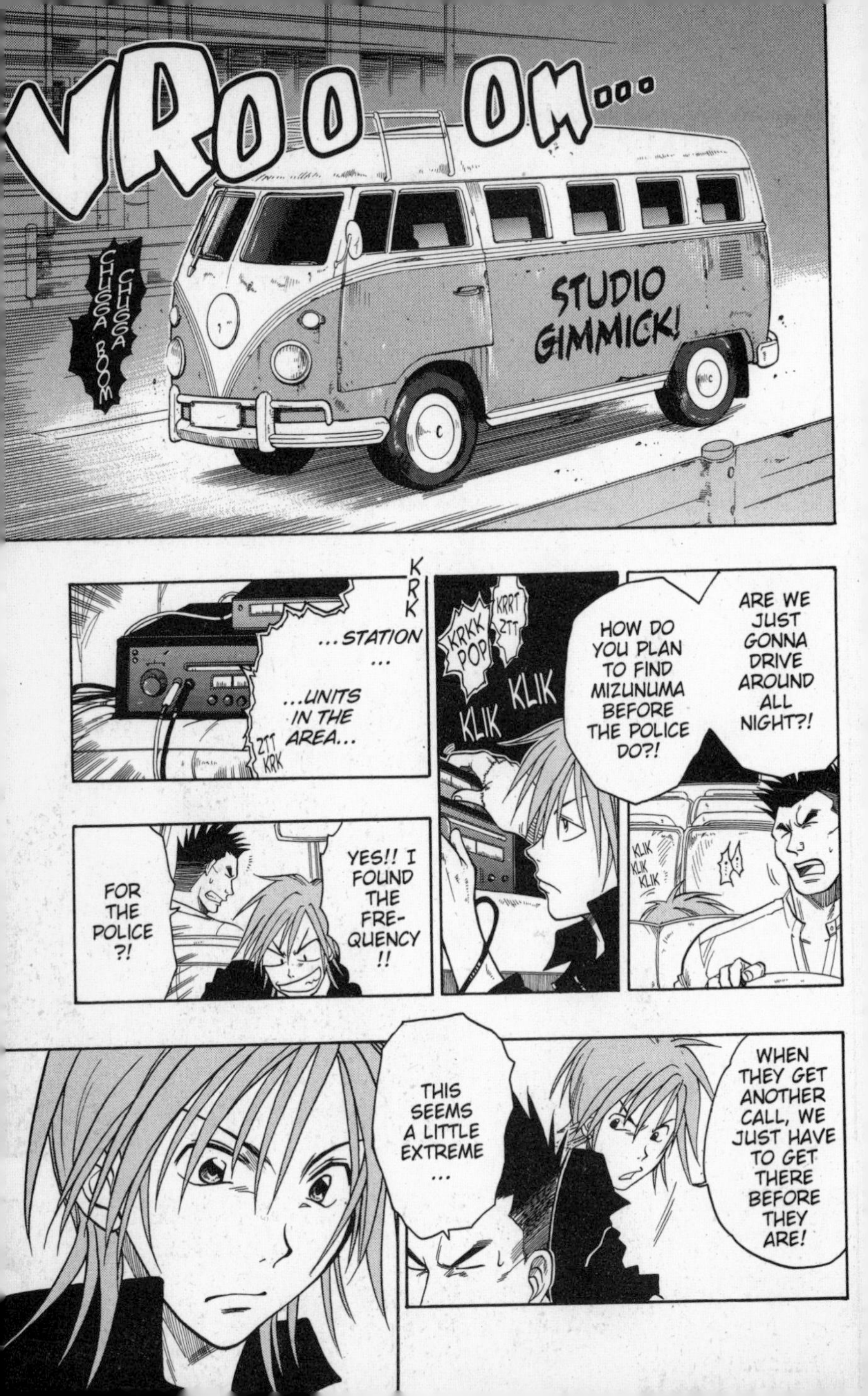
VROOOOM...
CHUGGA CHUGGA BOOM
STUDIO GIMMICK!
ARE WE JUST GONNA DRIVE AROUND ALL NIGHT?!
KLIK KLIK KLIK
HOW DO YOU PLAN TO FIND MIZUNUMA BEFORE THE POLICE DO?!
KRRT ZTT
KRKK POP
KLIK
KLIK
KRK
...STATION...
...UNITS IN THE AREA...
ZTT KRK
YES!! I FOUND THE FRE-QUENCY!!
FOR THE POLICE?!
WHEN THEY GET ANOTHER CALL, WE JUST HAVE TO GET THERE BEFORE THEY ARE!
THIS SEEMS A LITTLE EXTREME...

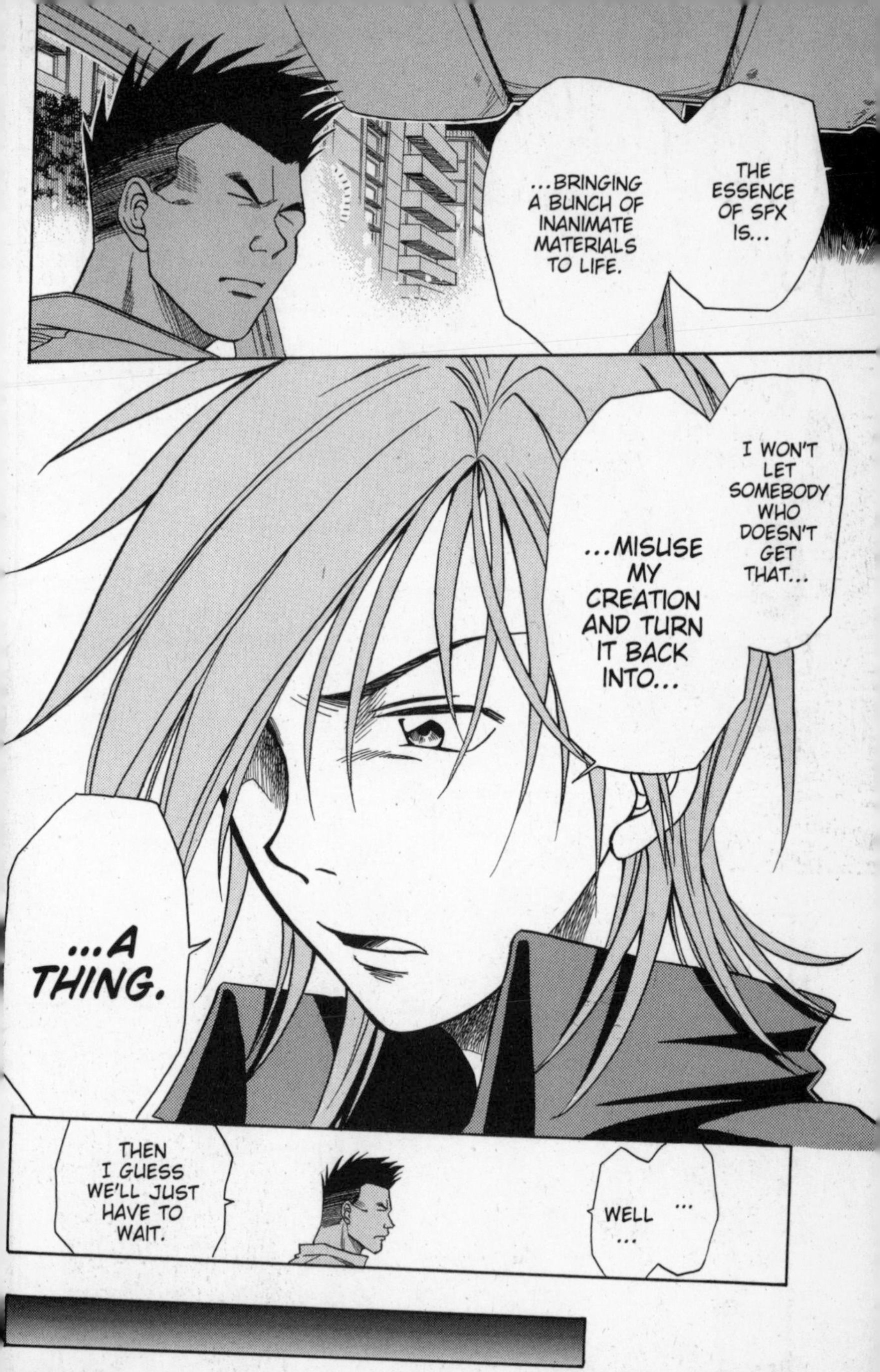
THE ESSENCE OF SFX IS...
...BRINGING A BUNCH OF INANIMATE MATERIALS TO LIFE.
I WON'T LET SOMEBODY WHO DOESN'T GET THAT...
...MISUSE MY CREATION AND TURN IT BACK INTO...
...A THING.
WELL ... ...
THEN I GUESS WE'LL JUST HAVE TO WAIT.

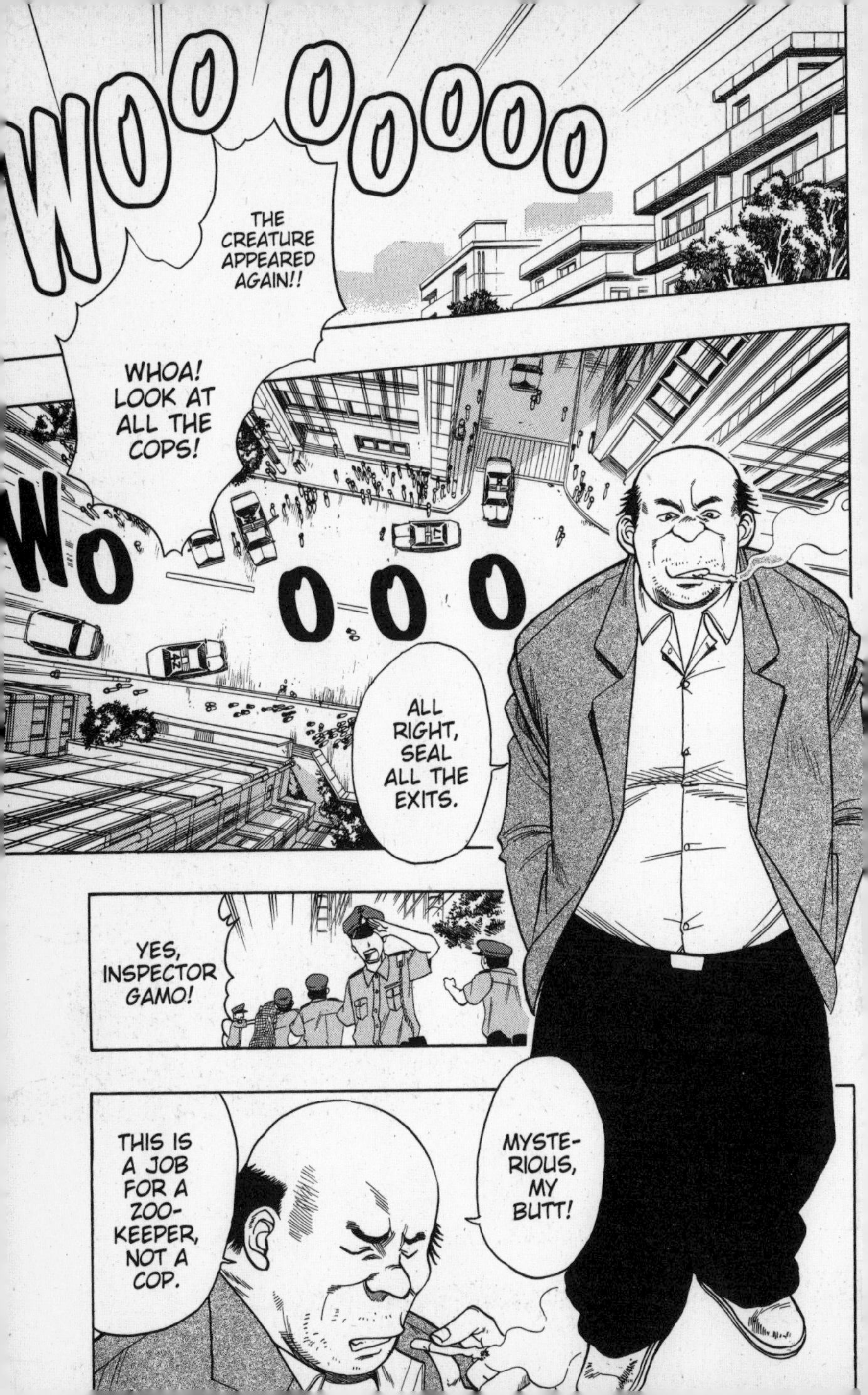
WOO OOOOO
THE CREATURE APPEARED AGAIN!!
WHOA! LOOK AT ALL THE COPS!
WO OOO
ALL RIGHT, SEAL ALL THE EXITS.
YES, INSPECTOR GAMO!
MYSTE-RIOUS, MY BUTT!
THIS IS A JOB FOR A ZOO-KEEPER, NOT A COP.

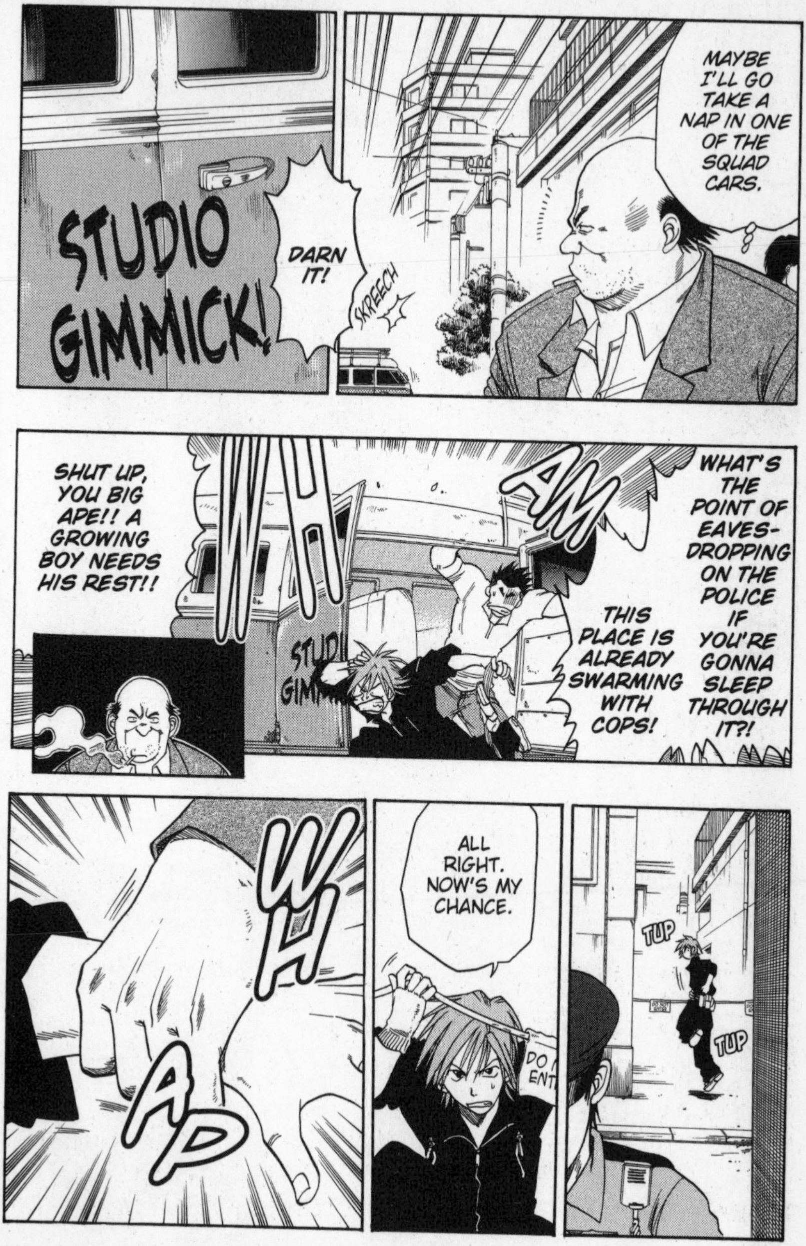
MAYBE I'LL GO TAKE A NAP IN ONE OF THE SQUAD CARS.
SKREECH
DARN IT!
STUDIO GIMMICK!
WHAT'S THE POINT OF EAVES-DROPPING ON THE POLICE IF YOU'RE GONNA SLEEP THROUGH IT?!
THIS PLACE IS ALREADY SWARMING WITH COPS!
WAH
AM
SHUT UP, YOU BIG APE!! A GROWING BOY NEEDS HIS REST!!
TUP
TUP
ALL RIGHT. NOW'S MY CHANCE.
WH
AP

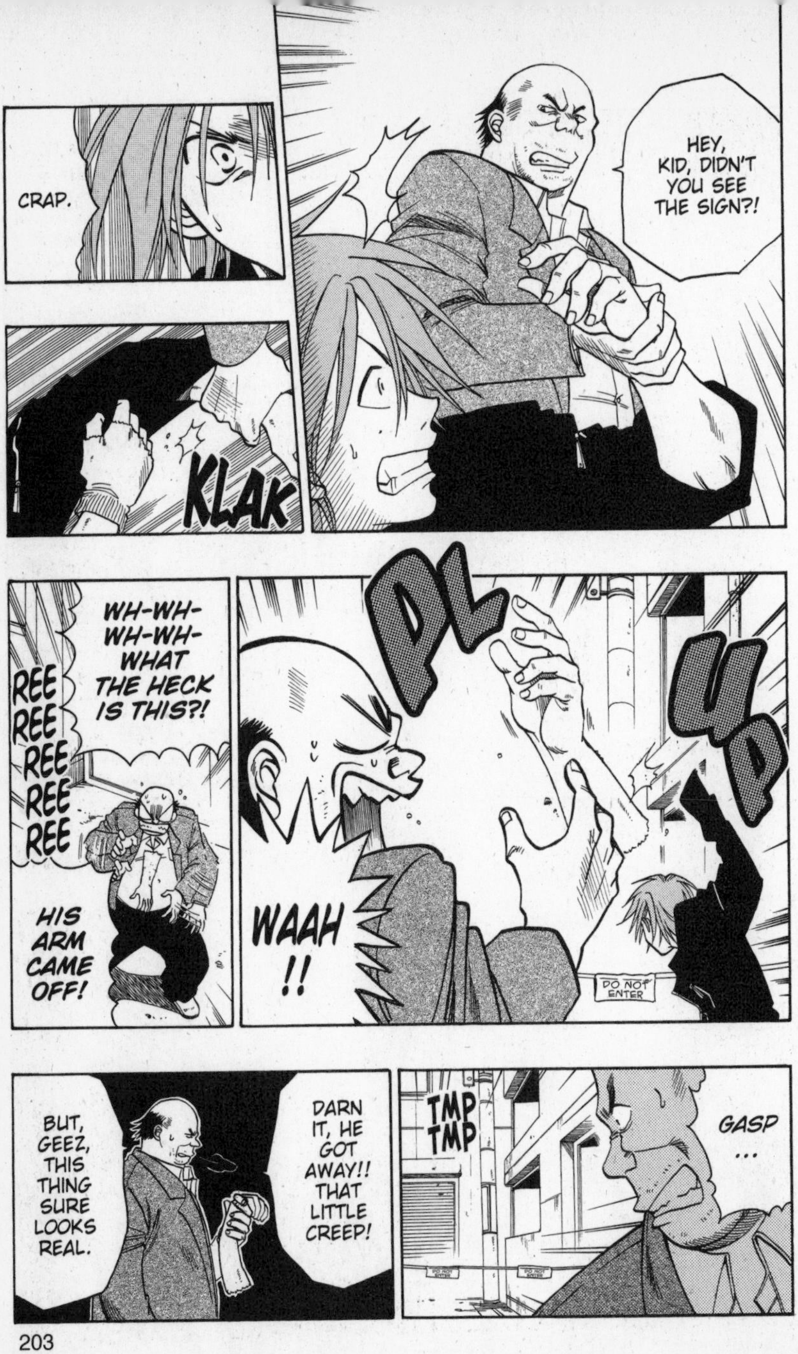
HEY, KID, DIDN'T YOU SEE THE SIGN?!
CRAP.
KLAK
PLUP
WAAH!!
DO NOT ENTER
WH-WH-WH-WH-WHAT THE HECK IS THIS?!
REE REE REE REE REE
HIS ARM CAME OFF!
GASP...
TMP TMP
DARN IT, HE GOT AWAY!! THAT LITTLE CREEP!
BUT, GEEZ, THIS THING SURE LOOKS REAL.

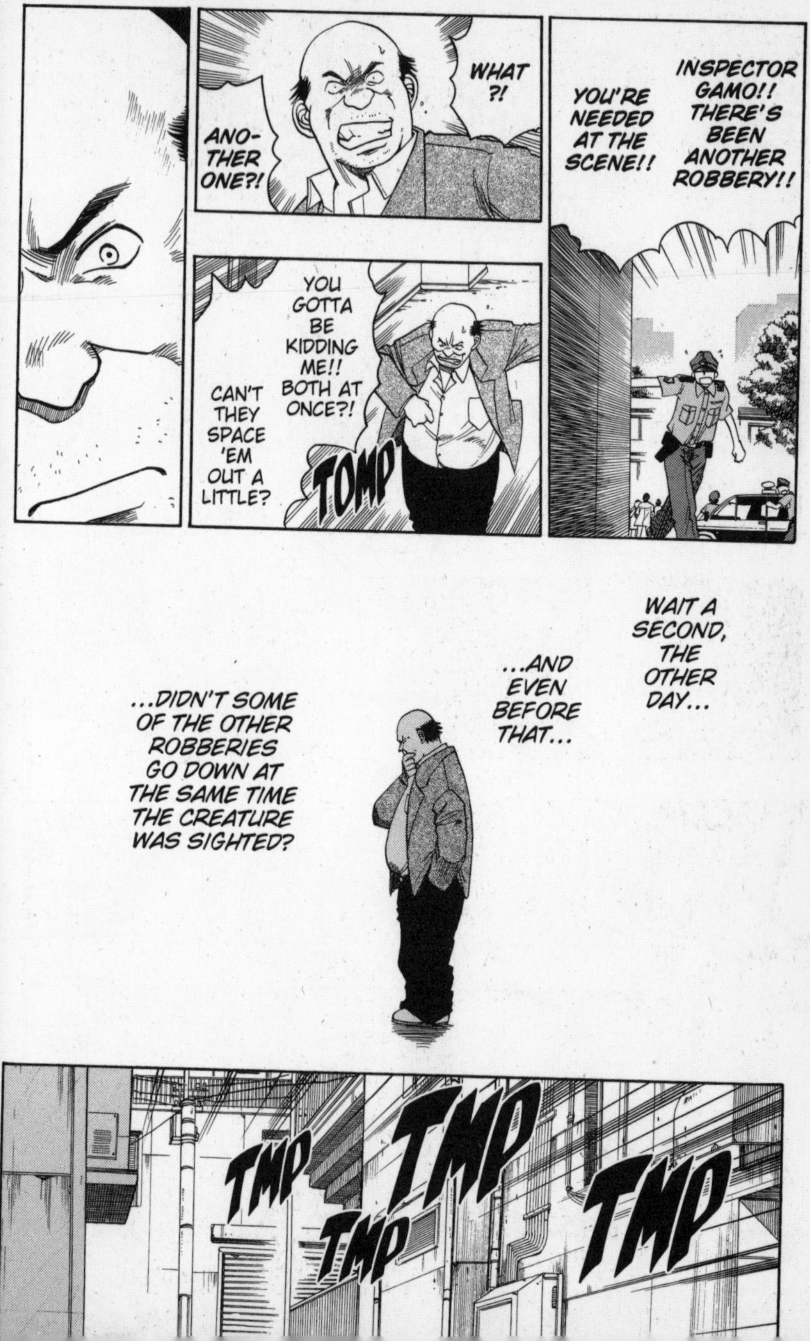
INSPECTOR GAMO!! THERE'S BEEN ANOTHER ROBBERY!!
YOU'RE NEEDED AT THE SCENE!!
WHAT ?!
ANOTHER ONE?!
YOU GOTTA BE KIDDING ME!! BOTH AT ONCE?!
CAN'T THEY SPACE 'EM OUT A LITTLE?
TOMP
WAIT A SECOND, THE OTHER DAY...
...AND EVEN BEFORE THAT...
...DIDN'T SOME OF THE OTHER ROBBERIES GO DOWN AT THE SAME TIME THE CREATURE WAS SIGHTED?
TMP
TMP
TMP
TMP

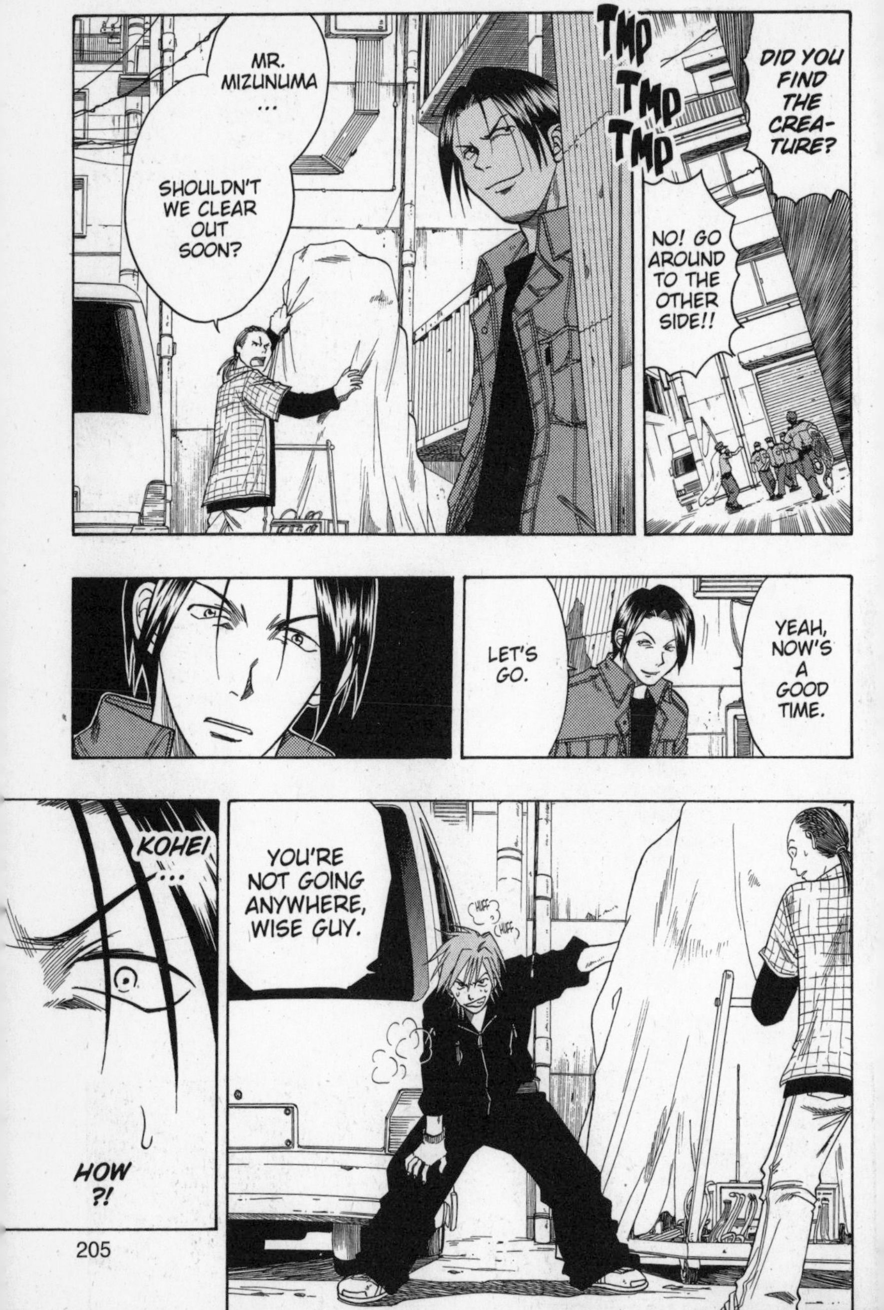
DID YOU FIND THE CREATURE?
NO! GO AROUND TO THE OTHER SIDE!!
TMP TMP TMP
MR. MIZUNUMA ...
SHOULDN'T WE CLEAR OUT SOON?
YEAH, NOW'S A GOOD TIME.
LET'S GO.
YOU'RE NOT GOING ANYWHERE, WISE GUY.
HUFF HUFF
KOHEI ...
HOW ?!

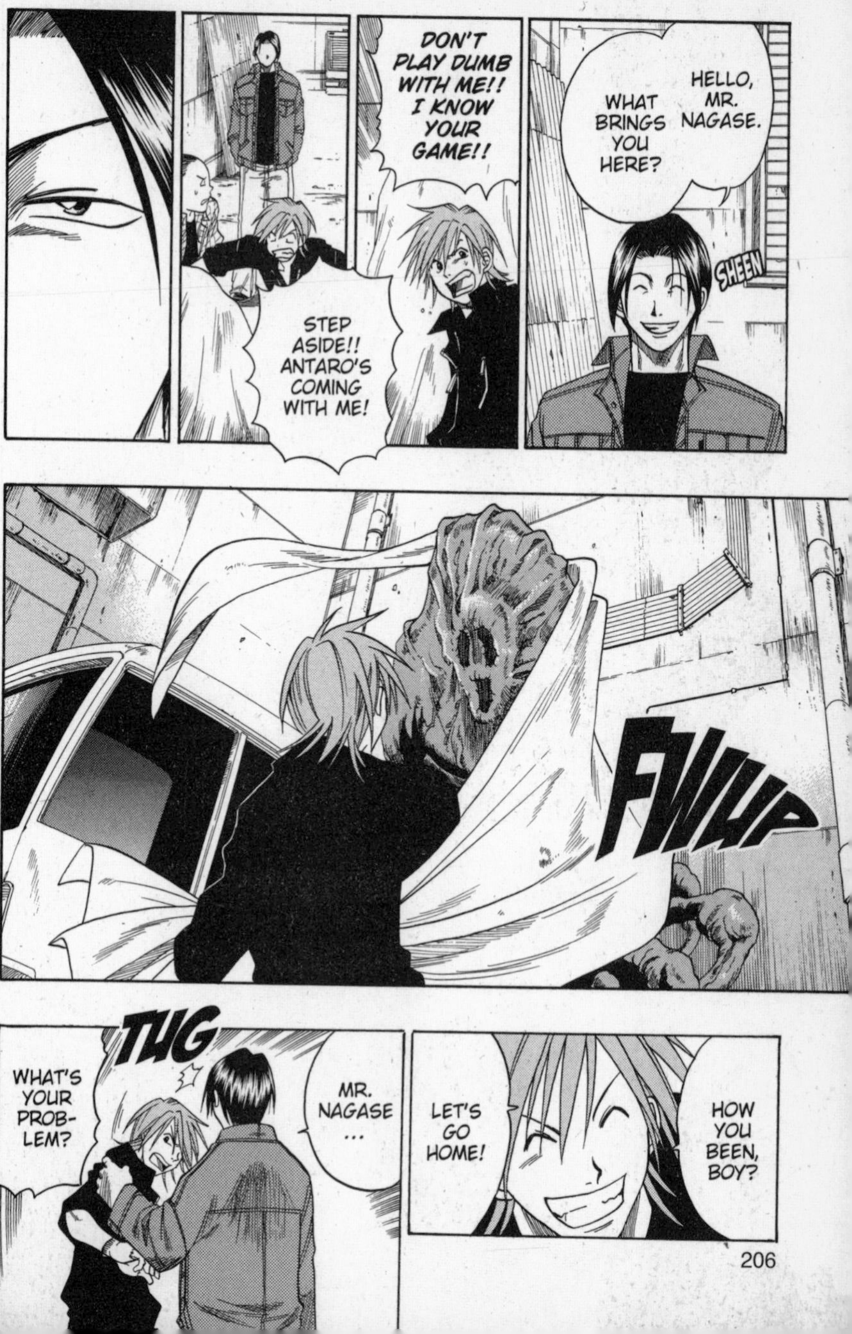
HELLO, MR. NAGASE.
WHAT BRINGS YOU HERE?
SHEEN
DON'T PLAY DUMB WITH ME!! I KNOW YOUR GAME!!
STEP ASIDE!! ANTARO'S COMING WITH ME!
FWUP
HOW YOU BEEN, BOY?
LET'S GO HOME!
MR. NAGASE...
TUG
WHAT'S YOUR PROB-LEM?

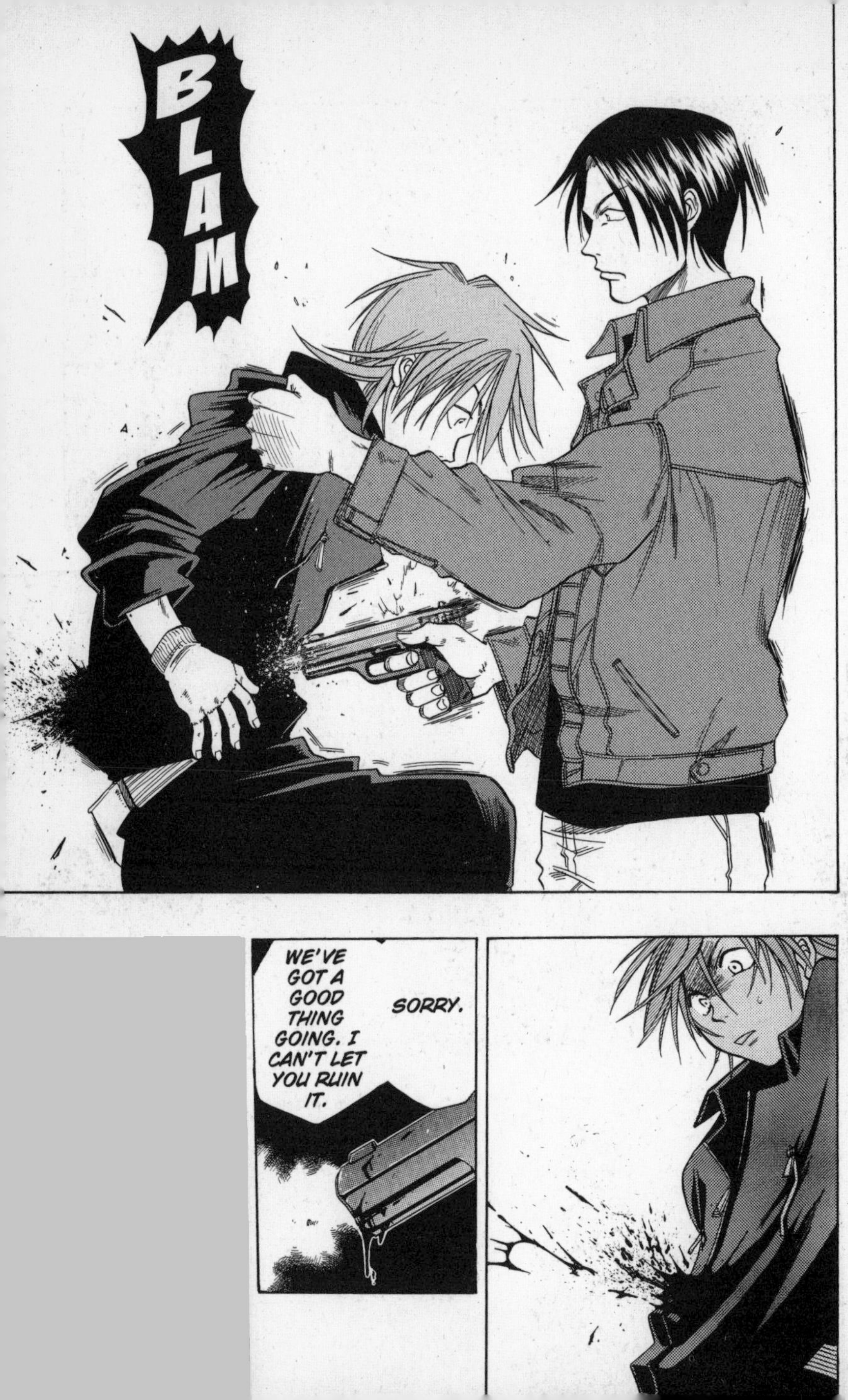
BLAM
SORRY.
WE'VE GOT A GOOD THING GOING. I CAN'T LET YOU RUIN IT.

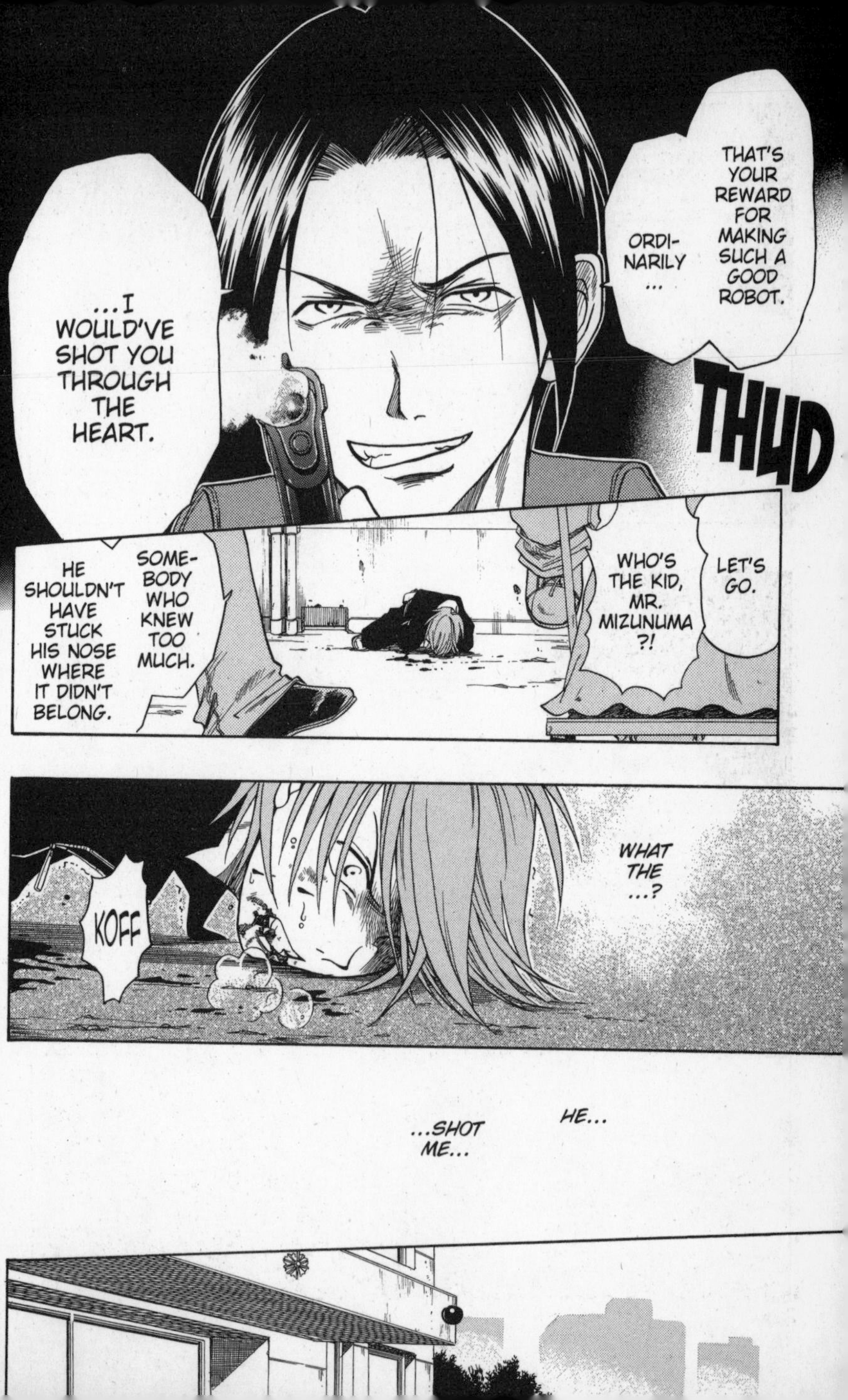
THAT'S YOUR REWARD FOR MAKING SUCH A GOOD ROBOT.
ORDI-NARILY ...
...I WOULD'VE SHOT YOU THROUGH THE HEART.
THUD
LET'S GO.
WHO'S THE KID, MR. MIZUNUMA?!
SOME-BODY WHO KNEW TOO MUCH.
HE SHOULDN'T HAVE STUCK HIS NOSE WHERE IT DIDN'T BELONG.
WHAT THE ...?
KOFF
HE...
...SHOT ME...

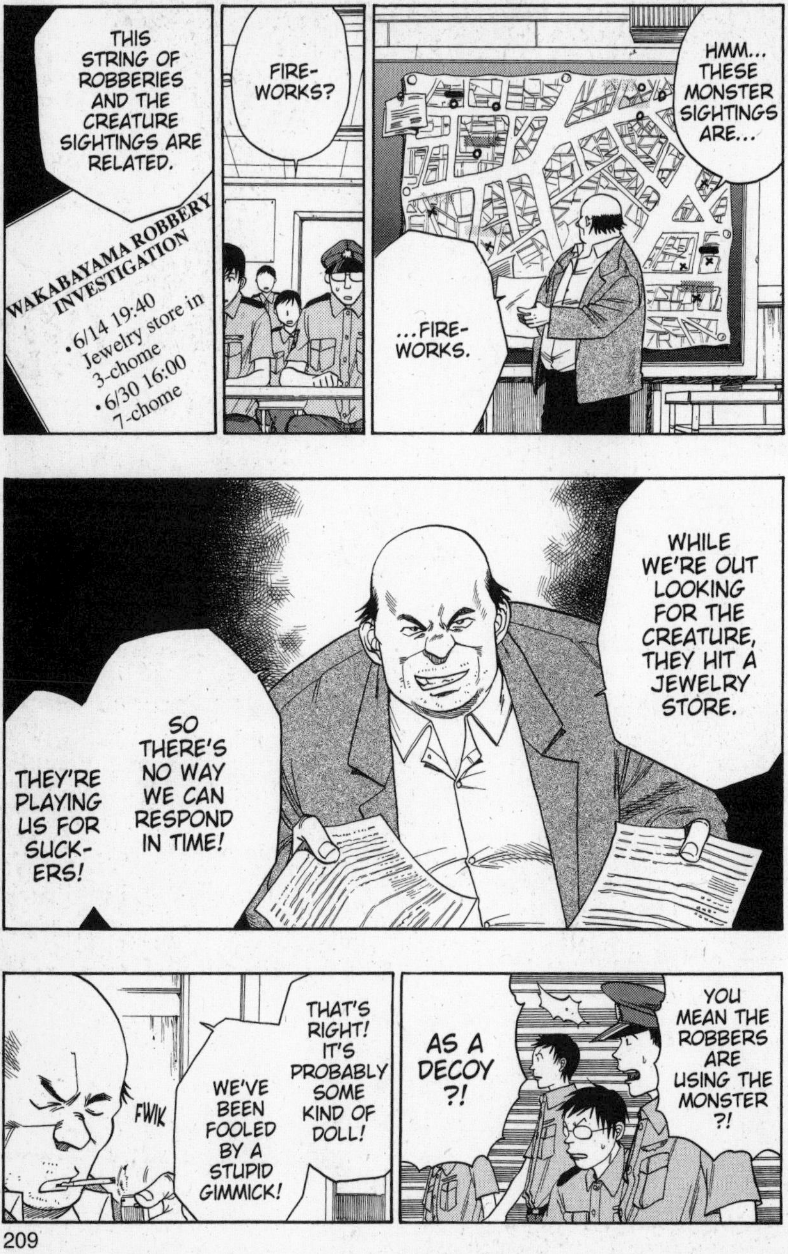
HMM... THESE MONSTER SIGHTINGS ARE...
...FIRE-WORKS.
FIRE-WORKS?
THIS STRING OF ROBBERIES AND THE CREATURE SIGHTINGS ARE RELATED.
WAKABAYAMA ROBBERY INVESTIGATION
•6/14 19:40 Jewelry store in 3-chome
•6/30 16:00 7-chome
WHILE WE'RE OUT LOOKING FOR THE CREATURE, THEY HIT A JEWELRY STORE.
SO THERE'S NO WAY WE CAN RESPOND IN TIME!
THEY'RE PLAYING US FOR SUCK-ERS!
YOU MEAN THE ROBBERS ARE USING THE MONSTER ?!
AS A DECOY ?!
THAT'S RIGHT! IT'S PROBABLY SOME KIND OF DOLL!
WE'VE BEEN FOOLED BY A STUPID GIMMICK!
FWIK

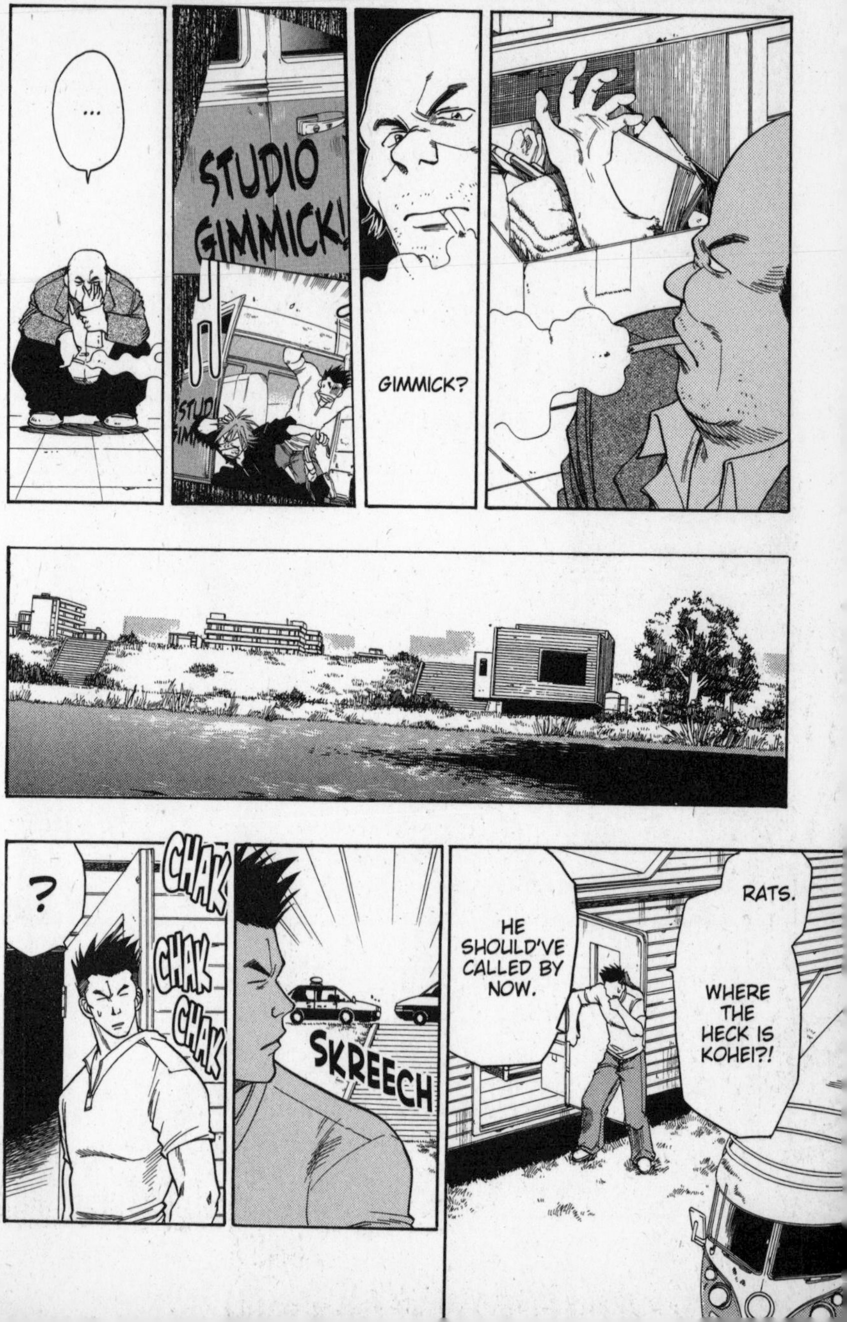
GIMMICK?
STUDIO GIMMICK!
STUDI GIM
...
RATS.
WHERE THE HECK IS KOHEI?!
HE SHOULD'VE CALLED BY NOW.
SKREECH
CHAK
CHAK
CHAK
?

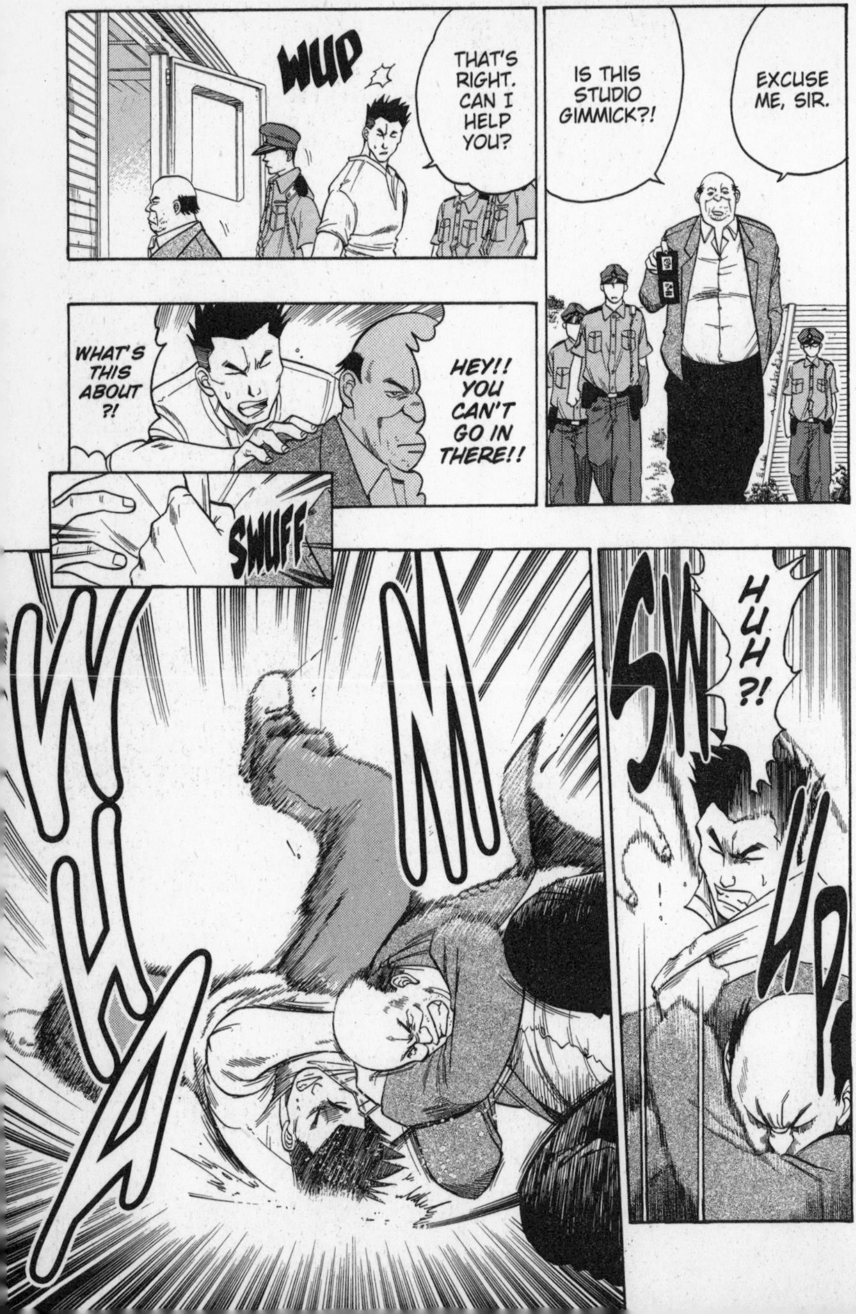
EXCUSE ME, SIR.
IS THIS STUDIO GIMMICK?!
THAT'S RIGHT. CAN I HELP YOU?
WUP
HEY!! YOU CAN'T GO IN THERE!!
WHAT'S THIS ABOUT ?!
SWUFF
HUH?!
SWUP
WHAM

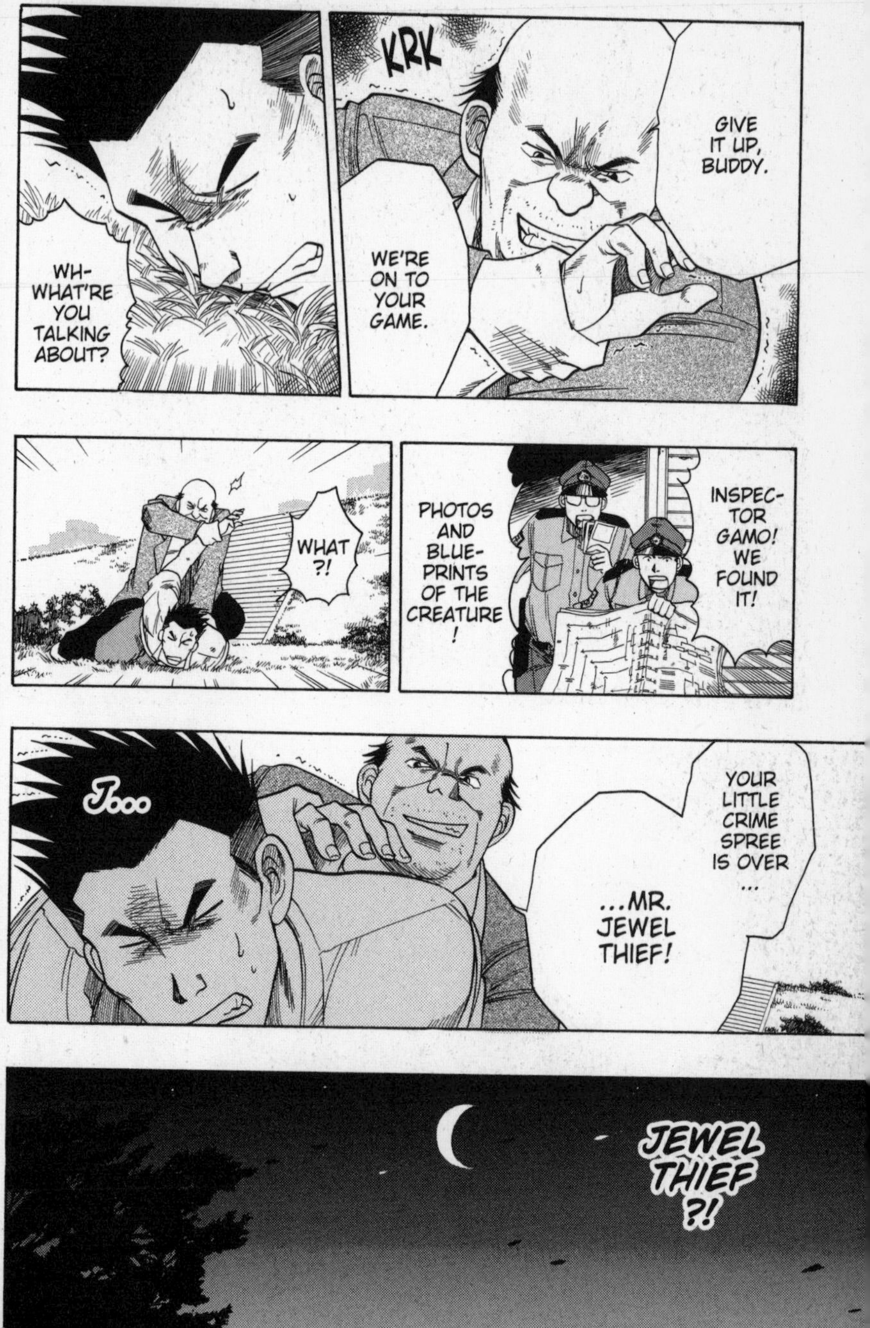
KRK
GIVE IT UP, BUDDY.
WE'RE ON TO YOUR GAME.
WH- WHAT'RE YOU TALKING ABOUT?
INSPECTOR GAMO! WE FOUND IT!
PHOTOS AND BLUEPRINTS OF THE CREATURE!
WHAT?!
YOUR LITTLE CRIME SPREE IS OVER...
...MR. JEWEL THIEF!
JEWEL THIEF?!

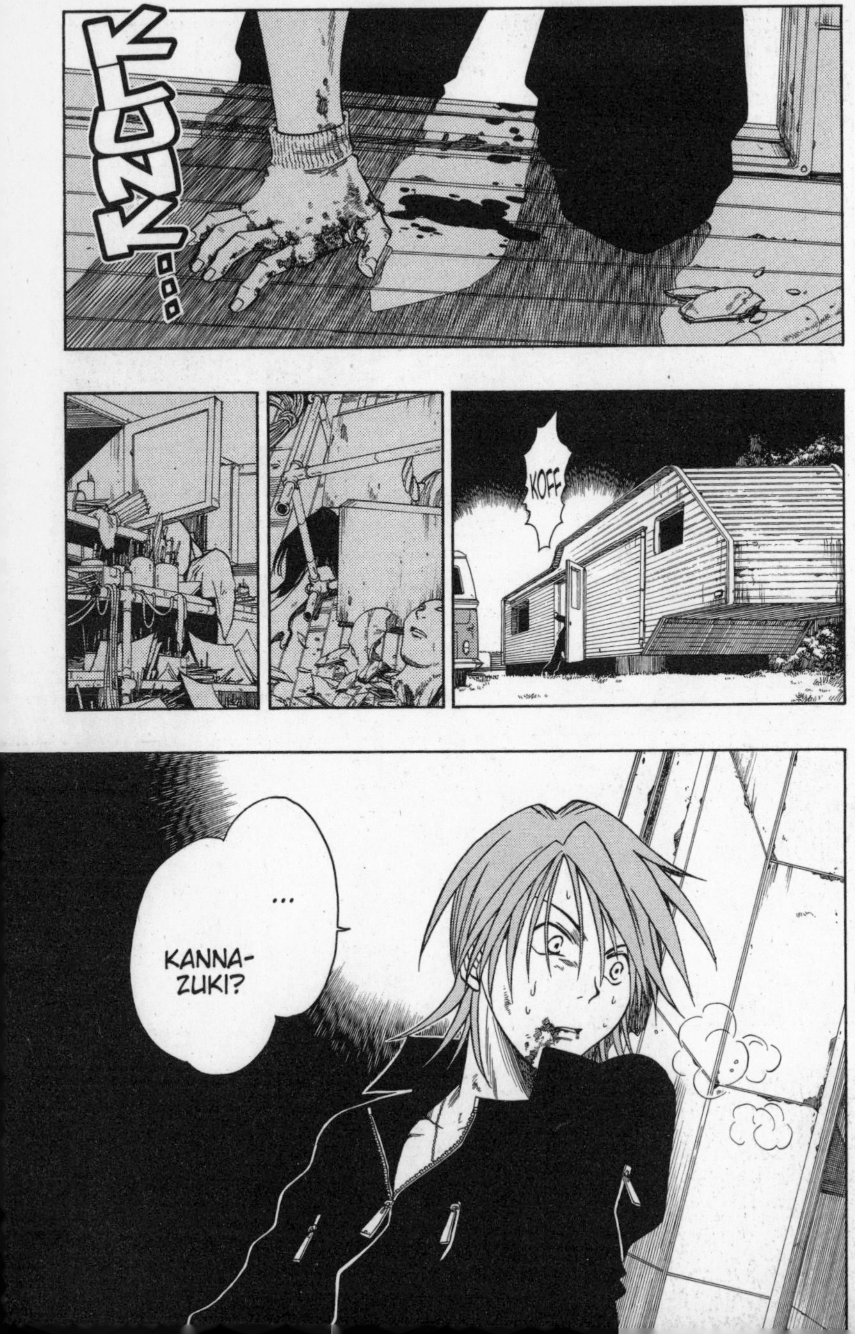
KLUNK...
KOFF
...
KANNA-
ZUKI?

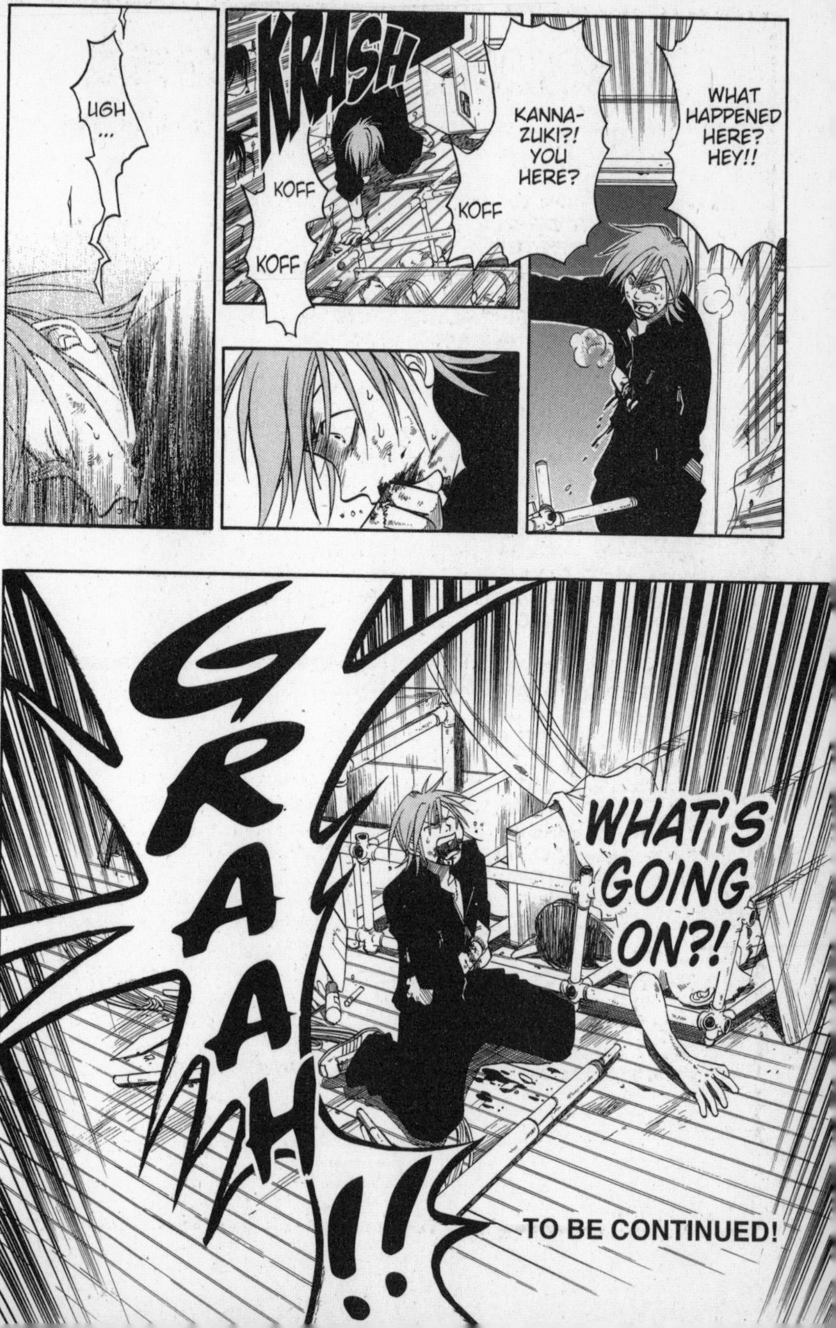
WHAT HAPPENED HERE? HEY!!
KANNA-ZUKI?! YOU HERE?
KRASH
KOFF
KOFF
KOFF
UGH ...
GRAAAH!!
WHAT'S GOING ON?!
TO BE CONTINUED!

THE MAKING OF GIMMICK!

By Youzaburou Kanari

THE IDEA FOR *GIMMICK!* CAME TO ME BACK IN DECEMBER OF 2003. I'VE ALWAYS LOVED MOVIES AND BEEN INTERESTED IN SPECIAL EFFECTS AND SCIENCE FICTION. MY EDITOR, MR. I-TANI (NICKNAME), LIKED THE IDEA AND GOT ON BOARD RIGHT AWAY. SO WE VISITED A LOT OF COMPUTER GRAPHICS AND SPECIAL EFFECTS STUDIOS OVER THE NEXT YEAR.

WHILE WE WERE DOING OUR RESEARCH, I CAME UP WITH SOME IDEAS FOR STORIES AND SETTINGS, BUT WE WEREN'T ABLE TO FIND AN ARTIST. WE OFFERED IT TO ONE THAT WE THOUGHT WAS RIGHT FOR THE PROJECT, BUT IT DIDN'T PAN OUT. AS A RESULT, *GIMMICK!* WAS PUT ON HOLD, AND, RELUCTANTLY, WE STARTED WORK ON ANOTHER PROJECT. THAT WAS AROUND APRIL OF 2004. BUT EVEN THOUGH WE'D DECIDED TO SAVE *GIMMICK!* UNTIL WE'D FOUND THE RIGHT ARTIST, WE WERE WORRIED SICK THAT SOMEBODY ELSE WOULD DO THE CONCEPT BEFORE WE DID.

THEN YABUGUCHI APPEARED LIKE AN ANGEL ANSWERING THE PRAYERS OF THE DESPERATE. (A LITTLE MELODRAMA.) ONE FRIDAY IN JULY OF 2004, WE HANDED YABUGUCHI A FEW PAGES OF STORY WE'D COME UP WITH TO SEE WHAT SHE THOUGHT, PREPARED TO WAIT WEEKS FOR A RESPONSE. BUT TO OUR ASTONISHMENT, ON THE FOLLOWING TUESDAY WE RECEIVED A STORYBOARD!! WE LATER LEARNED THAT YABUGUCHI WAS EXCITED ABOUT THE IDEA TOO. AFTER THAT, *GIMMICK!* STARTED TO GAIN MOMENTUM.

THAT STORYBOARD EVENTUALLY BECAME THE FIRST SCRIPT, AND IN DECEMBER IT WAS PUBLISHED IN *YOUNG JUMP* AS A ONE-SHOT STORY IN TWO INSTALLMENTS. TO OUR DELIGHT, IT WAS WELL RECEIVED BY THE READERS AND WE BEGAN WORK ON A SEQUEL, BUT... ONCE AGAIN, SOMETHING INCREDIBLE HAPPENED, SOMETHING NONE OF US EVER SAW COMING...

CONTINUED IN VOLUME 2

GIMMICK!

RESEARCH TRIP ANECDOTES

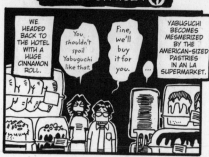

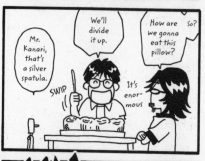

EDITOR: ITAYAN

STORY: YOUZABUROU KANARI

ART: KUROKO YABUGUCHI

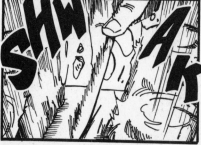

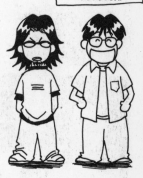

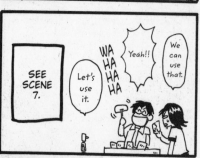

SILVER SPATULA 7

YABUGUCHI BECOMES MESMERIZED BY THE AMERICAN-SIZED PASTRIES IN AN LA SUPERMARKET.
...
Fine, we'll buy it for you.
You shouldn't spoil Yabuguchi like that.
WE HEADED BACK TO THE HOTEL WITH A HUGE CINNAMON ROLL.
So?
How are we gonna eat this pillow?
We'll divide it up.
It's enormous
Mr. Kanari, that's a silver spatula.
SWIP
SHWAK
We can use that.
Yeah!!
WA HA HA HA
Let's use it.
SEE SCENE 7.

SILVER SPATULA 2

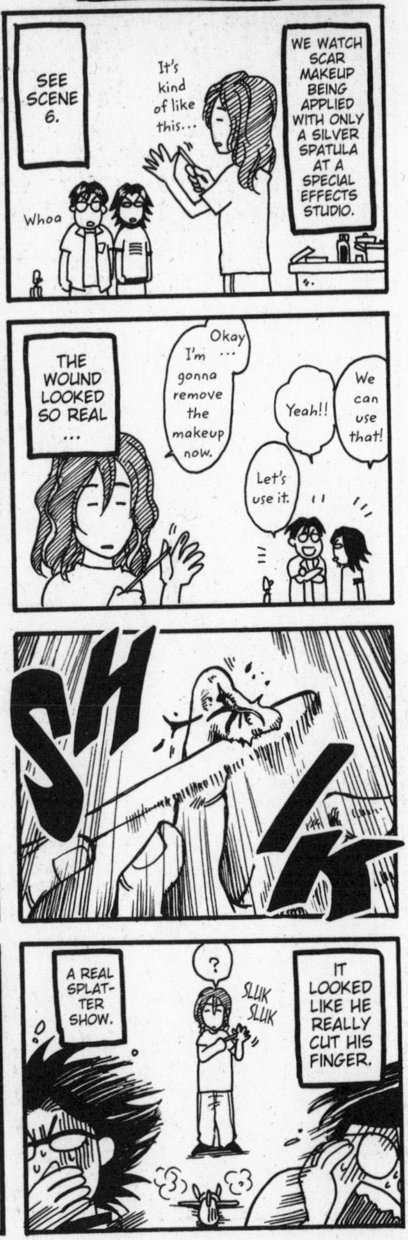

WE WATCH SCAR MAKEUP BEING APPLIED WITH ONLY A SILVER SPATULA AT A SPECIAL EFFECTS STUDIO.
It's kind of like this...
SEE SCENE 6.
Whoa
We can use that!
Yeah!!
Let's use it.
Okay... I'm gonna remove the makeup now.
THE WOUND LOOKED SO REAL...
SHIK
IT LOOKED LIKE HE REALLY CUT HIS FINGER.
SLUK SLUK
?
A REAL SPLAT-TER SHOW.

SILVER SPATULA 3

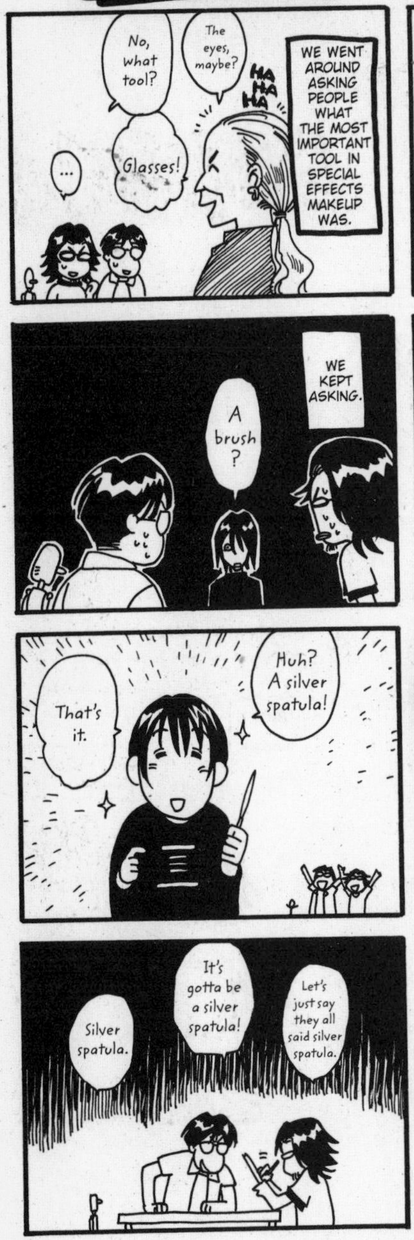

WE WENT AROUND ASKING PEOPLE WHAT THE MOST IMPORTANT TOOL IN SPECIAL EFFECTS MAKEUP WAS.
HA HA HA
The eyes, maybe?
No, what tool?
Glasses!
...
WE KEPT ASKING.
A brush?
Huh? A silver spatula!
That's it.
Let's just say they all said silver spatula.
It's gotta be a silver spatula!
Silver spatula.

GIMMICK! THIS IS OUR WORK PLACE.

IT'S A ROOM THAT FACES NORTH. ON DAYS BEFORE DEADLINES WHEN THE ASSISTANTS ARE THERE, HEAVY METAL, CLASSICAL MUSIC, AND "ROCKY'S THEME" ARE PLAYED.

I HAVE THE PRIVILEGE OF WORKING ON *GIMMICK!* EVERY WEEK WITH THE SUPPORT OF MANY PEOPLE. IT'S A MANGA ARTIST'S ROOM WITH NO MANGA. IT'S TINY.

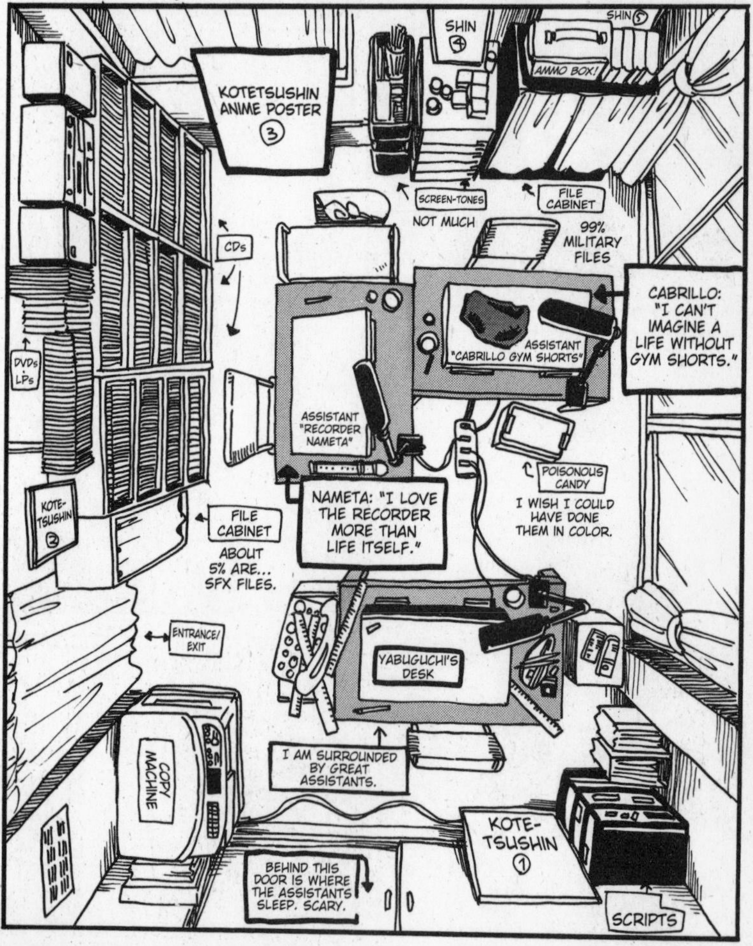

SHIN 5
AMMO BOX!
SHIN 4
KOTETSUSHIN ANIME POSTER 3
FILE CABINET
SCREEN-TONES
NOT MUCH
99% MILITARY FILES
CDs
CABRILLO: "I CAN'T IMAGINE A LIFE WITHOUT GYM SHORTS."
ASSISTANT "CABRILLO GYM SHORTS"
DVDs LPs
ASSISTANT "RECORDER NAMETA"
POISONOUS CANDY
I WISH I COULD HAVE DONE THEM IN COLOR.
NAMETA: "I LOVE THE RECORDER MORE THAN LIFE ITSELF."
FILE CABINET
ABOUT 5% ARE... SFX FILES.
KOTE-TSUSHIN 2
YABUGUCHI'S DESK
ENTRANCE/EXIT
I AM SURROUNDED BY GREAT ASSISTANTS.
COPY MACHINE
KOTE-TSUSHIN 1
SCRIPTS
BEHIND THIS DOOR IS WHERE THE ASSISTANTS SLEEP. SCARY.

EXTRA

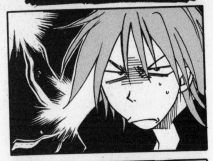

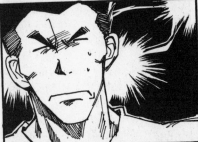

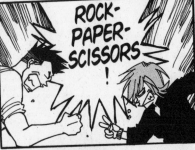

ROCK-PAPER-SCISSORS!
But it's my house...

EVERY DAY IS LIKE CAMPING OUT.

The rice is ready.
Curry again?

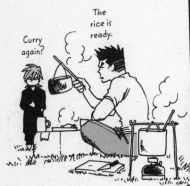

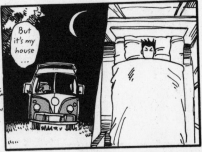

GIMMICK!

Vol. 1

Story by Youzaburou Kanari
Art by Kuroko Yabuguchi

English Adaptation/Lance Caselman
Translation/Joe Yamazaki
Touch-up Art & Lettering/Rina Mapa
Design/Amy Martin
Editor/Kit Fox

Editor in Chief, Books/Alvin Lu
Editor in Chief, Magazines/Marc Weidenbaum
VP of Publishing Licensing/Rika Inouye
VP of Sales/Gonzalo Ferreyra
Sr. VP of Marketing/Liza Coppola
Publisher/Hyoe Narita

Printed in the U.S.A.

Published by VIZ Media, LLC
P.O. Box 77010
San Francisco, CA 94107

10 9 8 7 6 5 4 3 2 1
First printing, June 2008

www.viz.com

store.viz.com

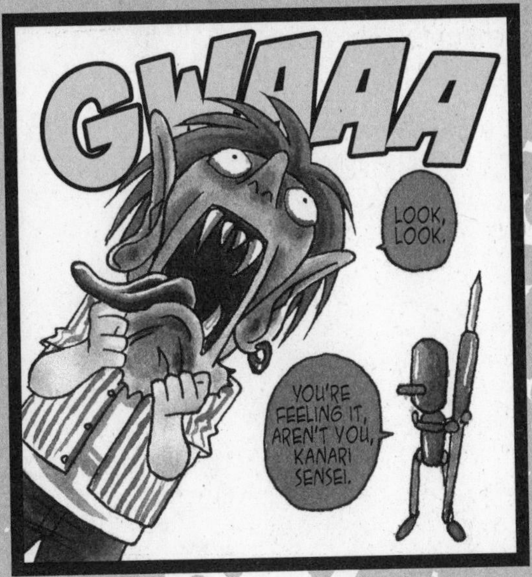
GWAAA
LOOK, LOOK.
YOU'RE FEELING IT, AREN'T YOU, KANARI SENSEI.

Roman Holiday is a great old black-and-white movie from 50 years ago. If only I could write a story like that.

—Kanari

I'm having a great time illustrating *Gimmick!* I want to share this joy with as many people as I can.

—Yabuguchi

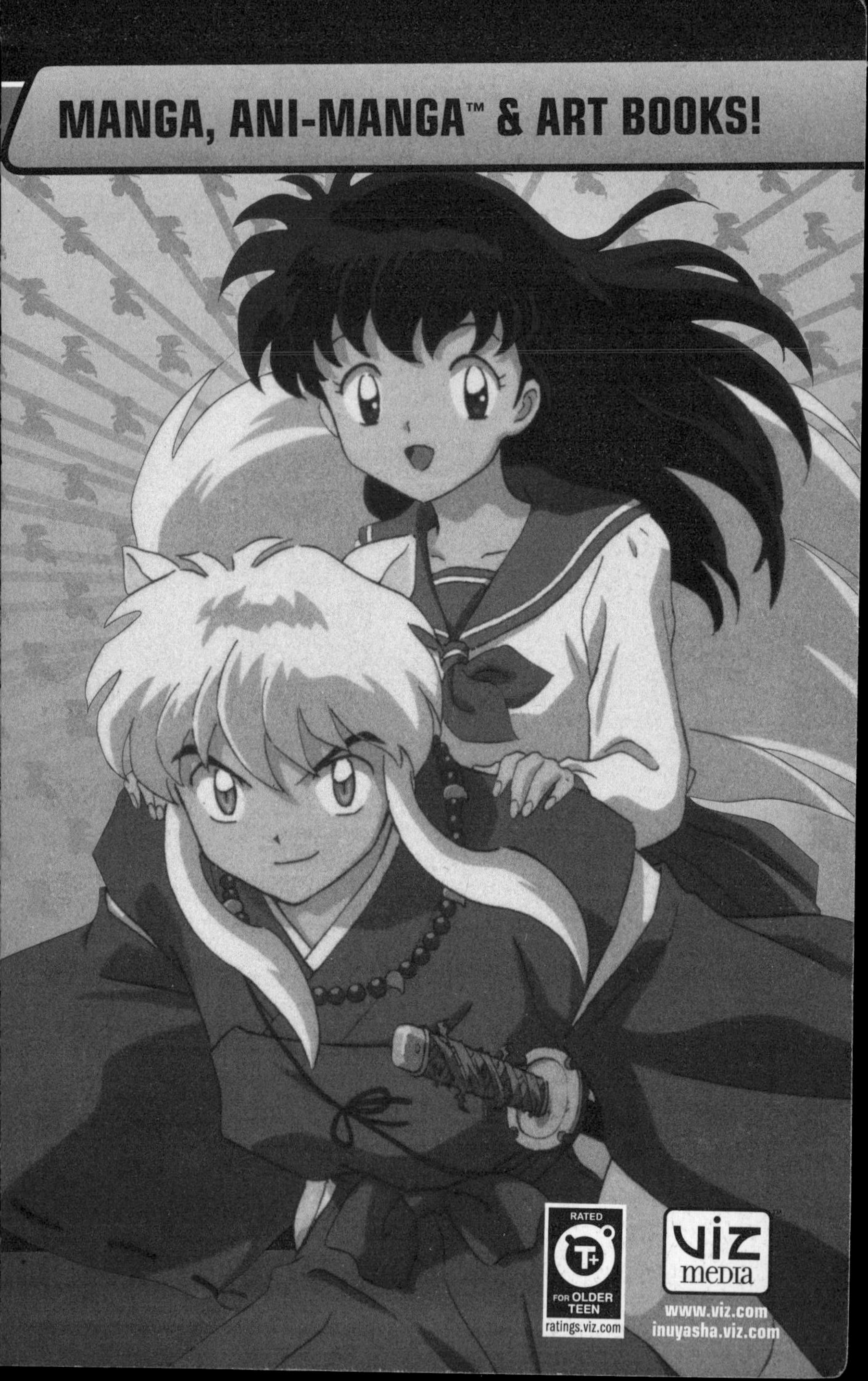
MANGA, ANI-MANGA™ & ART BOOKS!
RATED
T+
FOR OLDER TEEN
ratings.viz.com
viz media
www.viz.com
inuyasha.viz.com

INUYASHA

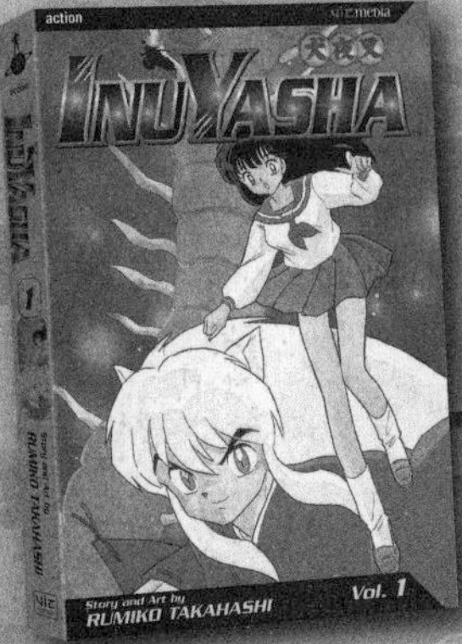
action
INUYASHA
犬夜叉
Story and Art by
RUMIKO TAKAHASHI
Vol. 1

Read the action from the start with the original manga series

Full color adaptation of the popular TV series

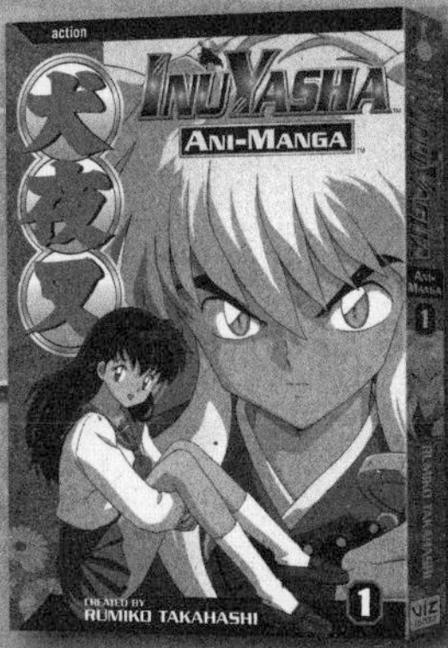
action
INUYASHA
ANI-MANGA
犬夜叉
CREATED BY
RUMIKO TAKAHASHI
1

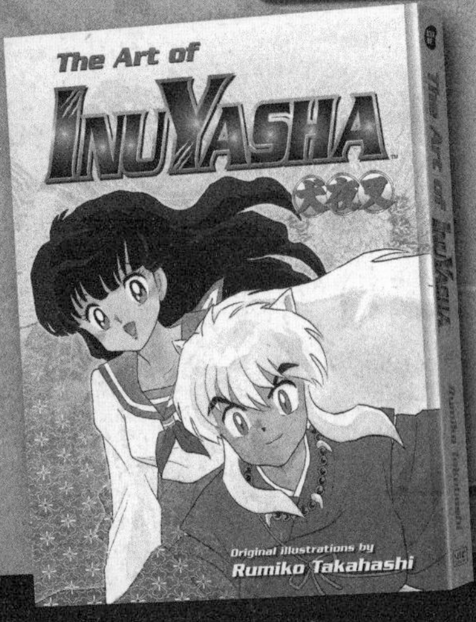
The Art of
INUYASHA
犬夜叉
Original illustrations by
Rumiko Takahashi

Art book with cel art, paintings, character profiles and more